T0235674

Lecture Notes in Computer Science 11917

More information about this series at http://www.springer.com/series/7407

Andrea Tagarelli · Hanghang Tong (Eds.)

Computational Data and Social Networks

8th International Conference, CSoNet 2019
Ho Chi Minh City, Vietnam, November 18–20, 2019
Proceedings

 Springer

Editors
Andrea Tagarelli
University of Calabria
Rende, Italy

Hanghang Tong
University of Illinois
at Urbana-Champaign
Urbana, IL, USA

ISSN 0302-9743   ISSN 1611-3349 (electronic)
Lecture Notes in Computer Science
ISBN 978-3-030-34979-0   ISBN 978-3-030-34980-6 (eBook)
https://doi.org/10.1007/978-3-030-34980-6

LNCS Sublibrary: SL1 – Theoretical Computer Science and General Issues

This Springer imprint is published by the registered company Springer Nature Switzerland AG
The registered company address is: Gewerbestrasse 11, 6330 Cham, Switzerland

Preface

This book constitutes the refereed proceedings of the 8th International Conference on Computational Data and Social Networks (CSoNet 2019) held in Ho Chi Minh City, Vietnam, November 18–20, 2019. This conference provides a premier interdisciplinary forum to bring together researchers and practitioners from all fields of complex networks (e.g., social networks, communication networks, sensor networks), big data analysis, modeling, and learning. CSoNet 2019 welcomed not only the presentation of original research results, but also the exchange and dissemination of innovative, practical development experiences. The topics of CSoNet 2019 cover the fundamental background, theoretical technology development, and real-world applications associated with the aforementioned fields. Selected papers will be published in special issues of *Journal of Combinatorial Optimization, IEEE Transactions on Network Science and Engineering, and Computational Social Networks*.

The intended audience of this book mainly consists of researchers, research students, and practitioners in complex networks, machine and deep learning, data mining, and combinatorial optimization. The book is also of interest to researchers and industrial practitioners in emerging areas such as Internet of Things, blockchain modeling, cloud computing, fraud detection, rumor blocking, crime detection, intelligent transportation systems, and many more.

We would like to express our appreciation to all contributors and the conference committee members. A special thanks goes to Van Lang University for its support of this conference. Furthermore, without the tremendous efforts from local chair Tran Thi My Dieu and team members, publicity co-chairs Minh Hoang Ha, Meng Jiang, and Pasquale De Meo, financial chair Thang Dinh, and website chair Lan N. Nguyen, our conference would not have been so successful in its 8th year. In addition, we sincerely appreciate the consistent support and great efforts of Ms. Anna Kramer and Mr. Alfred Hofmann from Springer in publishing the proceedings of this conference.

November 2019

Andrea Tagarelli
Hanghang Tong

Organization

General Chairs

Rosa Benito   Universidad Politecnica de Madrid, Spain
My T. Thai   University of Florida, USA

TPC Co-chairs

Andrea Tagarelli   University of Calabria, Italy
Hanghang Tong   Arizona State University, USA

TPC Members

Rajdeep Bhowmik	Cisco Systems, Inc., USA
Erik Cambria	Nanyang Technological University, Singapore
K. Selcuk Candan	Arizona State University, USA
Nan Cao	TongJi University, China
Kevin Chang	University of Illinois at Urbana-Champaign, USA
Hocine Cherifi	University of Burgundy, France
Hasan Davulcu	Arizona State University, USA
Pasquale De Meo	University of Messina, Italy
Yuxiao Dong	Microsoft, USA
Nan Du	Google, Inc., USA
Hongwei Du	Harbin Institute of Technology (Shenzhen), China
Yuan Fang	Singapore Management University, Singapore
Reza Farahbakhsh	Institut Mines-Télécom, Télécom SudParis, France
Niloy Ganguly	Indian Institute of Technology Kharagpur, India
Wei Gao	Victoria University of Wellington, New Zealand
Yong Ge	UNC Charlotte, USA
Francesco Gullo	UniCredit, Italy
Jinyoung Han	Hanyang University, South Korea
Jingrui He	Arizona State University, USA
Ting Hua	Virginia Tech, USA
Dino Ienco	Irstea, France
Roberto Interdonato	CIRAD - UMR TETIS, France
Donghyun Kim	Kennesaw State University, USA
Pavel Kromer	Technical University of Ostrava, Czech Republic
Taekyoung Kwon	Seoul National University, South Korea
Liangyue Li	Arizona State University, USA
Gang Li	Deakin University, Australia
Huan Liu	Arizona State University, USA

Qi Liu	University of Science and Technology of China, China
Lorenzo Malandri	University of Milan-Bicocca, Italy
Julian Mcauley	University of California San Diego, USA
Amanda Minnich	Lawrence Livermore National Laboratory, USA
Franco Maria Nardini	ISTI-CNR, Italy
Huan Xuan Nguyen	Middlesex University, UK
Yue Ning	Stevens Institute of Technology, USA
Jia-Yu Pan	Google, Inc., USA
Spiros Papadimitriou	Rutgers University, USA
Jian Pei	Simon Fraser University, Canada
Ruggero G. Pensa	University of Turin, Itlay
Hai Phan	New Jersey Institute of Technology, USA
Hamid R. Rabiee	Sharif University of Technology, Iran
Mohsin Raza	Northumbria University, UK
Akrati Saxena	National University of Singapore, Singapore
Alexander Semenov	University of Jyväskylä, Finland
Huawei Shen	Chinese Academy of Sciences, China
Lei Shi	Institute of Software, Chinese Academy of Sciences, China
Fabrizio Silvestri	Facebook, UK
Anurag Signh	NIT Delhi, India
Dimitris Spiliotopoulos	University of Houston, USA
Cathleen M. Stuetzer	University of Technology Dresden (TUD), Germany
Jie Tang	Tsinghua University, China
Jiliang Tang	Michigan State University, USA
Lu-An Tang	NEC Labs America, USA
Xiaohui Tao	University of Southern Queensland, Australia
Gabriele Tolomei	University of Padua, Italy
Balazs Vedres	Central European University, Hungary
Xintao Wu	University of Arkansas, USA
Yanghua Xiao	Fudan University, China
Jingwei Xu	Nanjing University, China
Pei Yang	South China University of Technology, China
Yuan Yao	Nanjing University, China
Xinyue Ye	New Jersey Institute of Technology, USA
Hongzhi Yin	The University of Queensland, Australia
Si Zhang	Arizona State University, USA
Xin Zhao	Renmin University of China, School of Information, China
Jiayu Zhou	Michigan State University, USA

Publicity Co-chairs

Minh Hoang Ha	VNU University of Engineering and Technology, Vietnam
Meng Jiang	University of Notre Dame, USA
Pasquale De Meo	University of Messina, Italy

Local Organizing Committee Chair

Tran Thi My Dieu	Van Lang University, Vietnam

Financial Chair

Thang Dinh	Virginia Commonwealth University, USA

Web Chair

Lan N. Nguyen	University of Florida, USA

Contents

Combinatorial Optimization and Learning

Influence Modeling, Propagation, and Maximization

NLP and Affective Computing

Computational Methods for Social Good

User Profiling and Behavior Modeling

Combinatorial Optimization and Learning

A Probabilistic Divide and Conquer Algorithm for the Minimum Tollbooth Problem

Julian Nickerl$^{(\boxtimes)}$ (iD)

Institute of Theoretical Computer Science, Ulm University, Ulm, Germany
`julian.nickerl@uni-ulm.de`

Abstract. The tollbooth problem aims at minimizing the time lost through congestion in road networks with rational and selfish participants by demanding an additional toll for the use of edges. We consider a variant of this problem, the minimum tollbooth problem, which additionally minimizes the number of tolled edges. Since the problem is NP-hard, heuristics and evolutionary algorithms dominate solution approaches. To the best of our knowledge, for none of these approaches, a provable non-trivial upper bound on the (expected) runtime necessary to find an optimal solution exists.

We present a novel probabilistic divide and conquer algorithm with a provable upper bound of $\mathcal{O}^*(m^{opt})$ on the expected runtime for finding an optimal solution. Here, m is the number of edges of the network, and opt the number of tolled roads in an optimal solution. Initial experiments indicate that in practice significantly less time is necessary.

Keywords: Algorithmic game theory · Minimum tollbooth problem · Network congestion game · Social optimum · System optimal flow

1 Introduction

Rational but selfish behavior seldom leads to globally, or socially, good results [9,21]. In road networks, this can be observed as, unnecessary congestion and overall waiting times, i.e., a reduction of the overall performance, translating into a significant loss of time and money [1]. In this paper, we present a novel algorithm for an optimization problem in the field of algorithmic game theory that addresses this issue in non-atomic network congestion games. In this type of game, pairs of source and sink nodes are each associated with a commodity. Each commodity has an individual demand - an amount of infinitesimally small players, the participants of the network. Every player chooses a route from their source to their sink, suffering a cost for the traversal of edges. Typically, the more players use the same edge, the higher the cost for each player on that edge, simulating congestion. A common way to counteract unnecessary congestion due to selfish behavior in network congestion games is the levy of tolls on the use of certain edges. By meticulously calculating the tolls, the participants of the

© Springer Nature Switzerland AG 2019
A. Tagarelli and H. Tong (Eds.): CSoNet 2019, LNCS 11917, pp. 3–15, 2019.
https://doi.org/10.1007/978-3-030-34980-6_1

network can be motivated to choose strategies that lead to a global optimum, without sacrificing their rationality or selfishness. Under light restrictions, it is known that such tolls always exist and can be efficiently computed [7,10,13,20].

Since its introduction, several variants of this problem have emerged. For example, Bonifaci, Salek, and Schäfer [8] address the issue of some toll being very expensive, leading to unrealistically high cost for using single edges. They approach this with a bounded version of the tollbooth problem. Harks, Kleinert, and Klimm [15] note that allowing to place a tollbooth on any edge can be unrealistic. In practice, these booths would often be constructed on easily controllable landmarks like bridges. They analyze the problem while restricting the set of tollable edges to a given set. As a last and recent example, Colini-Baldeschi, Klimm, and Scarsini [11] consider a variant of the problem where knowledge about the number of participants in the network is incomplete.

The particular case we consider here is called the minimum tollbooth problem (**MINTB**), first introduced by Hearn and Ramana [17]. In addition to the goal of the tollbooth problem, we aim at minimizing the number of placed tollbooths. Fewer tollbooths mean both reduced administrative complexity, and less cost for maintenance (e.g., the yearly cost of a single manned tollbooth was estimated at 180.000\$ in 2005 [23]). As the social optimum, we apply the minimum of the sum of all experienced costs. **MINTB** is known to be NP-Hard, both for atomic [19] and non-atomic games [6]. Polynomial-time algorithms are known only for series-parallel networks in both cases [6,19]. We focus on non-atomic games in this work, i.e., every participant in the network is represented as an infinitesimally small amount of flow. Prominent heuristics and algorithms tackling the NP-hard problem are dynamic slope scaling [2], combinatorial Benders' cuts [3], genetic algorithms [16,22], and evolutionary algorithms [4,18]. While the dynamic slope scaling performs well, it may not be able to find the globally optimal solution. The genetic and evolutionary algorithms try to address this issue. However, they require the tuning of several parameters. Also, the choice of a practical target function is unclear.

In this work, we present a novel probabilistic divide and conquer algorithm that neither requires additional parameters, nor a target function and is capable of finding the optimal solution. We prove that the algorithm finds the optimal solution with a probability at least $\frac{1}{m^{opt}}$ per iteration, where m is the number of edges of the network, and opt the number of tollbooths in an optimal solution. This means that after probability amplification, the expected number of iterations of the algorithm before finding the optimal solution is in $\mathcal{O}(m^{opt})$. To the best of our knowledge, an algorithm with such a provable upper bound on the (expected) runtime has not been presented before for **MINTB**. We conduct experiments and observe that the actual required number of iterations is significantly lower in most cases. The algorithm is easily adaptable to similar problem formulations. The remainder of the paper is organized as follows. Section 2 formally defines the considered instances of non-atomic network congestion games in addition to some connected concepts. It also introduces definitions for the original tollbooth problem and its variant **MINTB**. Following a top-down approach, Sect. 3 describes the new algorithm and proves some of its properties. We present the results of initial experiments on random instances in Sect. 4. Section 5 serves as a conclusion and gives hints for future work in the presented field.

2   Preliminaries

We begin by defining the addressed problem. An *instance* $I = (G, K)$ consists of a set of commodities K, and a (directed) graph $G = \{V, E\}$, with a monotonically increasing cost function $c_e(x) : \mathbb{R}_0^+ \rightarrow \mathbb{R}_0^+$ associated with each edge $e \in E$. A number of *commodities* route flow through the network. A commodity k is defined by the tuple (s_k, t_k, d_k), where s_k is the source node, t_k the sink node, and d_k the demand of the commodity. The demand is the amount of flow the commodity sends from its source to its sink. To do so, it may split up the demand arbitrarily over all source-sink paths as long as the flow on each edge is non-negative, and the sum of the flows over each path sum up to the demand. To manage flows, we make use of a *flow profile* f. By $f[e, k]$ we refer to the flow associated with commodity k that is sent over edge e. If we consider the total flow on a single edge, we denote this by $f[e] = \sum_{\{k \in K\}} f[e, k]$.

We are interested in two kinds of states that can occur in such a network. One is the *system optimal flow* (SO) f^* (another name is the *social optimum*), which is a flow profile that minimizes $\sum_{\{e \in E\}} c_e(f[e]) f[e]$ while routing the demand of every commodity from the respective source to the respective sink. It minimizes the sum of the costs experienced by all participants of the network. However, it is a well-known result that the system optimal flow is seldom an equilibrium state. An *equilibrium flow* (EQ) f (other names include *user equilibrium*, *Nash equilibrium*, and *Wardrop equilibrium*) is reached when for all commodities k and all paths P_1 and P_2 from s_k to t_k with $f[e, k] > 0 \; \forall e \in P_1$, $\sum_{\{e \in P_1\}} c_e(f[e]) \leq \sum_{\{e \in P_2\}} c_e(f[e])$. In other words, if some flow associated with commodity k is sent over some path P_1 from s_k to t_k, in an equilibrium flow, there cannot be another path P_2 from s_k to t_k that is cheaper to send the flow over, even for an infinitesimal amount of flow.

The goal in the *tollbooth problem* (**TB**) is to turn the SO into an EQ by raising tolls on edges. For this, we introduce a value $\beta_e \geq 0 \; \forall e \in E$ called a *toll*. Given the SO f^*, a toll vector $\beta = (\beta_1, ..., \beta_m)$ with $m = |E|$ is a solution to **TB**, if f^* is an EQ after replacing the cost functions c_e by $c_e^\beta(x) = c_e(x) + \beta_e$.

In this work, we focus on a problem where we additionally minimize the number of edges with non-zero tolls, called the *minimum tollbooth problem* (**MINTB**). Let $y_e = 1$ if $\beta_e > 0$, and $y_e = 0$ otherwise, with $y = (y_{e_1}, ..., y_{e_m})$ for $m = |E|$. The goal in **MINTB** is to find tolls β that solve **TB**, s.t. the corresponding vector y minimizes $\sum_{i=1}^m y_{e_i}$. In the following, we call a vector y *feasible* or a *feasible solution* for a given instance, if there exists a corresponding toll vector that is a solution to **TB** on this instance. We call y an *optimal solution* if it is feasible and solves **MINTB**. Given y and a flow profile f, the feasibility of y is easily confirmed by verifying that a solution to the following set of linear (in-)equalities exists, making use of the conditions for **MINTB** introduced by Hearn and Ramana [17].

$$\sum_{\{e \in E\}} f[e](c_e(f[e]) + \beta_e) - \sum_{k \in K} d_k(\rho_{s_k}^k - \rho_{t_k}^k) = 0$$
$$c_e(f[e]) + \beta_e - (\rho_i^k - \rho_j^k) \geq 0, \forall e = (i, j) \in E, k \in K \qquad (1)$$
$$\beta_e \geq 0, \forall e : y_e = 1$$
$$\beta_e = 0, \forall e : y_e = 0$$

Here, β_e is the yet to determine the value of the toll on edge e and ρ_v^k are unknown variables with $\rho_v^k \in \mathbb{R}$. Figure 1 depicts a simple example instance that will appear several times in this work. It is a variant of Pigou's example [20], slightly extended in order to visualize better some of the properties of the upcoming algorithm.

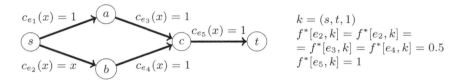

Fig. 1. An example network with one commodity. The flow profile f^* denotes the system optimal flow. However, in the user equilibrium, all flow is sent over the path $s - b - c - t$. Setting either $\beta_{e_2} = 0.5$ or $\beta_{e_4} = 0.5$ leads to an optimal solution.

3   A Probabilistic Divide and Conquer Algorithm

We introduce a new probabilistic algorithm for **MINTB**. The algorithm initially generates a random permutation of the graph's edges. Based on this permutation and following a divide and conquer approach, **MINTB** is solved on sub-instances and finally combined to a feasible solution of the original instance. The algorithm is repeated several times to amplify the probability of finding a good solution. Algorithm 1 displays the whole procedure. By $|y|$ we refer to the number of 1s in the binary vector y (y_{out} analogously).

The remainder of this section describes the functions used in Algorithm 1, namely Preprocess(I, f), a method that preprocesses the given flow profile, Divide(I, f, π), that divides the given instance into sub-instances based on the random permutation π, and Conquer($I_1, ..., I_m, f_1, ..., f_m, \pi$), that inductively solves the previously generated sub-instances, combining them to a feasible solution for the original instance.

3.1   Preprocessing

The algorithm requires a given flow profile f^*, typically the SO. In the following, we assume that the given flow profile is the SO. Additionally, we require the flow

Algorithm 1. Main

Data: Instance I, flow profile f^*
1 Let $I = (G = (V, E), K)$;
2 Set $I, f^* = \text{Preprocess}(I, f^*)$;
3 Initialize $y_{out} = (1, 1, ..., 1)$;
4 **for** $it = 1$ **to** $maxIterations$ **do**
5   Generate a random permutation π of the edges of E;
6   Set $I_1, ..., I_m, f_1, ..., f_m = \text{Divide}(I, f^*, \pi)$;
7   Set $y = \text{Conquer}(I_1, ..., I_m, f_1, ..., f_m, \pi)$;
8   **if** $|y| < |y_{out}|$ **then**
9   Set $y_{out} = y$;
10   Set $it = it + 1$;
11 **return** y_{out};

from the source to the destination node in f^* for every commodity to correspond to a single path. Any commodity can be split up, s.t. each sub-commodity sends its flow only over a single path. Recombining the paths leads to the flow as sent from the initial commodity in f^*. These paths are similar to augmenting paths in the Ford-Fulkerson maximum flow algorithm [14]. Algorithm 2 returns a set of commodities and a fitting flow profile with this property for any given instance and initial flow profile while increasing the number of commodities to at most $|K| \cdot |E|$.

Algorithm 2. Preprocess

Data: Instance $(G, \hat{K})$, system optimal flow f^*
1 Initialize $K = \emptyset$;
2 **for** $k \in \hat{K}$ **do**
3   **while** $d_k \neq 0$ **do**
4   Compute a path P from s_k to t_k in G, s.t. $f^*[e, k] > 0 \; \forall e \in P$;
5   Set $\delta_{min} = \min\{f^*[e, k] : e \in P\}$;
6   Create a new commodity $\lambda = (s_k, t_k, \delta_{min})$;
7   Set $f^*[e, \lambda] = 0 \; \forall e \notin P$;
8   Set $f^*[e, \lambda] = \delta_{min} \; \forall e \in P$;
9   Set $f^*[e, k] = f^*[e, k] - \delta_{min} \; \forall e \in P$;
10   Set $d_k = d_k - \delta_{min}$;
11   Set $K = K \cup \{\lambda\}$;
12 **return** instance (G, K), updated system optimal flow f^*;

One iteration in the while loop computes a path from s_k to t_k, such that (according to the given flow profile) commodity k sends flow over each edge of the path in f^*. This path is extracted as a new commodity. The demand for the new commodity is the flow the original commodity sends over this path.

The flow profile and demand of the original commodity get updated, and the whole process repeated until the original commodity has no demand left. Note that for each iteration of the while loop, the flow of the commodity on at least one edge gets reduced to 0, ensuring that the number of commodities grows to at most $|K| \cdot |E|$. Flows that are a SO or an EQ in the original instance have an analogous representation in the new instance generated by Algorithm 2, fulfilling the same properties. Figure 2 shows the result of applying Algorithm 2 to our example instance.

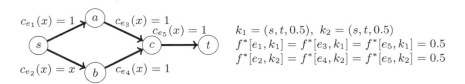

Fig. 2. The example instance after applying CreatePaths. The commodity has been split in two. All unlisted values of $f^*[e_i, k_j]$ are 0.

3.2   Dividing the Instance

Given a random permutation π of the graph's edges, Algorithm 3 splits the original instance into sub-instances.

Following the given permutation π of edges, Algorithm 3 step by step removes single edges, creating new commodities when necessary. The central part of the algorithm is lines 7 to 17. Assume edge $e_{\pi(i)}$ is to be removed. With f^* as a given SO the goal is to create an instance s.t. if $f[e_{\pi(j)}] = f^*[e_{\pi(j)}]$ for all edges $e_{\pi(j)}$ with $j > i$, f is a SO of the new instance. This is reached by splitting every commodity k that sends flow over e_i in two, namely k_1 and k_2. After applying Algorithm 2, we can guarantee that every commodity sends its flow through the network following a single path. We set the source of commodity k_1 as the source of k. Now following the path, we will reach edge $e_{\pi(i)} = (v_1, v_2)$. We update the flow profile of commodity k_1 to send all of its flow over the path's edges, just like k but set the sink node as v_1. Analogously, k_2 sends all of its flow from v_2 as its source to the sink of k using the path's edges after v_2. Afterward, we remove k and add k_1 and k_2 to the set of commodities. We repeat the process until no flow is sent over $e_{\pi(i)}$ anymore. Then we can remove $e_{\pi(i)}$ and continue with edge $e_{\pi(i+1)}$. The resulting instances and flow profiles created by Algorithm 3 applied to our example instance are displayed in Fig. 3.

3.3   Conquer the Original Instance

In the following, we inductively solve the previously generated sub-instances in order to create a feasible solution for the original instance I.

Algorithm 3. Divide

Data: Instance (G, K), system optimal flow f^*, permutation π

1 Let $G = (V, E)$ with $|E| = m$;

2 Initialize $K_1 = K$ and $K_2, ..., K_m = \emptyset$;

3 Initialize flow profiles $f_1, ..., f_m = f^*$;

4 **for** $\xi = 2$ *to* m **do**

5   Set $K_\xi = K_{\xi-1}$;

6   Set $f_\xi = f_{\xi-1}$;

7   **for** $k \in K_\xi : f_\xi[e_{\pi(\xi-1)}, k] > 0$ **do**

8   Let $e_{\pi(\xi-1)} = (v_1, v_2)$;

9   Let P be the path from s_k to t_k with $f_\xi[e, k] > 0 \; \forall e \in P$;

10   Create commodity $k_1 = (s_k, v_1, d_k)$;

11   Create commodity $k_2 = (v_2, t_k, d_k)$;

12   Set $f_\xi[e, k_1] = d_k$ for all edges e that come before $e_{\pi(\xi-1)}$ in P;

13   Set $f_\xi[e, k_1] = 0$ for all other edges;

14   Set $f_\xi[e, k_2] = d_k$ for all edges e that come after $e_{\pi(\xi-1)}$ in P;

15   Set $f_\xi[e, k_2] = 0$ for all other edges;

16   Set $K_\xi = K_\xi \backslash \{k\}$;

17   Set $K_\xi = K_\xi \cup \{k_1, k_2\}$;

18 Create graphs $G_i = (V, E_i)$ with $E_i = \{e_{\pi(j)} \in E : j \geq i\}$;

19 Create instances $I_i = (G_i, K_i)$;

20 **return** instances $I_1, ..., I_m$ and flow profiles $f_1, ..., f_m$;

In Algorithm 4, we assume for every instance I_i, $i \in \{1, ..., m\}$, that we have already found a feasible solution for instance I_{i+1} (an exception is instance I_m, since instance I_{m+1} does not exist. Interpret instance I_{m+1} as an instance without any edges). Regarding the edges, the instances I_i and I_{i+1} only differ in the edge $e_{\pi(i)}$, which is contained in I_i, but not in I_{i+1}. Accordingly, we extend the solution for instance I_{i+1} by setting $y_{e_{\pi(i)}} = 0$. If the vector $(y_{e_{\pi(i)}}, ..., y_{e_{\pi(m)}})$ is feasible for instance I_i, we continue with instance I_{i-1}. Otherwise we try placing a tollbooth on $e_{\pi(i)}$ by setting $y_{e_{\pi(i)}} = 1$. Again, if it is feasible, we continue to instance I_{i-1}. Otherwise, the algorithm cannot create a feasible solution from this permutation, and returns as a solution the vector where a tollbooth is placed on every edge, which is always feasible, albeit usually a bad solution. Figure 4 displays the situation after reinserting edge $e_4 = e_{\pi(1)}$ into the graph in instance I_1 of our example instance.

3.4 Properties of the Algorithm

In this section, we present some properties of the algorithm. We prove that a permutation π of edges that results in an optimal solution for **MINTB** always exists and give a lower bound on the probability of success for a single run of the algorithm.

Theorem 1. *For any given instance of **MINTB**, there exists at least one permutation π of edges $e_1, ..., e_m$, such that Algorithm 4 returns an optimal solution.*

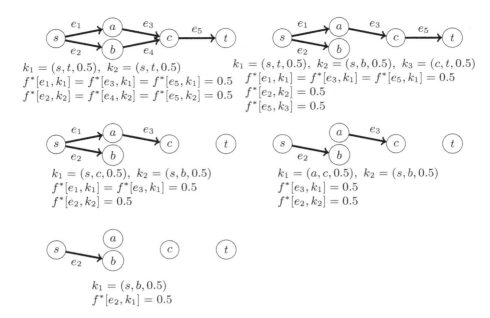

$k_1 = (s, t, 0.5), \ k_2 = (s, t, 0.5)$
$f^*[e_1, k_1] = f^*[e_3, k_1] = f^*[e_5, k_1] = 0.5$
$f^*[e_2, k_2] = f^*[e_4, k_2] = f^*[e_5, k_2] = 0.5$

$k_1 = (s, t, 0.5), \ k_2 = (s, b, 0.5), \ k_3 = (c, t, 0.5)$
$f^*[e_1, k_1] = f^*[e_3, k_1] = f^*[e_5, k_1] = 0.5$
$f^*[e_2, k_2] = 0.5$
$f^*[e_5, k_3] = 0.5$

$k_1 = (s, c, 0.5), \ k_2 = (s, b, 0.5)$
$f^*[e_1, k_1] = f^*[e_3, k_1] = 0.5$
$f^*[e_2, k_2] = 0.5$

$k_1 = (a, c, 0.5), \ k_2 = (s, b, 0.5)$
$f^*[e_3, k_1] = 0.5$
$f^*[e_2, k_2] = 0.5$

$k_1 = (s, b, 0.5)$
$f^*[e_2, k_1] = 0.5$

Fig. 3. Applying divide on the example instance for permutation $\pi = (1, 4, 3)(2, 5)$. Cost functions and commodities whose source is equal to their sink are omitted. All unlisted values of $f^*[e_i, k_j]$ are 0.

Proof. We consider an instance $I = (G, K)$ with $G = (V, E)$ and $|E| = m$. Let $y^* = (y^*_{e_1}, ..., y^*_{e_m})$ be a possible optimal solution. Additionally, assume without loss of generality, that the edges are permuted such that $y^*_{e_{\pi(i)}} = 1$ for $i \le opt$, and $y^*_{e_{\pi(i)}} = 0$ for $i > opt$, where opt is the number of non-zero tolls in an optimal solution.

Lemma 1. *Given y^* and a permutation π of the edges as mentioned above, Algorithm 4 sets $y_{e_{\pi(i)}} = 0$ for all $i : i > opt$.*

Proof. For each instance I_i with $i > opt$ (starting with m and decreasing to $opt + 1$), the algorithm will decide whether it is necessary to place a tollbooth on edge $e_{\pi(i)}$. Aiming for a proof by contradiction, assume that there is an instance I_i with $i > opt$ s.t. the algorithm decides that placing a tollbooth on edge $e_{\pi(i)}$ is necessary. Let i be additionally the largest value for which this is the case. The algorithm deciding to place a tollbooth on $e_{\pi(i)}$ implies that there exists a commodity (s, t, d) that can divert some of its flow away from the SO to a path P that includes $e_{\pi(i)}$. This shortcut equally exists in the original instance I, though potentially for a different commodity. Hence, with $y_e = 0$ for all $e \in P$, to solve **MINTB** on I a tollbooth has to be placed on a (currently untolled) edge of P, which is a contradiction to y^* being a feasible solution.

Algorithm 4. Conquer

Data: Instances $I_1, ..., I_m$, flow profiles $f_1, ..., f_m$, permutation π

1 Initialize $y = (y_{e_1}, ..., y_{e_m})$ with $y_{e_i} = 0$ for all $i \in \{1, ..., m\}$;

2 **for** $\xi = m$ *to* 1 **do**

3   **if** $(y_{e_{\pi(\xi)}}, ..., y_{e_{\pi(m)}})$ *is not a feasible solution for* I_ξ *with* f_ξ **then**

4   Set $y_{e_{\pi(\xi)}} = 1$;

5   **if** $(y_{e_{\pi(\xi)}}, ..., y_{e_{\pi(m)}})$ *is not a feasible solution for* I_ξ *with* f_ξ **then**

6   Set $y_{e_i} = 1$ for all $i \in \{1, ..., m\}$;

7   **return** y;

8 **return** y;

$$k_1 = (s, t, 0.5), \quad k_2 = (s, t, 0.5)$$
$$f^*[e_1, k_1] = f^*[e_3, k_1] = f^*[e_5, k_1] = 0.5$$
$$f^*[e_2, k_2] = f^*[e_4, k_2] = f^*[e_5, k_2] = 0.5$$

Fig. 4. Conquer decides to place a tollbooth on an edge only in the last step when reinserting edge e_4, based on the random permutation $\pi = (1, 4, 3)(2, 5)$. Reinserting e_4 creates a shortcut for k_1: $e_2 - e_4 - e_5$ (2.5) is currently shorter than $e_1 - e_3 - e_5$ (3).

In the second phase, we show that there exists a permutation of the edges with $y^*_{e_{\pi(i)}} = 1$, such that the algorithm sets $y_{e_{\pi(i)}} = 1$ for all these edges if $i \leq opt$. However, first, we require the notion of a shortcut:

Definition 1. *Given nodes v_1 and v_2, and a SO f^*, s.t. there exists a commodity k that sends flow from v_1 to v_2 in the SO. A shortcut is a path P_1 from v_1 to v_2 such that there exists a path P_2 with $f^*[e, k] > 0$ $\forall e \in P_2$ s.t. $\sum_{\{e \in P_1\}} c(f^*[e]) < \sum_{\{e \in P_2\}} c(f^*[e])$. We call such a path a shortcut of second order if it only exists through a toll being raised on a different edge. Otherwise, we call it a shortcut of first order.*

Intuitively, any solution to the tollbooth problem must block all shortcuts of first order with tollbooths. However, depending on the solution, different shortcuts of second order may emerge that have to be blocked additionally.

Lemma 2. *If all edges that do not require tollbooths due to y^* already exist, there exists an edge that if introduced, produces a shortcut of first order.*

Proof. Let $\mathcal{P} = \{P \subseteq E \mid P \text{ defines a shortcut of first order}\}$. We show that there always exists a $P \in \mathcal{P}$, s.t. for precisely one edge $e \in P$, $y^*_e = 1$. Assume, that for every $P \in \mathcal{P}$, there are at least two edges $e \in P$ with $y^*_e = 1$. Then we could choose any edge with $y^*_e = 1$ that appears in one of these shortcuts and set $y^*_e = 0$. Still, all shortcuts will be blocked by tollbooths, and since only tollbooths have been removed, the number of shortcuts of second order did not increase.

Therefore, y^* with $y_e^* = 0$ is still a feasible solution for **MINTB**. However, y^* was optimal, which is a contradiction.

Lemma 1 demonstrates that the order of the edges $e_{\pi(opt)+1}, ..., e_{\pi(m)}$ does not matter, as long as $y_e^* = 0$ for all those edges. From Lemma 2, we can conclude that edge $e_{\pi(opt)}$ is the one that if introduced, produces a shortcut of first order. Consequently, since an unblocked shortcut over this edge exists now, the algorithm will place a tollbooth on $e_{\pi(opt)}$. We can apply Lemma 2 again by acting as though $y_{e_{\pi(opt)}}^* = 0$ while removing all shortcuts blocked by $y_{e_{\pi(opt)}}$ from $\mathcal{P}$. This update will turn some of the shortcuts of second order into shortcuts of first order, including those in $\mathcal{P}$. With an analogous argument, this results in an option for $e_{\pi(opt-1)}$. Applying the same technique several times inductively results in a complete permutation of the edges, concluding the proof.   □

Since the order of the edges without tollbooths in an optimal solution does not matter, we have a lower bound on the number of permutations that lead to an optimal solution of $(m - opt)!$. Thus, a lower bound on the probability of success of a single run of the algorithm is $\frac{(m-opt)!}{m!} > \frac{1}{m^{opt}}$, and the expected number of iterations before finding the optimal solution is in $\mathcal{O}(m^{opt})$.

Corollary 1. *A single iteration in Algorithm 1 finds an optimal solution with probability at least $\frac{1}{m^{opt}}$.*

4   Experiments

In order to get a grasp on the capabilities of the algorithm, we have evaluated it on different types of small randomly generated instances, used to model different types of scenarios. For all instances, we choose the number of nodes to be $n = 48$ and the number of commodities to be $|K| = 5$. The types of instances differ in the way the networks are generated. The first type follows the Erdős-Rényi model [12], i.e., we decide for each edge with a probability $p = 0.05$ whether it exists or not, leading to graphs with a Poisson degree distribution. The second is grid networks. The combinations of rows and columns were chosen uniformly at random under the condition that the number of nodes is 48. The last type of random network is generated with the preferential attachment method following the Barabási-Albert model [5], leading to graphs whose degree distributions correspond to heavy-tail distributions. For each edge e, the cost function was of form $c_e(x) = T(1 + (\frac{x}{C})^P)$, with $T \in \{1, ..., 10\}$, $C \in \{10, ..., 25\}$, and $P \in \{0, 1\}$ chosen uniformly at random. Source, sink, and demand with $d \in \{5, ..., 15\}$ were chosen uniformly at random as well for each commodity. For each type of random network, 100 instances were generated. We compare our algorithm to the results found by the dynamic slope scaling procedure improved by first improvement local search (DSSP+FILS), introduced by Bai, Hearn, and Lawphongpanich [2]. For each instance, we measure the number of iterations until a solution is found that is equal or better in quality to one found with DSSP+FILS, up to a maximum of 1000 iterations. All algorithms were written in Java with IBM's CPLEX. Table 1 displays the results.

Table 1. Overview over experimental results. The first row shows the number of instances where the algorithm found a feasible (but potentially not optimal) solution after at most 1000 iterations. The other rows display the number of instances for which a solution was found that was at least as good as the DSSP+FILS solution after the respective number of iterations.

	Grid	Poisson	HeavyTail
Solution found	60	99	99
≤ 100 iterations	33	84	77
≤ 500 iterations	48	94	91
<1000 iterations	56	96	95

The difference from the fourth row to the first row are instances, where the algorithm found a solution that was slightly worse than the solution from DSSP+FILS (most of the time just one tollbooth off). We see that after at most 1000 iterations the algorithm found a feasible solution for 258 of 300 instances, 247 of which were at least as good as the DSSP+FILS solution. Considering the upper bound on the expected number of iterations of $\mathcal{O}(m^{opt})$, it is a surprising result that for a total of 194 instances, so above 60%, as little as 100 iterations were sufficient to find a good solution.

5   Conclusion and Future Work

This work introduces a new algorithm for solving **MINTB** based on a probabilistic divide and conquer approach. Unlike many previous methods, this approach does not require any parameters. Hence no additional effort has to be put into their tuning. At the same time, the algorithm is capable of finding an optimal solution with a non-zero probability of at least $\frac{1}{m^{opt}}$ for each iteration, leading to an expected number of iterations in $\mathcal{O}(m^{opt})$. Experiments on several randomly generated instances indicate that in practice significantly fewer iterations suffice.

The algorithm, in its current form, presents several indications for further improvements and should be seen as the introduction of a new concept for algorithms for **MINTB**. As a first step, the "failed" permutations should be salvaged to always lead to at least feasible solutions. Instead of creating a whole new permutation once an infeasible vector is reached, one could reassign the parts of the permutation within the edges that have been considered up to that point. In another approach without reconsidering the permutation, first experiments show, that infeasible solutions in sub-instances can often be turned into feasible ones by allowing a single additional tollbooth on a previously considered edge.

The presented approach is easily adaptable to similar problem formulations regarding **MINTB**. Updating the constraints in the system of (in-)equalities that check the feasibility of a toll vector can tailor the algorithm to many further problem formulations in a simple way while leaving the rest of the algorithm untouched.

References

1. Arnott, R., Small, K.: The economics of traffic congestion. Am. Sci. **82**(5), 446–455 (1994)
2. Bai, L., Hearn, D.W., Lawphongpanich, S.: A heuristic method for the minimum toll booth problem. J. Global Optim. **48**(4), 533–548 (2010)
3. Bai, L., Rubin, P.A.: Combinatorial benders cuts for the minimum tollbooth problem. Oper. Res. **57**(6), 1510–1522 (2009)
4. Bai, L., Stamps, M.T., Harwood, R.C., Kollmann, C.J.: An evolutionary method for the minimum toll booth problem: the methodology. J. Manage. Inf. Decis. Sci. **11**(2), 33 (2008)
5. Barabási, A.L., Albert, R.: Emergence of scaling in random networks. Science **286**(5439), 509–512 (1999)
6. Basu, S., Lianeas, T., Nikolova, E.: New complexity results and algorithms for the minimum tollbooth problem. In: Markakis, E., Schäfer, G. (eds.) WINE 2015. LNCS, vol. 9470, pp. 89–103. Springer, Heidelberg (2015). https://doi.org/10.1007/978-3-662-48995-6_7
7. Beckmann, M., McGuire, C.B., Winsten, C.B.: Studies in the Economics of Transportation. Yale University Press, New Haven (1956)
8. Bonifaci, V., Salek, M., Schäfer, G.: Efficiency of restricted tolls in non-atomic network routing games. In: Persiano, G. (ed.) SAGT 2011. LNCS, vol. 6982, pp. 302–313. Springer, Heidelberg (2011). https://doi.org/10.1007/978-3-642-24829-0_27
9. Christodoulou, G., Koutsoupias, E.: The price of anarchy of finite congestion games. In: Proceedings of STOC, pp. 67–73. ACM (2005)
10. Cole, R., Dodis, Y., Roughgarden, T.: Pricing network edges for heterogeneous selfish users. In: Proceedings of STOC, pp. 521–530. ACM (2003)
11. Colini-Baldeschi, R., Klimm, M., Scarsini, M.: Demand-independent optimal tolls. arXiv preprint arXiv:1708.02737 (2017)
12. Erdős, P., Rényi, A.: On random graphs i. Publ. Math. Debrecen **6**, 290–297 (1959)
13. Fleischer, L., Jain, K., Mahdian, M.: Tolls for heterogeneous selfish users in multi-commodity networks and generalized congestion games. In: Proceedings of FOCS, pp. 277–285. IEEE (2004)
14. Ford, L.R., Fulkerson, D.R.: Maximal flow through a network. Can. J. Math. **8**, 399–404 (1956). https://doi.org/10.4153/CJM-1956-045-5
15. Harks, T., Kleinert, I., Klimm, M., Möhring, R.H.: Computing network tolls with support constraints. Networks **65**(3), 262–285 (2015)
16. Harwood, R.C., Kollmann, C.J., Stamps, M.T.: A genetic algorithm for the minimum tollbooth problem (2005)
17. Hearn, D.W., Ramana, M.V.: Solving congestion toll pricing models. In: Marcotte, P., Nguyen, S. (eds.) Equilibrium and Advanced Transportation Modelling. Centre for Research on Transportation, pp. 109–124. Springer, Heidelberg (1998). https://doi.org/10.1007/978-1-4615-5757-9_6
18. Krömer, P., Nowaková, J., Hasal, M.: Towards a new evolutionary algorithm for the minimum tollbooth problem. In: Chen, X., Sen, A., Li, W.W., Thai, M.T. (eds.) CSoNet 2018. LNCS, vol. 11280, pp. 116–125. Springer, Cham (2018). https://doi.org/10.1007/978-3-030-04648-4_10
19. Nickerl, J.: The minimum tollbooth problem in atomic network congestion games with unsplittable flows. arXiv preprint arXiv:1906.09865 (2019)
20. Pigou, A.C.: The Economics of Welfare. McMillan&Co., London (1920)

21. Roughgarden, T., Tardos, É.: How bad is selfish routing? JACM **49**(2), 236–259 (2002)
22. Stefanello, F., et al.: On the minimization of traffic congestion in road networks with tolls. Ann. Oper. Res. **249**(1–2), 119–139 (2015)
23. Todd, J.: Duke student math aims to alleviate tollbooth lines. Duke University News and Communications (2005)

Distributed Core Decomposition in Probabilistic Graphs

Qi Luo[1], Dongxiao Yu[1(✉)], Feng Li[1(✉)], Zhenhao Dou[1], Zhipeng Cai[2],
Jiguo Yu[3(✉)], and Xiuzhen Cheng[1]

[1] School of Computer Science and Technology, Shandong University,
Qingdao, People's Republic of China
{luoqi2018,dxyu,fli,douzhenhao,xzcheng}@sdu.edu.cn
[2] Department of Computing Science, Georgia State University, Atlanta, USA
zcai@gsu.edu
[3] School of Computer Science and Technology, Qilu University of Technology,
Jinan, People's Republic of China
jiguoyu@sina.com

Abstract. This paper initializes distributed algorithm studies for core decomposition in probabilistic graphs. Core decomposition has been proven to be a useful primitive for a wide range of graph analyses, but it has been rarely studied in probabilistic graphs, especially in a distributed environment. In this work, under a distributed model underlying Pregel and live distributed systems, we present the first known distributed solutions for core decomposition in probabilistic graphs, where there is an existence probability for each edge. In the scenario that the existence probability of edges are known to nodes, the proposed algorithm can get the exact coreness of nodes with a high probability guarantee. In the harsher case that the existence probability is unknown, we present a novel method to estimate the existence probability of edges, based on which the coreness of nodes with small approximation ratio guarantee can be computed. Extensive experiments are conducted on different types of real-world graphs and synthetic graphs. The results illustrate that the proposed algorithms exhibit good efficiency, stability and scalability.

Keywords: Uncertain graph · Core decomposition · Distributed algorithm

1 Introduction

Uncertainty has been an inherent feature of graph date in real-world applications, which may be caused by a variety of reasons such as noisy measurements and inconsistent information sources [11]. Dealing with uncertainty is necessary in graph analytics, but needs new efficient and effective methods. In this work, we consider graphs with the common edge uncertainty, i.e., probabilistic graphs [9], where each edge is assigned a probability of existence. This type of

© Springer Nature Switzerland AG 2019
A. Tagarelli and H. Tong (Eds.): CSoNet 2019, LNCS 11917, pp. 16–32, 2019.
https://doi.org/10.1007/978-3-030-34980-6_2

uncertain graphs arise in several emerging applications including social, biological and mobile networks. In Protein-Protein Interaction (PPI) networks [2], the edges represent interactions between proteins, which are derived through noisy and error-prone lab experiments and therefore entail uncertainty. In social networks, link prediction and peer influence motivate the need to model interactions between users with uncertainty, and in mobile ad-hoc networks, mobile nodes move and connect to each other, and a link between nodes can be unreliable and may fail with a certain probability.

One of the major issues in graph analytics is identifying cohesive subgraphs and communities [21]. There are lots of indexes to depict the cohesiveness of a graph, such as cliques, k-truss, k-core, F-groups, n-clans and so on [33], among which k-core is recognized as one of the most efficient and helpful ones. One of its most appealing features is that, unlike other notions of dense subgraphs, it can be computed linearly in the size of the input graph. Given a graph G, the k-core is the largest subgraph in G, such that the minimum degree of the subgraph is at least k. The coreness of a node v is defined as the largest k such that there exists a k-core containing v. In static graphs, the computation of the coreness of each node is known as the core decomposition problem. Besides the analysis of cohesive subgroup, core decomposition is also widely used in a large number of applications to analyze the structure and function of a network, e.g., analyzing the topological structure of Internet [4,10], identifying influential spreader in complex networks [26,36], analyzing the structure of large-scale software systems [19,29,34,35], predicting the function of biology network [6], and visualizing large networks [3,7] and so on.

Although k-core without uncertainty have been extensively studied in the literature, their counterparts for probabilistic graphs have not been investigated until very recently [9,31]. In [9], Bonchi et al. presented a counterpart concept of k-core, called (k, η)-core, which is a subgraph consisting of nodes that have at least k neighbors with probability at least η. Based on (k, η)-core, the probabilistic coreness of each node can well defined similar to the coreness in static graphs. It has been shown that such a definition of coreness keeps the appealing feature that can be computed very efficiently. Figure 1 shows an example of (k, η)-core. But the proposed solution is a centralized one. It is still unknown whether the probabilistic coreness can be efficiently derived in a distributed environment. In this work, we answer this question affirmatively.

We study the probabilistic core decomposition problem in a distributed model underlying Pregel [27] and live distributed systems [25]. Specifically, the distributed system we consider is composed of a set of hosts. Each node u in the graph represents a host. Each node can send and receive messages through probabilistic edges and perform local computations in each round. This model represents the reality in many real distributed systems, such as P2P overlays [26], that self-inspect their topologies (peers are nodes in the graph, and their network connections are edges). Clearly, distributed solutions can greatly improve the parallelization of the computation.

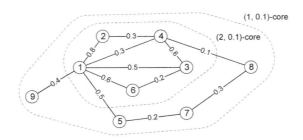

Fig. 1. An example of (k, η)-core

However, it faces a great challenge to compute the probabilistic coreness in the distributed setting, as nodes can only exchange information between neighboring nodes connected by unreliable edges. We prove a locality property of the probabilistic coreness computation, such that the design of distributed coreness computation becomes possible. Our main contributions are summarized as follows:

- We first consider the scenario that the existence probability of edges is known to nodes. In this case, we propose a distributed algorithm that efficiently compute the probabilistic coreness of nodes exactly with a high probability guarantee.
- We then consider the harsher case that the existence probability of edges is unknown to nodes. By first presenting a novel distributed algorithm for estimating the existence probability of edges, we give an algorithm that can compute the probabilistic coreness with small approximation ratio guarantee.

The remaining of the paper is organized as follows. The related work will be introduced in Sect. 2. The problem formulation and preliminaries will be discussed in Sect. 3. In Sects. 4 and 5, the algorithms dealing with cases of knowing and unknowing probability will be presented, respectively. The experimental results will be analyzed in Sect. 6. At last, the paper is concluded in Sect. 7.

2   Related Work

In this section, we make a brief review of related works in core decomposition and probabilistic graphs.

In deterministic graphs, the problem of computing the coreness of nodes, known as the core decomposition problem, has been widely studied [8,13,15,24, 37]. The best known result was given in [8], where the proposed algorithm can compute the coreness of nodes in $O(m)$ time, where m is the number of edges in the graph. As for distributed solutions, in [30], Montresor et al. proposed a distributed algorithm, which can compute the coreness of nodes in $O(n)$ rounds, where n is the number of nodes in the network. The problem how to implement centralized algorithms in real distributed systems was studied in [5,28].

There have been some problems studied in the probabilistic graphs, such as k-nearest-neighbor queries [32], k-truss decomposition [20] and clustering [11]. As for the probabilistic core decomposition, there are only very few recent works focusing on this problem. In [9], the counterpart of k-core in probabilistic graphs, (k, η)-core, was proposed. It was shown that (k, η)-core decomposition can be accomplished in $O(m\Delta)$ time. In [31], Peng et al. proposed another probabilistic coreness, called (k, θ)-core, and showed that the core decomposition can be completed in $O(sm)$ time, where s is number of sample graphs. All above results are done in a centralized setting. To the best of our knowledge, there have been no distributed solutions proposed for probabilistic core decomposition.

3   Problem Formulation and Preliminaries

We consider a probabilistic graph $\mathcal{G} = (V, E, p)$, where $p : E \rightarrow [0, 1]$ defines an existence probability on each edge $e \in E$. Each edge is typically assumed to exist independently [23]. A well-know approach to analyzing and reasoning about probabilistic graphs is to use *possible worlds*: each possible world is a deterministic graph instantiation of $\mathcal{G}$. Notice that by definition, a possible world retains all nodes of $\mathcal{G}$. An $e = (u, v) \in E$ is called a probabilistic edge of u (v). Denote by N_u the set of all probabilistic edges adjacent to u, and let $d_u = |N_u|$. We denote by Δ the max degree of $\mathcal{G}$.

A probabilistic graph can be viewed as a probability space whose outcomes, referred to as possible graphs, are graphs $G = (V, E')$ where any edge $e \in E$ is included in E' with probability $p(e)$, independently of the other edges.

Definition 1 (Possible Graph). *Given a probabilistic graph $\mathcal{G} = (V, E, p)$, $|E| = m$, there are 2^m possible deterministic graphs, each of which containing a subset of the edges in E. More precisely, an probabilistic graph $\mathcal{G} = (V, E, p)$ yields a set of possible graphs $\{G = (V, E_G)\}_{E_G \subseteq E}$, and the probability of observing a possible graph G is:*

$$Pr(G) = \prod_{e \in E_G} p_e \prod_{e \in E \setminus E_G} (1 - p_e).$$

For a node v of the input probabilistic graph $\mathcal{G}$, the probability $Pr[deg(v) \geq k]$ can be expressed as:

$$Pr[deg(v) \geq k] = \sum_{G \sqsubseteq \mathcal{G}_{deg(v) \geq k}} Pr(G),$$

where $\mathcal{G}_{deg(v) \geq k}$ is the set of all possible graphs drawn from $\mathcal{G}$ in which v has degree at least k.

Given a threshold $\eta \in [0, 1]$, for every node v in the graph $\mathcal{G}$, there exists a value $\hat{k} \in [0, deg(v)]$, such that for all $h \leq \hat{k}$, $Pr[deg(v) \geq h] \geq \eta$, and for all $h > \hat{k}$, $Pr[deg(v) \geq h] < \eta$. We then call $\hat{k}$ the η-degree of node v. Formally,

$$\eta\text{-}deg(v) = max\{k | Pr[deg(v) \geq k] \geq \eta\}.$$

In a probabilistic graph, if the η-degree of every node in a subgraph $\mathcal{H}$ is not smaller than a threshold η, we call the subgraph as a (k, η)-core.

Definition 2 ((k, η)-Core). *Given a probabilistic graph $\mathcal{G} = (V, E, p)$, a non-negative integer k and a threshold $\eta \in [0, 1]$, the (k, η)-core is a subgraph H in which for each node $v \in V_H : \eta\text{-}deg(v) \geq k$.*

Definition 3 (η-Coreness). *Given a graph $\mathcal{G} = (V, E, p)$ and threshold η, the η-coreness of a node $u \in \mathcal{G}$, denoted by $\eta\text{-}core(u)$, is the largest k, such that there exists a (k, η)-core containing u.*

The problem of computing the η-coreness of all nodes in a probabilistic graph is called *probabilistic core decomposition*.

System Model. We next present the distributed system. The distributed system we consider is composed of a set of hosts. Each node $u \in V$ in $\mathcal{G}$ represents a host, which is used to compute the η-coreness of node u, and connections among hosts are the edges. The existence probability of an edge can be thought as the communication success rate of hosts. Each node can send and receive messages through probabilistic edges and perform local computations in each round. Only if the edge between a pair of nodes exists in a round, the transmissions between this pair of nodes succeeds.

Locality Property. We next show a locality property for the computation of (k, η)-core, i.e., the η-coreness of a node u is only determined by the η-coreness of nodes in N_u. The locality property ensures the possibility of computing the η-coreness based on local communication, such that efficient distributed solutions can be devised.

Theorem 1 (Locality). $\forall u \in V : \eta\text{-}core(u) = k$ *if and only if*

(i) *there exist a subset $V_k \subset N_u$ such that $|V_k| = k$ and $\forall v \in V_k : \eta\text{-}core(v) \geq k$ and*

(ii) *there is no subset $V_{k+1} \subset N_u$ such that $|V_{k+1}| = k + 1$ and $\forall v \in V_{k+1} : \eta\text{-}core(v) \geq k + 1$.*

Proof. We give the proof of adequacy and necessity respectively.

$\Rightarrow$ According to the definition of η-coreness, for a node u, $\eta\text{-}core(u) = k$. For a given threshold η, assume $u \in H_k$ where H_k is a (k, η)-core. By the definition, there does not exist a $(k + 1, \eta)$-core H_{k+1} such that $u \in H_{k+1}$.
The part (i) follows from the fact that for any node $u \in H_k$, $\eta\text{-}deg(v) \geq k$, and hence at least k neighbors of v are in H_k and each neighbor has η-degree not smaller than k.
For part (ii), assume there are $k+1$ neighbors of u with η-coreness not smaller than $k + 1$. Denote these $k + 1$ neighbors as $\{v_1, \ldots, v_{k+1}\}$. Let H_{k+1} be the $(k+1, \eta)$-core containing $v_1, \ldots, v_{k+1}$ except u. Clearly, the induced subgraph by adding u into H_{k+1} is also a $(k + 1, \eta)$-core, which contradicts with the assumption that $\eta\text{-}core(u) = k$.

$\Leftarrow$ For each node $v_i \in V_k$, η-$core(v_i) \geq k$. Let H_k be a (k, η)-core containing V_k. Let H'_k be the induced subgraph by adding u into H_k. It is easy to see that in H'_k, the η-degree of every node is at least k, and hence H'_k is also a (k, η)-core. So η-$core(u) \geq k$.

Now consider η-$core(u) = k' \geq k + 1$. This means that there is a (k', η)-core containing u, i.e., u has at least $k' \leq k + 1$ neighbors whose η-degree is at least k', which contradicts with our hypothesis (ii). Then we can conclude that η-$core(u) = k$.

The locality property ensures that the η-coreness of the neighbors of a node is sufficient to compute the η-coreness of the node itself. Based on this property, we present distributed core decomposition algorithms in probabilistic graphs for both scenarios where the existence probabilities of edges are known and unknown in prior, with the intuition as follows: each node tries to transmit its current estimation of η-coreness to its neighbors in each round; every node then updates its estimate of the η-coreness based on the received messages from neighbors. We show that our algorithms can ensure the estimates convergent to the true η-coreness of nodes.

4   Distributed Probabilistic Core Decomposition with Known Probability

In this section, we consider the scenario that the edge probabilities are known to nodes in advance. It is possible that in some systems the nodes already know in advance the probabilities of success in communicating with the neighbors nodes. At the beginning, the initial estimate of the η-coreness of every node is set to be its η-degree, which can be computed using the algorithm given in [9], the *changed* flag is set to *true*. Only nodes with non-zero η-degree join the algorithm execution. In each round, for a node v, if the *changed* flag is *true*, v tries to transmit the estimate to its neighbors. If v receives new estimates from its neighbors, it updates its own estimate based on the locality property. If v's estimate changed, it keeps the *changed* flag as *true*, and *false* otherwise. The pseudo codes for the core decomposition algorithm and core estimation are given in Algorithms 1 and 2, and we can get the following result for core decomposition. Due to the space limitation, the proof is put in the full version [38].

Theorem 2. *With high probability, the η-coreness of nodes can be computed after $O(\frac{m \log n}{\eta})$ rounds by DPCD (Algorithm 1). The message complexity of the algorithm is $O(\frac{m^2 \log n}{\eta})$.*

Algorithm 1: DPCD: Distributed Probabilistic Core Decomposition with Known Probability

---

Input : probabilistic graph $\mathcal{G}(V, E, p)$, a threshold η
Output: probabilistic coreness of each node

Initialization

1 | changed ← true;
2 | $est[u] ← \eta\text{-}deg(u)$;
3 | **foreach** $v \in neighbor(u)$ **do** $est[v] ← \infty$

4   **if** $\eta\text{-}deg(u) > 0$ **then**
    | **repeat**
5 | | **if** *changed* **then**
6 | | | send $< u, est[u] >$ to $neighbor(u)$;
7 | | | changed ← false ;
8 | | **if** receive $< v, k >$ **then**
9 | | | **if** $k < est[v]$ **then**
10 | | | | $est[v] ← k$;
11 | | | | $t ←$ computeEstCore $(est, u, \eta\text{-}deg(u))$;
12 | | | | **if** $t < est[u]$ **then**
13 | | | | | $est[u] ← t$;
14 | | | | | changed ← true ;

---

5   Distributed Probabilistic Core Decomposition with Unknown Probability

In this section, we consider the scenario where the existence probability of edges are unknown to nodes. In this case, we need to first estimate the existence probability of every edge, and then using the estimated probability to compute the η-coreness of nodes.

We first present an algorithm that consists of two stages: the first stage is used for estimating the existence probability of edges, and the second stage is for the computation of the coreness. Then, we give an algorithm which makes the two operations executed in parallel. By the experimental results given in the next section, the latter algorithm can greatly reduce the computation time while sacrificing a the computation accuracy a bit.

5.1   Distributed Probabilistic Core Decomposition with Probability Estimation

The algorithm consists of two stages. The first stage contains $\mathcal{R} = \frac{c \log n}{\eta}$ rounds, where η is the given threshold on the coreness computation. In each round, every node tries to transmit a message to neighboring nodes through probabilistic

---

Algorithm 2: computeEstCore $(est, u, \eta\text{-}deg(u))$

---

1 **for** $i = 1$ **to** k **do** $count[i] \leftarrow 0$;
2 $d \leftarrow \eta\text{-}deg(u)$;
3 $N'_V(u) \leftarrow$ take d neighbors in descending order of edge probability from $N_V(u)$;
4 **foreach** $v \in N'_V(u)$ **do**
5 $\quad j \leftarrow min(k, est[v])$;
6 $\quad count[j] = count[j] + 1$;

7 **for** $i = k$ **to** 2 **do**
8 $\quad count[i-1] \leftarrow count[i-1] + count[i]$;

9 $i \leftarrow k$;
10 **while** $i > 1$ **and** $count[i] < i$ **do**
11 $\quad i \leftarrow i - 1$

12 **return** i ;

---

edges. After the stage, for each node u and an edge $e = (u, v)$, the estimate of the existence probability of e at node u is set as the ratio of the number of messages u received from v and $\mathcal{R}$. As shown later, this estimate can be very close to the true probability by a factor up to δ, where δ can be any constant.

In the second stage, with the estimate of the existence probability of edges, Algorithm 1 is invoked to compute the approximate coreness. The pseudo code of the algorithm is given in Algorithm 3, and we can get the following result for the algorithm. Due to the space limitation, the proof of Theorem 3 is put in the full version [38].

Theorem 3. *With high probability, the η-coreness of nodes with approximation ratio ϵ for any constant ϵ can be computed in $O(\frac{m \log n}{\eta})$ rounds by DPCD-PE. The message complexity of the algorithm is $O(\frac{m^2 \log n}{\eta})$.*

5.2 Parallel Execution of Two Stages

To further improve the efficiency of the coreness computation, we present Algorithm 4 which makes the operations in the two stages of probability estimation and coreness estimation executed in parallel. In particular, in each round, every node first estimates the existence probabilities of connected edges, and then estimate the coreness based on the estimated existence probability. The details are given in Algorithm 4. Using a very similar analysis as that for Algorithm 3, we can show the correctness of Algorithm 4. As shown in the subsequent section, Algorithm 4 is much more efficient than Algorithm 3 in reality.

Algorithm 3: DPCD-PE: Distributed core Decomposition by Probability Estimation

---

Input : probabilistic graph without probabilities $\mathcal{G}(V, E)$, a threshold η
Output: probabilistic coreness of each node

Stage 1

 Initialization

1   **foreach** $v \in neighbor(u)$ **do**
2    $count[v] \leftarrow 0$;

3 **repeat**
4   **send** $< u, \text{bit} >$ to $neighbor(u)$;
5   **if** receive $< v, \text{bit} >$ **then**
6    $count[v] \leftarrow count[v] + 1$;

 until $\mathcal{R}$ *rounds*;

7 $p_{(u,v)} \leftarrow \frac{count[v]}{R}$;
8 **return** p ;

Stage 2
9 DPCD $(\mathcal{G}(V, E, p), \eta)$;

---

6 Experiments

In this section, we evaluate the effectiveness and efficiency of the proposed algorithms. We conducted experiments to evaluate the running time and the accuracy of our algorithms in the real-world graphs and the synthetic graphs, respectively. The baseline we used is the (k, η)-core decomposition algorithm in [9]. All programs were implemented in standard C++ and compiled with Visual Studio 2017. All experiment were performed on a machine with Intel Core i7-7700 3.6 GHz and 24 GB DDR3-RAM in Windows 10.

6.1 Evaluation on Real-World Graphs

For real-world graphs, four probabilistic graph data sets are used. Three of them are protein-protein interaction (PPI) networks with different distribution of edge probabilities. In a PPI network, two proteins are connected if they are likely to interact. **Collins** [14] is mainly composed of high probability edges; **Gavin** [17], most edges in this graph have low existence probabilities; **Krogan** [22], 25% edges in this graph have existence probability larger than 0.9, and the existence probability of the rest edges are almost uniform distributed between 0.27 and 0.9. **DBLP** [11], nodes are authors in the graph and two authors are connected by an edge if they have co-authored at least one journal paper together. Each edge has an existence probability $1 - e^{\frac{x}{2}}$, where x is the number of collaborations between the two authors. About 80% of the edges have an existence probability

---

Algorithm 4: DPCD-PSE: Distributed Probabilistic Core Decomposition with Parallel Stage Execution

---

Input : probabilistic graph without probabilities $\mathcal{G}(V, E, p)$, a threshold η

Output: probabilistic coreness of each node

Initialization

1    $R \leftarrow 1$;
2   changed $\leftarrow$ true;
3    $est[u] \leftarrow deg(u)$;
4   **foreach** $v \in neighbor(u)$ **do**
5      $est[v] \leftarrow \infty$;
6      $count[v] \leftarrow 0$;

7 **Repeat**
8   **if** *changed* **then**
9   send $< u, est[u] >$ to $neighbor(u)$;
10   changed $\leftarrow$ false ;

11   **if** receive $< v, k >$ **then then**
12      $est[v] \leftarrow k$;
13      $count[v] \leftarrow count[v] + 1$;
14      $Pr[v] \leftarrow count[v]/R$;
15   compute η-$deg(u)$ by est and η ;
16      $t \leftarrow$ computeEstCore$(est, u, \eta$-$deg(u))$;
17   **if** $t \neq est[u]$ **then**
18        $est[u] \leftarrow t$;
19   changed $\leftarrow$ true ;

20    $R \leftarrow R + 1$;

---

of 0.39, 12% have a probability of 0.63, and the remaining 8% have a higher probability. The statistics of the four graphs are summarized in Table 1(a).

We first evaluate the running time of the algorithms on each datasets under different η values. The evaluation results are given in Fig. 2.

It can be seen that all algorithms can compute the coreness very efficiently, even if in the large graph DBLP. DPCD always takes the smallest number of rounds to compute the coreness, but it needs to know the existence probability of edges in prior. On almost all graphs, DPCD can compute the coreness after only dozens of rounds. As η increases, the running time of all algorithms decreases. This is because when η is larger, less nodes and edges need to be considered in the computation. Comparing with DPCD-PE, DPCD-PSE takes less time in all cases.

Table 1. Statistics of data sets. d_{avg} is the average degree. d_{max} is the max degree. p_{avg} is the average existence probability of edges.

(a) Real-world graphs.

Datasets	Nodes	Edges	d_{avg}	d_{max}	p_{avg}
Collins	1622	9074	11.1886	127	0.7821
Gavin	1855	1669	8.2684	48	0.3564
Krogan	3674	14317	7.7979	213	0.4155
DBLP	636781	2366461	7.4329	446	0.4593

(b) Synthetic graphs.

Scale	Nodes	Edges	$\hat{d}_{avg}$	d_{max}	p_{avg}
10^3	1024	1541	3.4308	18	0.4955
10^4	16384	34524	4.6345	50	0.5009
10^5	131072	335381	5.5659	123	0.5004
10^6	1048576	3156528	6.4785	273	0.4998

We next evaluate the accuracy of the algorithms. We compare the computed coreness of nodes computed by the proposed algorithms with the baseline algorithm. The evaluation is conducted on all four data sets. Because the existence probability distribution of the four graphs are significantly different, we conduct the evaluation on four graphs with different threshold η. The evaluation results are shown in Fig. 3. From the figure, it can be seen that all three algorithms can correctly compute the coreness for almost all nodes. In comparison, DPCD has the highest accuracy, which can correctly compute the coreness for all nodes. This is consistent with our theoretical analysis.

6.2   Evaluation on Synthetic Graphs

Internet topology and peer-to-peer networks follow the power-laws degree distribution [16], while still have a small diameter [1]. The Recursive Matrix (R-MAT) model [12], which can naturally generates power-law degree distributions, is used to generate synthetic graph data in different scale. The synthetic graphs what we used have the same parameter setting, which ensures the similar attributes among them. The parameters of the R-MAT model used in our experiment are $\{a = 45, b = 15, c = 15, d = 25\}$. The probability of an edge is determined by the frequency of duplicated edges in the graph generation process in the R-MAT model. The range of edge probabilities is $[0.01, 1]$ in our experiments. The scale of nodes increases from 10^3 to 10^6. The statistics of the synthetic graphs are shown in Table 1(b).

We first evaluate the running time of the three algorithms on synthetic graphs. The evaluation results are illustrated in Fig. 4. It can be seen that in all

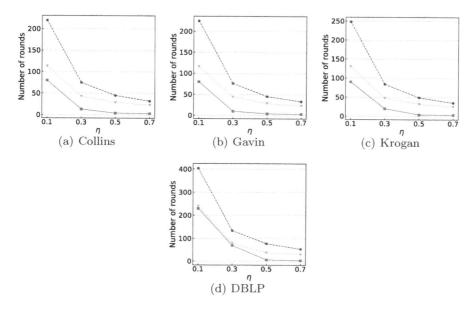

(a) Collins   (b) Gavin   (c) Krogan

(d) DBLP

Fig. 2. The running time of the proposed algorithms under different η on real-world graphs.

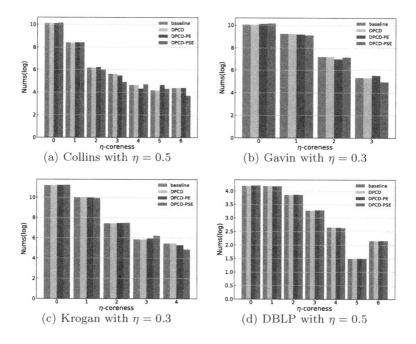

(a) Collins with $\eta = 0.5$ (b) Gavin with $\eta = 0.3$

(c) Krogan with $\eta = 0.3$ (d) DBLP with $\eta = 0.5$

Fig. 3. Comparisons of computed coreness on real-world graphs.

Table 2. The errors of the computed η-coreness in synthetic graphs

η	0.1				0.3				0.5				0.7			
Algorithm	DPCD-PE		DPCD-PSE		DPCD-PE		DPCD-PSE		DPCD-PE		DPCD-PSE		DPCD-PE		DPCD-PSE	
ED	1	2	1	2	1	2	1	2	1	2	1	2	1	2	1	2
10^3	16	2	458	47	194	39	381	12	144	2	233	4	5	2	22	0
10^4	931	18	4731	161	3071	51	6858	312	1606	4	2441	6	7	0	138	2
10^5	20805	1746	44967	2547	24393	141	40108	2276	10068	6	14610	2	41	2	556	0
10^6	179715	12947	708129	16875	219682	330	411134	18572	94260	11	136132	2	334	0	5036	0

cases, the coreness can be efficiently computed using all three algorithms. Similar as that in the real-world graphs, DPCD has the best performance, but it needs to know the existence probability of edges in prior. Furthermore, as the number of nodes increases, the running time of all three algorithm increases. However, it can be found that the running time increase linearly when the number of nodes increases exponentially. In comparision, the running time of DPCD-PSE is roughly half of that for DPCD-PE.

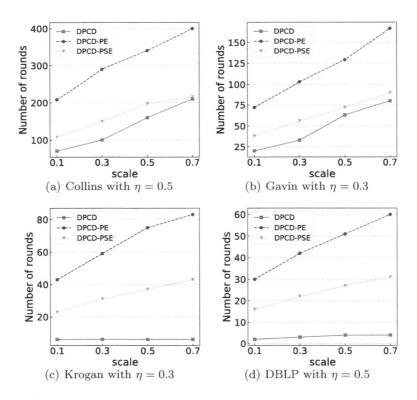

(a) Collins with $\eta = 0.5$ (b) Gavin with $\eta = 0.3$

(c) Krogan with $\eta = 0.3$ (d) DBLP with $\eta = 0.5$

Fig. 4. The running time of the proposed algorithms when the graph size changes.

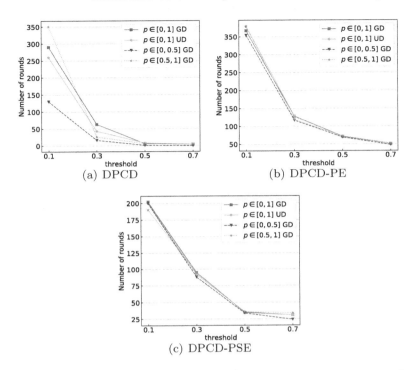

Fig. 5. The running time of the proposed algorithms under different edge probability distributions. UD and GD represent the uniform distribution and the gaussian distribution, respectively.

In order to test the performance of the algorithms under different probability distributions, we conduct the experiments on synthetic graphs with four different probability distributions. We adopt the node scale is 10^5 for the synthetic graph and the four distributions are gaussian distribution with $p \in [0, 1]$, uniform distribution with $p \in [0, 1]$, gaussian distribution with $p \in [0, 0.5]$ and gaussian distribution with $p \in [0.5, 1]$. The evaluation results are given in Fig. 5. It can be seen that different probability distributions influence the performance of DPCD heavier than the other two algorithms. The two algorithms without needing prior knowledge on the existence probability of edges are insensitive to the probability distribution.

In the scenario of the edge probabilities are unknown, the η-coreness of nodes may differ from the true value due to the probabilities of edges are estimated in our algorithms. To evaluate the errors, we conduct experiments on synthetic graphs under different thresholds. The evaluation results are summarized in Table 2. The experimental results showed that over 80% of the η-coreness of nodes can be computed correctly by DPCD-PE, and over 60% of the nodes' coreness are correctly computed by DPCD-PSE. Furthermore, almost all of the error η-coreness differs from the true value by ±1. Only a few nodes have error difference of 2, and none have error difference larger than 2.

7   Conclusion

We studied the problem of designing distributed algorithms for core decomposition in probabilistic graphs. By presenting a locality property, we showed that distributed algorithm design is possible for the (k, η)-coreness, a counterpart in the probabilistic graph of the extensively studied k-core in deterministic graphs. Based on the locality property, efficient algorithms for probabilistic core decomposition were proposed for both scenarios that the existence probability of edges are known or unknown to nodes. Extensive experiments on real-world graphs and synthetic graphs demonstrate the efficiency of the proposed algorithms in reality.

This work initiates distributed algorithm studies in probabilistic graphs. It is meaningful to investigate whether efficient distributed solutions can be derived for other fundamental problems in graph analytics.

Acknowledgement. This work is partially supported by NSFC (No. 61971269, 61832012, 61672321, 61771289, 61702304) and Shandong Provincial Natural Science Foundation (No. ZR2017QF005).

References

1. Albert, R., Barabási, A.: Statistical mechanics of complex networks. CoRR cond-mat/0106096 (2001)
2. Altaf-Ul-Amin, M., Koma, T., Kurokawa, K., Kanaya, S.: Prediction of protein functions based on protein-protein interaction networks: a min-cut approach. In: Proceedings of the 21st International Conference on Data Engineering Workshops, ICDE, p. 1156 (2005)
3. Alvarez-Hamelin, J.I., Dall'Asta, L., Barrat, A., Vespignani, A.: Large scale networks fingerprinting and visualization using the K-core decomposition. In: Neural Information Processing Systems, NIPS, pp. 41–50 (2005)
4. Alvarez-Hamelin, J.I., Dall'Asta, L., Barrat, A., Vespignani, A.: K-core decomposition of internet graphs: hierarchies, self-similarity and measurement biases. NHM **3**(2), 371–393 (2008)
5. Aridhi, S., Brugnara, M., Montresor, A., Velegrakis, Y.: Distributed K-core decomposition and maintenance in large dynamic graphs. In: Proceedings of the 10th ACM International Conference on Distributed and Event-based Systems, DEBS, pp. 161–168 (2016)
6. Bader, G.D., Hogue, C.W.V.: An automated method for finding molecular complexes in large protein interaction networks. BMC Bioinform. **4**, 2 (2003)
7. Batagelj, V., Mrvar, A., Zaversnik, M.: Partitioning approach to visualization of large graphs. In: Proceedings of the 7th International Symposium Graph Drawing, GD 1999, Stirín Castle, Czech Republic, pp. 90–97, September 1999
8. Batagelj, V., Zaversnik, M.: An o(m) algorithm for cores decomposition of networks. CoRR cs.DS/0310049 (2003)
9. Bonchi, F., Gullo, F., Kaltenbrunner, A., Volkovich, Y.: Core decomposition of uncertain graphs. In: The 20th ACM SIGKDD International Conference on Knowledge Discovery and Data Mining, KDD 2014, pp. 1316–1325 (2014)

10. Carmi, S., Havlin, S., Kirkpatrick, S.: From the cover: a model of internet topology using K-shell decomposition. Proc. Nat. Acad. Sci. **104**(27), 11150–11154 (2007)
11. Ceccarello, M., Fantozzi, C., Pietracaprina, A., Pucci, G., Vandin, F.: Clustering uncertain graphs. PVLDB **11**(4), 472–484 (2017)
12. Chakrabarti, D., Zhan, Y., Faloutsos, C.: R-mat: a recursive model for graph mining. In: Proceedings of the Fourth SIAM International Conference on Data Mining, pp. 442–446 (2004)
13. Cheng, J., Ke, Y., Chu, S., Özsu, M.T.: Efficient core decomposition in massive networks. In: Proceedings of the 27th International Conference on Data Engineering, ICDE, pp. 51–62 (2011)
14. Collins, S.R., Kemmeren, P., Zhao, X.C., Greenblatt, J.F., Spencer, F., Holstege, F.C., Weissman, J.S., Krogan, N.J.: Toward a comprehensive atlas of the physical interactome of saccharomyces cerevisiae. Mol. Cell. Proteomics Mcp **6**(3), 439 (2007)
15. Dasari, N.S., Ranjan, D., Zubair, M.: Park: an efficient algorithm for K-core decomposition on multicore processors. In: IEEE International Conference on Big Data, ICBD, pp. 9–16 (2014)
16. Faloutsos, M., Faloutsos, P., Faloutsos, C.: On power-law relationships of the internet topology. In: Proceedings of the ACM SIGCOMM Conference on Applications, Technologies, Architectures, and Protocols for Computer Communication, SIGCOMM, pp. 251–262 (1999)
17. Gavin, A.C., et al.: Proteome survey reveals modularity of the yeast cell machinery. Nature **440**(7084), 631–636 (2006)
18. Hahn, G.J., Doganaksoy, N.: A career in statistics. Wiley Online Library (2011)
19. Huang, X., Cheng, H., Li, R., Qin, L., Yu, J.X.: Top-K structural diversity search in large networks. PVLDB **6**(13), 1618–1629 (2013)
20. Huang, X., Lu, W., Lakshmanan, L.V.S.: Truss decomposition of probabilistic graphs: semantics and algorithms. In: Proceedings of the International Conference on Management of Data, SIGMOD, pp. 77–90 (2016)
21. Li, C., Tang, Y., Lin, H., Chengzhe, Y., Mai, H.: Parallel overlapping community detection algorithm in complex networks based on label propagation. Scientia Sinica **46**(2), 212 (2016)
22. Krogen, N.J.: Global landscape of protein complexes in the yeast saccharomyces cerevisiae. Nature **440**(7084), 637–643 (2006)
23. Jin, R., Liu, L., Aggarwal, C.C.: Discovering highly reliable subgraphs in uncertain graphs. In: Proceedings of the 17th ACM SIGKDD International Conference on Knowledge Discovery and Data Mining, pp. 992–1000 (2011)
24. Khaouid, W., Barsky, M., Venkatesh, S., Thomo, A.: K-core decomposition of large networks on a single PC. PVLDB **9**(1), 13–23 (2015)
25. Krepska, E., Kielmann, T., Fokkink, W., Bal, H.E.: A high-level framework for distributed processing of large-scale graphs. In: Proceedings of The 12th International Conference Distributed Computing and Networking, ICDCN, pp. 155–166 (2011)
26. Kitsak, M., et al.: Identification of influential spreaders in complex networks. Nature Phys. **6**(11), 888–893 (2010)
27. Malewicz, G., et al.: Pregel: a system for large-scale graph processing. In: Proceedings of the ACM SIGMOD International Conference on Management of Data, SIGMOD, pp. 135–146 (2010)
28. Mandal, A., Hasan, M.A.: A distributed K-core decomposition algorithm on spark. In: IEEE International Conference on Big Data, ICBD, pp. 976–981 (2017)

29. Meyer, P., Siy, H.P., Bhowmick, S.: Identifying important classes of large software systems through K-core decomposition. Adv. Complex Syst. **17**(7–8), 1550004 (2014)
30. Montresor, A., Pellegrini, F.D., Miorandi, D.: Distributed K-core decomposition. In: Proceedings of the 30th Annual ACM Symposium on Principles of Distributed Computing, PODC, pp. 207–208 (2011)
31. Peng, Y., Zhang, Y., Zhang, W., Lin, X., Qin, L.: Efficient probabilistic K-core computation on uncertain graphs. In: 34th IEEE International Conference on Data Engineering, ICDE, pp. 1192–1203 (2018)
32. Potamias, M., Bonchi, F., Gionis, A., Kollios, G.: K-nearest neighbors in uncertain graphs. PVLDB **3**(1), 997–1008 (2010)
33. Robert, A.H., Mark, R.: Introduction to social network methods. Department of Sociology, University of California Riverside (2005)
34. Sariyüce, A.E., Seshadhri, C., Pinar, A., Çatalyürek, Ü.V.: Finding the hierarchy of dense subgraphs using nucleus decompositions. In: Proceedings of the 24th International Conference on World Wide Web, WWW, pp. 927–937 (2015)
35. Zhang, H., Zhao, H., Cai, W., Liu, J., Zhou, W.: Using the k-core decomposition to analyze the static structure of large-scale software systems. J. Supercomput. **53**(2), 352–369 (2010)
36. Zhao, X., Liu, F., Xing, S., Wang, Q.: Identifying influential spreaders in social networks via normalized local structure attributes. IEEE Access **6**, 66095–66104 (2018)
37. Zhu, R., Zou, Z., Li, J.: Diversified coherent core search on multi-layer graphs. In: 34th IEEE International Conference on Data Engineering, ICDE, pp. 701–712 (2018)
38. Full version. https://pan.baidu.com/s/1DK_XjOqkUhNm_NHDLgTK5w

Sampled Fictitious Play on Networks

Alexander Nikolaev[1], Alexander Semenov[2(✉)], and Eduardo L. Pasiliao[3]

[1] University at Buffalo, 312 Bell Hall, Buffalo, NY 14260, USA
`anikolae@buffalo.edu`
[2] University of Jyväskylä, P.O. Box 35, 40014 Jyväskylä, Finland
`alexander.v.semenov@jyu.fi`
[3] Air Force Research Laboratory, Eglin AFB, FL 32542, USA
`eduardo.pasiliao@us.af.mil`

Abstract. We formulate and solve the problem of optimizing the structure of an information propagation network between multiple agents. In a given space of *interests* (e.g., information on certain targets), each agent is defined by a vector of their desirable information, called *filter*, and a vector of available information, called *source*. The agents seek to build a directed network that maximizes the value of the desirable source-information that reaches each agent having been filtered *en route*, less the expense that each agent incurs in filtering any information of no interest to them. We frame this optimization problem as a game of common interest, where the Nash equilibria can be attained as limit points of Sampled Fictitious Play (SFP), offering a method that turns out computationally effective in traversing the huge space of feasible networks on a given node set. Our key idea lies in the creative use of history in SFP, leading to the new History Value-Weighted SFP method. To our knowledge, this is the first successful application of FP for network structure optimization. The appeal of our work is supported by the outcomes of the computational experiments that compare the performance of several algorithms in two settings: centralized (full information) and decentralized (local information).

Keywords: Social networks · Information diffusion · Fictitious play

1 Introduction

Social networks is an ideal medium for information diffusion. Most successful social media sites have millions of users, with Facebook serving over two billion people. Typically, users share the information available to them with and through their peers; in other words, information tends to spread in a cascading fashion, where each user gets to see the information they like and consider worth spreading as well as the information they do not like and have to filter through.

Social media sites allow users to add and remove peers from their friendship circles. Consequently, as it has been shown [1], users tend to polarize: the users who share opinions and interests of like-minded peers add those peers as friends,

© Springer Nature Switzerland AG 2019
A. Tagarelli and H. Tong (Eds.): CSoNet 2019, LNCS 11917, pp. 33–44, 2019.
https://doi.org/10.1007/978-3-030-34980-6_3

and un-friend (un-follow) those peers whose interests are not favored. Up to now, however, little attention has been paid to the fact that in reality each user has an array of different interests: two users may be in agreement on the appeal of certain topics, while at the same time disagreeing on others. For instance, if users A and B support the same basketball team, but discover they do not like each other's posts about politics (perhaps because of the differences in the views), should they stay friends a social media site? Here, we assume that both of them get to see all the information posted on each other's feeds. If user A decides to un-follow user B, and start following user C who shares A's political likings, then A would have to worry about getting the news about their basketball team from another source; besides, user C might have other interests, too, that would not perfectly align with those of A. Moreover, some peers of user A may now decide to un-follow A because they would not be receiving the basketball news from A anymore. Due to such considerations, the friendship-followship network structure might never stabilize, ever undergoing the domino effect-like changes. In fact, strategically, social network users would be better off finding and keeping some good connection structure, which would serve them all in accordance with their values in terms of the desired quality of information received, and perhaps, desired popularity also.

A similar objective can be foreseen as desirable for a team of unmanned aerial vehicles (UAVs) the communicating agents, each transmitting at its own frequency. Here, the agents build information propagation channels by deciding whose frequencies to read, with each agent having its own preference regarding which information (on which targets) should be viewed as important and be retransmitted, and which should be viewed as unimportant and be filtered out. In this case, the objective of the entire UAV team is for each to receive as much relevant information as possible, at as little total energy cost as possible.

Both cases described above can be treated by a general optimization problem of building a network between a given set of agents that maximizes some global objective, with this objective being expressed as a given function of the agents' attributes and the network structure. In this paper, we store the agents' interests as vectors; each vector element corresponds to a certain "topic/target. Information is assumed to diffuse through the network in a cascading fashion. Without loss of generality, we assume that each agent is a *source* of the information on some topics/targets; also, each agent has its own *filter* that reflects the information on which topics/targets is of interest to them. Whenever an agents (re-)transmits information to a peer, the peer filters it first and then spreads it on. Striving to maximize the global communication value objective, the agents build the network progressively by taking *actions*: an eligible action can have an agent connect to some peer(s), or disconnect from some peer(s), or make no change.

With the objective of identifying such a network configuration that would result in the best utility for all agents combined, the key challenge of this problem lies in the vastness of its solution space. Indeed, the size of the feasible solution set equals the number of distinct directed graphs that have the same number of nodes. For n nodes, this number is $2^{n\,(n-1)}$, which amounts to 2^{90} possible states for a problem on just 10 nodes. Further, all the actions are available in all the states, so there exists no convenient state dependency structure that could help guide the traversal of the states in an organized manner.

Our main contributions towards solving the stated problem are as follows:

- we formulate the problem of network formation given attribute-rich nodes,
- we present a novel approach and a set of algorithms for finding optimal network configurations, employing the theory for solving games of common interests,
- we analyze the performance of both the centralized and decentralized versions of our algorithms, and confirm their scalability and practical value.

The rest of the paper is structured as follows: the next section states our problem formally; another section offers the necessary background on the theory of fictitious play and sampled fictitious play, and presents our approach; next, we set up and discuss the results of our computational experiments; the final section offers concluding remarks.

2   Formal Problem Statement

Given a set of nodes (communicating agents), N. For every node $i \in N$, given are two K-dimensional binary vectors: *filter* f_i and *source* s_i. The elements of these node-defining attribute vectors are interpreted as the topics/targets of possible interest to the agents; the filter describes what kind of information node i would like to have, while the source describes what kind of information node i has by default, i.e., from its private source.

Define a space of directed graphs G with the elements of the form $g = g(N, E) \in G$, $E = \{e_{ij}\}$, where each binary variable e_{ij}, $i \in N$, $j \in N$, assumes the value of one if the edge from node i to node j exists (the direct communication channel is open), and the value of zero otherwise (the direct communication channel is closed). With each of the variables e_{ij}, $i \in N$, $j \in N$, set to either one or zero, the resulting directed graph $g \in G(N, E)$ defines the information propagation channel structure between the nodes.

The outcome of the information propagation process over all the available directed paths, for every node $i \in N$, is captured by two K-dimensional binary vectors, *reception* r_i and *knowledge* k_i, such that the equalities

$$r_i(g) = \cup_{\{j:\, e_{ji}=1\}} k_j(g),$$

$$k_i(g) = s_i \cup r_i(g) \cap f_i$$

hold simultaneously for all $i \in N$. This ensures that the source information s_j that reaches node i can be found as a union over all the directed paths from j to i, where for each path, all the intermediary nodes on the path together apply their filters to s_j. This described mechanism is similar to that which is implemented on Twitter, assuming that each user will tweet/re-tweet everything they like, and disregard (filter out) everything that they receive but do not like.

To illustrate how the above described information spread process can be captured mathematically, see Fig. 1. Assuming that only node 1 has source information in this network configuration, the information propagates to node 6 simultaneously along two paths:

$$s1 \rightarrow f2 \rightarrow f3 \rightarrow f5 \rightarrow \text{node}\,6,$$

$$s1 \rightarrow f2 \rightarrow f4 \rightarrow f5 \rightarrow \text{node}\,6.$$

In vector form, the information that node 6 thereby *receives* can be expressed as

$$r_6 = s_1 \odot f_2 \odot f_3 \odot f_5 + s_1 \odot f_2 \odot f_4 \odot f_5,$$

with $\odot$ denoting the Hadamard product [6]. The information that node 6 keeps as *knowledge* (for potential further sharing) is

$$k_6 = r_6 \odot f_6.$$

Fig. 1. Two source-information propagation paths from node 1 to node 6.

We now define the local objective function for node $i \in N$ in graph $g \in G$ as the *weighted difference* between (1) the number of topics that $i \in N$ receives information about and which align with its interests, and (2) those which do not align with its interests,

$$o_i(g) = (k_i(g) - \gamma\,(r_i(g) - r_i(g) \cap f_i))^T\,\mathbf{1},$$

with the weight $\gamma \in (0,1)$ defining the tradeoff of how much filtering effort an agent would agree to expend to receive one extra unit of information of interest. The global objective function value for graph $g \in G$ is defined as

$$o(g) = \sum_i o_i(g).$$

We are now ready to formulate an optimization problem of building such a communication network between a given set of agents that maximizes this global objective over the space of feasible graphs $g \in G$,

$$E^* = argmax_{\{e_{ij}\}_{i \in N, j \in N}}\,o(g). \tag{1}$$

Example. Given four nodes, with the filter and source vectors shown in Tables D and E of Fig. 2, the task is to construct a graph that solves (1). Three feasible solutions – graphs A, B, and C – are shown at the top of Fig. 2; Table F gives the individual objective values achieved by the nodes, and the total value, for each solution. Graph A is an optimal solution (verified by complete enumeration), with $o_{G_A} = 4.4$. Graph B is a solution returned by the greedy algorithm, with $o_{G_B} = 3.8$. Another suboptimal solution, graph C, is built by adding an extra edge (1,2) to graph A: it gives $o_{G_C} = 4.1$. There is a difference in nine edges between graphs G_A and G_B.

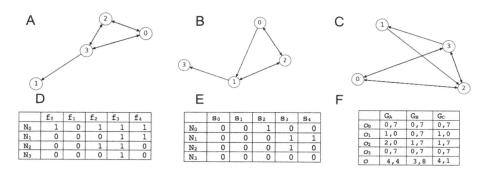

	f_0	f_1	f_2	f_3	f_4
N_0	1	0	1	1	1
N_1	0	0	0	1	1
N_2	0	0	1	1	0
N_3	0	0	0	1	0

	s_0	s_1	s_2	s_3	s_4
N_0	0	0	1	0	0
N_1	0	0	0	1	1
N_2	0	0	0	1	0
N_3	0	0	0	0	0

	G_A	G_B	G_C
o_0	0,7	0,7	0,7
o_1	1,0	0,7	1,0
o_2	2,0	1,7	1,7
o_3	0,7	0,7	0,7
o	4,4	3,8	4,1

Fig. 2. An illustrative example: a network formation problem and three feasible solutions.

The following section will re-frame Problem 1 as a game of common interests, solvable using the fictitious play paradigm.

3   Solution Methodology

This paper presents a general approach to solving network formation problems that relies on the developments in the theory of fictitious play. In order to properly position our contribution with respect to existing literature, we begin with an overview of the important historical, and also, the most recent advances in this field.

Fictitious Play (FP) was introduced in 1951 [2,9] as an observation that holds for finite mixed strategy games in strategic form where two players are engaged in a repeated play. The observation is that an equilibrium in any such game can be found iteratively: the players observe the actions taken in previous stages, update their beliefs about their opponents' strategies, and choose myopic pure best responses against these beliefs. Much later, it was found and proven that every n-person game with identical interests has the FP property [8]: an equilibrium is attained if every player acts in accordance to their beliefs of the mixed strategies of all other players; here, the belief of every player (except player i) about i's actions in future plays comes from the empirical distribution of i's previous actions. More recently, it was shown that Sampled FP (SFP) has nice convergence properties, and allows for a practically efficient implementation [7]: algorithms based on SFP solve optimization problems where the objective function $u(\cdot)$ comes from a black box, e.g., a simulation model. For example, a variant of SFP [4] was shown to converge almost surely to optimal policies in a model-free, finite-horizon stochastic Dynamic Program (DP); the DP states here were viewed as players, with the common interest of maximizing the total multi-period expected reward starting in a fixed initial state. Further, if the decision in each DP state is a multi-dimensional vector, SFP can be applied to a sequence of DPs with a one-dimensional action-space [5]. Very recently, in a practical application to maritime navigation, a parameter-free SFP finds a high quality solution after only a few iterations, in contrast with traditional methods [3].

Still, the network formation problems considered in this paper boast much larger state spaces than in the above mentions works. Moreover, all the actions are available to each network node in all the states, and therefore, the lack of a convenient state dependency structure prevents us from framing and solving the problem as a DP. Thus, further advances in FP theory are required to make it useful in the network formation domain. Indeed, over time, we saw that the practically useful definitions of the FP process may depend on first move rules, weights assigned to initial beliefs, and tie breaking rules determining the particular best replies chosen at each stage.

We present a parameter-free, History Value-Weighted SFP (HVWSFP) approach for tackling network formation problems using SFP principles. In HVWSFP the history of plays is creatively used to ensure and speed up convergence. The logic of HVWSFP is as follows:

Step 0: Initialization. For each player e_{ij}, $i \in N$, $j \in N$, select an action from A_i uniformly at random, and set H_{ij}^1 equal to that action. Set $k = 1$.

Step 1: Draw. For every player e_{ij}, $i \in N$, $j \in N$, draw an action from the history of the most recent plays $H^{d|k}$ (at most d last elements of the history H^k)), for every other player in $E \setminus e_{ij}$ uniformly at random.

Step 2: Best Action. For each player e_{ij}, $i \in N$, $j \in N$, compute a best current action. The best action here is defined as the action from the action space A that maximizes the average global objective function value for this action, with the average taken over the entire history.

Step 3: Update. Append the best replies computed in Step 2 to the history of each player, to get H^{k+1} for e_{ij}, $i \in N$, $j \in N$. Set $k = k + 1$ and go back to Step 1.

Note that in Step 2, the best action calculation is performed independently for each player. Player e_{ij}, $i \in N$, $j \in N$ chooses the best action based on the *value gain* of a possible action, with respect to the draws in all prior plays. This is different from just computing a *best reply* to a single draw, as is done in applications of conventional SFP to large problems, e.g., DPs [3]. By taking the average this way, first, we emulate the generation of more than one samples in the current play: it works since the history-based distribution of all players' actions does not change much between consecutive plays, and also, the improving actions of the players in the more recent plays eventually outweigh the impact of the draws from the far past. And second, the contribution of each sample (here equivalent to a draw) into the decision on an action depends on how much better one action (e.g., to build a link) is in value in comparison with the other. Hence the name "History Value Weighted" SFP. As will be seen in the next section, in practice, HVWSFP manages to both effectively explore the solution space of a network formation problem and converge faster than the competition.

4 Computational Results

We compare four algorithms: Centralized and Decentralized Greedy, and Centralized and Decentralized HVWSFP. In all these algorithms, we let each edge e_{ij}, $i \in N$, $j \in N$, be a player with a two-element action space $A_{ij} = \{0,1\}$. The total objective function value $o(g)$ is computed using an exhaustive, recursive information propagation procedure from every source.

Algorithm 1: GREEDY Centralized Greedy algorithm

Input: Graph $G(N, E)$, vector s, vector s, vector k
Output: E^*, o
while *True* do
    $rewards \leftarrow$ empty 2D array size $N * N$
    for $i \leftarrow 0$ *to* N do
        for $j \leftarrow 0$ *to* N do
            $G_c(N_c, E_c) \leftarrow G(N, E)$ $O_c \leftarrow o(G)$
            if $i == j$ then
                ⌊ continue
            if $(i, j) \in E_c$ then
                ⌊ $E_c \leftarrow E_c \setminus (i, j)$
            else
                ⌊ $E_c \leftarrow E_c \cup (i, j)$
            $PROP(G_c)$
            $rewards(i, j) \leftarrow o(G_c) - O_c$
    $(i_{max}, j_{max}) \leftarrow argmax(rewards)$
    if $rewards(i_{max}, j_{max}) > 0$ then
        if $(i, j) \in E$ then
            ⌊ $E \leftarrow E \setminus (i_{max}, j_{max})$
        else
            ⌊ $E \leftarrow E \cup (i_{max}, j_{max})$
    else
        ⌊ break
    $PROP(G)$
return E, o

Algorithm 2: GREEDY Decentralized Greedy algorithm

Input: Graph $G(N, E)$, vector s, vector s, vector k
Output: E^*, o
$S \leftarrow 1000$ **for** $step \leftarrow 0$ **to** S **do**

    $rewards \leftarrow$ empty array size N
    $i \leftarrow random(0, N)$
    for $j \leftarrow 0$ **to** N **do**

        $G_c(N_c, E_c) \leftarrow G(N, E)$
        $O_c \leftarrow o_j(G)$
        if $i == j$ **then**
            L continue
        if $(i, j) \in E_c$ **then**
            L $E_c \leftarrow E_c \setminus (i, j)$
        else
            L $E_c \leftarrow E_c \cup (i, j)$
        $PROP(G_c)$
         L $rewards(j) \leftarrow o_j(G_c) - O_c$
    $j_{max} \leftarrow argmax(rewards)$
    if $rewards(j_{max}) > 0$ **then**

        if $(i, j_{max}) \in E$ **then**
            L $E \leftarrow E \setminus (i, j_{max})$
        else
            L $E \leftarrow E \cup (i, j_{max})$

    else
     L break
     $PROP(G)$

  return E, o

Greedy Centralized (GC). See Algorithm 1 for the pseudocode of the Centralized greedy implementation. In each step of this algorithm, we compute the global objective improvement for all the actions of all the players e_{ij}, $i \in N$, $j \in N$, and choose the best action – edge addition or removal – myopically, until no improvement is possible. An empty graph is always taken as an initial solution.

Greedy Decentralized (GD). Algorithm 2 gives the pseudocode of this method. Here, in each step, a node (i) is chosen randomly, and a local objective improvement is compared over the actions of players e_{ij}, $j \in N$; the best action of these actions is then chosen myopically. Because this algorithm does not converge, we run it for a predefined number of steps. An empty graph is used as an initial solution.

Centralized HVWSFP. The pseudocode of the original HVWSFP described in the previous section is given in Algorithm 3.

Decentralized HVWSFP (DHVWSFP). The difference between this algorithm and the original Centralized HVWSFP is that here, the action choice (in

---

Algorithm 3: Centralized HVWSFP

Input: Graph $G(N, E)$, vector **s**, vector **s**, vector **k**, history depth d
Output: E^*, o
$S \leftarrow 500$
$A \leftarrow$ adjacency matrix of random graph with N nodes;
$H.append(A)$
$\Delta \leftarrow ((0,0)_0, ..., (0,0)_{N*N})$
for $step \leftarrow 0$ **to** S **do**
    $M \leftarrow \emptyset_{N*N}$
    for $i \leftarrow 0$ **to** N **do**
        for $j \leftarrow 0$ **to** N **do**
            $M_d \leftarrow M_0$
            $G_c \leftarrow G(N, E)$
            $E_c \leftarrow \emptyset$
            for $k \leftarrow 0$ **to** N **do**
                for $l \leftarrow 0$ **to** N **do**
                    $c \leftarrow random(0, d)$
                    $M_d(k, l) \leftarrow H_{kl}^{|H|-c}$
                    if $p * 100 < d * \lambda^{step}$ **then**
                        $\lfloor$ $M_d(k, l) \leftarrow 1$
                    if $i == k$ *and* $j == l$ **then**
                        $\lfloor$ $M_d(k, l) \leftarrow 1$
            $PROP(G_c)$
            $O_1 \leftarrow o(G_c)$
            $E_c \leftarrow E_c \setminus (i, j)$
            $O_2 \leftarrow o(G_c)$
            $\Delta_{i*N+j}^0 \leftarrow \Delta_{i*N+j}^0 + \frac{O_1 - \Delta_{i*N+j}^0}{step}$
            $\Delta_{i*N+j}^1 \leftarrow \Delta_{i*N+j}^1 + \frac{O_2 - \Delta_{i*N+j}^1}{step}$
            if $\Delta_{i*N+j}^0 > \Delta_{i*N+j}^1$ **then**
                $M(i, j) \leftarrow 1$
                $\lfloor$ $E \leftarrow E \cap (i, j)$
    $H.append(M)$
    $PROP(G)$ $o \leftarrow o(G)$
return E, o

Step 2) is made by *each* player based on their own objective function value, computed with an increment of $\frac{1+\alpha}{2} \sum_{k=1}^{|E_{i=k}|} \frac{1}{2*(k+1)}$ that slightly encourages each node to serve as an intermediary for information transfer to its k out-neighbors.

We implemented the above four algorithms in C++, and added a modification of algorithm 3 with depth of history $d = 2$. We created four setups, summarized in Table 1. Each setup was executed 50 times with synthetically generated input graphs. In all the setups, vectors f and s were filled with uniform random numbers (0 and 1), $P_{f_i=1} = 0.7$. Table 1 gives the sum-totals of

---

Algorithm 4: Decentralized HVWSFP

Input: Graph $G(N, E)$, vector s, vector s, vector k, history depth d
Output: E^*, o
$S \leftarrow 500$
$A \leftarrow$ adjacency matrix of random graph with N nodes;
$H.append(A)$
$\Delta \leftarrow ((0,0)_0, ..., (0,0)_{N*N})$
for $step \leftarrow 0$ **to** S **do**
   $M \leftarrow \emptyset_{N*N}$
   for $i \leftarrow 0$ **to** N **do**
      for $j \leftarrow 0$ **to** N **do**
         $M_d \leftarrow M_0$
         $G_c \leftarrow G(N, E)$
         $E_c \leftarrow \emptyset$
         for $k \leftarrow 0$ **to** N **do**
            for $l \leftarrow 0$ **to** N **do**
               $c \leftarrow random(0, d)$
               $M_d(k, l) \leftarrow H_{kl}^{|H|-c}$
               if $p * 100 < d * \lambda^{step}$ **then**
                  $M_d(k, l) \leftarrow 1$
               if $i == k$ *and* $j == l$ **then**
                  $M_d(k, l) \leftarrow 1$
         $PROP(G_c)$
         $O_1 \leftarrow o_j(G_c) + \frac{1+\alpha}{2} \sum_{k=1}^{|E_{i=k}|} \frac{1}{2*(k+1)}$
         $E_c \leftarrow E_c \setminus (i, j)$
         $O_2 \leftarrow o_j(G_c) + \frac{1+\alpha}{2} \sum_{k=1}^{|E_{i=k}|} \frac{1}{2*(k+1)}$
         $\Delta_{i*N+j}^0 \leftarrow \Delta_{i*N+j}^0 + \frac{O_1 - \Delta_{i*N+j}^0}{step}$
         $\Delta_{i*N+j}^1 \leftarrow \Delta_{i*N+j}^1 + \frac{O_2 - \Delta_{i*N+j}^1}{step}$
         if $\Delta_{i*N+j}^0 > \Delta_{i*N+j}^1$ **then**
            $M(i, j) \leftarrow 1$
            $E \leftarrow E \cap (i, j)$
  $H.append(M)$
  $PROP(G)$ $o \leftarrow o(G)$
return E, o

---

the objective function values over all the instances. Figures 3a, b and 4 illustrate the typical convergence dynamics for some of the algorithms. We observe that on average, the Centralized HVWSFP outperforms GC, and the Decentralized HVWSFP with short history beats GD. The latter suggests that this work can inform individual agents, both in small (e.g., UAV) and large (e.g., social media portal user) agent groups.

Table 1. Experimental results: objective value sum-totals over multiple instances, for (in order) Short-Memory HVWSFP ($d = 2$), HVWSFP, GC, DHVWSFP, GD.

Setup	Alg. 3'	Alg. 3	Alg. 1	Alg. 4	Alg. 2
K = 20, N = 10, $P_{s_i=1} = 0.8$	919,6	904,6	928,3	798,6	159,5
K = 40, N = 5, $P_{s_i=1} = 0.3$	856,3	838,1	841,3	829,8	471,6
K = 40, N = 5, $P_{s_i=1} = 0.8$	526,7	519,2	520,4	512,4	166,7
K = 100, N = 10, $P_{s_i=1} = 0.8$	3424,4	3083,4	3441,4	3109,7	1100,3

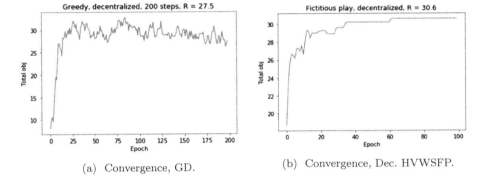

(a) Convergence, GD.   (b) Convergence, Dec. HVWSFP.

Fig. 3. Convergence of decentralized algorithms

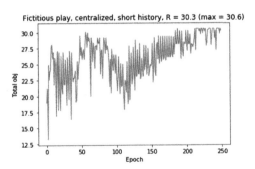

Fig. 4. Convergence, HVWSFP ($d = 2$)

5   Conclusions

Our investigations show promise for using FP theory-based methods for network formation. Our most interesting discovery is the appeal of the Decentralized HVWSFP, as it is highly scalable. As for improvement ideas, the ideas of edge ordering manipulation appears interesting: by fixing the order of edges, in which actions can be taken only once, one can convert the problem into a DP.

Acknowledgements. Work of A. Semenov was funded in part by the AFRL European Office of Aerospace Research and Development (grant no. FA9550-17-1-0030). This material is based upon work supported by the AFRL Mathematical Modeling and Optimization Institute.

References

1. Adamic, L.A., Glance, N.: The political blogosphere and the 2004 U.S. election: divided they blog. In: Proceedings of the 3rd International Workshop on Link Discovery, LinkKDD 2005, pp. 36–43. ACM, New York (2005). https://doi.org/10.1145/1134271.1134277
2. Brown, G.W.: Iterative solution of games by fictitious play (1951)
3. Dolinskaya, I.S., Epelman, M.A., Şişikoğlu Sir, E., Smith, R.L.: Parameter-free sampled fictitious play for solving deterministic dynamic programming problems. J. Optim. Theory Appl. **169**(2), 631–655 (2016). https://doi.org/10.1007/s10957-015-0798-5
4. Epelman, M., Ghate, A., Smith, R.L.: Sampled fictitious play for approximate dynamic programming. Comput. Oper. Res. **38**(12), 1705–1718 (2011). https://doi.org/10.1016/j.cor.2011.01.023. http://www.sciencedirect.com/science/article/pii/S0305054811000451
5. Ghate, A., Cheng, S.F., Baumert, S., Reaume, D., Sharma, D., Smith, R.L.: Sampled fictitious play for multi-action stochastic dynamic programs. IIE Trans. **46**(7), 742–756 (2014)
6. Horn, R.A.: The hadamard product. In: Proceedings of Symposium in Applied Mathematics, vol. 40, pp. 87–169 (1990)
7. Lambert, T.J., Epelman, M.A., Smith, R.L.: A fictitious play approach to large-scale optimization. Oper. Res. **53**(3), 477–489 (2005). https://doi.org/10.1287/opre.1040.0178. http://dx.doi.org/10.1287/opre.1040.0178
8. Monderer, D., Shapley, L.S.: Fictitious play property for games with identical interests. J. Econ. Theory **68**(1), 258–265 (1996). https://doi.org/10.1006/jeth.1996.0014. http://www.sciencedirect.com/science/article/pii/S0022053196900149
9. Robinson, J.: An iterative method of solving a game. Ann. Math. **54**, 296–301 (1951)

Outlier Detection Forest for Large-Scale Categorical Data Sets

Zhipeng Sun[1], Hongwei Du[1(✉)], Qiang Ye[2], Chuang Liu[1],
Patricia Lilian Kibenge[2], Hui Huang[2], and Yuying Li[3]

[1] Department of Computer Science and Technology, Harbin Institute of Technology
(Shenzhen), Shenzhen, China
`sgsunzhipeng@gmail.com`, {`hongwei.du,chuangliu`}`@ieee.org`
[2] Faculty of Computer Science, Dalhousie University, Halifax, Canada
`qye@cs.dal.ca`, {`p.kibenge,hz344590`}`@dal.ca`
[3] Department of Economics and Management, Harbin Institute of Technology
(Shenzhen), Shenzhen, China
`liyuying426@hotmail.com`

Abstract. Outlier detection is one of the most important data mining problems, which has attracted much attention over the past years. So far, there have been a variety of different schemes for outlier detection. However, most of the existing methods work with numeric data sets. And these methods cannot be directly applied to categorical data sets because it is not straightforward to define a practical similarity measure for categorical data. Furthermore, the existing outlier detection schemes that are tailored for categorical data tend to result in poor scalability, which makes them infeasible for large-scale data sets. In this paper, we propose a tree-based outlier detection algorithm for large-scale categorical data sets, Outlier Detection Forest (ODF). Our experimental results indicate that, compared with the state-of-the-art outlier detection schemes, ODF can achieve the same level of outlier detection precision and much better scalability.

Keywords: Categorical data · Outlier detection · Big data · Entropy

1 Introduction

Outlier detection, also known as anomaly detection, aims to detect the unusual data items whose characteristic is exceptional compared with that of the majority data items in the data set [4]. Outlier detection can be used in two different scenarios. In the scenario that outliers are considered noise, they need to be removed before a data set can be utilized for knowledge discovery purposes. In the scenario that outliers are the targets (e.g. frequent buyers in an online electronics store), they need to be carefully identified [10]. Due to the effectiveness of outlier detection, it has become an important technology for a wide range of applications, such as intrusion detection, fraud detection in financial transactions, and disease detection. Specifically, outlier detection can be used to identify

© Springer Nature Switzerland AG 2019
A. Tagarelli and H. Tong (Eds.): CSoNet 2019, LNCS 11917, pp. 45–56, 2019.
https://doi.org/10.1007/978-3-030-34980-6_4

a moving target in realtime surveillance video. In addition, it can help detect fraudulent transactions among a large set of data for credit card companies. Furthermore, it can discover the brain signals that may indicate early development of brain cancer.

Over the past years, many outlier detection techniques have been proposed. The existing outlier detection techniques can be divided into three categories: statistical distribution based methods [3], distance-based methods [1,9–11,15], clustering-based methods [8,18]. Statistical distribution-based methods assume that the data points under investigation follows a specific distribution. Consequently, the distribution is utilized to identify outliers. Distance-based methods identify outliers by counting the number of neighbours that each data point has. In other words, a data point with few neighbours is identified as an outlier. Since distance-based methods need to calculate the distance between each pair of points in the data set, the execution time of this type of methods is at least quadratic with respect to the number of objects, which is unacceptable if the data set is very large. Clustering-based methods detect outliers by placing data points into different clusters. Most of the existing outlier detection techniques are designed for data sets numerical attributes. It is often infeasible to apply these techniques to categorical data sets because it is not straightforward to define a practical similarity measure for categorical data.

In this paper, a tree-based outlier detection algorithm for large-scale categorial data sets, Outlier Detection Forest (ODF), is proposed. In our research, we first proposed a primitive outlier detection algorithm named Outlier Detection Tree (ODT). With ODT, a classification tree is constructed to classify the data set into two classes: one normal class and one abnormal class. Each data point is categorized as an outlier or a normal one with the if-then rules of the tree. Thereafter, we proposed an advanced algorithm named ODF, which is based on ODT, to improve the accuracy and scalability of outlier detection. Our experimental results indicate that ODF can achieve the same level of outlier detection precision and much better scalability.

The remainder of this paper is organized as follows. The related work is presented in Sect. 2. In Sect. 3, the preliminary definition and concepts are provided. In Sect. 4, the proposed algorithms are described. Section 5 includes the experimental results and discussions. Our conclusions are presented in Sect. 6.

2   Related Work

In this paper, we implement and experiment on categorical data. Some entropy-based algorithms were investigated in the area of outlier mining for categorical data. He et al. [6,7] proposed entropy-based outlier detection methods. Their algorithm use a local-search heuristic to find outliers. Their algorithm calculate the impact of each object on data set entropy, then sort these objects by their effects and select the points with the greatest impact as outliers. However, to detect p outliers in a data set, this algorithm requires p scans over the data, which is computationally expensive for large data sets. Koufakou et al. [12] proposed an algorithm called Attribute Value Frequency(AVF) which detects oultier by a metric named AVF Score based on frequency of each attribute. Objects with low scores are considered as outliers. This algorithm detects objects with infrequent attribute values as outliers. However, when the number of attribute values and number of objects is similar, each attribute value is infrequent. A distance-based method for outlier detection in high-dimensional categorical data proposed in [13] using the notion of common-neighbor-based distance to measure the distance of a pair of objects. Though the better result of this method can be achieved in their experiment, their method take to much time to achieve that result. A ranking-based algorithm is proposed in [17]. The proposed algorithm has its merit in detecting outliers of different types employing two independent ranking schemes based on the attribute value frequencies and the distance between each object and clustering center founf in the given data. Although the performance of their algorithm has been experimentally evaluated and demonstrate the effectiveness, the algorithm use too many computing resources.

3   Preliminaries

In this section, the definition of categorical data is first presented. Thereafter, an overview of entropy is provided.

3.1   Categorical Data

A large portion of data sets is often presented as categorical attributes in the real world such as transaction data, financial records in commercial banks or demographic data. Normally, categorical data are assumed to be stored in a table, where an object is represented by a row (tuple). More formally, a categorical data table can be defined as a quadruple $DT = (U, A, V, f)$, where:

- U is a nonempty set of objects;
- A is a nonempty set of attributes;
- V is the union of attribute domains, i.e., $V = \bigcup_{a \in A} V_a$; where V_a is the value domain of attribute a;
- $f : U \times A \to V$ is a function such that, $\forall a \in A$ and $\forall x \in U$, $f(x, a) \in V_a$.

3.2   Entropy

Information entropy and its variants are the most common uncertainty measures of data sets. The entropy of a system defined by Shannon gives a measure of uncertainty about its actual structure. Entropy is a measure of the uncertainty of random variables [16]. More formally, if X is a random variable, and $S(X)$ is the set of values that X can take, and the probability function of X is $p(x)$, then the entropy $E(X)$ is defined as:

$$E(X) = - \sum_{x \in S(x)} p(x) \log p(x) \qquad (1)$$

Since the objective of outlier detection is to detect the rare objects which have abnormal properties or abnormal atttribute values. And uncertainty can be recognized as a kind of abnormal measure. Therefore, entropy can be used for outlier detection. Next, we will use entropy to calculate uncertainty in each attribute domain and use entropy gain to calculate the abnormal degree of an attribute value in the corresponding attribute domain. Supposed that X is an multivariate vector from U, $X = \{X_1, X_2, ..., X_m\}$(a multidimensional data set containing m attributes). Entropy of X_i, is defined as:

$$E(X_i) = - \sum_{x_{ij} \in V_{X_i}} p(x_{ij}) \log p(x_{ij}) \tag{2}$$

$\frac{|x_{ij}|}{|U|}$ Supposed that $V_{X_i} = V_a$, where $a \in A$, is the attribute corresponding to X_i. $p(x_{ij}) = \frac{|x_{ij}|}{|U|}$, where $|x_{ij}|$ represents the amount of x_{ij} in U with respect to i-th attribute. In the above definition, $E(X_i)$ represents the complexity of attribute X_i.

Inspired by [6], define $E(X_i, x_{ij})$ as:

$$E(X_i, x_{ik}) = - \sum_{x_{ij} \in V_{X_i}} \acute{p}(x_{ij}) \log \acute{p}(x_{ij}) \tag{3}$$

where $p(x_{ij})$ is recomputed after one record of which i-th attribute is equal to x_{ik} is removed from U, denoted as $\acute{p}(x_{ij})$.

Through the bias between $E(X_i)$ and $E(X_i, x_{ik})$, we can observe the influence of x_{ik} on the entropy of X_i. In order to measure the change in $E(X_i)$ caused by x_{ik}, define $G(X_i, x_{ik})$ as follow:

$$G(X_i, x_{ik}) = E(X_i) - E(X_i, x_{ik}) \tag{4}$$

Later in this paper, G is used to indicate the general meaning of $G(X_i, x_{ik})$. Intuitively, the outliers for categorical data are those points with highly irregular values. Additionally, an ideal outlier in a categorical data set is the one whose some or all of the attribute values are extremely irregular or infrequent compared with others. The irregular-ness of an attribute value can be measured by computing the entropy decrease based on G. $G(X_i, x_{ik})$ is the entropy impact in terms of X_i caused by x_{ik}. The larger the value of $G(X_i, x_{ik})$ is, the more significant the distribution of X_i change. In other words, The larger the $G(X_i, x_{ik})$, the more x_{ik} is like an abnormal attribute value in V_{X_i}. We will use $G(X_i, x_{ik})$ as a indicator later to judge an attribute value is abnormal or not in each attribute.

4   ODF: A Tree-Based Outlier Detection Algorithm

In this section, we first present a tree-based outlier detection algorithm, Outlier Detection Tree (ODT). Later the details of an improved algorithm based on ODT, Outlier Detection Forest (ODF), will be discussed.

4.1 Overview

The proposed algorithms, ODT and ODF, utilize the idea of decision tree algorithm and an ensemble algorithm called random forest in supervised learning.

C4.5 [14] is one of the most common and most classic decision tree generation algorithms. The core of this algorithm is to apply the information gain ratio to each node on the decision tree to select features, and recursively construct the decision tree. The specific method is: starting from the root node, calculating the information gain of all possible features for the node. Then, the feature with the largest information gain is selected as the feature of the node, the child nodes are constructed by different values of the feature; and recursively calling the child node above The method constructs a decision tree; until the information gain ratio of all features is less than a certain predefined threshold or no features can be selected. Finally get a decision tree.

The classification decision tree model is a tree structure that represents classification of instances based on features. A decision tree can be transformed into a set of if-then rules, or regarded as a conditional probability distribution defined on feature space partitioning.

In this paper, the decision tree algorithm in supervised learning is adjusted to unsupervised case. The proposed algorithm ODT, first, "(4)" is used as a new partitioning metric. Then, the feature with $G(X_i, x_{ik})$ larger than a predefined threshold is selected as the feature of the node, the child nodes are constructed by x_{ik}, i.e. build two nodes according to whether the i-th attribute of a data record is equal to x_{ik}. Finally, the part of the nodes which are consistent with x_{ik} in each division are marked as 'outlier'. Based on ODT, ODF is proposed. In a ODF, multiple ODTs are merged together to make the clustering results more accurate and realistic.

The data processing steps are presented in Algorithm 1. We construct a tree which is able to distinguish outliers. To achieve this goal, we first count the number of each attribute value in the data set U and store the result in $Dtable$ which is a two-dimensional dictionary or two-dimensional array. Specifically, $Dtable[i][j]$ represents the number of attribute value j from attribute i. Then, with $Dtable$, we can calculate G to store in $Gtable$ according to "(4)" which has the same data structure as $Dtable$. Specifically, $Gtable[i][j]$ represents the information gain $G(X_i, j)$.

After G is calculated, we begin to construct the tree. $ROOT$ represents the root node of the ODT. α is a threshold that determines outlier attribute value. we construct ODT recursively, for any $G(i, j)$ greater than α, divide the node into two sub-nodes according to attribute value j. One of the sub-nodes is marked as 'outlier' whose i-th attribute is consistent with j, and the other repeats this division process whose i-th attribute is different from j. In the subsequent division process, B that was previously classified as outlier attribute value is removed from $Dtable$, and $Gtable$ is recalculated according to newly generated $Dtable$. This iterative process stops when all values in the $Gtable$ are smaller than α and the last node containing the remaining attribute values is marked as 'normal'.

4.2 Outlier Detection Forest (ODF)

Observed that the working principle of an ODT is that a data is judged to be outlier, when there is at least one attribute value in this data point is marked as abnormal. Is this way of judging the abnormality of data points too strict? ODF is an improvement of ODT to solve this problem. In our algorithm, an ODF contains multiple trees, and its output is determined by the mode of output of individual trees. To construct a ODF, the tree construction method Algorithm 1 must first be modified to Algorithm 3 showed below.

Algorithm 1. ODT

Require:
    U // the categorical database;
    α // the threshold of G;
Ensure:
    A set of outliers, O;
  1: Let $O = \varnothing, Dtable = \varnothing, Gtable = \varnothing, ROOT \leftarrow \forall records \in U$;
  2: **for** each $record \in U$ **do**
  3:    **for** each $i \in [1, len(record)]$ **do**
  4:        $Dtable[i][record[i]] + +$;
  5:    **end for**
  6: **end for**
  7: **while** $\exists G(i,j) \in G, G(i,j) > \alpha$ **do**
  8:    partion $ROOT$ into two children nodes L, R;
  9:    **for** each $record \in Root$ **do**
10:      **if** $record[i] \neq j$ **then**
11:        $L \leftarrow record, O = O \cup \{record\}$;
12:      **else**
13:        $R \leftarrow record$;
14:      **end if**
15:    **end for**
16:    $ROOT = R$
17:    remove $Dtable[i][j]$ from D, update$G$
18: **end while**
19: **return** O;

4.3 Outlier Detection Tree (ODT)

In Algorithm 3, After calculating $Gtable$, for each attribute whose G is greater than α, split the node with P as the probability. In this case, if multiple trees are built, each tree will have different characteristics for outlier detection. Then the mode of multiple results of such trees will be regarded as the final result which is an outlier or not. Forest construction is shown in Algorithm 2.

    The computational complexity of the proposed ODF algorithm is mainly contributed by the second half which generates the ODT. Supposed that k trees is in the forest, if the maximum number of unique values of an attribute is s, m is the number of attributes and n is the number of record in data set U, then the algorithm requires $O(knms)$ computations. Typically, s is known to be a small quantity compared to n and k does not need to be set to a large value.

5 Experimental Results

To study the performance of ODF, the proposed outlier detection algorithm, we used three real categorical data sets and two categorical simulated data sets to in our research. The performance of ODF in terms of detection accuracy and scalability is compared to that of two state-of-the-art schemes: ROAD [17] and LSA [6]. All the experiments were carried out on a Windows 10 PC with an Intel Core i5-8300 CPU and 8-Gigabit memory. All the outlier detection algorithms under investigation are code using Python 3.5.

Algorithm 2. ODF

Require:
    U // the categorical database;
    P // the pruning probability;
    k // number of trees;
    α // the threshold of G;
Ensure:
    A set of outliers, O;
 1: Let $O = \varnothing, O_1, O_2, ..., O_k = \varnothing$
 2: construct k trees by Algorithm 3, the result of i-th tree is O_i
 3: construct O by voting through $O_i, i = 1, 2, ..., k$
 4: **return** O;

5.1 Details of Data Sets

The experimental evaluation of the proposed method includes three categorical data sets taken from the UCI ML Repository [2].

Lymphography data set contains 148 objects and 18 categorical attributes and class attribute. These objects are partitioned into four classes, those rare objects in classes 1 and 4 are considered as the outliers.

Wisconsin breast cancer data set was collected by Dr. William H. Wolberg at the University of Wisconsin Madison Hospitals. There are 699 records in this data set. Each record has nine attributes, which are graded on an interval scale from a normal state of 1–10, with 10 being the most abnormal state. In this database, 241 records are malignant and 458 records are benign. We follow the experimental technique of Harkins et al. [5,19]. We randomly remove some of the records to form a unbalanced distribution. The resultant data set had 29

Algorithm 3. ODT Modified

Require:
    U // the categorical database;
    P // the pruning probability;
    α // the threshold of G;
Ensure:
    A set of outliers, O;
 1: Let $O = \varnothing, Dtable = \varnothing, Gtable = \varnothing, ROOT \leftarrow \forall records \in U$;
 2: **for** each $record \in U$ **do**
 3:    **for** each $i \in [1, len(record)]$ **do**
 4:       $Dtable[i][record[i]] + +$;
 5:    **end for**
 6: **end for**
 7: **while** $\exists G(i,j) \in G, G(i,j) > \alpha$ **do**
 8:    partion $ROOT$ into two children nodes L, R with probability P;
 9:    **if** L, R is not $\varnothing$ **then**
10:       **for** each $record \in Root$ **do**
11:          **if** $record[i] \neq j$ **then**
12:             $L \leftarrow record, O = O \cup \{record\}$;
13:          **else**
14:             $R \leftarrow record$;
15:          **end if**
16:       **end for**
17:       $ROOT = R$
18:    **end if**
19:    remove $Dtable[i][j]$ from D, update$G$
20: **end while**
21: **return** O;

(6%) malignant objects and 453 (94%) benign objects. That is to say, there are 29 outliers in this data set.

Letter recognition data set contains character image features of 26 capital letters in the English alphabet. Each object is described by 16 attributes seen as categorical attributes in the experiment. In order to form an imbalanced data for outlier detection, we follow the processing method of [20], choose all the objects labeled A and some of objects labeled B to form a new data set including 789 objects with label A and 50 objects with label B considered as outlier.

5.2   Details of Experimental Results

The experimental results produced by the ODF algorithm against the ROAD algorithm and the LSA algorithm on lymphography data set are summarized in Table 1. Here, the top ratio is ratio of the number of objects specified as outliers to that of the objects in the data set. The coverage is ratio of the number of detected rare classes to that of the rare classes in the data set. For example, we let outlier detection algorithm find the top six outliers with the top ratio of 4%. By examining these six objects, we found that 5 of them belonged to the rare classes. For fairness, we adjust their parameters so that they can have the same top ratio as our algorithm.

Table 1. Detected rare classes in lymphography data set

Top ratio(Number of records)	Number of rare classes included(Coverage)		
	ODF	ROAD	LSA
%4(6)	5(83%)	5(83%)	5(83%)
%5(9)	6(100%)	5(83%)	6(100%)
%7(12)	6(100%)	6(100%)	6(100%)

From Table 1, both ODF and LSA algorithms performed the best for all cases and can find all the records in rare classes when top ratio at 5%. From the above results, our proposed algorithm achieves the same performance as that of LSA algorithm on lymphography data set.

The experimental results produced by the forest algorithm against the ROAD algorithm and the LSA algorithm on Wisconsin breast cancer data set and letter recognition are summarized in Tables 2 and 3.

Table 2. Wisconsin breast cancer data set

Top ratio(Number of records)	Number of rare classes included(Coverage)		
	ODF	ROAD	LSA
%4(20)	14(48%)	14(48%)	15(51%)
%5(24)	18(62%)	19(65%)	17(58%)
%6(28)	21(72%)	21(72%)	19(65%)
%7(32)	24(83%)	26(89%)	23(79%)
%8(38)	27(93%)	28(96%)	27(93%)
%9(44)	29(100%)	29(100%)	29(100%)

From Tables 2 and 3, in comparison to other algorithms, the performance of our algorithm on this data set is not as good as others in four cases in total, but their performance are very close. And next in this Section, we will show that our algorithm is faster for large data sets.

We manually copy and expand on the basis of the original lymphography data set to verify the performance of our algorithm under different data volumes. We prepare to expand the lymphography data set 500 times to test the time performance of these algorithms, but because the time spent on the LSA is too large and hard to calculate. We only use 50 times of the lymphography data set

Table 3. Letter recognition data set

Top ratio(Number of records)	Number of rare classes included(Coverage)		
	ODF	ROAD	LSA
%13(100)	34(68%)	36(72%)	34(68%)
%15(120)	43(86%)	45(90%)	43(86%)
%18(140)	47(94%)	47(94%)	47(94%)
%20(160)	48(96%)	48(96%)	47(94%)
%23(180)	48(96%)	48(96%)	48(96%)
%25(200)	50(100%)	50(100%)	50(100%)

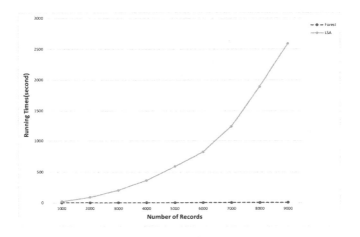

Fig. 1. Running time of LSA and ODF

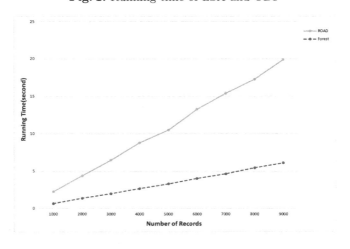

Fig. 2. Running time of ROAD and ODF

to compare with the LSA. Through Fig. 1, we can observe that the algorithm we proposed is much faster than LSA under different data volumes.

Figure 2 is a comparison of the running time of ROAD and our algorithm. We can observe that although the running time of our proposed algorithm is only a few seconds faster than ROAD in the case of a small amount of data, as the amount of data increase, the difference in running time between two algorithms is increasing to dozens of seconds.

Overall, the experimental results mentioned previously indicate that, compared with ROAD and LSA, ODF leads to much better scalability and similar outlier detection accuracy.

6 Conclusion

In this paper, two unsupervised outlier detection algorithms, ODT and ODF, are proposed for large-scale categorical data sets. ODF is based on ODT and leads to satisfactory detection accuracy and scalability. Technically, ODF involves two parameters: the threshold α and the pruning probability P. The threshold α is used to tune the sensitivity of judging an attribute value as an outlier value. The pruning probability P is employed to set the sensitivity of judging an object as an outlier. These parameters can be configured to work well with varied categorical data sets. In our research, the performance of ODF was experimentally evaluated with a few large-scale categorical data sets. Our experimental results indicate that, compared with the state-of-the-art outlier detection schemes, ODF can achieve the same level of outlier detection precision and much better scalability.

Acknowledgement. This work was supported by National Natural Science Foundation of China No. 61772154.

References

1. Aggarwal, C.C., Yu, P.S.: Outlier detection for high dimensional data. In: ACM Sigmod Record, vol. 30, pp. 37–46. ACM (2001)
2. Bache, K., Lichman, M.: UCI machine learning repository (2013)
3. Barnett, V., Lewis, T.: Outliers in Statistical Data. Wiley, New York (1994)
4. Chandola, V., Banerjee, A., Kumar, V.: Anomaly detection: a survey. ACM Comput. Surv. (CSUR) **41**(3), 15 (2009)
5. Hawkins, S., He, H., Williams, G., Baxter, R.: Outlier detection using replicator neural networks. In: Kambayashi, Y., Winiwarter, W., Arikawa, M. (eds.) DaWaK 2002. LNCS, vol. 2454, pp. 170–180. Springer, Heidelberg (2002). https://doi.org/10.1007/3-540-46145-0_17
6. He, Z., Deng, S., Xu, X.: An optimization model for outlier detection in categorical data. In: Huang, D.-S., Zhang, X.-P., Huang, G.-B. (eds.) ICIC 2005. LNCS, vol. 3644, pp. 400–409. Springer, Heidelberg (2005). https://doi.org/10.1007/11538059_42

7. He, Z., Deng, S., Xu, X., Huang, J.Z.: A fast greedy algorithm for outlier mining. In: Ng, W.-K., Kitsuregawa, M., Li, J., Chang, K. (eds.) PAKDD 2006. LNCS (LNAI), vol. 3918, pp. 567–576. Springer, Heidelberg (2006). https://doi.org/10.1007/11731139_67

8. Jiang, M.F., Tseng, S.S., Su, C.M.: Two-phase clustering process for outliers detection. Pattern Recogn. Lett. **22**(6–7), 691–700 (2001)

9. Knorr, E.M., Ng, R.T.: Finding intensional knowledge of distance-based outliers. VLDB **99**, 211–222 (1999)

10. Knorr, E.M., Ng, R.T., Tucakov, V.: Distance-based outliers: algorithms and applications. VLDB J. Int. J. Very Large Data Bases **8**(3–4), 237–253 (2000)

11. Knox, E.M., Ng, R.T.: Algorithms for mining distancebased outliers in large datasets. In: Proceedings of the International Conference on Very Large Data Bases, pp. 392–403. Citeseer (1998)

12. Koufakou, A., Ortiz, E.G., Georgiopoulos, M., Anagnostopoulos, G.C., Reynolds, K.M.: A scalable and efficient outlier detection strategy for categorical data. In: 19th IEEE International Conference on Tools with Artificial Intelligence (ICTAI 2007), vol. 2, pp. 210–217. IEEE (2007)

13. Li, S., Lee, R., Lang, S.D.: Mining Distance-Based Outliers from Categorical Data (2007)

14. Quinlan, J.R.: C4. 5: Programs for Machine Learning. Elsevier (2014)

15. Ramaswamy, S., Rastogi, R., Shim, K.: Efficient algorithms for mining outliers from large data sets. In: ACM Sigmod Record, vol. 29, pp. 427–438. ACM (2000)

16. Shannon, C.E.: A mathematical theory of communication. Bell Syst. Tech. J. **27**(3), 379–423 (1948)

17. Suri, N., Murty, M.N., Athithan, G.: A ranking-based algorithm for detection of outliers in categorical data. Int. J. Hybrid Intell. Syst. **11**(1), 1–11 (2014)

18. Tang, C., Wang, S., Xu, W.: New fuzzy c-means clustering model based on the data weighted approach. Data Knowl. Eng. **69**(9), 881–900 (2010)

19. Williams, G., Baxter, R., He, H., Hawkins, S., Gu, L.: A comparative study of RNN for outlier detection in data mining. In: 2002 IEEE International Conference on Data Mining, 2002, Proceedings, pp. 709–712. IEEE (2002)

20. Zhao, X., Liang, J., Cao, F.: A simple and effective outlier detection algorithm for categorical data. Int. J. Mach. Learn. Cybern. **5**(3), 469–477 (2014)

Neural Networks with Multidimensional Cross-Entropy Loss Functions

Alexander Semenov[1]([✉]), Vladimir Boginski[2], and Eduardo L. Pasiliao[3]

[1] University of Jyväskylä, P.O.Box 35, 40014 Jyväskylä, Finland
`alexander.v.semenov@jyu.fi`
[2] University of Central Florida, 12800 Pegasus Dr., Orlando, FL 32816, USA
`vladimir.boginski@ucf.edu`
[3] Air Force Research Laboratory, Eglin AFB, FL 32542, USA
`eduardo.pasiliao@us.af.mil`

Abstract. Deep neural networks have emerged as an effective machine learning tool successfully applied for many tasks, such as misinformation detection, natural language processing, image recognition, machine translation, etc. Neural networks are often applied to binary or multiclass classification problems. In these settings, cross-entropy is used as a loss function for neural network training. In this short note, we propose an extension of the concept of cross-entropy, referred to as multidimensional cross-entropy, and its application as a loss function for classification using neural networks. The presented computational experiments on a benchmark dataset suggest that the proposed approaches may have a potential for increasing the classification accuracy of neural network based algorithms.

Keywords: Neural networks · Cross-entropy loss functions

1 Introduction

Deep neural networks are successfully applied for many important practical tasks in machine learning, including misinformation detection, natural language processing, image recognition, speech recognition, machine translation, and many others. Many of these tasks can be formulated as supervised machine learning classification problems: a neural network approximates a function based on labelled training data. Such classification problems can be distinguished by the following major types:

- *Binary classification*: two labels (i.e., classifying whether a patient has certain disease, whether a transaction is a fraudulent, whether an email is a spam, etc.)
- *Multiclass classification*: multiple exclusive labels (i.e., classifying images, classifying hand-written digits digits from 0 to 9, etc.)
- *Multilabel classification*: multiple non-exclusive labels (i.e., classifying genres of a movie)

A. Tagarelli and H. Tong (Eds.): CSoNet 2019, LNCS 11917, pp. 57–62, 2019.
https://doi.org/10.1007/978-3-030-34980-6_5

In order to perform a classification task, a *classifier* function should be defined. This function assigns labels to unseen data items based on historical (training) data. This classifier should be *trained* on historical data by solving an optimization problem that seeks to minimize a *loss* function. There are many different loss functions that can be defined and used for different purposes, such as hinge loss, cross-entropy loss, among others.

There have been several recent attempts to propose new types of loss functions in the context of neural networks. For instance, Chen et al. [2] introduced the *quadruplet loss* as an extension of the *triplet loss* used in Siamese neural networks [1]. *Large-margin Softmax Loss*, a loss function that contains a parameter to control decision margin between the classes, was proposed in [3]. *Large Margin Cosine Loss* was proposed in [5]: this loss function aims at further increasing inter-class variance. Multiple modifications of cross-entropy loss have been proposed in the literature. The authors of the paper [6], which recently appeared in the well-known NIPS conference, proposed the *generalized cross entropy* as a noise-robust alternative to the ordinary cross entropy loss. In addition, the *class-weighted cross-entropy* was proposed in [4].

In this study, we introduce new types of cross-entropy loss function in the context of neural networks and test their potential applicability and benefits on a standard benchmark dataset (CIFAR-10).

2   Proposed Approach

In this section, we formally introduce the problem and present the proposed three types of multidimensional cross-entropy loss functions.

2.1   Formal Problem Statement

Following the standard concepts from the classification (or, supervised learning) problem setup, consider a training dataset $D_T = \{(x_i, y_i)\}_{i=1}^{N}, x \in \mathcal{X}, y \in \mathcal{Y}$, consisting of N training examples x_i and corresponding labels y_i. The goal of a supervised learning task is to learn a function $g : \mathcal{X} \rightarrow \mathcal{Y}$, such that $\hat{y}_j = g(x_j, \theta)$, where $\hat{y}_j$ is the predicted label for the item x_j, and θ is the vector of model parameters. In this paper we represent the function g as the deep neural network (DNN) with softmax output layer. In order to find optimal parameters θ for function g we need to solve the optimization problem that minimizes the loss function $\mathcal{L}(y, g(x, \theta)), x \in \mathcal{X}$ between actual and predicted labels. If g is represented as a DNN, then the loss can be minimized using a stochastic gradient descent algorithm.

There are multiple ways to set up the loss function $\mathcal{L}$. For instance, in regression settings it could be the mean average loss $\frac{1}{N} \sum_{j=1}^{N} |y_j - g(x_j, \theta)|$ or the mean squared loss $\frac{1}{N} \sum_{j=1}^{N} (y_j - g(x_j, \theta))^2$. However, a typical choice of such function in classification settings is *cross-entropy loss* defined as

$$\mathcal{L}_{CE}(\cdot,\cdot) = -\sum_{j=1}^{N} y_j \log(g(x_j, \boldsymbol{\theta})).$$

Further, in the special case of binary classification, the cross-entropy loss function can be formulated as

$$\mathcal{L}_{CE}(\cdot,\cdot) = -y_1 \log(g(x_1, \boldsymbol{\theta})) - (1 - y_1) \log(1 - g(x_1, \boldsymbol{\theta})).$$

2.2 Proposed Multidimensional Cross-Entropy Loss Functions

Motivated by the works mentioned above, we propose to "expand" the output layer of the neural network, which leads to the following three definitions of multidimensional cross-entropy losses (referred to as **CE1**, **CE2**, **CE3** below for brevity).

- **CE1:** In this modification we include an extra term into the cross-entropy loss function as follows:

$$\mathcal{L}_{CE1}(\cdot,\cdot) = -\sum_{j=1}^{N} y_j \log(g_1(x_j, \boldsymbol{\theta})) - \sum_{j=1}^{N} (1 - y_j) \log(1 - g_1(x_j, \boldsymbol{\theta}));$$

- **CE2:** In this modification we expand output layer, by adding another copy of the output (as depicted in Fig. 1(a)):

$$\mathcal{L}_{CE2}(\cdot,\cdot) = -\sum_{j=1}^{N} y_j \log(g_2(x_j, \boldsymbol{\theta})) - \sum_{j=N+1}^{2N} (y_j) \log(g_2(x_j, \boldsymbol{\theta}));$$

- **CE3:** In this modification we create a "square" output layer, as depicted in Fig. 1(b):

$$\mathcal{L}_{CE3}(\cdot,\cdot) = -\sum_{j=0}^{(N-1)} \sum_{i=Nj+1}^{N(j+1)} y_i \log(g_3(x_i, \boldsymbol{\theta})).$$

Here g_1, g_2, and g_3 correspond to neural networks with different size of output layer; output layer of neural network g_1 does not change, while outputs of g_2, and g_3 are expanded in accordance with the corresponding loss functions. In the next section, we present the results of computational experiments performed on a well-known benchmark dataset in order to evaluate potential benefits of introducing the aforementioned loss functions into neural network based classifiers.

$C_{\{1\}}$	$C_{\{2\}}$	$C_{\{3\}}$	$C_{\{4\}}$	$C_{\{5\}}$	$C_{\{6\}}$	$C_{\{7\}}$	$C_{\{8\}}$	$C_{\{9\}}$	$C_{\{10\}}$
0	**1**	0	0	0	0	0	0	0	0
0	**1**	0	0	0	0	0	0	0	0

(a) Illustration of CE2 loss function.

$C_{\{1\}}$	$C_{\{2\}}$	$C_{\{3\}}$	$C_{\{4\}}$	$C_{\{5\}}$	$C_{\{6\}}$	$C_{\{7\}}$	$C_{\{8\}}$	$C_{\{9\}}$	$C_{\{10\}}$
0	**1**	0	0	0	0	0	0	0	0
0	**1**	0	0	0	0	0	0	0	0
0	**1**	0	0	0	0	0	0	0	0
0	**1**	0	0	0	0	0	0	0	0
0	**1**	0	0	0	0	0	0	0	0
0	**1**	0	0	0	0	0	0	0	0
0	**1**	0	0	0	0	0	0	0	0
0	**1**	0	0	0	0	0	0	0	0
0	**1**	0	0	0	0	0	0	0	0
0	**1**	0	0	0	0	0	0	0	0

(b) Illustration of CE3 loss function.

Fig. 1. Illustrative examples of multidimensional cross-entropy loss functions CE2 and CE3 for 10 output classes.

3   Results and Discussion

In order to draw preliminary conclusions about the performance of deep neural network based classification algorithms with the aforementioned modifications to the loss functions, we tested them on a well-known dataset CIFAR-10. The reason for choosing this dataset was the fact that it is commonly used as a benchmark in related literature and it is rather challenging for the known classification algorithms to achieve high accuracy on this dataset.

Specifically, we have implemented a 10-layer deep neural network (DNN) that had two subsequent blocks of two 3×3 2D convolution layers followed by max-pooling and dropout layers, followed by a dense layer, and the resulting softmax layer. For this DNN, we have then implemented new loss functions as described above, as well as the standard ("default") cross-entropy loss function. We did not change any other network parameters except output layer size needed for our loss functions. For prediction, we use only one level of resulting expanded outputs. For the considered dataset, we used a 84%/16% split for training and test datasets, and we evaluated the accuracy of classification using our cross-entropy modifications on 16% unseen data (10.000 items) after 10 epochs. The respective results are shown in Fig. 2 and Table 1.

As it can be observed from the results, it appears that all of the proposed modifications of cross-entropy loss functions provide a slight increase in accuracy compared to the "default" approach on the training dataset, whereas only CE1 and CE2 provide such an increase on the test dataset. In fact, the modification based on CE2 ("duplicate" output layer) gives the best improvement in accuracy by a slim margin. Although these results are clearly of preliminary nature, we believe that they are noteworthy due to the fact that an increase in classification accuracy on a rather challenging dataset was achieved by applying very simple modifications to the standard approaches based on cross-entropy loss functions. It turns out that introducing a small amount of "redundancy" (or, "duplication"), either to the cross-entropy loss function itself or to the output layer, is sufficient to provide a more than 1% increase in classification accuracy on both training and test datasets. Interestingly, adding even more redundancy, as shown in the definition on the CE3 loss function, does not produce the same increase in accuracy on the test dataset. Thus, one may hypothesize that there may be some "optimal" amount of redundancy that could be beneficial for DNN-based classification algorithms. Since this is a preliminary study, we did not perform such in-depth analysis of these hypothesized phenomena; however, we believe that this is an interesting research direction that can be addressed from both theoretical (e.g., mathematical/statistical analysis) and computational (e.g., performing extensive computational experiments on a variety of datasets) perspectives. Last but not least, the proposed modifications to cross-entropy loss functions could be used in combination with other enhancements to DNN-based classification algorithms, which may potentially provide larger increases in classification accuracy.

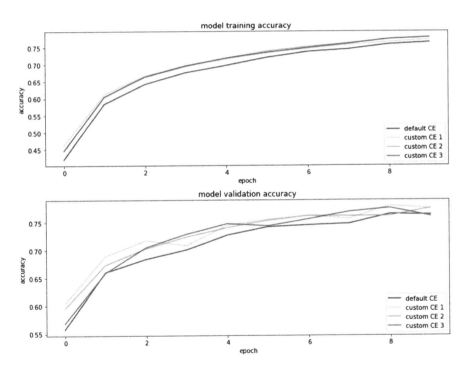

Fig. 2. Computational results on CIFAR-10 dataset. It can be observed that on the training dataset, classifiers that use each of the three introduced new multidimensional cross-entropy loss functions outperform the standard ("default") approach based on cross-entropy loss function. On the test dataset, CE1 and CE2 consistently outperform the default technique at almost all of the epochs, whereas CE3 exhibits results similar to the default approach.

Table 1. Summary of computational results on CIFAR-10 (test dataset, after 10 epochs) for three proposed cross-entropy loss functions and the standard ("default") approach. The results suggest that CE1 and CE2 provide a slight increase ($\sim$1%) in accuracy compared to the standard approach, whereas the accuracy of CE3 and the standard approach is similar.

Loss function	Validation accuracy
Standard	76.2%
CE1	77.3%
CE2	**77.4%**
CE3	75.9%

Acknowledgements. The work of A. Semenov was funded in part by the AFRL European Office of Aerospace Research and Development (grant no. FA9550-17-1-0030). This material is based on the work supported by the AFRL Mathematical Modeling and Optimization Institute.

References

1. Chechik, G., Sharma, V., Shalit, U., Bengio, S.: Large scale online learning of image similarity through ranking. J. Mach. Learn. Res. **11**, 1109–1135 (2010). http://dl.acm.org/citation.cfm?id=1756006.1756042
2. Chen, W., Chen, X., Zhang, J., Huang, K.: Beyond triplet loss: a deep quadruplet network for person re-identification. In: The Conference on Computer Vision and Pattern Recognition (2017)
3. Liu, W., Wen, Y., Yu, Z., Yang, M.: Large-margin softmax loss for convolutional neural networks. In: Proceedings of the 33rd International Conference on International Conference on Machine Learning, ICML 2016, vol. 48, pp. 507–516. JMLR.org (2016). http://dl.acm.org/citation.cfm?id=3045390.3045445
4. Panchapagesan, S., et al.: Multi-task learning and weighted cross-entropy for DNN-based keyword spotting. In: Interspeech 2016, pp. 760–764 (2016). https://doi.org/10.21437/Interspeech.2016-1485
5. Wang, H., et al.: Cosface: large margin cosine loss for deep face recognition. In: The IEEE Conference on Computer Vision and Pattern Recognition (CVPR), June 2018
6. Zhang, Z., Sabuncu, M.R.: Generalized cross entropy loss for training deep neural networks with noisy labels. In: Proceedings of the 32nd International Conference on Neural Information Processing Systems, NIPS 2018, pp. 8792–8802. Curran Associates Inc., New York (2018). http://dl.acm.org/citation.cfm?id=3327546.3327555

A RVND+ILS Metaheuristic to Solve the Delivery Man Problem with Time Windows

Ha-Bang Ban$^{(\boxtimes)}$

School of Information and Communication Technology,
Hanoi University of Science and Technology, Hanoi, Vietnam
BangBH@soict.hust.edu.vn

Abstract. The Delivery Man Problem with Time Windows (DMPTW) is an extension of the Delivery Man Problem (DMP). The objective of DMPTW is to minimize the sum of travel durations between a depot and several customer locations while the delivery made in a specific time window given by the customers. It has many practical applications in network, e.g., whenever servers have to accommodate a set of requests so as to minimize clients' total (or average) waiting time. To solve medium and large size instances, two-phase metaheuristic algorithm is proposed. The first stage constructs a feasible solution using Neighborhood Descent with Random neighborhood ordering (RVND), and the optimization stage improves the feasible solution with an Iterated Local Search (ILS). The proposed algorithm is tested on the DMPTW benchmark instances from the literature. The results indicate that the developed algorithm has improved the best solutions for 34 instances in a reasonable computation time.

Keywords: DMPTW · ILS · RVND

1 Introduction

The Delivery Man Problem with Time Windows (DMPTW), in some special cases, has been studied in the number of previous work [1–5], and is often called as Minimum Latency Problem (MLP), Traveling Repairman Problem (TRP). It has many practical applications in network and scheduling, e.g., whenever deliverymen or servers have to accommodate a set of requests so as to minimize their total (or average) waiting time [1,2,4,5]. The literature on the DMPTW is very limited. The papers that we are aware of are those from Ban et al. [4], Tsitsiklis [13] and Heilporn [9]. In this paper, we formulate the DMPTW as followings: Given an complete graph $K_n = (V, E)$, where $V = 1, 2, ..., n$ is a set of vertices representing the depot and client places, and E the set of edges connecting the vertices, a DMPTW tour is a list of visiting each vertex exactly once. Assume that, a tour represents as $T = (v_1 = s, v_2..., v_n)$, and v_k denotes the index of the vertex at the k-th position of the tour. For each edge $(v_i, v_j) \in E$,

© Springer Nature Switzerland AG 2019
A. Tagarelli and H. Tong (Eds.): CSoNet 2019, LNCS 11917, pp. 63–69, 2019.
https://doi.org/10.1007/978-3-030-34980-6_6

which connects the two vertices v_i and v_j, there exists a cost $c(v_i, v_j)$. This cost describes the service time at vertex v_i plus the travel time between vertex v_i and v_j. A time window $[e_i, l_i]$ is associated to each vertex $v_i \in V$, which indicates when service time at vertex v_i can start. This implies that a vertex v_i may be reached before the start e_i, but service cannot start until e_i and no latter than l_i of its time window. Therefore, given a particular tour T, let $D(v_k)$ be the times at which service begins at v_k. It is calculated as follows: $D(v_k) = \max\{A(v_k), e_k\}$, where $A(v_k) = D(v_{k-1}) + c(v_{k-1}, v_k)$ is the arrival time at vertex v_k in the tour. We also define the travel duration of vertex v_i as the difference between the beginning of service at vertex v_i and the beginning of service at s. A tour is feasible, if and only if $A(v_k) \leq l_k$ for all vertices. The DMPTW consists in determining a tour, starting at the depot s, so as to minimize the sum of travel durations over all vertices while respecting time windows.

DMPTW is also NP-hard because it is a generalization case of DMP. Salvesbergh [14] argues that even building a feasible solution to the problem is a NP-hard problem. For NP-hard problems, there are several three common approaches to solve the problem, namely, (1) exact algorithms, (2) approximation algorithms, (3) heuristic (or metaheuristic) algorithms. Previously, only two works based on heuristic have been proposed for DMPTW [4,9]. Heilporn et al. [9] propose an insertion heuristic that gradually builds the tour. After that, Ban et al.'s solutions [4] are obtained by using metaheuristic based on Variable Neighborhood Search (VNS). The experimental results from [4,9] indicate that metaheuristic is a suitable approach to solve the problem. In this work, we developed a two phase metaheuristic consisting of a constructive and an optimization stage. The construction stage seeks a feasible solution, whereas the improvement stage tries to improve the solution using the feasible solution produced in the previous phase as a starting point. Our metaheuristic combines RVND with ILS, in which ILS ensures the diversification while RVND maintains the intensification. This combination maintains the simplicity spirit of RVND while it effectively explores the search space. Extensive numerical experiments on benchmark instances show that our algorithm reaches the better solutions than the-state-of-art metaheuristics in many cases.

The rest of this paper is organized as follows. Section 2 presents the proposed algorithm. Computational evaluations are reported in Sect. 3 and Sect. 4 concludes the paper.

2 Two-Phase Algorithm

2.1 Neighborhoods

We used neighborhoods widely applied in the literature to explore the solution space of this problem [14]. The main operation in exploring the neighborhood is the calculation of a neighboring solutions' cost. In straightforward implementation in the worst case, this operation requires $Tsol = O(n)$. Assume that T, and n are a tour and its size, respectively. We describe more details about seven neighborhoods as follows: (1) **move-up** moves a vertex forward one position

Algorithm 1. RVND+ILS

Input: $v_1, V, N_i(T)(i = 1, ..., 7), level$ are a starting vertex, the set of vertices in K_n, the set of neighborhoods, the parameter to control the strength of the perturbation procedure, respectively.

Output: the best solution T^*.

  for $i \leftarrow 1, ..., I_{max}$ **do**

    $T \leftarrow$ **Construction**(v_1, V);{Construction phase}

    $T' \leftarrow T$;

    $iterILS \leftarrow 0$;

    while $iterILS < m$ **do**

      Initialize the Neighborhood List NL;

      while $NL \neq 0$ **do**

        Choose a neighborhood N in NL at random

        $T'' \leftarrow$ arg min $N(T)$;

        if $(L(T'') < L(T))$ or $(L(T'') < L(T^*)))$ **then**

          $T \leftarrow T''$

          Update NL;

          if $(L(T'') < L(T^*))$ and (T'' must be an feasible solution) **then**

            $T^* \leftarrow T''$;

        else

          Remove N from the NL;

      $T \leftarrow T''$;

      if $L(T) < L(T')$ **then**

        $T' \leftarrow T$;

        $iterILS \leftarrow 0$;

      $T \longleftarrow$ Perturbation$(T, level)$;

      $iterILS + +$;

  return T^*;

---

in T; (2) textbfmove-down moves a vertex backward one position in T; (3) **shift** relocates a vertex to another position in T; (4) **swap-adjacent** attempts to swap each pair of adjacent vertices in the tour; (5) **swap neighborhood** tries to swap the positions of each pair of vertices in the tour; (6) **2-opt** removes each pair of edges from the tour and reconnects them; (7) **Or-opt**: Three adjacent customers are reallocated to another position of the tour.

2.2 RVND+ILS

Our proposed algorithm works iteratively in two stages. The construction stage seeks a feasible solution, whereas the improvement stage tries to improve the solution using the feasible solution produced in the previous phase as a starting point. A local search is used in the construction phase and a RVND+ILS is used in the improvement phase. Algorithm 1 depicts the whole process.

The Construction Phase: Algorithm 2 shows the constructive procedure. The objective function used in this procedure is the sum of all positive differences between the time to reach each customer and its due date, that is,

---

Algorithm 2. Construction

Input: $v_1, V, k, \alpha, level$ are a starting vertex, the set of vertices in K_n, the number of vehicles and the size of RCL, the parameter to control the strength of the perturbation procedure, respectively.

Output: An initial solution T.

1: $LT = \phi$; {LIT is the list of infeasible tours}
2: $T = \phi$; {T is a tour}
3: **while** $|T| < n$ **do**
4:     Create RCL that includes α nearest vertices to v_e; {v_e is the last vertex in T}
5:     Select randomly vertex $v = \{v_i | v_i \in RCL \text{ and } v_i \notin T\}$;
6:     $T \leftarrow T \cup v_i$
7: **if** T is a feasible solution **then**
8:     **return** T;
9: **else**
10:    $level = 1$;
11:    **while** ((T is infeasible solution) and ($level \leq level\_max$)) **do**
12:      $T' = $ Perturbation($T, level$);
13:      $T' = $ Shift(T');
14:      **if** $L(T') < L(T)$ **then**
15:        $T \leftarrow T'$;
16:      **if** $L(T') == L(T)$ **then**
17:        $level \leftarrow 1$;
18:      **else**
19:        $level + +$;
20: **return** T;

$\min \sum_{i=1}^{n} \max(0, D(v_i) - l_i)$. The algorithm works iteratively until it finds a feasible solution. At next Step, a restricted candidate list (RCL) is determined by ordering all non selected vertices in term of a greedy function that measures the benefit of including them in the tour. After that, one element will be chosen randomly from RCL Since all vertices are visited, the algorithm stops and the initial solution is returned. If any feasible solution is found, it is considered as an initial solution. Conversely, a local search procedure using the shift neighborhood, and the algorithm iterates until finding a feasible solution or $level\_max$ is reached.

The Improvement Phase: After the construction of a feasible initial solution, the heuristic tries to improve it. The optimization phase applies a RVND heuristic [11]. In this phase, the objective function is to minimize $\sum_{i=1}^{n} D(v_k)$. Our algorithm begin with a feasible solution in the first phase. ILS is a single-solution based solution approach comprised of main components: an improvement procedure and a perturbation mechanism. At the beginning of an ILS execution, the initial solution from the first phase and local search mechanisms are successively applied. After that, perturbation and local search procedures are iteratively applied to the current solution to obtain better solutions.

In the local search procedure, the Neighborhood List (NL) is initialized with all neighborhoods. In the main loop, a given neighborhood is selected at random from the *NL*. Neighbor solutions are evaluated and the feasible solution with the best cost is stored. In the case of improvement, *NL* is repopulated with all neighborhoods. Otherwise, we removed from *NL*. The procedure terminates when *NL* becomes empty.

In the Perturbation mechanism design, the perturbation mechanism, called double-bridge, was originally developed in [12]. It consists in removing and re-inserting four arcs in such a way that a feasible tour is generated.

The last aspect to discuss is the stop criterium of our algorithm. Here, the algorithm stops if no improvement is found after the number of loop.

3   Evaluations

Our algorithm is run on a Pentium 4 core i7 2.40 GHz processor with 8 GB of RAM. On all experiments, parameters α, $level\_max$, m, and I_{max} were respectively set to 10, 5, 50, and 10.

3.1   Instances

We implement the algorithm in two sets of instances. The first is proposed by Dumas et al. [6] while the second is from Gendreau et al. [8].

3.2   Results

We define the improvement of our algorithm with respect to *Best.Sol* (*Best.Sol* is the best solution found by our algorithm) in comparison with the-state-of-the-art metaheuristic algorithms for the problem as followings: $Gap[\%] = \frac{Best.Sol - BKS}{BKS} \times 100\%$. In the tables, *BKS*, *Best.Sol*, *Aver.Sol*, and *T*, correspond to the best known solution, best solution, the average solution, and the average time in seconds of ten executions obtained by our algorithm, respectively. *cTime* represents scaled run times, estimated on a Pentium IV by means of the factors of Dongarra[1]. Tables from 1 to 3 compare the results of our algorithm with the known best solutions from the other algorithms, respectively. Due to the paper limit, all Tables can be found in[2].

Table 1 shows the results on the Dumas et al.'s [6] instances and compares them with the results obtained by the algorithm in [4]. The quality of our solutions is much better than Ban et al.'s in [4] in 24 instances. The average best result is slightly better (0.31%) than the one obtained by VNS, but the run time is the same on average. In Table 2, our result is comparable with G. Heilporn et al.'s algorithm [9]. Specifically, it reaches the better solutions for 10 out of 21 instances. The improvement is significant when G. Heilporn et al.'s algorithm is the state-of-the art.

---

[1] Dongarra, J. J., 2011. Performance of various computers using standard linear equations software. Tech. Rep. CS-89-85.

[2] https://sites.google.com/a/soict.hust.edu.vn/dmptw/.

Computation times of our algorithm grow quite moderate compared to the G. Heilporn et al.'s algorithm [9] while it is the same as Ban et al.'s algorithm [4].

From Table 3, we know that most algorithms are developed for a specific variant, that are not applicable to other variants. Our algorithm can run well to multiple variants of TRPTW. In comparison with the best known solution in [10, 14], our algorithm's solutions obtain the optimal solutions for the instances with up to 40 vertices. The average gap between the optimal solution and our result is about 0.73% for the instances with 100 vertices. It shows that our results are very close to the optimal solutions.

4   Conclusions

In this paper, we propose a metaheuristic algorithm which combines the ILS and RNVD for DMPTW. The experimental results show that our algorithm is able to find the optimal solutions for the small instances, which is up to with 40 vertices in some seconds. For the larger instances, our solution's quality is comparable with the state-of-the-art metaheuristic algorithms, moreover, for many instances it provides the new best solutions.

References

1. Ban, H.B., Nguyen, D.N.: Improved genetic algorithm for minimum latency problem. In: Proceedings of SOICT, pp. 9–15 (2010)
2. Ban, H.B., Nguyen, K., Ngo, M.C., Nguyen, D.N.: An efficient exact algorithm for minimum latency problem. J. PI **10**, 1–8 (2013)
3. Ban, H.B., Nghia, N.D.: A meta-heuristic algorithm combining between tabu and variable neighborhood search for the minimum latency problem. J. FI **156**(1), 21–44 (2017)
4. Ban, H.B., Nghia, N.D.: Metaheuristic for the minimum latency problem with time windows. In: Proceedings of RIVF, pp. 1–6 (2017)
5. Blum, A., Chalasani, P., Coppersmith, D., Pulleyblank, W., Raghavan, P., Sudan, M.: The minimum latency problem. In: Proceedings of STOC, pp. 163–171 (1994)
6. Dumas, Y., Desrosiers, J., Gélinas, E.: An optimal algorithm for the traveling salesman problem with time windows. J. Oper. Res. **43**, 367–371 (1995)
7. Feo, T.A., Resende, M.G.C.: Greedy randomized adaptive search procedures. J. Global Opt. **6**(2), 109–133 (1995)
8. Gendreau, M., Hertz, A., Laporte, G., Stan, M.: A generalized insertion heuristic for the traveling salesman problem with time windows. J. Oper. Res. **43**, 330–335 (1998)
9. Heilporn, G., Cordeau, J.F., Laporte, G.: The delivery man problem with time windows. Discrete Optim. **7**(4), 269–282 (2010)
10. Lopez-Ibanez, M., Blum, C.: Beam-ACO for the traveling salesman problem with time windows. J. Comput. Oper. Res. **37**(9), 1570–1583 (2010)
11. Mladenovic, N., Hansen, P.: Variable neighborhood search. J. Oper. Res. **24**(11), 1097–1100 (1997)

12. Johnson, D.S., McGeoch, L.A.: The traveling salesman problem: a case study in local optimization. In: Aarts, E., Lenstra, J.K. (eds.) Local Search in Combinatorial Optimization, pp. 215–310

13. Tsitsiklis, J.N.: Special cases of traveling salesman and repairman problems with time windows. J. Netw. **22**, 263–283 (1992)

14. Ohlmann, J.W., Thomas, B.W.: A compressed-annealing heuristic for the traveling salesman problem with time windows. J. Inform. **19**(1), 80–90 (2007)

Star2vec: From Subspace Embedding to Whole-Space Embedding for Intelligent Recommendation System (*Extended Abstract*)

Quang Nguyen[✉], Vu Nguyen, Doi Tran, Trung Mai, and Tho Quan[✉]

Ho Chi Minh City University of Technology, 268 Ly Thuong Kiet, District 10,
Ho Chi Minh City, Vietnam
quang.nguyen2016@ict.jvn.edu.vn, qttho@hcmut.edu.vn

Recommendation systems are powerful tools that can alleviate system overload problems by recommending the most relevant items (contents) to users. Recommendation systems allow users to find useful, interesting items from a significantly large space and also enhance the user's browsing experience. Relevant items are determined by predicting user's ratings on different items. Two traditional techniques used in recommendation system are Content-Based filtering and Collaborative-Filtering. Content-Based filtering uses content of the items that the user has involved in the past to discover items that the user might be interested in. On the other hands, Collaborative-Filtering determine the similarity between users and recommends items chosen by *similar* users.

Similarity measure is to evaluate the similarity of objects. These studies can be roughly categorized into two types: feature based approaches and link based approaches. The feature based approaches measure the similarity of objects based on their feature values. Similarity search via feature based approaches has been extensively studied for traditional categorical and numerical data types in relational data. However, the joining operations [1] that allows the combining of related tuples from relations on different attribute schemes are executed frequently with highly computational cost. The link based approaches measure the similarity of objects based on their link structures in a graph. For example, Personalized PageRank [2] evaluates the probability starting from a source object to a target object by randomly walking with restart, and SimRank [3] evaluates the similarity of two objects by their neighbors similarities. The key problem of multi-modal retrieval is to find an effective embedding mechanism, which maps data from different modalities into a common latent space. An effective mapping mechanism would preserve both intra-modal semantics and inter-modal semantics well in the latent space, and thus generates good retrieval performance. This becomes a challenge task due to the diversity of the ontologies, and the semantic richness of the concepts, which makes it really hard to generate proper and universally applicable graph embeddings.

In this paper, we exploit the advantages of knowledge graph embedding and propose a novel approach to build robust recommendation systems. The main idea of our approach is to embed domain knowledge captured by an ontology into

© Springer Nature Switzerland AG 2019
A. Tagarelli and H. Tong (Eds.): CSoNet 2019, LNCS 11917, pp. 70–71, 2019.
https://doi.org/10.1007/978-3-030-34980-6_7

latent features to support efficient retrieval for recommendation. Unlike emerging embedding techniques which embed knowledge of the same kind, considered a *subspace* in the knowledge space, our approach can embed the *whole space* of ontological knowledge, including instances of different concepts, into a single vector space.

In order to do so, we firstly construct *Knowledge Graphs* (KGs), i.e. sets of *(subject,predicate, object)* triples. As an ontology can be represented by T-box and A-box, we can merge those two representations into a single knowledge graph.

Next step is to perform *knowledge graph embedding*, which is to embed elements of a KG including subjects and relations into continuous vector spaces, to obtain a simplification of the manipulation while maintaining the fundamental structure of the KG. Knowledge graph embedding earned much attention recently because it can benefit a lot of tasks such as KG completion and relation extraction.

The knowledge graph embedding involves network representation learning, which aims to learn a low-dimensional representation of nodes in the network. There are several works in network representation learning which can be classified based on their approach to mapping a node into the embedding space: shallow and deep encoders. Techniques that use shallow encoders [4,5] construct a unique embedding for each node directly. These techniques are sometimes faster to train and do not require knowing the node features. On the other hand, deep encoder approaches [6,7] consider node neighborhood to generate node embedding. In this research, our graph embedding technique is also a variant of a deep encoder approach. However, our graph embedding technique differs from traditional deep encoder approach as we also capture the ontology of information network into the embedded space.

References

1. Musto, C., et al.: Word Embedding Techniques for Content-based Recommender Systems: An Empirical Evaluation. RecSys Posters (2015)
2. Bobadilla, J., et al.: Recommender systems survey. Knowl. Based Syst. **46**, 109–132 (2013)
3. Ozsoy, M.G.: From word embeddings to item recommendation. arXiv preprint arXiv:1601.01356 (2016)
4. Yera, R., Martinez, L.: Fuzzy tools in recommender systems: a survey. Int. J. Comput. Intell. Syst. **10**(1), 776–803 (2017)
5. Perozzi, B., Al-Rfou, R., Skiena, S.: DeepWalk: online learning of social representations. In: Proceedings of the 20th ACM SIGKDD International Conference on Knowledge Discovery and Data Mining. ACM (2014)
6. Goyal, P., Ferrara, E.: Graph embedding techniques, applications, and performance: a survey. Knowl. Based Syst. **151**, 78–94 (2018)
7. Pirotte, A., Renders, J.-M., Saerens, M.: Random-walk computation of similarities between nodes of a graph with application to collaborative recommendation. IEEE Trans. Knowl. Data Eng. **3**, 355–369 (2007)

Approximation Algorithm for the Squared Metric Soft Capacitated Facility Location Problem (*Extended Abstract*)

Lu Han[1], Dachuan Xu[2], Yicheng Xu[3], and Dongmei Zhang[4(✉)]

[1] Academy of Mathematics and Systems Science, Chinese Academy of Sciences, Beijing 100190, People's Republic of China
[2] Department of Operations Research and Scientific Computing, Beijing University of Technology, Beijing 100124, People's Republic of China
[3] Shenzhen Institutes of Advanced Technology, Chinese Academy of Sciences, Shenzhen 518055, People's Republic of China
[4] School of Computer Science and Technology, Shandong Jianzhu University, Jinan 250101, People's Republic of China
zhangdongmei@sdjzu.edu.cn

Abstract. We consider the squared metric soft capacitated facility location problem (SMSCFLP), which includes both the squared metric facility location problem (SMFLP) and the soft capacitated facility location problem (SCFLP) as special cases. As our main contribution, we propose a primal-dual based 10-approximation algorithm for the SMSCFLP. Our work also extends the applicability of the primal-dual technique.

Keywords: Facility location problem · Squared metric · Soft capacitated · Approximation algorithm · Primal-dual

The facility location problem (FLP) is one of the most essential problems in operations management and computer science [6,7]. The most classical model of the FLP is the uncapacitated facility location problem (UFLP). The UFLP is a well-known NP-hard problem and for the metric version of the UFLP extensive approximation algorithms have been proposed for it.

The soft capacitated facility location problem (SCFLP) is one of the most well-studied variants [1,3–5] of the UFLP. In the SCFLP, a facility set $\mathcal{F}$ and a client set is given. For any facility $i \in \mathcal{F}$, it has a capacity u_i and an opening cost f_i. Every facility can be opened multiple times. If facility i is opened l times, facility i can be connected by at most lu_i clients and costs lf_i to open l copies of itself. Every facility-client pair has a connection cost, which is equal to the distance between them. Under the assumption that the distances are metric, we want to open some facilities (once or multiple times) and connect every client to an opened facility without violating the capacity constraint such that the total opening costs as well as connection costs is minimized. In some practical

© Springer Nature Switzerland AG 2019
A. Tagarelli and H. Tong (Eds.): CSoNet 2019, LNCS 11917, pp. 72–73, 2019.
https://doi.org/10.1007/978-3-030-34980-6_8

applications, the distances plays a more important role for the total cost than it is in the UFLP model. Fernandes et al. [2] consider the squared metric facility location problem (SMFLP).

In this paper, we propose the squared metric soft capacitated facility location problem (SMSCFLP), which is a variant for both the SMFLP and the SCFLP. The SMSCFLP is similar to the SCFLP, except that the connection cost of a facility-client pair is equal to the square of the distance between them. We state the following result as our main contribution.

Theorem 1. *For the SMSCFLP, there exists a primal-dual 10-approximation algorithm.*

The result is inspired by the brilliant work of Jain and Vazirani [4] on the SCFLP. Compared with the SCFLP, the triangle inequality does not hold for the connection costs anymore in the SMSCFLP. When designing primal-dual algorithm for the SMSCFLP, the crucial challenge is to carefully design the algorithm in order to make sure that the analysis of the algorithm can provide a dual-related upper bound for the total connection costs.

Acknowledgements. The second author is supported by Natural Science Foundation of China (No. 11531014). The third author is supported by Natural Science Foundation of China grant (No. 11901558) and China Postdoctoral Science Foundation funded project (No. 2018M643233). The fourth author is supported by Natural Science Foundation of China (No. 11871081).

References

1. Arya, V., Garg, N., Khandekar, R., Meyerson, A., Munagala, K., Pandit, V.: Local search heuristics for *k*-median and facility location problems. SIAM J. Comput. **33**, 544–562 (2004)
2. Fernandes, C.G., Meira, L.A.A., Miyazawa, F.K., Pedrosa, L.L.C.: A systematic approach to bound factor-revealing LPs and its application to the metric and squared metric facility location problems. Math. Program. **153**, 655–685 (2015)
3. Jain, K., Mahdian, M., Markakis, E., Saberi, E., Vazirani, V.V.: Greedy facility location algorithms analyzed using dual fitting with factor-revealing LP. J. ACM **50**, 795–824 (2003)
4. Jain, K., Vazirani, V.V.: Approximation algorithms for metric facility location and *k*-median problems using the primal-dual schema and Lagrangian relaxation. J. ACM **48**, 274–296 (2001)
5. Mahdian, M., Ye, Y., Zhang, J.: Improved approximation algorithms for metric facility location problems. In: Jansen, K., Leonardi, S., Vazirani, V. (eds.) APPROX 2002. LNCS, vol. 2462, pp. 229–242. Springer, Heidelberg (2002). https://doi.org/10.1007/3-540-45753-4_20
6. Stollsteimer, J.F.: A working model for plant numbers and locations. J. Farm Econ. **45**, 631–645 (1963)
7. Teo, C.P., Shu, J.: Warehouse-retailer network design problem. Oper. Res. **52**, 396–408 (2004)

An Efficient Algorithm
for the k-Dominating Set Problem
on Very Large-Scale Networks
(*Extended Abstract*)

Minh Hai Nguyen[1,2], Minh Hoàng Hà[1(✉)], Dinh Thai Hoang[2],
Diep N. Nguyen[2], Eryk Dutkiewicz[2], and The Trung Tran[3]

[1] ORLab, VNU University of Engineering and Technology, Hanoi, Vietnam
minhhoangha.vth@gmail.com
[2] Faculty of Engineering and Information Technology,
University of Technology, Sydney, Australia
[3] FPT Technology Research Institute, Hanoi, Vietnam

The minimum dominating set problem (MDSP) aims to construct the minimum-size subset $D \subset V$ of a graph $G = (V, E)$ such that every vertex has at least one neighbor in D. The problem is proved to be NP-hard [5]. In a recent industrial application, we encountered a more general variant of MDSP that extends the neighborhood relationship as follows: a vertex is a k-neighbor of another if there exists a linking path through no more than k edges between them. This problem is called the minimum k-dominating set problem (MkDSP) and the dominating set is denoted as D_k. The MkDSP can be used to model applications in social networks [2] and design of wireless sensor networks [3]. In our case, a telecommunication company uses the problem model to supervise a large social network up to 17 millions nodes via a dominating subset in which k is set to 3.

Unlike MDSP that has been well investigated, the only work that addressed the large-scale MkDSP was published by [2]. In this work, the MkDSP is converted to the classical MDSP by connecting all non-adjacent pairs of vertices whose distance is no more than k edges. The converted MDSP is then solved by a greedy algorithm that works as follows. First, vertex v is added into the set D_k, where v is the most covering vertex. Then, all vertices in the set of k-neighbors of v denoted by $\mathcal{N}(k, v)$ are marked as covered. The same procedure is then repeated until all the vertices are covered. The algorithm, called *Campan*, could solve instances of up to 36,000 vertices and 200,000 edges [2]. However, it fails to provide any solution on larger instances because computing and storing k-neighbor sets of all vertices are very expensive.

The telecommunication company currently uses a simple greedy algorithm whose basic idea is to sort the vertices in decreasing order of degree. We then check each vertex in the obtained list. If the considering vertex v is uncovered, it is added to D_k and the vertices in $\mathcal{N}(k, v)$ become covered. Our experiments show that this algorithm, called HEU_1, is faster but provides solutions that are often worse than *Campan*.

© Springer Nature Switzerland AG 2019
A. Tagarelli and H. Tong (Eds.): CSoNet 2019, LNCS 11917, pp. 74–76, 2019.
https://doi.org/10.1007/978-3-030-34980-6_9

Table 1. Comparisons among three algorithms.

			k = 1						k = 3					
			HEU₁		Campan		HEU₂		HEU₁		Campan		HEU₂	
Instances	|V|	|E|	Sol	Time (s)	Sol	Time (s)	Sol	Time (s)	Sol	Time (s)	Sol	Time (s)	Sol	Time (s)
ca-GrQc	4k	13k	1210	0.00	803	0.15	776	1.38	251	0.01	120	0.35	102	2.71
ca-HepPh	11k	118k	2961	0.01	1730	1.54	1662	6.49	430	0.02	138	14.63	117	53.76
ca-AstroPh	18k	197k	3911	0.02	2175	1.79	2055	15.22	438	0.06	122	75.60	106	203.18
ca-CondMat	21k	91k	5053	0.04	3104	4.20	2990	21.35	898	0.02	302	5.82	266	63.16
email-enron-large	34k	181k	12283	0.10	2005	4.48	1972	37.71	724	0.14	-	-	92	203.72
soc-BlogCatalog	89k	2093k	49433	0.72	4896	26.89	4915	1839.26	87	0.06	-	-	15	1616.70
soc-delicious	536k	1366k	215261	19.07	56066	1464.84	56600	5679.63	14806	2.44	-	-	1505	1695.77
soc-flixster	2523k	7919k	1452450	999	-	-	91543	27374.44	20996	29.71	-	-	313	3333.45
hugebubbles	2680k	2161k	1213638	2087.83	-	-	1169394	7498.20	843077	649.47	-	-	688817	17221.76
soc-livejournal	4033k	27933k	1538044	2689.72	-	-	930632	75185.96	211894	394.98	-	-	83710	42600.51
soc-tc-0	17642k	33397k	6263241	64228.04	-	-	29278	26740.42	6337	55.57	-	-	5158	5200.1448
soc-tc-1	16819k	26086k	4129393	19109.00	-	-	38303	38644.65	12807	78.3	-	-	10905	5481.59

Our main contribution is to propose an algorithm that yields better solutions at the expense of reasonably longer computational time than *Campan*. More specially, unlike *Campan*, our algorithm can handle very large real-world networks. The algorithm, denoted as HEU_2, includes three phases: preprocessing, solution construction, and post-optimization. In the first phase, we remove the connected components whose radius is less than $k + 1$. The construction phase is similar to HEU_1 except that if the considering vertex v is covered but itself covers more than θ uncovered vertices, then v is added to D_k. We repeat this process with different integer values of θ from 0 to 4, and select the best result. In the post-optimization phase, we reduce the size of D_k by two techniques. First, the vertices in D_k are divided into disjoint subsets; each contains about 20,000 vertices with the degree less than 1000, e.g. if there are 45,000 vertices in D_k that have degree less than 1000 then they are divided in to three subsets which have 20,000, 20,000 and 5000 vertices respectively. For each set B, we define set $\bar{B} = \cup_{v \in B} N(v, 1)$ and X, the set of all vertices covered by B, but not by $D_k \setminus B$. A Mixed Integer Programming (MIP) model is used to find a better solution B' which replaces B in D_k. The second technique is removing redundant vertices. A vertex $v \in D_k$ is redundant if there exists a subset $U \subset D_k \setminus \{v\}$, such that $\mathcal{N}(k, v) \subset \cup_{u \in U} \mathcal{N}(k, u)$.

Experiments are performed on a computer with Intel Core i7-8750h 2.2 Ghz and 24 GB RAM. Three algorithms are implemented in *Python* using *IBM CPLEX* 12.8.0 whenever we need to solve the MIP formulations. The summarized results are shown in Table 1. The first ten instances are from the Network Data Repository source [4]. The last two instances are taken from the data of the telecommunication company mentioned above. The values of k are set to 1 and 3. The results clearly demonstrate the performance of our proposed algorithm. It outperforms the current algorithm used by the company (HEU_1) in terms of solution quality and provides better solutions than *Campan* on 10 over 12 instances. More specially, it can handle 13 very large instances that *Campan* cannot (results marked "-" in *Campan* columns).

References

1. Fan, Y., et al.: Efficient local search for minimum dominating sets in large graphs. In: Li, G., Yang, J., Gama, J., Natwichai, J., Tong, Y. (eds.) DASFAA 2019. LNCS, vol. 11447, pp. 211–228. Springer, Cham (2019). https://doi.org/10.1007/978-3-030-18579-4_13
2. Campan, A., Truta, T.M., Beckerich, M.: Approximation algorithms for d-hop dominating set problem. In: 12th International Conference on Data Mining, p. 86 (2016)
3. Rieck, M.Q., Pai, S., Dhar, S.: Distributed routing algorithms for wireless adhoc networks using d-hop connected d-hop dominating sets. Comput. Netw. **47**, 785–799 (2005)
4. Ryan, A.R., Nesreen, K.A.: The network data repository with interactive graph analytics and visualization. In: AAAI (2015)
5. Wang, Y., Cai, S., Chen, J., Yin, M.: A fast local search algorithm for minimum weight dominating set problem on massive graphs. In: IJCAI 2018, pp. 1514–1522 (2018)

Strategy-Proof Cost-Sharing Mechanism Design for a Generalized Cover-Sets Problem (*Extended Abstract*)

Longkun Guo[1], Chenchen Wu[2(✉)], Huahui Yu[3], and Xiaoyan Zhang[3]

[1] College of Mathematics and Computer Science, Fuzhou University,
Fuzhou 350116, People's Republic of China
[2] College of Science, Tianjin University of Technology,
Tianjin 300384, People's Republic of China
wu_chenchen_tjut@163.com
[3] School of Mathematical Science, Institute of Mathematics,
Nanjing Normal University, Jiangsu 210023, China

Abstract. In this work, we extend the set cover game, which is called as "generalized cover-sets game". We propose several approximate cost allocation methods for three different game settings.

Keywords: Set cover · Cost sharing · Mechanism design

1 Introduction

Set cover problem is a classical NP-hard problem. It has applications in lots of fields such as social network, location, and so on. Formally speaking, there is a ground set $U = \{e_1, e_2, \cdots, e_n\}$ and its collection set $\mathcal{S} = \{S_1, S_2, \cdots, S_m\}$ $(S_i \subseteq U)$ in the set cover problem. We need to choose a subset of $\mathcal{S}$ to cover all elements in U such that the carnality of the subset is minimized. In this work, we propose a generalized version of the set cover problem. We call it as "cover-sets problem". In fact, we are given a ground set $U = \{e_1, e_2, \cdots, e_n\}$. Also, we are given two collection sets $\mathcal{S} = \{S_1, S_2, \cdots, S_m\}$ and $\mathcal{S}' = \{S'_1, S'_2, \cdots, S'_m\}$ that are service suppliers set and service receivers set, respectively. Each elements in $S_i \in \mathcal{S}$ has a coverage requirement r_i, that is, there is at least r_i elements in S_i are covered by some elements in $\mathcal{S}'$. Each $S'_j \in \mathcal{S}'$ has a cost c_j. We need to choose a subsets $\mathcal{T}$ of $\mathcal{S}'$ such that $|S_i \cap (\cup_{S' \in \mathcal{T}} S')| \geq r_i$ for each $S_i \in \mathcal{S}$. The goal of the problem is the total cost of the subset $\mathcal{T}$ is minimized. Obviously, the cover-sets problem is a generalization of the set cover problem. If $S_i = e_i$ and $r_i = 1$, the cover-sets problem is the set cover problem.

Mechanism design is one of the most important fields in Operations Research. Typically, the following well-known constraints are required to be imposed on a mechanism.

© Springer Nature Switzerland AG 2019
A. Tagarelli and H. Tong (Eds.): CSoNet 2019, LNCS 11917, pp. 77–78, 2019.
https://doi.org/10.1007/978-3-030-34980-6_10

- α-*value efficient*: if for any private information of each player, the outcome is no less than α times the optimal total value.
- α-*budget balance*: for any players subset $\tilde{S}$, let $C(\tilde{S})$ and $\xi(i, \tilde{S})$ be the total cost for all players and the cost-sharing cost for the player i in $\tilde{S}$, respectively. A mechanism is called as budget balance, if
  - cost recovery: $\sum_{S_i \in \tilde{S}} \xi(i, \tilde{S}) \geq C(\tilde{S})$,
  - competitiveness: $\sum_{S_i \in \tilde{S}} \xi(i, \tilde{S}) \leq C(\tilde{S})$.
  However, it is hard to achieve. A mechanism is called as α-*budget balance* if $\alpha C(\tilde{S}) \leq \sum_{S_i \in \tilde{S}} \xi(i, \tilde{S}) \leq C(\tilde{S})$.
- Strategyproofness: if each selfish player gets the most benefit only when it reports the true information.

Set cover problem is studied well (c.f. [1,2]). Li et al. [3] consider the set cover games that is the most important literature for our work.

2   Main Results

In this work, we consider generalized cover-sets games under three different settings: unselfish players, selfish suppliers, and selfish receivers. Based on the greedy scheme, we can obtain the following results.

Theorem 1

- *There is a $H(k)$-budget balance mechanism if all players are unselfish.*
- *There is a $H(k)$-value efficient strategyproof mechanism if the service suppliers are selfish.*
- *There is a $H(k)$-value efficient strategyproof mechanism if the service receivers are selfish.*

Acknowledgements. The research of the first author is supported by Natural Science Foundation of China (No. 61772005) and Natural Science Foundation of Fujian Province (No. 2017J01753). The second author is supported by Natural Science Foundation of China (No. 11971349). The last author is supported by National Natural Science Foundation of China (No. 11871280 and No. 11471003) and Qing Lan Project.

References

1. Feige, U.: A threshold of $\ln n$ for approximating set cover. J. ACM **45**(4), 634–652 (1998)
2. Gupta, A., Krishnaswamy, R., Kumar, A., Panigrahi, D.: Online and dynamic algorithms for set cover. In: Proceedings of the 49th Annual ACM SIGACT Symposium on Theory of Computing, pp. 537–550. ACM, Montreal (2017)
3. Li, X.Y., Sun, Z., Wang, W.Z., Lou, W.: Cost sharing and strategyproof mechanisms for set cover games. J. Comb. Optim. **3**, 259–284 (2010)

Influence Modeling, Propagation, and Maximization

Hybrid Centrality Measures for Service Coverage Problem

Anuj Singh[1], Rishi Ranjan Singh[1(✉)], and S. R. S. Iyengar[2]

[1] Department of Electrical Engineering and Computer Science,
Indian Institute of Technology, Bhilai, Chhattisgarh, India
{anujs,rishi}@iitbhilai.ac.in
[2] Department of Computer Science and Engineering,
Indian Institute of Technology, Ropar, Punjab, India
sudarshan@iitrpr.ac.in

Abstract. Service Coverage Problem aims to find an ideal node for installing a service station in a given network such that services requested from various nodes are satisfied while minimizing the response time. Centrality Measures have been proved to be a salient computational science tool to find important nodes in networks. With increasing complexity and vividness in the network analysis problems, there is a need to modify the existing traditional centrality measures. In this paper we propose a new way of hybridizing centrality measures based on node-weighted centrality measures to address the service coverage problem.

Keywords: Complex network analysis · Centrality measures · Weighted networks · Hybrid centrality

1 Introduction

Flow networks are those networks where information, people, commodities, etc. move from one node to another while traversing on the links. Each node starts with a limited bandwidth of resources for convening the flow and these resources prone to collapse/degrade/reduce over time due to the continuous participation of the node in fostering the flow. Due to this, such networks require uninterrupted maintenance/replenishment service on a regular basis for the proper functioning of the network. Keeping this in mind, service facilities are installed at nodes that meet the service demand of other nodes from time to time.

After a service request is made by some node for more resources or reviving the node after a failure occurs, the service team is sent from the service center to meet the demand. The *response time* to meet the service demand is defined as the time taken between the request for service and start of the service work on the demanding node. The response-time depends on the distance between the node requesting a service and the node with the service stations. It is under the assumption that the service-centers have sufficient resources to meet the demand of other nodes. The *response-efficiency* of a node is inversely correlated

© Springer Nature Switzerland AG 2019
A. Tagarelli and H. Tong (Eds.): CSoNet 2019, LNCS 11917, pp. 81–94, 2019.
https://doi.org/10.1007/978-3-030-34980-6_11

to the response-time, i.e., when the response-time is least, the node is said to be maximum response-efficient and most suitable for installing service stations. A node with a higher response-time possesses a smaller response-efficiency and is not an appropriate choice for installing service stations.

Given an unweighted network, the objective of *Service Coverage Problem (SCP)* is to find a best-suited node to install a service station facility such that the expected response-time is reduced. In blue other words, the goal is to find a node with the highest expected response-efficiency, i.e. the service should reach faster at the nodes that request for service more often than the nodes with moderate or seldom demands. Therefore, the service center should be installed closer to the nodes with frequent demands.

Randomly choosing a node to install a service facility is certainly not the best solution. It is because the randomly picked node may be very far from the nodes with higher demand. In such a case where a node with a higher load fails, severe damage would have already been caused before the maintenance service reaches it. Thus, we require a measure to evaluate the importance of nodes for the candidacy to install a station covering service requests.

Centrality measures are an important tool in social and complex network analysis to quantify the eminence of nodes. These measures remain invariant under the isomorphic transformation of a network [10]. By definition, a centrality measure is a quantification of the structural importance of a node based on its location, connectivity, or any other structural property. These have been used not only by the network scientists but also by biologists, sociologists, physicists, psychologists, and economists over time. Several measures are coined in literature. The most popular centrality measures for network analysis (traditional measures) are degree, closeness, betweenness and eigenvector centrality. Readers are referred to the books by Jackson [16] and Brandes and Erlebach [10] for a detailed survey on the centrality indices and their applications. There exist several other measures that either extend or generalize these traditional measures or limit them to a restricted application. Moreover, various variants of these centrality measures have been proposed which consider a set of nodes and compute its collective centrality, called *group-centrality* [14]. Yet another direction is to combine various centrality measures to achieve better results for answering more complex problems. Such measures are termed as *Hybrid-centralities* and few of them are summarized in Sect. 2.

In this paper, we propose two hybrid centrality measures to address the service coverage problem. These measures are motivated from the definition of node-weighted centrality measures. Related works to hybrid centrality measures are summarized in Sect. 2. Section 4 introduces the new hybridization of centrality measures for solving the Service Coverage problem based on the definitions of node-weighted centrality measures which are summarized in Sect. 3. The experimental comparison between the newly proposed hybrid centrality measures and traditional centrality measures on real-world networks is comprised in Sect. 5. Finally, in Sect. 6, we conclude and discuss the prospective future directions.

2   Related Work

Centrality measures are the tools to find application specific importance of a node. Unweighted Centrality measures mentioned earlier, are the most widely used measures but for complex problems and applications, these measures are inefficient. In that case, a combination of these centrality measures produces better analysis than using them individually. In a recent study [3], authors have proposed a new set of hybrid centralities; Degree-Degree, Degree Closeness, and Degree Betweenness. They noticed that the newly defined centrality measures are different than the traditional centrality measures. On real-world co-authorship networks, they found that all the newly defined hybrid centrality measures are significantly correlated to the authors' performance (sum of citations of authors' h-index). A similar study [2] on weighted collaboration networks was done and three new sets of collaborative centrality measures were proposed. The traditional collaborative centrality measures for an author node (h-index, a-index, g-index) are used to propose new centrality measures. Newly defined set of measures were highly correlated with the traditional performance measures of scholars (Publication Count, Citation Count, h-index, a-index, g-index). Zhang et al. [33] proposed a new hybrid centrality measure to measure a node's importance in satellite communication networks. This measure is also based on the combination of closeness and betweenness centrality but the considered measure in their paper punishes the betweenness importance with a different factor. Qiao et al. [24] proposed a hybrid page scoring algorithm based on degree centrality, betweenness centrality, closeness centrality and the PageRank algorithm. Lee and Djauhari [19] proposed a hybrid centrality measure which was a linear combination of the degree, closeness, betweenness, and eigenvector centrality measures. The proposed measures were used to find the most significant or influential stocks. A hybrid centrality based on the linear combination of degree centrality and cohesion centrality was proposed was Qiu et al. [25] and further used for community detection by Li-Qing et al. [21]. Wang et al. [30] proposed a hybrid centrality measure based on the combination of degree, the degree of neighbors and betweenness. In another study by Buechel and Buskens [12], authors analyze a hybrid centrality model as a combination of extended closeness (a variation of closeness for disconnected networks), betweenness and degree measures. None of the above studies attempt to solve the service coverage problem.

3   Node-Weighted Centrality

Most of the centrality measures proposed in literature were first defined for unweighted graphs i.e. all of the nodes and all the edges were assumed homogeneous in the beginning of centrality computation. We refer to these measures as *unweighted centrality measures*. Freeman's [15] Degree, Closeness and Betweenness Centralities and Bonach-ich's [8] Eigenvector Centrality are some popular examples. After realizing the existence and understanding the necessity and importance of weights on the edges, centrality measures for unweighted graphs were extended to *edge-weighted centrality measures*. These measures take weights on the edges into consideration for ranking the nodes while analyzing the networks but still assuming equal weights on the nodes. A substantial part of the present-day research in the analysis of weighted networks considers only edge weights to determine the topological significance of nodes [22].

One basic reason to ignore the weights on nodes is the hardness and complexity in figuring out the non-trivial mapping from attributes of nodes to real values. Another reason is to avoid the complexity of the analysis process, but sometimes the ignorance of node weights might lead to a wrong analysis of the given network. Therefore, it becomes essential to also consider weights on nodes in the process for a better analysis fully weighted networks. Due to this reason, there was a need to upgrade the previously defined unweighted and edge-weighted centrality measures so that weights at the nodes can also be taken into account for the analysis.

Therefore, while considering the weights on the nodes, there can be two possible extensions of the unweighted and edge-weighted centrality measures:

– *Node-weighted centrality measures*: Consider only the node weights for the analysis while taking all edge weights as one.
– *Fully weighted centrality measures*: Consider both types of weights, edge weights and node weights for the analysis.

In most of the studies done so far on fully weighted networks, while considering weighted edges, weights on the nodes were completely ignored. Meanwhile, only a little work has been accomplished while considering the weights on nodes in the real-world networks [2,3,5,32].

This section summarizes centrality measures that take into consideration the weights on the nodes while giving equal priority to the edges in a given network. These fall in the category of node-weighted centrality measures. We only mention these here to avoid the complexity of including weights on both edges and nodes. Once, these measures are understood, we recommend the readers to combine these measures with the edge-weighted centrality measures given in [22] to derive the definition for fully weighted centrality measures. Let $G = \{V, E\}$ denote an undirected unweighted graph. We add an extra element, weights on the nodes defined as a function $W : V \to R$, where R is set of real numbers. Let W_x be the weight given at node x. We do not directly use W_x in the definitions, but at place of it, we use a function f of W_x (or a function of W_x and W_y depending on the number of parameters) without losing the generality. This gives us the flexibility to tune the function of weights on the nodes according to our need. Here, in this paper we take $f(W_x) = W_x$ for the simplicity. To normalize the new centrality measures, we divide by the maximum possible value that any node can score in the numerator of below-given formulas. We start with degree centrality.

– **Node Weighted Degree centrality**: In [3], weights on nodes are considered and the definition of degree centrality is modified to accommodate the node weights. Abbasi and Hossain [3] considered centrality scores as weights on the nodes. Following it, node weighted centrality of a node u is calculated as:

$\dfrac{\sum\limits_{v\in V\setminus\{u\}}(f(W_v)\cdot a_{u,v})}{\sum\limits_{x\in V} f(W_x)}$. This measure assigns higher importance to those nodes which are in the immediate neighborhood of highly weighted nodes. Next two measures extend the consideration to all the nodes to compute the eminence of a node.

– **Node Weighted Closeness/Harmonic Centrality**: To target the wider applicability, we define node weighted harmonic centrality (which also can be used in the case of closeness centrality computation as both are highly correlated). Node weighted harmonic centrality of a node u in a network is defined as: $\dfrac{f(W_u)+\sum\limits_{v\in V\setminus\{u\}}\frac{f(W_v)}{d_{u,v}+1}}{\sum\limits_{x\in V} f(W_x)}$. This measure depends on two factors: weight of the node u under consideration and the effective weights of other nodes corresponding to their distances from node u. It assigns a higher value to the nodes that are of high weights and closer to the nodes with high weights. We refer this measure as *harmonically attenuated node weighted centrality measure*.

– **Node Weighed Decay**: Weighted decay of a node u in a network as defined as $\dfrac{f(W_u)+\sum\limits_{v\in V\setminus\{u\}}(\delta^{d_{u,v}}\cdot f(W_v))}{\sum\limits_{x\in V} f(W_x)}$ where δ lies between 0 and 1. Here also the computation of importance depends on the same two factors as in NWCC. But, the contribution of weights of other nodes decays exponentially with distance. Weighted decay assigns a higher value to the nodes that are of high weights and very close to the nodes with high weights. We refer this measure as *exponentially attenuated node weighted centrality measure*.

– **Node Weighted Betweenness Centrality**: In [23], a factor denoting the importance of communication between two pairs is multiplied in the core formula while computing the betweenness centrality. The node weighted betweenness centrality of a node u was defined as $\dfrac{\sum\limits_{s,t,u\in V:|\{s,t,v\}|=3}f(W_s,W_t)\cdot\frac{\sigma_{st}(u)}{\sigma_{st}}}{\sum\limits_{x,y,u\in V:|\{x,y,v\}|=3}f(W_x,W_y)}$ where $f(W_x,W_y)$ can be assumed to map the weights given on node x and y to a real value denoting the importance of flow happening between x and y.

Eigenvector centrality is a measure where it is still open how to include the effect of node weights.

4   New Hybrid Centrality Measures

This section defines two new hybrid measures to solve the Service Coverage Problem. We define these measures for networks without weights on edges. These can be easily further extended to edge-weighted version of hybrid centralities following the ideas for edge-weighted centrality measures given in [22].

Betweenness centrality is used to predict the importance of nodes in a number of flow-based networks e.g. Power Grid networks, Public-transit networks,

Gas Line networks, and Communication networks. The betweenness scores of the nodes in such networks have been considered as the load on the nodes in literature. Several models for understanding and replicating the cascading phenomena have been proposed [13,17]. Some of these models observe that failure of a node with a high load may cause a severe cascading failure and hence result in the breakdown of the whole network system. After a node fails, the best way to reduce the damage is to recover the failed node as soon as possible. We cannot prevent a node from failure but we can definitely put a maintenance mechanism on some of the nodes in the network.

4.1   Formulation

In the Service Coverage Problem in flow networks, the load of the nodes (when no other information is provided) can be assumed to be proportional to the betweenness centrality of the nodes. This is because a node with large flow through it, is expected to degrade faster than other nodes and if such a node shuts down, a large amount of flow will be affected. Thus we take the probability of node j requesting for a maintenance service over a fixed time-interval as $Pr[Node\ j\ request\ for\ service] = \frac{BC(j)}{\sum_{k \in V} BC(k)}$, where $BC(j)$ is the betweenness centrality of node j. Let X_{ij}, be the response-efficiency of a node i to meet service demand from node j if the service station is going to be installed on node i. Certainly, X_{ij} depends on the distance between the node requesting for a service (node j) and the node with the service stations (node i). Harmonic decay can be considered in applications where the nodes are more robust and the service requirement is not urgent while exponential decay might be a more appropriate simplified model in applications like real-time systems where service requests need to be met on an urgent basis.

   If the response-efficiency decays harmonically in a given application, i.e. the node is maximum efficient (efficiency value$=1$) for itself while it is half efficient (efficiency value$=0.5$) for each of its neighbors and so on, then we can formulate for the value of response-efficiency $X_{ij} = \frac{1}{d_{i,j}+1}$. Recall, $d_{u,v}$ denotes the distance, i.e., length of the shortest path from node u to node v in the given network. Let χ_i be the total response-efficiency of a node i if the service station is going to be installed on node i. Then, $\chi_i = \sum_{j \in V} X_{ij} \cdot Pr[Node\ j\ request\ for\ service]$. The expected response-efficiency of node i ($E[\chi_i]$) is computed by taking expectation over that node's response-efficiency to service all the nodes in network. $E[\chi_i] = \sum_{j \in V} \frac{1}{d_{i,j}+1} \cdot \frac{BC(j)}{\sum_{k \in V} BC(k)}$. We define the following hybrid centrality measures based on the above formulation:

Harmonically-Attenuated-Betweenness Centrality (HABC): This measure is based on the harmonic attenuation of importance with respect to the distance. The harmonically-attenuated-betweenness centrality of a node u is defined as,

$$HABC(u) = \frac{BC(u) + \sum_{v \in V \setminus \{u\}} \frac{BC(v)}{d_{u,v}+1}}{\sum_{w \in V} BC(w)}$$

where $BC(u)$ is the unweighted betweenness centrality of node u. This hybrid measure assigns a value that is calculated based on an averaging function of distances and betweenness centrality. This measure assigns a higher value to the nodes that are of high betweenness and closer to other high betweenness central nodes. This measure solves the SCP problem in flow networks where the response-efficiency decays harmonically.

In few complex systems, response-time plays very crucial roles in the functionality of networks and the response-efficiency decays exponentially. In such networks, the response-efficiency decays faster, i.e., the node is maximum efficient (efficiency value $= 1$) for itself while it decays by a multiplicative factor α (efficiency value $= \alpha$) for each of it's neighbors and so on. Here, α is a severity factor that lies in interval $[0, 1]$. Then we can formulate for the value of response-efficiency $X_{ij} = \alpha^{d_{i,j}}$. Similar to the previous analysis, the expected efficiency of a node i to be a service station, when efficiency decays exponentially by a factor α is $E[\chi_i] = \sum_{j \in V} \alpha^{d_{i,j}} \cdot \frac{BC(j)}{\sum_{k \in V} BC(k)}$. We define the following hybrid centrality measures based on the above formulation:

Exponentially-Attenuated-Betweenness Centrality (EABC): This measure is based on an exponential attenuation in the power of distance. The Exponentially-attenuated-betweenness centrality of a node u is defined as,

$$EABC(u) = \frac{BC(u) + \sum_{v \in V \setminus \{u\}} \alpha^{d_{u,v}} \cdot BC(v)}{\sum_{w \in V} BC(w)} .$$

where $BC(u)$ is the betweenness centrality of node i. α is the attenuation factor that is used in the exponential function to the power of distance. It is used to sharply punish the service time. This hybrid measure assigns a value that is calculated based on betweenness centrality of nodes and an exponential function in the power of distances. This measure assigns a higher value to the nodes that are of high betweenness and very close to other high betweenness central nodes. This centrality measure is a sharp attenuation variant of harmonically-attenuated-degree centrality. This measure solves the service coverage problem when the service is required on a very urgent basis.

Let m be the number of links and n be the number of nodes in a given network. The over all time to compute proposed hybrid centrality measure is $O(mn)$ in unweighted and $O(mn + n^2 \log n)$ in weighted graphs. It is due to the time complexity for computing betweenness centrality [9]. Efficient algorithms for updating and estimating betweenness centrality measures in dynamic and large-size networks are discussed in [4, 27, 28].

5   Experimental Results

In this section, we discuss the simulation results on various real-world networks. First, we discuss the experimental setup. Then, we mention all the data set used for experimentation. Next, we provide a comparison of traditional centrality measures: degree (DC), closeness (CC), betweenness (BC) and, eigenvector (EC)

Table 1. Considered real-world networks

Instance name	n	Avg. Deg.	$\hat{C}$	Network type
Chicago Road [18]	1467	1.7696	0.0001	Transport network
Chilean Power Grid [29]	347	2.55908	0.0865	Energy network
Euroroad [18]	1174	2.41397	0.0167	Transport network
London Metro [6]	266	2.31579	0.0363	Transport network
Madrid Metro [6]	209	2.29665	0.0056	Transport network
Mexico Metro [6]	147	2.23129	0.0034	Transport network
Minnesota Road [26]	2642	2.50038	0.016	Transport network
Moscow Metro [6]	134	2.32836	0.0174	Transport network
New York Metro [6]	433	2.194	0.0173	Transport network
Oldenburg Road [11]	6105	2.3027	0.0108	Transport network
Openflights [6]	2939	10.66825	0.4526	Transport network
Osaka Metro [6]	108	2.27778	0.0001	Transport network
p2p-Gnutella08 [20]	6301	6.59483	0.0109	Internet peer-to-peer network
Paris Metro [6]	299	2.38127	0.0204	Transport network
as20000102 [20]	6474	4.29255	0.2522	Autonomous systems graph
Seoul Metro [6]	392	2.22959	0.006	Transport network
Shanghai Metro [6]	148	2.13514	0.0029	Transport network
Tokyo Metro [6]	217	2.41475	0.0237	Transport network
US Air [7]	332	12.80723	0.6252	Transport network
US Power Grid [31]	4941	2.6691	0.0801	Energy network
NRPG Data [1]	246	3.03252	0.1071	Energy network

and the proposed hybrid centrality measure (HABC, EABC(α = 0.5), EABC(α = 0.75)) in the considered networks. The experiments are performed on a Linux system with 8 GB RAM and Intel Core i5-8250U CPU at 1.6 GHz. Implementation is done in Python 3.6.7 with the help of Networkx library.

Real-World Data Sets: The proposed solution to solve service coverage problem discussed in this paper hybridizes betweenness centrality within closeness/harmonic and decay centrality. Betweenness centrality is first used to compute the load on each node, therefore, we have selected 26 real-world flow networks. We provide a brief summary of these networks in Table 1 and [1,6,7,11,18,20,26,29,31] can be referred for a detailed description of the networks. We have considered various types of transport networks, energy networks, internet peer to peer network, etc. The columns of Table 1 consist of names of the network instances, the number of nodes (n), the average degree of the networks (Avg. Deg.), average clustering coefficient ($\hat{C}$) and the network type respectively.

Simulation: We have conducted simulations for evaluating the performance of various traditional centrality measures and the hybrid measures proposed in this

Table 2. Expected response-time of the proposed hybrid measures and the traditional centrality measures when the most central node is made the service center

Instance name	BC	DC	CC	EC	HABC	EABC($\alpha = 0.5$)	EABC($\alpha = 0.75$)
Chicago Metro	**0.49**	**0.49**	**0.49**	**0.49**	**0.49**	**0.49**	**0.49**
Chilean Power Grid	**0.29**	0.33	**0.29**	0.33	**0.29**	**0.29**	**0.29**
Euroroad	**0.88**	**0.88**	0.89	1.05	**0.88**	**0.88**	**0.88**
London Metro	0.83	0.83	**0.80**	0.83	**0.80**	**0.80**	**0.80**
Madrid Metro	0.46	0.46	0.44	0.66	0.46	0.46	**0.42**
Mexico Metro	**0.50**	**0.50**	0.54	**0.50**	**0.50**	**0.50**	0.54
Minnesota Road	2.29	3.21	2.15	3.11	3.29	**2.29**	3.45
Moscow Metro	0.40	0.40	**0.37**	0.39	0.39	0.39	**0.37**
Newyork Metro	**1.11**	1.3	1.12	1.3	**1.11**	**1.11**	**1.11**
Oldenburg Road	**1.66**	**1.66**	1.68	2.64	**1.66**	**1.66**	**1.66**
Openflights	**0.16**	**0.16**	**0.16**	**0.16**	**0.16**	**0.16**	**0.16**
Osaka Metro	0.48	0.48	0.44	0.48	0.48	0.48	**0.42**
p2p-Gnutella08	0.29	**0.27**	**0.27**	**0.27**	**0.27**	**0.27**	**0.27**
Paris Metro	0.55	0.55	0.55	0.56	**0.51**	**0.51**	**0.51**
as20000102	**0.12**	**0.12**	**0.12**	**0.12**	**0.12**	**0.12**	**0.12**
Seoul Metro	1.06	1.25	1.06	1.23	**1.02**	**1.02**	**1.02**
Shanghai Metro	**0.53**	**0.53**	0.64	**0.53**	0.64	**0.53**	0.64
Tokyo Metro	0.57	0.57	0.57	0.57	0.57	0.57	**0.49**
US Air	**0.10**	**0.10**	**0.10**	**0.10**	**0.10**	**0.10**	**0.10**
US Power Grid	0.92	1.34	**0.83**	2.12	**0.83**	**0.83**	**0.83**
NRPG	**0.30**	0.45	**0.30**	0.37	**0.30**	**0.30**	**0.30**

paper which have been summarized in Table 2. The performance of a centrality measure is evaluated by computing the expected response-time in terms of the average distance of the service requesting nodes from the top central node as per this centrality measure.

Betweenness centrality has been used as one of the best measure to map loads on nodes in flow networks [17]. A node having higher load will be more frequent in requesting for services. Therefore, we consider the probability of a node requesting for services proportional to the betweenness centrality of that node. The expected response-time is computed over $\lceil n/10 \rceil$ service requests where n is the number of nodes in respective real-world networks. The first column in the table contains label of the considered real-world network instances. The next columns lists the expected response-time of the traditional centrality measures (BC, CC, DC, EC) and the proposed hybrid measures (HABC, EABC($\alpha = 0.5$), and EABC($\alpha = 0.75$)).

It is evident from Table 2 that no traditional measure can consistently find an ideal service center. While at least one of the proposed hybrid centrality measures are always able to minimize the average response-time for all considered networks. In some cases such as Madrid Metro, Paris Metro, Osaka Metro,

Table 3. Ranking list of top three central nodes using the proposed hybrid measures and the traditional centrality measures on considered real-world networks given in Table 1

Instance Name	HABC			EABC(α = 0.5)			EABC(α = 0.75)			BC			CC			DC			EC		
	R1	R2	R3	R1	R2	R3	R1	R2	R3	R1	R2	R3	R1	R2	R3	R1	R2	R3	R1	R2	R3
Chicago Road	1156	1157	1147	1156	1157	1147	1156	1157	1147	1156	1157	1147	1156	1157	1147	552	922	10	1156	1147	1150
Chilean Power Grid	178	105	147	178	105	147	178	105	147	178	105	108	178	105	147	108	6	178	108	264	29
Euroroad	*402*	284	277	402	284	277	402	284	277	*402*	284	277	401	402	403	284	7	39	7	43	454
London Metro	*115*	29	12	115	29	12	115	29	12	12	115	180	*115*	29	214	12	164	305	214	115	219
Madrid Metro	*80*	162	146	80	162	146	162	80	146	*80*	146	162	162	80	235	80	15	9	15	54	40
Mexico Metro	*26*	70	23	26	70	78	70	26	54	*26*	70	25	70	26	23	26	127	61	26	70	23
Minnesota Road	300	328	280	1821	2069	300	280	328	300	1821	2069	2063	1356	1820	1109	2418	35	32	1927	1930	1987
Moscow Metro	59	71	25	59	71	25	71	59	73	25	74	59	73	71	25	24	59	21	59	25	73
New York Metro	*424*	191	410	424	191	410	424	191	410	*424*	191	148	84	424	410	273	228	410	273	228	188
Oldenburg Road	*831*	714	731	831	714	711	831	714	803	*831*	714	593	714	731	712	831	1657	1571	1677	1683	1691
Openflights	53	65	57	53	57	65	53	57	65	53	65	1576	53	65	57	53	65	59	53	59	65
Osaka Metro	*25*	70	95	25	70	95	70	95	25	*25*	99	70	95	70	25	25	54	42	25	81	54
p2p-Gnutella08	*123*	367	127	123	367	127	123	127	367	5831	1317	424	*123*	127	1317	123	127	367	367	123	145
Paris Metro	150	57	235	150	57	235	150	57	235	57	150	106	57	150	235	57	177	246	186	150	235
as20000102	2	10	7	2	10	7	2	10	7	2	7	10	2	10	7	2	10	7	2	10	7
Seoul Metro	220	480	357	220	444	391	220	480	357	220	444	391	220	480	357	254	444	391	103	254	125
Shanghai Metro	*136*	16	113	136	16	213	136	113	16	16	136	65	*136*	113	97	16	136	220	16	137	138
Tokyo Metro	150	85	53	150	85	53	85	150	60	150	53	85	150	60	85	150	53	120	150	120	36
US Air	118	261	201	118	201	47	118	201	47	118	8	261	118	261	67	118	261	255	118	261	255
US Power Grid	*1378*	1365	2685	1378	1365	2685	1378	1365	1678	651	559	1365	*1378*	1678	2944	2847	602	932	4422	4436	4419
NRPG Data	*233*	235	238	233	235	238	233	235	238	70	235	213	*233*	238	70	194	65	56	239	213	215

Seoul Metro, and Tokyo Metro, the proposed measures even outperform all the traditional measures.

Node Ranks: Here, we discuss the ranking result of nodes by various centrality measures. Table 3 contains the ranking list of the top three central nodes using the proposed hybrid measures and the traditional centrality measures on the considered real-world networks given in Table 1. Due to space constraints, only the data of top three central nodes have been presented in the paper. The first column in the table contains the label of the considered real-world network instances. The next columns in a group of three lists top 3 central nodes using the proposed hybrid measures (HABC, EABC($\alpha = 0.5$), and EABC($\alpha = 0.75$)) and the traditional centrality measures (BC, CC, DC, EC).

Finding only the most central node might not be useful in the cases when the top central node does not allow it to be made as a service facility due to some constraints. In that case, finding the first top-k potential centers are important. It is evident from the experimental results that the proposed measures are results of hybridizations between closeness centrality and betweenness centrality.

We have emphasized the top-ranking node for a few entries in the table and have written them in bold to exhibit the above phenomenon. For some networks, the top-ranking node as per HABC is the same as BC but not as CC and vice-versa. The ranking on two networks (Minnesota Road and Moscow Metro) also provide evidence that top-ranking nodes due to the proposed centrality measures are different from closeness and betweenness centrality. In addition to these two, another network (Openflights) shows that these proposed measures also rank nodes differently than each other.

Table 4. Spearman's rank correlation between the proposed and the traditional centrality measures and on considered real-world networks given in Table 1

Instance Name	HABC				EABC($\alpha = 0.5$)				EABC($\alpha = 0.75$)			
	BC	CC	DC	EC	BC	CC	DC	EC	BC	CC	DC	EC
Chicago Road	0.2087	0.3688	0.2393	0.2027	0.2040	0.3437	0.2351	0.2024	0.2035	0.3241	0.1985	0.1515
Chilean Power Grid	0.0691	-0.0620	0.0132	0.0057	0.0224	0.0274	0.0506	0.0163	0.0929	0.0867	-0.0200	0.0850
Euroroad	0.7707	0.0144	0.2019	-0.0010	0.7985	0.0190	0.1675	-0.0174	0.7656	0.0214	0.1834	-0.0227
London Metro	0.1625	0.1450	0.0296	0.0312	-0.0291	0.0323	0.0917	0.0636	0.0432	0.1496	-0.0837	0.0324
Madrid Metro	0.0540	0.1561	-0.0912	0.0149	0.0284	0.0891	-0.0949	0.1213	0.0109	0.0814	-0.1316	0.0049
Mexico Metro	-0.0598	0.2043	0.0428	0.1145	0.1267	-0.0479	0.0516	0.1401	-0.0037	0.2043	-0.0716	0.1522
Minnesota Road	-0.0068	-0.0358	-0.0777	-0.1648	0.0286	-0.0221	0.0075	-0.0393	0.0015	-0.0552	0.0345	-0.1444
Moscow Metro	0.0824	0.0474	0.1245	0.0570	-0.1814	-0.1215	-0.2326	0.0627	0.1012	0.0468	0.0331	-0.1045
New York Metro	0.0386	0.0865	-0.0061	0.0760	0.0599	0.0394	-0.0382	-0.0222	0.0083	-0.0139	-0.0651	-0.0156
Oldenburg Road	0.0098	0.1332	0.0094	-0.0222	0.0075	0.0593	0.0202	0.0169	0.0113	0.0991	0.0039	-0.0083
Openflights	0.0018	0.1090	0.0263	0.0799	0.0055	0.1417	0.0318	0.0898	0.0032	0.1305	0.0200	0.0618
Osaka Metro	0.0110	0.1728	0.0262	0.1440	0.0482	0.1662	0.0402	0.1398	0.0795	0.1031	-0.0713	0.0656
p2p-Gnutella08	0.0537	0.0760	0.0880	0.0491	0.0636	0.0634	0.0775	0.0485	0.0660	0.0529	0.0754	0.0561
as20000102	0.1327	0.5878	0.1837	0.4513	0.1408	0.5881	0.1810	0.4423	0.1309	0.6273	0.1912	0.4392
Seoul Metro	0.0520	-0.0055	-0.0048	-0.0389	0.0257	0.0143	0.0480	0.0775	-0.0427	0.0109	-0.0643	0.0136
Shanghai Metro	0.1104	-0.0165	0.1168	0.0977	0.0721	0.1124	0.0326	0.1617	0.0014	0.0922	0.1809	0.0610
US Air	0.0855	0.1707	0.0522	0.0608	0.1171	0.2246	0.0059	0.0674	0.0503	0.2372	0.0243	0.1065
US Power Grid	0.0450	0.0831	0.0830	0.0437	0.0350	0.0279	0.0345	0.0038	0.0436	0.0598	0.0622	0.0436
Paris Metro	-0.1077	0.0421	-0.0625	0.1169	0.0302	0.0846	-0.0271	0.0351	0.0175	0.1305	-0.0914	0.0309
Tokyo Metro	0.1693	0.0920	0.0064	0.0460	0.0555	0.0883	0.0958	0.0511	0.0646	0.1071	-0.0794	0.1039
NRPG Data	0.0118	0.1334	-0.0693	0.0934	0.0445	0.0975	-0.1389	0.1395	-0.0867	0.1659	-0.1322	0.0936
Average Correlation	0.0902	0.1192	0.0444	0.0694	0.0811	0.0966	0.0305	0.0858	0.0744	0.1268	0.0094	0.0574
Standard Deviation	0.1729	0.1441	0.0907	0.1152	0.1802	0.1485	0.1043	0.1042	0.1701	0.1432	0.1069	0.1139

It is evident that no single standard centrality measure is a perfect substitute for our proposed centrality measures. As our measures follow directly from the requirements of the Service Coverage Problem, it is evident that current centrality measures are not sufficient to solve the problem adequately.

The popular Spearman's rank correlation coefficient is computed to evaluate the correlation between the proposed hybrid centralities and the four traditional centrality measures on the considered real-world networks. These results are summarized in Table 4. The first column in the table contains the label of the considered real-world network instances. The next four columns comprise of the rank correlation between HABC and the traditional centrality measures (BC, CC, DC, EC). Similarly the next four columns contain the rank correlation values between and EABC($\alpha = 0.5$) and BC, CC, DC, EC respectively. The last four columns are the rank correlation between EABC($\alpha = 0.75$) and the traditional centrality measures.

The experimental results in Table 4 make it evident that ranking by the proposed hybrid measures is different than traditional centrality measures. The average correlation coefficient between the proposed measures and traditional measures, although is positive but very small. The standard deviation is larger than the average coefficient values for most of the computation of rank correlation. It is due to several negative correlation coefficient values. Based on the average rank correlation coefficient values, HABC is best correlated with CC and then BC among the traditional measures. EABC($\alpha = 0.75$) also exhibits similar pattern as the decay rate is slower than EABC($\alpha = 0.5$). EABC($\alpha = 0.5$) is best correlated with the CC and then EC among the traditional measures. The proposed measures are least correlated with DC. Therefore, the existing traditional measures do not provide the solution to the service coverage problem. The top-ranked nodes by the proposed hybrid centrality measures are more appropriate in this application.

6   Conclusion

In this paper, we have proposed two new hybrid centrality measures based on closeness (harmonic), betweenness and decay measures. The hybridization is used to solve service coverage problem in flow networks where the demand for services is assumed to be proportional to the betweenness centrality. The proposed hybridization of centrality measures is based on the node weighted centrality measures. The experimental results on several real-world networks show that the proposed measures rank the nodes differently than traditional measures. Our measures perform well in simulations, and give statistically different results than the traditional centrality measures. The proposed measures can also be used in another application that requires installing a facility farthest from the failure prone nodes. The solution, in this case, will be the node with the minimum expected response-efficiency. Analyzing these measures on various other real-world networks and at the place of betweenness, hybridizing other measures specific to some particular applications are the possible future directions. The analysis of real-world networks where non-uniform weights are given at nodes using node weighted centrality measures is another open direction.

References

1. NRPG-DATA.   https://www.iitk.ac.in/eeold/facilities/Research_labs/Power_System/NRPG-DATA.pdf
2. Abbasi, A.: h-Type hybrid centrality measures for weighted networks. Scientometrics **96**(2), 633–640 (2013)
3. Abbasi, A., Hossain, L.: Hybrid centrality measures for binary and weighted networks. In: Menezes, R., Evsukoff, A., González, M. (eds.) Complex Networks. Studies in Computational Intelligence, vol. 424, pp. 1–7. Springer, Heidelberg (2013). https://doi.org/10.1007/978-3-642-30287-9_1
4. Agarwal, M., Singh, R.R., Chaudhary, S., Iyengar, S.R.S.: An efficient estimation of a node's betweenness. In: Mangioni, G., Simini, F., Uzzo, S.M., Wang, D. (eds.) Complex Networks VI. SCI, vol. 597, pp. 111–121. Springer, Cham (2015). https://doi.org/10.1007/978-3-319-16112-9_11
5. Akanmu, A.A., Wang, F.Z., Yamoah, F.A.: Clique structure and node-weighted centrality measures to predict distribution centre location in the supply chain management. In: Science and Information Conference (SAI), pp. 100–111. IEEE (2014)
6. Barthelemy, M.: https://www.quanturb.com/data.html
7. Batagelj, V., Mrvar, A.: Pajek datasets (2006). http://vlado.fmf.uni-lj.si/pub/networks/data
8. Bonacich, P.: Factoring and weighting approaches to status scores and clique identification. J. Math. Sociol. **2**(1), 113–120 (1972)

9. Brandes, U.: A faster algorithm for betweenness centrality. J. Math. Sociol. **25**(2), 163–177 (2001). https://doi.org/10.1080/0022250X.2001.9990249
10. Brandes, U., Erlebach, T. (eds.): Network Analysis. LNCS, vol. 3418. Springer, Heidelberg (2005). https://doi.org/10.1007/b106453
11. Brinkhoff, T.: A framework for generating network-based moving objects. GeoInformatica **6**(2), 153–180 (2002)
12. Buechel, B., Buskens, V.: The dynamics of closeness and betweenness. J. Math. Sociol. **37**(3), 159–191 (2013)
13. Buldyrev, S.V., Parshani, R., Paul, G., Stanley, H.E., Havlin, S.: Catastrophic cascade of failures in interdependent networks. Nature **464**(7291), 1025–1028 (2010)
14. Everett, M.G., Borgatti, S.P.: The centrality of groups and classes. J. Math. Sociol. **23**(3), 181–201 (1999)
15. Freeman, L.C.: Centrality in social networks conceptual clarification. Soc. Netw. **1**(3), 215–239 (1979)
16. Jackson, M.O.: Social and Economic Networks. Princeton University Press, Princeton (2008)
17. Kinney, R., Crucitti, P., Albert, R., Latora, V.: Modeling cascading failures in the north american power grid. Eur. Phys. J. B-Condens. Matter Complex Syst. **46**(1), 101–107 (2005)
18. Kunegis, J.: http://konect.uni-koblenz.de/networks/
19. Lee, G.S., Djauhari, M.A.: An overall centrality measure: the case of us stock market. Int. J. Electr. Comput. Sci. **12**(6) (2012)
20. Leskovec, J., Krevl, A.: SNAP Datasets: Stanford large network dataset collection, June 2014. http://snap.stanford.edu/data
21. Li-Qing, Q., Yong-Quan, L., Zhuo-Yan, C.: A novel algorithm for detecting local community structure based on hybrid centrality. J. Appl. Sci. **14**, 3532–3537 (2014)
22. Opsahl, T., Agneessens, F., Skvoretz, J.: Node centrality in weighted networks: generalizing degree and shortest paths. Soc. Netw. **32**(3), 245–251 (2010)
23. Puzis, R., Elovici, Y., Zilberman, P., Dolev, S., Brandes, U.: Topology manipulations for speeding betweenness centrality computation. J. Complex Netw. **3**(1), 84–112 (2014)
24. Qiao, S., Peng, J., Li, H., Li, T., Liu, L., Li, H.: WebRank: a hybrid page scoring approach based on social network analysis. In: Yu, J., Greco, S., Lingras, P., Wang, G., Skowron, A. (eds.) RSKT 2010. LNCS (LNAI), vol. 6401, pp. 475–482. Springer, Heidelberg (2010). https://doi.org/10.1007/978-3-642-16248-0_67
25. Qiu, L., Liang, Y., Chen, Z., Fan, J.: A new measurement for the importance of nodes in networks. In: Control Engineering and Information Systems, pp. 483–486 (2014)
26. Rossi, R.A., Ahmed, N.K.: The network data repository with interactive graph analytics and visualization. In: Proceedings of the Twenty-Ninth AAAI Conference on Artificial Intelligence (2015). http://networkrepository.com
27. Singh, R.R., Goel, K., Iyengar, S., Gupta, S.: A faster algorithm to update betweenness centrality after node alteration. Internet Math. **11**(4–5), 403–420 (2015)
28. Singh, R.R., Iyengar, S., Chaudhary, S., Agarwal, M.: An efficient heuristic for betweenness estimation and ordering. Soc. Netw. Anal. Mining **8**(1), 66 (2018)
29. Son, S.W., Kim, H., Olave-Rojas, D., lvarez Miranda, E.: Edge information of chilean power grid with tap. Figshare. Dataset (2018)
30. Wang, J., Rong, L., Guo, T.: A new measure of node importance in complex networks with tunable parameters. In: 4th International Conference on Wireless Communications, Networking and Mobile Computing, WiCOM 2008, pp. 1–4. IEEE (2008)

31. Watts, D.J., Strogatz, S.H.: Collective dynamics of small-world networks. Nature **393**(6684), 440–442 (1998)
32. Wiedermann, M., Donges, J.F., Heitzig, J., Kurths, J.: Node-weighted interacting network measures improve the representation of real-world complex systems. EPL (Europhys. Lett.) **102**(2), 28007 (2013)
33. Zhang, X.J., Wang, Z.L., Zhang, Z.X.: Finding most vital node in satellite communication network. In: Applied Mechanics and Materials, vol. 635, pp. 1136–1139. Trans Tech Publications (2014)

Hop-Based Sketch for Large-Scale Influence Analysis

Phuc D. Thai$^{(\boxtimes)}$ and Thang N. Dinh

Virginia Commonwealth University, Richmond, VA 23284, USA
{pdthai,tndinh}@vcu.edu

Abstract. Quantifying users' influence in social networks is an important topic with many applications including viral marketing, political studies, and fake news propagation. For the last few years, the novel sketching technique, termed RIS, by Borgs. et al. has inspired a series of scalable approaches for influence analysis.

In this paper, we propose a new sketching technique, termed hop-based influence sketches or HIS that provides a more compact yet more accurate estimation. Unlike ad hoc heuristics, HIS-based approaches can solve influence estimation and influence maximization tasks with rigorous statistical guarantees on errors. Finally, we provide initial experiments on real-world networks to demonstrate the efficiency of our new sketch comparing to the existing influence sketches.

1 Introduction

Given many applications, influence analysis is an important topic in social network analysis. Several applications include viral marketing, propaganda, and fake news propagation. The two famous problems in this topic are *influence estimation* [3,8,14] (evaluating the influence of a group of individuals) and *influence maximization* [1,3,5,12,17,18] (finding a small group of individuals with highest influence).

However, diffusion analysis is challenging in large scale networks. Recently, efficient sketching techniques are introduced in [1]. That leads to a series of scalable approaches for influence analysis, including TIM/TIM+[18], IMM [17], SSA/D-SSA [12], and SKIS [9]. While the current sketch techniques provides efficient identification of nodes or groups of nodes with high influences, it is less robust with respect to nodes with small influences.

In this paper, we propose a hybrid sketching technique, termed Hop-based Influence Sketch or HIS. The influence of nodes are estimated by adding (1) the exact 'local influence' of S as a heuristic with (2) an estimate of the 'remote influence' of S via sketch. The exact computation of 'local influence' helps to reduce the variation, increase the estimation accuracy, especially for those of small influence. Even for nodes that do not appear in the RIS sketch due to small influence can be estimated and ranked against each other. Especially, the recently proposed sketch SKIS [9] can be seen as a special case of our sketch when the number of hop(s) $h = 0$.

© Springer Nature Switzerland AG 2019
A. Tagarelli and H. Tong (Eds.): CSoNet 2019, LNCS 11917, pp. 95–107, 2019.
https://doi.org/10.1007/978-3-030-34980-6_12

We further carry-out initial experiments to demonstrate the effectiveness of our sketch in estimating influence and finding solution for the influence maximization problems. We also provide the recommendation for the number of hops that provide the best time-quality trade-off for our sketch.

Related Work. Borgs et al. [1] proposed a new technique, that captures the influences in a reverse manner. We refer this technique as reverse influence sampling or RIS. This approach has been applied in many follow up works in finding the seed set with maximum influence, i.e. influence maximization.

Ohsaka et al. [14] use RIS sketches to estimate influences in dynamic graphs. [15] reduce the space usage of RIS by storing the data structure on the hard drive of the machine. RIS sketch finds extensive applications in Influence Maximization problem, [11–13, 17, 18].

Nguyen et al. [9] provides an improvement of RIS by removing singular samples (samples of size one) from the sketch. Also, they propose an important sampling procedure to produce non-singular samples that speed up the sketch generation in case of small edge probabilities. We note that their sketch can be seen as a special case of our sketch when $h = 0$.

Nguyen et al. [10] introduce a new influence measure, called outward influence, defined as the expected number of influenced nodes, excluding the nodes in seed set. They use the important sampling procedure as in [9], plus a robust mean estimation method to minimize the number of samples.

Cohen et al. [3] investigate the bottom-k min-hash sketch of the set of reachable nodes. They show small estimation errors for estimating influences. However, since the size of each sketch is fixed, this method does not work well for large influences. A similar scheme was applied for continuous-time model [4].

For a more comprehensive cover of literature on influence maximization, we refer to [17] and [9].

Organization. The rest of the paper is organized as follows: In Sect. 2, we introduce the independent cascade [5] model. We propose our HIS sketch in Sect. 3. Algorithm to solve influence maximization using our new sketch is presented in Sects. 4. Experiments results are present in Sect. 5.

2   Preliminaries

Consider a social network abstracted as a directed graph $\mathcal{G} = (V, E, w)$. Each edge $(u, v) \in E$ is associated with a weight $w(u, v) \in [0, 1]$ specifying the probability that node u will influence v once u is influenced. To model the influence dynamic in the network, we focus on the popular *Independent Cascade* (IC) model [5] and then. Our techniques can easily be extended to the Linear Threshold (LT).

2.1   Independent Cascade Model

Given a graph $\mathcal{G}$, for a subset of nodes $S \subseteq V$, called the seed set, the influence propagation from S happens in discrete rounds. At round 0, only nodes in S are influenced. At any round $t \geq 0$, each newly activated node u will have a single chance to influence each neighbor v of u with probability $w(u,v)$. All influenced nodes remain influenced till the end of the diffusion propagation. The process stops when no more nodes get influenced at that round.

Sample Graphs. A node $u \in V$ can influence each of its neighbor v with probability $w(u,v)$. This can be thought of as flipping a biased coin that gives head with probability $w(u,v)$ to determine node u whether or not influences v. If the coin lands head, u influences v and we call (u,v) a *live-edge*. We generate a deterministic graph g by determining the live-edges through flipping coins. We refer g as a *sample graph*.

We note that all the influences of nodes are independent, it does not matter when coins are flipped. Thus, we can use the sample graph g to determine weather or not a node u influences its neighbor when u is influenced.

A sample graph $g = (V, E' \subseteq E)$ (where E' is the set of live-edges), is generated from $\mathcal{G}$ with probability

$$\Pr[g \sim \mathcal{G}] = \prod_{(u,v) \in E'} w(u,v) \prod_{(u,v) \notin E'} (1 - w(u,v)). \tag{1}$$

Influence Spread. In IC model, the measure *Influence Spread* (or simply *influence*) of a seed set S is defined as the expected number of nodes, that are activated by S, in the end of the diffusion propagation. Given a sample graph $g \sim \mathcal{G}$ and a seed set $S \subset V$, we denote $\eta_g(S)$ the set of nodes reachable from S (including nodes in S themselves). The influence spread of S is defined as follows,

$$\mathbb{I}(S) = \sum_{g \sim \mathcal{G}} |\eta_g(S)| \Pr[g \sim \mathcal{G}]. \tag{2}$$

3   Hop-Based Sketch & Influence Estimation

Given a probabilistic graph $\mathcal{G}$ and a seed set of nodes $S \subseteq V$, one common task in social network analysis is to find a close estimation $\hat{\mathbb{I}}(S)$ of the influence spread $\mathbb{I}(S)$. The problem is known as influence estimation (IE). We begin with the introduction of the RIS sketch method [1] to estimate influence.

3.1   Reverse Influence Sketch (RIS) [1]

Reverse Influence Sketch (RIS), proposed in [1], provides a novel approach to estimate nodes' influence in networks. The sketch is constructed by generating a collection of reverse reachability sets (aka RIS samples). A reverse reachability set of a node v is the set of nodes that are reached by v in a sample graph. We generate a RIS sample as follows.

(1) Select a random node $v \in V$.

(2) Generate a sample graph $g \sim \mathcal{G}$.

(3) Return the set R_j of nodes that can reach v in g.

The 2nd step is often implemented with a Breadth-first-search from v, reversing the edges' direction in G, and edge existence are determined as they encountered a long the algorithm.

Given an RIS sketch $\mathcal{R} = \{R_1, R_2, \ldots, R_T\}$ where T is the number of samples, the influence of a subset of nodes $S \subseteq V$, referred to as seed nodes, can be estimated as

$$\hat{\mathbb{I}}_{\mathcal{R}}(S) = n \cdot \left(\frac{1}{T} \sum_{j=1}^{T} \mathbb{1}_{R_j \cap S \neq \emptyset} \right), \tag{3}$$

where $n = |V|$ is the number of nodes in $\mathcal{G}$. For simplicity, we often ignore $\mathcal{R}$ when the context is clear.

This unbiased estimation is based on the fact that

$$\mathbb{I}(S) = n \cdot \Pr[R_j \cap S \neq \emptyset]. \tag{4}$$

We can easily prove the above Eq. 4 from Eq. 2 (please see Observation 3.2 in [1] for more detail).

While RIS is very efficient in identify node or group of nodes with large influence, major of nodes in the network have small influence and, thus, their estimation are not effective for ranking their relative influence. The reason is that the memory limit prevents the sketch from having sufficient coverage of all nodes in the network.

3.2 More Efficient Estimators

We propose an hybrid approach that estimate the influence of a seed set S by adding (1) the exact 'local influence' of S with (2) an estimate of the 'remote influence' of S via sketch. The exact computation of 'local influence' helps to reduce the variation, increase the estimation accuracy, especially for those of small influence. Even for nodes that do not appear in the RIS sketch due to small influence can be estimated and ranked against each other.

h-hop Estimators: Let $h \in \{0, 1, 2\}$ be the radius of the 'local influence', we want to estimate. We cap h at 2 as computing 'local influence' for larger values of h is not scalable for large networks.

Sketch Generation. We build a HIS sketch as follows.

- Obtain a RIS sketch $\mathcal{R} = \{R_1, R_2, \cdots, \mathcal{R}_T\}$.
- For each reachability set R_j, decompose it into two disjoint subsets $R_j = (R_j^{(h)}, R_j^{(h^+)})$, where $R_j^{(h)}$ contain nodes in R_j that are at most h hops away from its source node and $R_j^{(h^+)} = R_j \setminus R_j^{(h)}$.
- If $R_j^{(h^+)} = \emptyset$, discard R_j.

We separate the influence spread into two parts as follows,

$$\mathbb{I}^{(h)}(S) = l^{(h)}(S) + r^{(h)}(S), \tag{5}$$

where $l^{(h)}(S)$ is the local influence and $r^{(h)}(S)$ is the normalized remote influence. $l^{(h)}(S)$ and $r^{(h)}(S)$ are computed as follows,

$$l^{(h)}(S) = n \cdot \Pr[R_j^{(h)} \cap S \neq \emptyset],$$

$$r^{(h)}(S) = n \cdot \Pr[S \oplus R_j = \text{true}],$$

where

$$S \oplus R_j = \begin{cases} \text{true} & \text{if } R_j^{(h+)} \cap S \neq \emptyset \text{ AND } R_j^{(h)} \cap S = \emptyset, \\ \text{false} & \text{otherwise.} \end{cases} \tag{6}$$

We also say S *covers* R_j if $S \oplus R_j = \text{true}$.

Lemma 1. *For $h \in \{0, 1, 2\}$, a seed set $S \subseteq V$, and a random reachability set $R_j = (R_j^{(h)}, R_j^{(h+)})$, we have*

$$\mathbb{I}(S) = \mathbb{I}^{(h)}(S) = l^{(h)}(S) + r^{(h)}(S)$$

Proof.

$$\begin{aligned}
\mathbb{I}(S) &= n \cdot \Pr[R_j \cap S \neq \emptyset] \\
&= n \cdot \Pr[(R_j^h \cap S) \cup (R_j^{(h+)} \cap S) \neq \emptyset] \\
&= n \cdot \Pr[R_j^h \cap S \neq \emptyset] + n \cdot Pr[R_j^{(h+)} \cap S \neq \emptyset \text{ AND } R_j^{(h)} \cap S = \emptyset] \\
&= l^{(h)}(S) + n \cdot Pr[S \oplus R_j = \text{true}] = l^{(h)}(S) + r^{(h)}(S)
\end{aligned}$$

In an h-hop estimator, we compute the exact value of the local influence and estimate the remote influence based on the HIS sketch, i.e.,

$$\hat{\mathbb{I}}(S) = l^{(h)}(S) + \hat{r}^{(h)}(S). \tag{7}$$

Local Influence. $l^{(h)}(S)$ is defined as the expected numbers of nodes that are activated by S within at most h round(s). The local influence has been used many times before, e.g. [2], to approximate the nodes' influence. We note that such approximation provides no statistical guarantee on the estimation error. In contrast, our hybrid approach that relies on sketch technique can provide estimation with arbitrary small statistical guarantees. For the sake of completeness, we present here the definition of local influence for $h = 0, 1$, and 2.

Case $h = 0$: The local influence is simply

$$l^{(0)}(S) = |S|. \tag{8}$$

Algorithm 1: Influence estimation on HIS sketch

Input: A graph $\mathcal{G}$, HIS sketch $\mathcal{R}$ and the size of the seed set k

Output: h-hop influence estimation $\hat{\mathbb{I}}^{(h)}(S)$

1 Compute local influence $l^{(h)}(S)$;

2 Set $c(S) \leftarrow 0$;

3 $T \leftarrow |\mathcal{R}|$;

4 for $R_j \in \mathcal{R}$ **do**

5 $\quad$ **if** $S \oplus R_j = true$ **then**

6 $\quad\quad$ $c(S) \leftarrow c(S) + 1$;

7 $\hat{r}^{(h)}(S) \leftarrow n \cdot \frac{c(S)}{T}$;

8 $\hat{\mathbb{I}}^{(h)}(S) = l^{(h)}(S) + \hat{r}^{(h)}(S)$;

9 return $\hat{\mathbb{I}}^{(h)}(S)$;

Case $h = 1$: Denote by $D(S, h)$ the set of nodes at distance h from S and $\pi_h(u)$ the probability that u gets activated (for the first time) at round h. We have

$$\pi_1(S, u) = 1 - \prod_{s \in S, (s,u) \in E} (1 - p(s, u)) \ \forall u \in D(S, 1).$$

The local influence of S within 1 hop is then

$$l^{(1)}(S) = l^{(0)} + \sum_{u \in D(S,1)} \pi_1(S, u). \tag{9}$$

Case $h = 2$: Similarly, the local influence of S within 2 hop is

$$l^{(2)}(S) = l^{(1)} + \sum_{v \in D(S,1) \cup D(S,2)} \pi_2(v) \tag{10}$$

where

$$\pi_2(S, v) = (1 - \pi_1(S, v)) \left(1 - \prod_{(u,v) \in E} (1 - \pi_1(S, u)p(u, v)) \right)$$

with a note that $\pi_1(S, v) = 0$ for $v \in D(S, 2)$.

Remote Influence. The remote influence is estimated on the set of reverse reachability sets generated in HIS sketch. The estimator for remote influence is then defined as

$$\hat{r}^{(h)}(S) = n \cdot \frac{c(S, \mathcal{R})}{T}, \tag{11}$$

where $c(S) = |\{R_j \in \mathcal{R} : S \oplus R_j = true\}|$ is the number of reachability sets in $\mathcal{R}$ that are covered by S.

We summarize the influence estimation using our sketch in Algorithm 1.

Statistical Guarantees on Errors. We define $\hat{X}$ is an (ϵ, δ)-approximation of a random variable X if

$$\Pr[(1 - \epsilon)\hat{X} \leq X \leq X(1 + \epsilon)\hat{X}] \geq 1 - \delta. \tag{12}$$

Follow concentration bounds in Lemma 3 in [10], we have, $\hat{r}^{(h)}(S)$ is an (ϵ, δ)-approximation of $r^{(h)}(S)$ if

$$T = O\left(\frac{1}{\epsilon^2} \log\left(\frac{1}{\delta}\right) \frac{n}{r^{(h)}(S)}\right) \tag{13}$$

We note, we can follow Algorithm 2 in [10] to achieve this approximation guarantee with out knowing the value of $r^{(h)}(S)$.

Furthermore, since the influence also contains the exact value of local influence, the relative error of the approximation of the influence is smaller than the approximation of the remote influence.

Lemma 2. *For any $\epsilon, \delta \in [0, 1]$ and ϵ' such that*

$$\epsilon' = \frac{\mathbb{I}(S) - l^{(h)}(S)}{\mathbb{I}(S)} \epsilon = \frac{r^{(h)}(S)}{\mathbb{I}(S)} \epsilon. \tag{14}$$

If $\hat{r}^{(h)}(S)$ is an (ϵ, δ)-approximation of $r^{(h)}(S)$, then $\hat{\mathbb{I}}^{(h)}(S)$ is an (ϵ', δ)-approximation of $\mathbb{I}^{(h)}(S)$

Thus h-hop estimator needs a fewer number of samplers than using RIS sketch approximations to achieve the same approximation guarantee. From Eqs. 13 and 14, the number of samples reduces by a fraction of $\left(\frac{r^{(h)}(S)}{\mathbb{I}(S)}\right)^2$. Plus, when h increases, i.e., $r^{(h)}(S)$ decreases, the number of samples also reduces.

Memory Saving. As we only count samples R_j that $R_j^{(h+)}$ intersects with the seed set S, any samples R_j with $R_j^{(h+)} = \emptyset$ can be safely discarded from the sketch. For network with small edge probabilities, this can reason in significant saving in memory. A similar approach that discards samples of size one was studied in [9]. Our approach with $h = 0$ achieves the same memory saving with the one in [9] and achieve even better memory saving for $h = 1$ and $h = 2$.

Time vs. Accuracy Trade-Off. The larger value of h, the better estimation for the 'local influence' and, thus, the more robust estimation for nodes with small influence. However, the larger h also result in more computing time. In our experiments, $h > 1$ is not practical for large networks with billions of edges. And, thus, the best trade-off is achieved when $h = 1$.

4 HIS-Based Influence Maximization

Given a probabilistic graph $\mathcal{G}$, a budget k, the influence maximization (IM) [5] problem asks to identify a subset $S \subset V$ with the maximum influence among all subsets of size at most k,

$$S = \underset{S' \subseteq V, |S'| \leq k}{\arg\max} \ \mathbb{I}(S'). \tag{15}$$

Given a sketch $\mathcal{R} = \{R_1, R_2, \ldots, R_T\}$, we can approximate the influence maximization (IM) problem with finding a size-k seed set S that maximizes the estimated influence

$$S = \arg \max_{|S'|=k} \hat{\mathbb{I}}(S') = \arg \max_{|S'|=k} \left(l^{(h)}(S') + \hat{r}^{(h)}(S') \right). \tag{16}$$

For a large sketch, this approach gives a good approximate solutions for IM. Determining the right sketch size has been extensively investigated in previous research [11–13, 17, 18]

Greedy Algorithm. In the standard greedy algorithm for IM, we repeat k times and in each time select into the solution a node with maximum marginal gain. The marginal gain of a node v with respect to a current partial solution S on HIS sketch $\mathcal{R}$ is defined as

$$\Delta l(u, S) + n \cdot \frac{\Delta c(u, S)}{T}$$

where $\Delta l(u, S) = \left[l^{(h)}(S + \{u\}) - l^{(h)}(S) \right]$ is the local marginal gain and $\Delta c(u, S) = [c(S \cup \{u\}, \mathcal{R}) - c(S, \mathcal{R})]$ is the non-normalized remote marginal gain.

Algorithm 2: Greedy Algorithm on HIS sketch

Input: A graph $\mathcal{G}$, HIS sketch $\mathcal{R}$, and the size of the seed set k

Output: An approximate seed set S

1 $S \leftarrow \emptyset$;
2 $T \leftarrow |\mathcal{R}|$;
3 **for** $v \in V$ **do**
4 $\quad \Delta l(v, S) = l^{(h)}(\{v\})$;
5 $\quad \Delta c(v, S) = c(\{v\}, \mathcal{R})$;

6 **for** $i = 1 : k$ **do**
7 $\quad v \leftarrow \arg\max_{u \in V \setminus S} \left(\Delta l(u, S) + n \cdot \frac{\Delta c(u, S)}{T} \right)$
8 $\quad$ Add v to S
9 $\quad$ Update $\Delta l(u, S), \quad \forall u \in V \setminus S$;
10 $\quad$ Update $\Delta c(u, S), \quad \forall u \in V \setminus S$ using Algorithm 3;

11 **return** S

Update Local Marginal Gain. For $h = 0$ and $h = 1$, it is possible to maintain $\Delta l(u, S)$ explicitly. However, doing so for $h = 2$ incurs a very high cost as we basically need to examine all nodes that are at distance at most 4 from each selected node v. For $h = 2$, we employ a *partially lazy update*, that is inspired by the lazy update [7].

Algorithm 3: Update Remote Marginal Gain

    Input: HIS sketch $\mathcal{R}$, a set S, a node v, and the non-normalized marginal gain $\Delta c(u, S)$ for any node $u \in V \setminus S$.

    Output: The updated non-normalized marginal gain after adding node v to S and a new sketch $\mathcal{R}$.

1 $S \leftarrow S \cup \{v\}$;

2   **for** $R_j \in \mathcal{R}$ *such that* $v \in R_j$ **do**

3   **for** $u \in R_j^{(h^+)}$ **do**

4 $\Delta c(u, S) \leftarrow \Delta c(u, S) - 1$;

5   **if** $v \in R_j^{(h^+)}$ **then**

6   **for** $u \in R_j^{(h)}$ **do**

7 $\Delta c(u, S) \leftarrow \Delta c(u, S) - 1$;

8 $\mathcal{R} \leftarrow \mathcal{R} \setminus \{R_j\}$

9   **Return** $(\Delta c, \mathcal{R})$;

Update Remote Marginal Gain. For remote marginal gain, initialize, we set $\Delta c(u, S) = c(\{u\})$. After adding a node v to the seed set S to get the set S, i.e., $S = S \cup \{v\}$, we iterate through all sample R_j in the current sketch $\mathcal{R}$ such that $v \in R_j$ and update $\Delta c(u, S)$ as follows.

- For any node $u \in R_j^{(h^+)}$, we reduce $\Delta c(u, S)$ by 1. Since $v \in R_j$, either R_j is covered by S (if $v \in R^{(h^+)}$) or R_j can not be covered by any set $S' \supseteq S$ (if $v \in R_j^{(h)}$).

- If $v \in R_j^{(h^+)}$ (i.e., R_j is covered by S), for any node $u \in R_j^{(h)}$, we reduce $\Delta c(u, S)$ by 1 (by adding a node $u \in R_j^{(h)}$ to the seed set S, R_j is no longer covered by S).

Then we remove R_j from $\mathcal{R}$.

5   Experiments

We demonstrate the advantages of our HIS sketch through a comprehensive set of experiments on influence estimation and maximization problems. We report the results under the IC model.

Table 1. Datasets' statistics

Dataset	#Nodes	#Edges	Avg. Degree
NetPHY	$37 \cdot 10^3$	$181 \cdot 10^3$	9.8
Epinions	$75 \cdot 10^3$	$841 \cdot 10^3$	22.4
DBLP	$655 \cdot 10^3$	$2 \cdot 10^6$	6.1
Orkut	$3 \cdot 10^6$	$234 \cdot 10^6$	78.0
Twitter [6]	$41.7 \cdot 10^6$	$1.5 \cdot 10^9$	70.5

5.1   Experimental Settings

Datasets. We use 5 real-world datasets from [6, 16] with size of up to 65.6 million nodes and 3.6 billion edges. Table 1 gives a statistical summary of the testing datasets.

Algorithms Compared. We compare our HIS sketch with two other existing sketches

- RIS [1]: The well-known RIS sketch.
- SKIS [9]: The recently proposed sketch that ignores singular samples of size one. Note that the SKIS can be seen as a special case of our sketch with $h = 0$.

Following [14] and [9], we generate samples into HIS, SKIS, and RIS until the total size of all the samples reaches $c \cdot n \log n$ where $c \in \{5, 10\}$.

For quality assessment, we adopt the *relative difference* which is defined as $\frac{|\hat{\mathbb{I}}(S) - \mathbb{I}(S)|}{\max\{\mathbb{I}(S), \hat{\mathbb{I}}(S)\}} \cdot 100\%$, where $\hat{\mathbb{I}}(S)$ is the estimated influence, and $\mathbb{I}(S)$ is the "ground-truth" influence of S obtained from the authors of [9].

Weight Settings. We consider the widely-used model, termed *Weighted Cascade* (WC), [3, 12, 17, 18]. In the WC model, the weight of edge (u, v) is inversely proportional to the in-degree of node v, $d_{in}(v)$, i.e. $w(u, v) = \frac{1}{d_{in}(v)}$.

Environment. We implemented our algorithms in C++ and obtained the implementations of SKIS, data, and influence "ground truth" from the authors [9]. We conducted all experiments on a Linux machine with Intel 2.30 GHz CPUs and 200GB RAM. Only one core is used in our experiments.

5.2   Influence Estimation

The estimation errors, measured in relative difference, are shown in Table 2. Overall, HIS provides estimations with smaller errors than those of RIS and SKIS (0-hop) and the errors decrease when the number of hops h increases. Although, there is negligible gain in estimation quality when h increases from 1 to 2.

The time to build the sketches are roughly the same and are skipped due to the space limit. The average query times are present in Table 3. The query time for HIS increases together with the number of hops h. RIS results in the lowest query time, however, RIS results in higher errors as shown in Table 2.

Overall, HIS sketch with $h = 1$ provides the best trade-off between query time and estimation quality and is recommended as the default parameter for h.

Table 2. Average relative differences (Smaller is better).

$|S|$	Nets	$c(5)$				$c(10)$			
		0-hop	1-hop	2-hop	RIS	0-hop	1-hop	2-hop	RIS
	PHY	4.2	2.1	0.9	14.0	4.0	2.1	0.6	7.8
	Epin.	7.0	6.0	5.3	15.7	4.6	4.4	4.1	11.8
1	DBLP	4.8	1.9	1.0	13.7	4.8	1.4	0.3	11.6
	Orkut	10.2	10.5	10.2	13.5	9.2	8.8	8.3	8.8
	Twit.	10.9	10.5	10.1	21.4	10.7	9.1	8.2	16.0
	PHY	0.9	0.5	0.3	1.0	0.6	0.4	0.3	0.7
	Epin.	1.1	1.0	0.9	1.0	1.0	0.9	0.7	1.0
10^2	DBLP	1.6	1.2	1.3	1.9	1.5	1.3	1.3	1.4
	Orkut	0.9	0.9	0.9	1.1	0.7	0.7	0.7	0.7
	Twit.	1.3	1.4	1.3	1.3	1.0	1.1	1.0	1.1

Table 3. Query time (second) with $|S| = 1000$

Nets	$c(5)$				$c(10)$			
	0-hop	1-hop	2-hop	RIS	0-hop	1-hop	2-hop	RIS
Phy	0.38	0.50	0.81	0.42	0.74	0.66	1.12	0.86
Epin	0.47	0.76	1.97	0.50	0.96	1.26	2.09	1.02
DBLP	0.82	0.86	1.31	0.79	1.35	1.40	1.79	1.20
Orkut	1.44	2.60	12.42	1.32	1.59	3.44	13.5	1.7
Twitter	1.56	3.64	4.32	1.4	1.98	4.39	5.32	2.01

5.3   Influence Maximization

The solution quality, measured as influence spread, for different sketch sizes are provided in Fig. 1. When the number of samples are sufficiently large (100k), all sketches results in similar solution quality. However, for smaller number of samples, HIS performs better than RIS. Also, HIS with $h = 1$ and 2 performs better than SKIS (the same with 0-hop).

The running-time is omitted due to the space. The overall observation is that HIS with $h = 2$ does not scale for large network (cannot finish in Twitter). HIS $h = 1$ again provide the best trade-off between time-quality. It takes about 50% to 80% more times comparing to SKIS and RIS, however, provides solutions with significantly higher quality.

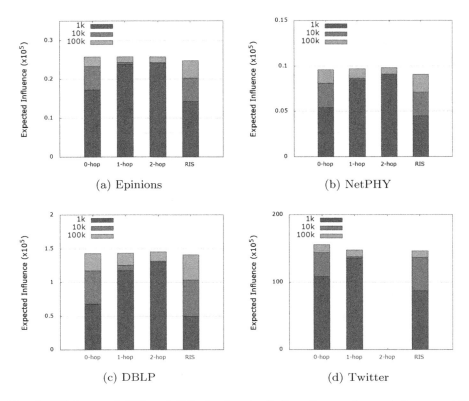

(a) Epinions   (b) NetPHY

(c) DBLP   (d) Twitter

Fig. 1. Efficiency of HIS and RIS sketches in finding the maximum influence with different seed set size (1k,10k,100k). The measures for SKIS are similar to those of HIS with 0-hop and ignored. HIS 2-hop did not finish in Twitter.

Acknowledgment. The work is partially supported by Subaward SUB00001739, NSF EFRI 1441231.

References

1. Borgs, C., Brautbar, M., Chayes, J., Lucier, B.: Maximizing social influence in nearly optimal time. In: Proceedings of the Twenty-Fifth Annual ACM-SIAM Symposium on Discrete Algorithms, pp. 946–957. SIAM (2014)
2. Chen, W., Wang, C., Wang, Y.: Scalable influence maximization for prevalent viral marketing in large-scale social networks. In: Proceedings of the 16th ACM SIGKDD International Conference on Knowledge Discovery and Data Mining, pp. 1029–1038. ACM (2010)
3. Cohen, E., Delling, D., Pajor, T., Werneck, R.F.: Sketch-based influence maximization and computation: scaling up with guarantees. In: CIKM, pp. 629–638. ACM (2014)
4. Du, N., Song, L., Gomez-Rodriguez, M., Zha, H.: Scalable influence estimation in continuous-time diffusion networks. In: NIPS, pp. 3147–3155 (2013)

5. Kempe, D., Kleinberg, J., Tardos, É.: Maximizing the spread of influence through a social network. In: KDD, pp. 137–146 (2003)
6. Kwak, H., Lee, C., Park, H., Moon, S.: What is twitter, a social network or a news media? In: WWW, pp. 591–600. ACM (2010)
7. Leskovec, J., Kleinberg, J., Faloutsos, C.: Graphs over time: densification laws, shrinking diameters and possible explanations. In: KDD, pp. 187. ACM (2005)
8. Lucier, B., Oren, J., Singer, Y.: Influence at scale: distributed computation of complex contagion in networks. In: KDD, pp. 735–744. ACM (2015)
9. Nguyen, H.T., Nguyen, T.P., Phan, N., Dinh, T.N.: Importance sketching of influence dynamics in billion-scale networks. In: 2017 IEEE International Conference on Data Mining (ICDM), pp. 337–346. IEEE (2017)
10. Nguyen, H.T., Nguyen, T.P., Vu, T.N., Dinh, T.N.: Outward influence and cascade size estimation in billion-scale networks. Proc. ACM Measur. Anal. Comput. Syst. 1(1), 20 (2017)
11. Nguyen, H.T., Thai, M.T., Dinh, T.N.: Cost-aware targeted viral marketing in billion-scale networks. In: INFOCOM, pp. 1–9. IEEE (2016)
12. Nguyen, H.T., Thai, M.T., Dinh, T.N.: Stop-and-stare: optimal sampling algorithms for viral marketing in billion-scale networks. In: SIGMOD, New York, NY, USA, pp. 695–710. ACM (2016)
13. Nguyen, H.T., Thai, M.T., Dinh, T.N.: A billion-scale approximation algorithm for maximizing benefit in viral marketing. IEEE/ACM Trans. Netw. 25(4), 2419–2429 (2017)
14. Ohsaka, N., Akiba, T., Yoshida, Y., Kawarabayashi, K.-I.: Dynamic influence analysis in evolving networks. VLDB 9(12), 1077–1088 (2016)
15. Popova, D., Ohsaka, N., Kawarabayashi, K.-I., Thomo, A.: Nosingles: a space-efficient algorithm for influence maximization. In: Proceedings of the 30th International Conference on Scientific and Statistical Database Management, p. 18. ACM (2018)
16. SNAP: Stanford network analysis project (2017). http://snap.stanford.edu
17. Tang, Y., Shi, Y., Xiao, X.: Influence maximization in near-linear time: a martingale approach. In: SIGMOD, pp. 1539–1554 (2015)
18. Tang, Y., Xiao, X., Shi, Y.: Influence maximization: Near-optimal time complexity meets practical efficiency. In Proceedings of the 2014 ACM SIGMOD International Conference on Management of Data, pp. 75–86. ACM (2014)

Profit Maximization Under Group Influence Model in Social Networks

Jianming Zhu[1]($\boxtimes$) (iD), Smita Ghosh[2], Weili Wu[2], and Chuangen Gao[3]

[1] School of Engineering Science, University of Chinese Academy of Sciences,
19A Yuquan Rd., Beijing, China
`jmzhu@ucas.ac.cn`
[2] Department of Computer Science,
University of Texas at Dallas, Richardson, TX, USA
{`smita.ghosh1,weiliwu`}`@utdallas.edu`
[3] Shandong University, Jinan, China
`gaochuangen@gmail.com`

Abstract. People with the same interests, hobbies or political orientation always form a group to share all kinds of topics in Online Social Networks (OSN). Product producers often hire the OSN provider to propagate their advertisements in order to influence all possible potential groups. In this paper, a group is assumed to be *activated* if β percent of members are activated. Product producers will gain revenue from all activated groups through group-buying behavior. Meanwhile, to propagate influence, producers need pay diffusion cost to the OSN provider, while the cost is usually relevant to total hits on the advertisements. We aim to select k seed users to maximize the expected profit that combines the benefit of activated groups with the diffusion cost of influence propagation, which is called *Group Profit Maximization* (GPM) problem. The information diffusion model is based on Independent Cascade (IC), and we prove GPM is NP-hard and the objective function is neither submodular nor supermodular. We develop an upper bound and a lower bound that both are difference of two submodular functions. Then we design an Submodular-Modular Algorithm (SMA) for solving difference of submodular functions and SMA is proved to converge to local optimal. Further, we present an randomized algorithm based on weighted group coverage maximization for GPM and apply Sandwich framework to get theoretical results. Our experiments verify the effectiveness of our method, as well as the advantage of our method against the other heuristic methods.

Keywords: Profit maximization · Group influence · Non-submodular · Social networks

---

The work is supported by the US National Science Foundation under Grant No. 1747818, National Natural Science Foundation of China under Grant No. 91324012 and Project of Promoting Scientific Research Ability of Excellent Young Teachers in University of Chinese Academy of Sciences.

A. Tagarelli and H. Tong (Eds.): CSoNet 2019, LNCS 11917, pp. 108–119, 2019.
https://doi.org/10.1007/978-3-030-34980-6_13

1   Introduction

In social society, no one is isolated and he must belong to some group. Understanding his feeling requires understanding his groups [4]. People's behavior is so often group behavior and much of the world's decision or work is done by groups and teams. Various kinds of groups exist both in real world society and Online Social Networks (OSN). Some groups may be smaller as only several members like family, while some groups may contains hundreds of members, such as such as a school, even a whole state or country. With explosive growth and rising population of large-scale social networks such as Facebook with 2.2B users, WeChat with 1.0B users and Twitter with 0.34B users etc. [11], hundreds of millions of people are able to become friends and share information with each other. People with same character such as interests or hobbies may form group on the SON platform to discuss the interested topics. Wechat platform as an example, Wechat public account, WeChat group or circle of friends are very popular for every Wechat user. Another group decision example is US Presidential Elections. Presidential candidate will win all votes in a state if he got the maximum number of tickets in this state.

Since group plays an important role both in real world society and online social networks, the producer (such as company) or government tries to activate group instead of care about personal influence. For example, a family usually makes one decision of purchasing some product according to the influence advertise from different brands. For another example, a company plans to purchase computers for each employee, while the company may use voting method to determine to purchase which brand of computer. The employee may influence by different brand of computer, but the final purchasing brand is just one brand. A group will be activated if a certain number of members are activated. Product producers often hire the OSN provider to propagate their advertisements in order to influence all possible potential groups. In this paper, a group is assumed to be *activated* if β percent of members are activated. Product producers will gain revenue from all activated groups through group behavior. Meanwhile, to propagate influence, producers need pay diffusion cost to the OSN provider, while the cost is usually relevant to total hits on the advertisements. In this paper, we aim to select k seed users to maximize the expected profit that combines the benefit of activated groups with the cost of influence propagation for the topic provider, which is called *Group Profit Maximization* (GPM) problem. Given a random social network $G = (V, E, P)$, P represents the influence probability on each directed edge (u, v) which means u will try to activate v with probability P when u becomes activated. A group is said to be *activated* if β percent of users in this group are activated. β is called activated threshold. For each group U, $b(U) \geq 0$ is the benefit when U is activated. While $c(v) \geq 0$ is the diffusion cost if v is activated for $v \in V$.

1.1 Related Works

Kempe et al. [8] formulated Influence Maximization (IM) Problem as an optimization problem. They proved IM to be NP-hard under Independent Cascade (IC) model. They also specified the objective function of IM under IC model was submodular, then greedy algorithm that yields $(1 - 1/e - \epsilon)$-approximate solutions for any $\epsilon > 0$ was proposed.

Maximizing the influence spread alone has been shown to be ineffective for optimizing the profit return of viral marketing [17], Since the number of seeds selected yields a tradeoff between the expense and reward of viral marketing. Several recent work studied profit maximization from the advertisers perspective [10,22]. These studies considered the cost of seed selection which is modular and implies that their profit metric is still submodular. [16] considered a profit maximization problem that takes into account the cost of information diffusion over the social network. The profit function is decomposed into the difference between two submodular functions.

The sampling method is the bottleneck of solving IM. Tang et al. [18,19] utilized a novel RIS sampling technique introduced by Borgs et al. [2]. TIM+ and IMM attempted to generate a $(1 - 1/e - \epsilon)$-approximate solution with minimal numbers of RIS samples. However, they may take days on billion-scale networks. Later, Nguyen et al. [13] made a breakthrough and proposed two novel sampling algorithms SSA and D-SSA. Unlike the previous heuristic algorithms, SSA and D-SSA are faster than TIM+ and IMM while providing the same $(1 - 1/e - \epsilon)$-approximate guarantee. SSA and D-SSA are the first approximation algorithms that use minimum numbers of samples, meeting strict theoretical thresholds characterized for IM. Zhu [21] presented an extended RIS sampling method for the weighted version of IM with a weight on each node or user.

Few results [6] are provided when the objective function of influence propagation model even slightly violates the submodularity. Note that function of group influences is not submodular which will be proved in the following section, we cannot adapt existing social influence maximization methods to solve the GPM. Schoenebeck [15] studied the 2-quasi-submodular function optimization problem which is a special case of non-submodular problem. Narasimhan and Bilmes [12] presented an approximation method for submodular + supermodular function by substituting the supermodular function to a modular function. In [1], Bach gave an general idea that any nonsubmodular function could represent as a difference of two submodular function. The latest approach is based on the sandwich [9] approximation strategy, which approximates the objective function by looking for its lower bound and upper bound. More relevant results can be found in [20].

1.2 Contributions

Motivated by the group decision in social society, we propose Group Profit Maximization (GPM) problem that aims select k seed users to maximize the expected profit that combines the benefit of activated groups with the cost of influence propagation under independent cascade (IC) model. We assess the challenges of the proposed profit maximization problem by analyzing computational complexity and properties of objective function. Firstly, we show the GPM is NP-hard under IC model. Moreover, the objective function of this problem is proved neither submodular nor supermodular. To achieve practical approximate solution, we develop a lower bound and upper bound of objective function. We prove that maximizing these two bounds are still NP-hard under IC model. However, we also prove that both lower bound and upper bound are difference of submodular functions. Motivated by RIS sampling method, we present a Submodular-Modular algorithm for solving the difference of submodular functions. For solving GPM, firstly we develop a weighted group coverage maximization algorithm. Secondly, We formulate a sandwich approximation framework, which preserves a theoretical analysis result. We verify our algorithm on real world dataset. The results show the effectiveness and the efficiency of the proposed algorithm.

The rest of this paper is organized as follows: First, we formulate the Group Profit Maximization (GPM) problem; then the statement of NP-hardness and properties of objective function will be discussed; after that, we develop a lower bound and upper bound and present our algorithms; experiments are presented in the following section; and finally, the paper is concluded.

2   Problem Formulation

The information diffusion model is first step for modelling IM problem. In this paper, we apply Independent cascade (IC) [8] model.

2.1   Group Profit Maximization

Given a directed graph $G = (V, E, P)$, a **group** U is defined as a subset of V. Let $\mathcal{U}$ be the set of groups and l be the number of total groups. Given an activation threshold $0 < \beta \leq 1$, a group is said to be **activated** if β percent of nodes in this group are activated under IC model. For each group U, $b(U) \geq 0$ is the benefit when U is activated. While $c(v) \geq 0$ is the diffusion cost if v is activated for $v \in V$.

Next, we introduce the concept of realization of random graph which helps to understand the IC model. Given a random directed graph $G = (V, E, P)$, a realization g of G is a graph where $V(g) = V(G)$ and $E(g)$ is a subset of $E(G)$. Each edge in $E(g)$ has the influence probability of 1 and is constructed in random. The construction process is as follows: (1) for each edge $e \in E(G)$, a random number r is generated from 0 to 1 in uniform; (2) this edge e appears in g if and only if $r \leq P_e$. Then, g is a deterministic directed graph. Let $\mathcal{G}$ be the set of all possible realizations of G. Obviously, there are $2^{|E(G)|}$ realizations in $\mathcal{G}$. Let $P[g]$ be the probability that g can be generated. Then,

$$P[g] = \prod_{e \in E(g)} P_e \prod_{e \in E(G) \setminus E(g)} (1 - P_e)$$

Let $\mathcal{U}_g(S)$ and $V_g(S)$ be the set of groups activated and the set of nodes activated by the initial seed set S respectively. Then, the expected benefit of activated groups is

$$\beta(S) = \sum_{g \in \mathcal{G}} P[g] \sum_{U \in \mathcal{U}_g(S)} b(U)$$

and the expected cost of activated nodes is

$$\gamma(S) = \sum_{g \in \mathcal{G}} P[g] \sum_{v \in V_g(S)} c(v).$$

Then we naturally define the profit as $\rho(S) = \beta(S) - \gamma(S)$. The Group Profit Maximization (GPM) considers information diffusion in social network under the IC model. The objective is to select k initially-influenced seed users to maximize the expected profit $\rho(S)$.

3 Properties of GPM

In this section, we first present statement of the hardness of the GPM. Then discuss the properties of the objective function $\rho(\cdot)$.

It is known that any generalization of a NP-hard problem is also NP-hard. The social Influence Maximization (IM) problem has been proved NP-hard [8], which is a special case of our problem when each node is considered as a group, $\beta = 1$, benefit of each group is 1 and cost of each node is 0. Therefore, the GPM is obvious NP-hard.

Theorem 1. *The Group Profit Maximization Problem is NP-hard.*

Given an instance of GPM, computing the objective $\rho(S)$ is difficult even for a given seed set S since the activation process is not determinate but randomized according the influence probability. For such a problem, Monte Carlo method is widely used to estimate $\rho(S)$ by generating a large number of sample graphs of G and computing $\rho(S)$ on each sample graph. At last, output the average value. How many graphs should we generate will be discussed in the next section. Since computing the objective of IM was proved #P-hard under the IC model [8], then we have the following result.

Theorem 2. *Given a seed node set S, computing $\rho(S)$ is #P-hard under the IC model.*

A set function $f : 2^V \leftarrow \mathbb{R}$ is said to be *submodular* [5] if for any subsets $A \subset B \subseteq V$ and $v \in V \setminus B$, it holds that $f(A \cup \{v\}) - f(A) \geq f(B \cup \{v\}) - f(B)$. While if for any subsets $A \subset B \subseteq V$ and $v \in V \setminus B$, it holds that $f(A \cup \{v\}) - f(A) \leq f(B \cup \{v\}) - f(B)$, f is *supermodular*. A set function $f : 2^V \leftarrow \mathbb{R}$ is said to be *monotone* nondecreasing if for any $A \subseteq B \subseteq V$, it satisfies $f(A) \leq f(B)$. f is called a *polymatroid function* if it is monotone nondecreasing, submodular and $f(\emptyset) = 0$, where $\emptyset$ denotes the empty set. Since $\rho(S) = \beta(S) - \gamma(S)$, it is obviously γ a polymatroid function.

Theorem 3. $\gamma(\cdot)$ *is monotone nondecreasing, submodular and* $\gamma(\emptyset) = 0$.

While although $\beta(\emptyset) = 0$ and $\beta(\cdot)$ is monotone nondecreasing, unfortunately $\beta(\cdot)$ is neither submodular nor supermodular under IC model.

Theorem 4. $\beta(\cdot)$ *is neither submodular nor supermodular under IC model even when* $b(U) = 1$ *for any* $U \in \mathcal{U}$.

4   Lower Bound and Upper Bound

There is no general method to optimize a non-submodular function. Lu et al. proposed a sandwich approximation strategy [9], which approximates the objective function by looking for its lower bound and upper bound. In this section, we will give a lower bound and an upper bound on $\rho(\cdot)$. Then, we will analysis the properties of the lower bound and upper bound.

4.1   The Upper Bound

We will define a new set function $\overline{\beta}(\cdot)$ satisfies $\beta(S) \leq \overline{\beta}(S)$ for any seed set $S \subseteq V$. Formulation process of such an upper bound in this paper can be divided into two steps. Given an instance of GPM $G = (V, E, P)$, in the first step, we get a relaxed GPM (r-GPM) problem for given GPM by changing the group activation rules. For r-GPM problem, a group will be activated if there exists at least 1 activated node in this group. In the second step, for each group, we add a super node to the graph and connect each node in this group to the super node with influence probability 1. Let W be the super node set and E' be the edge set for node in V to node in W. Then, we define an instance of general Weighted Influence Maximization (WIM) problem as follows. $V \cup W$ is the node set, $E \cup E'$ is the edge set, candidate seed set $C \subseteq V$ means k seed nodes must be selected from C. f is weight function of node which satisfy

$$f(v) = \begin{cases} b(v), & v \in W \\ 0, & v \in V \end{cases}$$

Assume S is the seed set. Let $\overline{\beta}(S) = \sum_v$ is activated $f(v)$ be the expected weight of eventually-influenced nodes. Then, $G = (V, C, E, P, f)$ is called general Weighted IM problem with candidate seed set $C \subseteq V$. $\overline{\beta}(\cdot)$ is monotone, submodular and $\beta(S) \leq \overline{\beta}(S)$ for any seed set $S \subseteq V$.

Theorem 5. *Given an instance GPM* $G = (V, E, P)$, $\overline{\beta}(\cdot)$ *is an upper bound of* $\beta(\cdot)$.

Certainly, let $\overline{\rho}(\cdot) = \overline{\beta}(\cdot) - \gamma(\cdot)$, then we have the following result:

Theorem 6. *Given an instance GPM* $G = (V, E, P)$, $\overline{\rho}(\cdot)$ *is an upper bound of* $\rho(\cdot)$ *and* $\overline{\rho}(\cdot)$ *is the difference of two submodular functions.*

4.2   The Lower Bound

Next, we will formulate a lower bound for GPM. The main idea is to delete some groups from G, and only keep such groups whose β percent of nodes can be activated at the same time. That means there exist at least 1 node connect to β percent nodes of this group in G. The general process is as follows. Given an instance of GPM $G = (V, E, P)$, for each group U_i with benefit b_i, suppose $H_i = \{v \in V | v$ connects to at least β percent nodes of $U_i\}$, if $H_i \neq \emptyset$, generate super node u_i and add directed edges $\{(v, u_i) | v \in H_i\}$. For each $v \in H_i$, assume U_i' contains all nodes in U_i which v connects to. Then, $p_{(v,u_i)} = \prod_{v' \in U_i'} p_{(v,v')}$, benefit of $b(u_i) = b_i$ and benefit of the other nodes equals 0. Finally, an instance of general Weighted Influence Maximization (WIM) problem could be formulated. $V \cup W$ is the node set, $E \cup E'$ is the edge set where E' contains all new added edges, candidate seed set $C \subseteq V$ means k seed nodes must be selected from C. f is weight function of node which satisfy

$$f(v) = \begin{cases} b(v), \, v \in W \\ 0, \quad v \in V \end{cases}$$

Assume S is the seed set. Let $\underline{\beta}(S) = \sum_v$ is activated $f(v)$ be the expected weight of eventually-influenced nodes. Then, $G = (V, C, E, P, f)$ is a general WIM problem with candidate seed set $C \subseteq V$. $\underline{\beta}(\cdot)$ is monotone, submodular and $\beta(S) \geq \underline{\beta}(S)$ for any seed set $S \subset V$.

Theorem 7. *Given an instance GPM $G = (V, E, P)$, $\underline{\beta}(\cdot)$ is an lower bound of $\beta(\cdot)$.*

Certainly, let $\underline{\rho}(\cdot) = \underline{\beta}(\cdot) - \gamma(\cdot)$, then we have the following result:

Theorem 8. *Given an instance GPM $G = (V, E, P)$, $\underline{\rho}(\cdot)$ is an lower bound of $\rho(\cdot)$ and $\underline{\rho}(\cdot)$ is the difference of two submodular functions.*

5   Algorithm

Since it is #P-hard to compute the objective function either for GPM or IM, we will extent Reverse Influence Set (RIS) sampling method [21] to estimate the value of $\overline{\rho}(\cdot)$ and $\underline{\rho}(\cdot)$. Then, we will present an Submodular-Modular algorithm for solving the lowerbound and upperbound problems whose objectives are a difference of two submodular functions. Next, an randomized algorithm base on weighted group coverage maximization strategy is designed for solving GPM. At the end, a sandwich approximation framework will be proposed for analyzing performance of our algorithm.

(ϵ, δ)-approximation in [3] will be used in our algorithm analysis. ϵ is absolute error of estimation and $(1 - \delta)$ is confidence. Define $\Upsilon = 4(e - 2) \ln(2/\delta)/\epsilon^2$ and $\Upsilon_1 = 1 + (1 + \epsilon)\Upsilon$, then the Stopping Rule Algorithm given in [3] has been proved to be (ϵ, δ)-approximation. Next, we will present an estimation procedure to compute $\phi(S)$ for given S. According to [3], Algorithm 1 guarantees (ϵ, δ)-approximation.

5.1 Submodular-Modular Algorithm for Difference of Submodular Functions

According to Theorems 6 and 8, $\overline{\rho}(\cdot)$ and $\underline{\rho}(\cdot)$ are difference of submodular functions. Furthermore, $\overline{\beta}(\cdot)$ and $\underline{\beta}(\cdot)$ are objective functions of WIM problems. Next, we will present a Submodular-Modular algorithm for such a function $\phi(S) - \gamma(S)$ while $\phi(\cdot)$ and $\gamma(\cdot)$ are submodular set functions.

Algorithm 1. Estimation Procedure (EP)

Input: An instance of WIM problem $G = (V, C, E, P, f)$, $0 \leq \epsilon, \delta \leq 1$, seed set S.
Output: $\widehat{\phi}(S)$ such that $\widehat{\phi}(S) \leq (1 + \epsilon)\phi(S)$ with at least $(1 - \delta)$-probability.
1: $\Upsilon = 1 + 4(1 + \epsilon)(e - 2)\ln(2/\delta)/\epsilon^2$
2: $\Upsilon_1 = 1 + (1 + \epsilon)\Upsilon$
3: $\mathcal{R} \leftarrow$ generate Υ random WRR sets
4: $L = Cov_{\mathcal{R}}(S)$
5: **while** $L < \Upsilon_1$ **do**
6:     $R' \leftarrow$ generate a new WRR set
7:     Add R' to $\mathcal{R}$
8:     $L = Cov_{\mathcal{R}}(S)$
9: **end while**
10: $\widehat{\phi}(S) \leftarrow \sum_{v \in V} f(v) \cdot WCov_{\mathcal{R}}(S) / \sum_{j=1}^{|\mathcal{R}|} w(R_j)$
11: **return** $\widehat{\phi}(S)$.

Firstly, we will present a modular upper bound set function and a modular lower bound set function for $\gamma(\cdot)$ according to [7]. The following two tight modular upper bounds that are tight at given set X:

$$m_X^1(S) \triangleq \gamma(S) - \sum_{j \in X \setminus S} \gamma(j | X \setminus \{j\}) + \sum_{j \in S \setminus X} \gamma(j | \emptyset) \tag{1}$$

$$m_X^2(S) \triangleq \gamma(S) - \sum_{j \in X \setminus S} \gamma(j | V \setminus \{j\}) + \sum_{j \in V \setminus X} \gamma(j | X) \tag{2}$$

For briefness, when referring either one we use m_X. A modular lower bound h_X that is tight at a given set X can be obtained as follows. Let π be any permutation of V that places all the nodes in X before the nodes in $V \setminus X$. Let $S_i^\pi = \{\pi(1), \pi(2), \cdots, \pi(i)\}$ be a chain formed by the permutation, where $S_0^\pi = \emptyset$ and $S_{|X|}^\pi = X$. Define

$$h_X^\pi(\pi(i)) = \gamma(S_i^\pi) - \gamma(S_{i-1}^\pi) \tag{3}$$

Then, $h_X^\pi(S) = \sum_{v \in S} h_X^\pi(v)$ is a lower bound of $\gamma(S)$, which is tight at X, i.e., $h_X^\pi(S) \leq \gamma(S)$ for any $S \subseteq V$ and $h_X^\pi(X) = \gamma(X)$. We have the following results:

Theorem 9. $\phi(S) - m_X(S) \leq \phi(S) - \gamma(S) \leq \phi(S) - h_X^\pi(S)$ and both are difference of submodular and modular functions.

Based on $\phi(S) - m_X(S) \leq \phi(S) - \gamma(S)$, we present the Submodular-Modular algorithm. In every iteration, run both maximization procedures with the two modular upper bounds and choose the one which is better. Although it can not guarantee any theoretical performance ratio, we can prove Algorithm 2 is guaranteed to converge to a local maxima.

Theorem 10. *Submodular-Modular Algorithm 2 monotonically increasing the objective value at every iteration. Moreover, assuming a submodular maximization procedure that reaches a local maxima of $\phi(X) - m_{X^t}(X)$, then if Algorithm 2 does not improve under both modular upperbounds then it reaches a local optima.*

Algorithm 2. Submodular-Modular Algorithm (SMA)

1: $X^0 = \emptyset; t \leftarrow 0$
2: **while** not converged (i.e., $(X^{t+1} \neq X^t)$) **do**
3:     Randomly choose a permutation π^t whose chain contains the set X^t
4:     $X^{t+1} := \arg\max_X \phi(X) - m_{X^t}(X)$
5:     $t \leftarrow t + 1$
6: **end while**
7: **return** X^t.

5.2   Sandwich Approximation Framework

We first present an algorithm for solving GPM based on weighted group coverage maximization method. Given $G = (V, E, P)$ and the set of groups $\mathcal{U}$, let $\mathcal{U}(S)$ be the set of groups that contains any one of nodes in S, i.e. $\mathcal{U}(S) = \{U \in \mathcal{U} | U \cap S \neq \emptyset\}$. Then the total benefit for $\mathcal{U}(S)$ is $b(\mathcal{U}(S)) = \sum_{U \in \mathcal{U}(S)} b(U)$. Group Coverage Maximization Algorithm (MC) is to select k nodes that total weighted covered groups is maximized. For GPM, we have provide a lower bound and an upper bound for $\rho(\cdot)$. Then, the sandwich approximation framework is shown in Algorithm 3.

Algorithm 3. Sandwich Approximation Framework

Input: Given an instance of CPM $G = (V, E, P)$, $0 \leq \epsilon, \delta \leq 1$ and k.
Output: a set of seed nodes, S.
1: Let S_L be the output seed set of solving the lowerbound $\underline{\rho}$ by Submodular-Modular algorithm (Algorithm 2)
2: Let S_Z be the output seed set of solving the upperbound $\overline{\rho}$ by Submodular-Modular algorithm (Algorithm 2)
3: Let S_A be the output seed set of solving $G = (V, E, P)$ by Algorithm MC.
4: $S = \arg\max_{S_0 \in \{S_L, S_Z, S_A\}} \text{EP}(G, \epsilon, \delta, S_0)$ (by Algorithm 1)
5: **return** S

6   Experiments

In this paper, we have used dataset from [14]. This dataset is Facebook-like Forum Network which was collected from a similar online community as the Facebook online social network. It records users activity in the forum. This dataset contains one-mode and two-mode data. The two-mode data is an interesting network of 899 users liking a topic among 522 topics. The one-mode data represents the relation among the 899 users. Each topic is assumed to be one group and the people who like the same topic are assumed to belong to a group.

For this datasets the one-mode data is used to build the graphs. The two-mode data is used to form the groups. Each group has a benefit and each node in the graph has a cost. The benefit of a group is defined by multiplying the size of the group by a factor of 10. The cost of each node is assigned as a random number between 0 and 1. The algorithms are applied to these graphs to determine the maximum profit. All the programs are written in Python 3.6.3 and run on a Linux server with 16 CPUs and 256 GB RAM.

Our Sandwich Approximation Framework (SAF) will be compared with Greedy Strategy (GS) presented by Kempe [8] and Maximum Outdegree (MO) method of selecting the first k nodes with largest outdegree. MC represents the Weighted Group Coverage Maximization Algorithm as shown in Algorithm MC. Experiment results will be shown in the following section.

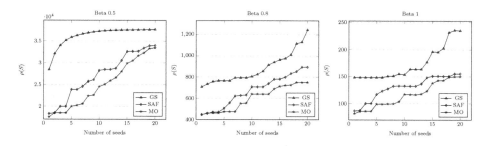

Fig. 1. Comparison of different strategies

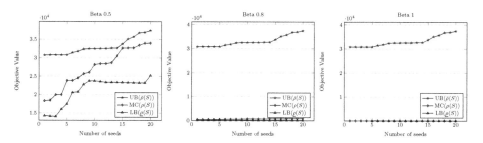

Fig. 2. Performance of sandwich framework vs lower bound and upper bound

6.1 Experimental Results

By comparing the different strategies of seed selection, it has been observed that the Greedy Strategy (GS) gives a comparatively higher output than the Sandwich Approximation Framework (SAF) and the Maximum Outdegree (MO) method, i.e., given a network, Greedy approach gives higher profit as compared to the others. The Maximum Outdegree initially gives higher profit than the Maximum Coverage but as the number of seed nodes increases, the SAF outperforms the MO but is still lower than the GS. The run time of the Greedy approach is however higher compared to that of the Maximum Coverage and the Maximum Outdegree approach as it iterates through the entire node set to get the k seed set. The observations of the experimental results are shown in Figs. 1 and 2. From the graphs the following results are obtained: (1) For Fixed Beta Value, Profit Increases with Increase in Seed Number; (2) With Increase in Beta, Profit Decreases; (3) Gap Observation between Upper Bound and Lower Bound.

7 Conclusion

In this paper, we investigated the profit maximization problem in social networks. We proposed a novel influence maximization model with consideration of group activation. The Group Profit Maximization (GPM) problem aims to select k seed users to maximize the expected profit that combines the benefit of activated groups with the cost of influence propagation. We showed GPM was NP-hard under Independent Cascade (IC) model and the objective function was neither submodular nor supermodular. For solving GPM, a weighted group coverage maximization strategy was proposed. Finally, We formulate a sandwich approximation framework, which preserves a theoretical analysis result and the experiment results showed effectiveness and the efficiency of the proposed algorithm. For future research, we are looking for an efficient method to solve nonsubmodular problems.

References

1. Bach, F., et al.: Learning with submodular functions: a convex optimization perspective. Found. Trends® Mach. Learn. **6**(23), 145–373 (2013)
2. Borgs, C., Brautbar, M., Chayes, J., Lucier, B.: Maximizing social influence in nearly optimal time. In: Proceedings of the Twenty-Fifth Annual ACM-SIAM Symposium on Discrete Algorithms, pp. 946–957. SIAM (2014)
3. Dagum, P., Karp, R., Luby, M., Ross, S.: An optimal algorithm for Monte Carlo estimation. SIAM J. Comput. **29**(5), 1484–1496 (2000)
4. Forsyth, D.R.: Group Dynamics. Cengage Learning, Belmont (2018)
5. Fujishige, S.: Submodular Functions and Optimization, vol. 58. Elsevier, Amsterdam (2005)
6. Hung, H.J., et al.: When social influence meets item inference. In: Proceedings of the 22nd ACM SIGKDD International Conference on Knowledge Discovery and Data Mining, pp. 915–924. ACM (2016)

7. Iyer, R., Bilmes, J.: Algorithms for approximate minimization of the difference between submodular functions, with applications. arXiv preprint arXiv:1207.0560 (2012)
8. Kempe, D., Kleinberg, J., Tardos, É.: Maximizing the spread of influence through a social network. In: Proceedings of the Ninth ACM SIGKDD International Conference on Knowledge Discovery and Data Mining, pp. 137–146. ACM (2003)
9. Lu, W., Chen, W., Lakshmanan, L.V.: From competition to complementarity: comparative influence diffusion and maximization. Proc. VLDB Endowment 9(2), 60–71 (2015)
10. Lu, W., Lakshmanan, L.V.: Profit maximization over social networks. In: 2012 IEEE 12th International Conference on Data Mining (ICDM), pp. 479–488. IEEE (2012)
11. Meeker, M., Wu, L.: Internet Trends Report 2018, vol. 5, p. 30. Kleiner Perkins (2018)
12. Narasimhan, M., Bilmes, J.A.: A submodular-supermodular procedure with applications to discriminative structure learning. arXiv preprint arXiv:1207.1404 (2012)
13. Nguyen, H.T., Thai, M.T., Dinh, T.N.: Stop-and-stare: optimal sampling algorithms for viral marketing in billion-scale networks. In: Proceedings of the 2016 International Conference on Management of Data. pp. 695–710. ACM (2016)
14. Opsahl, T.: Triadic closure in two-mode networks: redefining the global and local clustering coefficients. Soc. Netw. 35(2), 159–167 (2013)
15. Schoenebeck, G., Tao, B.: Beyond worst-case (in)approximability of nonsubmodular influence maximization. In: International Conference on Web and Internet Economics (2017)
16. Tang, J., Tang, X., Yuan, J.: Towards profit maximization for online social network providers. arXiv preprint arXiv:1712.08963 (2017)
17. Tang, J., Tang, X., Yuan, J.: Profit maximization for viral marketing in online social networks: algorithms and analysis. IEEE Trans. Knowl. Data Eng. 30(6), 1095–1108 (2018)
18. Tang, Y., Shi, Y., Xiao, X.: Influence maximization in near-linear time: a martingale approach. In: Proceedings of the 2015 ACM SIGMOD International Conference on Management of Data, pp. 1539–1554. ACM (2015)
19. Tang, Y., Xiao, X., Shi, Y.: Influence maximization: near-optimal time complexity meets practical efficiency. In: Proceedings of the 2014 ACM SIGMOD International Conference on Management of data, pp. 75–86. ACM (2014)
20. Wu, W.L., Zhang, Z., Du, D.Z.: Set function optimization. J. Oper. Res. Soc. China 3, 1–11 (2018)
21. Zhu, J., Zhu, J., Ghosh, S., Wu, W., Yuan, J.: Social influence maximization in hypergraph in social networks. IEEE Transactions on Network Science and Engineering, p. 1 (2018). https://doi.org/10.1109/TNSE.2018.2873759
22. Zhu, Y., Lu, Z., Bi, Y., Wu, W., Jiang, Y., Li, D.: Influence and profit: two sides of the coin. In: 2013 IEEE 13th International Conference on Data Mining (ICDM), pp. 1301–1306. IEEE (2013)

Importance Sample-Based Approximation Algorithm for Cost-Aware Targeted Viral Marketing

Canh V. Pham[1,2(✉)], Hieu V. Duong[1], and My T. Thai[3]

[1] People's Security Academy, Hanoi, Vietnam
maicanhki@gmail.com, dvhieubg95@gmail.com
[2] ORlab, University of Engineering and Technology,
Vietnam National University, Hanoi, Vietnam
[3] Department of Computer and Information Science and Engineering,
University of Florida, Gainesville, FL 32611, USA
mythai@cise.ufl.edu

Abstract. Cost-aware Targeted Viral Marketing (CTVM), a generalization of Influence Maximization (IM), has received a lot of attentions recently due to its commercial values. Previous approximation algorithms for this problem required a large number of samples to ensure approximate guarantee. In this paper, we propose an efficient approximation algorithm which uses fewer samples but provides the same theoretical guarantees based on generating and using important samples in its operation. Experiments on real social networks show that our proposed method outperforms the state-of-the-art algorithm which provides the same approximation ratio in terms of the number of required samples and running time.

Keywords: Viral marketing · Information diffusion · Approximation algorithm

1 Introduction

Online social networks (OSNs) have significantly contributed to the growth of the global economy base on providing a strong platform for communication and information dissemination. Many companies have leveraged the "word-of-mouth" effect of OSNs to conduct their marketing and advertising activities. One of the key problems in viral marketing in Online Social Networks (OSNs) is Influence Maximization (IM), which aims at selecting a set of k users, called a seed set, in a social network so that the expected number of influenced nodes is maximized. Kempe *et al.* [5] first introduced the IM problem under two classical information diffusion models, namely, Independent Cascade (IC) and Linear Threshold (LT), as a combinatorial optimization and designed a $(1 - 1/e)$-approximation algorithm. Due to its immense application potential, a vast amount of work focused

© Springer Nature Switzerland AG 2019
A. Tagarelli and H. Tong (Eds.): CSoNet 2019, LNCS 11917, pp. 120–132, 2019.
https://doi.org/10.1007/978-3-030-34980-6_14

on IM in many respects: designing effective algorithms [1,13,21,22] and studying variants with marketing applications [3,4,16,20,24,25] and its application for rumor/misinformation blocking [15,18,26].

Recently, Borgs *et al.* [1] make a theoretical breakthrough by proposing a reverse influence sketch (RIS) algorithm which is the foundation for later efficient algorithms. This algorithm captures the influences in a reverse manner and guarantees $(1-1/e-\epsilon)$-approximation solution with probability at least $1-n^{-1}$ where n is the number of nodes in the network. In a sequential work, Tang *et al.* [22] first presented a $(1-1/e)$-approximation algorithm that is scalable for billion-size networks with the running time reduces to $O((k+l)(m+n)\ln n\epsilon^{-2})$. [21] later proposed the IMM algorithm, which further reduced the number of samples of RIS process by using Martingale analysis. Nguyen *et al.* [11,13] SSA/DSSA algorithms to further reduce the running time up to orders of magnitude by modifying the original RIS framework.

In a more realistic scenario with taking into account both arbitrary cost for selecting a node and arbitrary benefit for influencing a node, Nguyen *et al.* [10] studied Cost-aware Targeted Viral Marketing (CTVM) problem, a generalization of IM, which aims to select a seed set within limited budget so that the expected total benefit over the influenced nodes (benefit function) is maximized. In this work, the benefit function can be estimated through benefit samples sampling algorithm, a generalized version of RIS and the authors proposed BCT algorithm, a $(1-1/\sqrt{e}-\epsilon)$-approximation algorithm with high probability with the number of required samples at least $O(n\ln(n^{k_{max}}/\delta)\epsilon^{-2})$ under IC model. In another direction, Li *et al.* [9] solved CTVM with an almost exact algorithm TIPTOP approach, which can return the solution within a ratio of $(1-\epsilon)$ with high probability. The algorithm needs at most $O(\frac{nk\log n}{\mathsf{OPT}_k\epsilon^2})$ samples and no bound on the time complexity as this is an exact approach, not the approximation algorithm approach. However, the authors have shown that TIPTOP can run on the Twitter datasets within four hours [9].

In this paper, we tackle CTVM via an approximation approach (not exact) with a goal of obtaining the same approximation ratio $(1-1/\sqrt{e}-\epsilon)$ as in [10], but significantly reducing the number of samples to $O(\rho n\log(k_{max}\binom{n}{k_0}/\delta)\epsilon^{-2})$ samples in the worst-case for $\rho < 1$. Our algorithm, namely Importance sample-based for Viral Marketing (IVM), contains two innovative techniques: (1) We note that importance samples (in the space of all benefit samples) can be used to estimate the benefit function. This leads to a general result of using importance sketches to estimate the influence spread function for IM [12]. (2) Base on that we design a new strategy to check approximation guarantee condition of candidate solutions. We develop two lower and upper bound functions to check approximation guarantee condition and adequate statistical evidence on the solution quality for termination. Our algorithm takes lower total samples than BCT, which is state of the art method with same approximation guarantee in both theoretical analysis and practical. In summary, the contributions of this paper are as follows.

- We first present Importance Benefit Sample (IBS) and Importance Benefit Sampling Algorithm (IBA), an algorithm to generate IBS. We then show that the benefit function can be estimated through IBS (Lemma 3).
- We proposed IVM, an efficient approximation algorithm which returns $(1 - 1/\sqrt{e} - \epsilon)$ with high probability and requires at most $O(\rho n \log(k_{max} \binom{n}{k_0})/\delta)\epsilon^{-2})$ samples in the worst-case for $\rho < 1$ under IC model.
- We conduct experiments on various real social networks. The experiments on some social networks suggest that IVM better than BCT, a current best method on CTVM with the same approximation guarantee, in terms of running time, number of required samples, and used memory. It achieves up to 153 times speed-up and the total required samples less than 112 times than that of BCT.

Organization. The rest of the paper is organized as follows. In Sect. 2, we present the model and the problem definition. Section 3 presents an analysis of generating IBS to estimate the benefit function. Our IVM algorithm along with its theoretical analysis are introduced in Sect. 4. Experimental results are shown in Sect. 5. Finally Sect. 6 concludes the paper.

2   Model and Problem Definitions

In this section, we present the well-known Independent Cascade (IC) model and the CTVM problem. The frequently used notations are summarized in Table 1.

Table 1. Table of symbols

Symbol	Notation	Symbol	Notation
n, m	# nodes and # of edges in G.	S	Seed set
$\mathbb{B}(S)$	The benefit of S	$\hat{\mathbb{B}}(S)$	An estimation of $\mathbb{B}(S)$
k_{max}	$k_{max} = \max\{k\|c(S) \leq B, \|S\| = k\}$	$\mathsf{Cov}(R_j, S)$	$\min\{1, \|R_j \cap S\|\}$
μ_{min}	$\sum_{v \in S}(1 - \gamma(v))\frac{b(u)}{\Gamma}$	μ_{max}	$\frac{\Phi}{\Gamma} + \sum_{v \in S}(1 - \gamma(v))\frac{b(u)}{\Gamma}$
ρ	$\mu_{max} - \mu_{min}$	p	$\min\{\mu_{max} - \mu_{min}, \mu_{max} + \mu_{min} - 2\sqrt{\mu_{min}\mu_{max}}\}$
S^*	An optimal solution	OPT	$\mathbb{B}(S^*)$.
Γ	$\Gamma = \sum_{u \in V} b(u)$	Φ	$\Phi = \sum_{u \in V} \gamma(u)b(u)$
$\alpha(\delta)$	$\left(1 - \frac{1}{\sqrt{e}}\right)(\ln \frac{2}{\delta})^{1/2}$	$\beta(\delta)$	$\left(1 - \frac{1}{\sqrt{e}}\right)\ln\left(\frac{2k_{max}}{\delta}\binom{n}{k_0}\right)^{1/2}$

In this model, a social network can be abstracted as a directed graph $G = (V, E)$ with a node set V and a directed edge set E, $|V| = n$ and $|E| = m$. Let $N_{in}(v)$ and $N_{out}(v)$ be the set of in-neighbors and out-neighbor of v, respectively. Each edge $e = (u, v) \in E$ has a probability $p(u, v) \in (0, 1)$ that represents the information transmission from u to v. The diffusion process from a seed set S to the rest of the network happens round by round as follows. At step 0, all nodes in S are activated while the rest of the nodes are inactive. At step $t \geq 1$, an active node u in the previous step $t - 1$ has a single chance to activate each currently inactive out neighbour node v with the successful probability $p(u, v)$. Once a node becomes activated, it remains in that state in all subsequent steps. The influence propagation stops when no more node can be activated.

Kempe *et al.* [5] showed IC model is equivalent to the reachability in a random graph g, called *live-edge* or *sample graph*. We generate a sample graph g with the set of nodes be V_g and the set of edges be E_g by: (1) setting $V_g \leftarrow V$, and (2) selecting $e = (u, v) \in E$ into E_g with probability $p(e) = p(u, v)$. The probability to generate g from G is: $\Pr[g \sim G] = \prod_{e \in E_g} p(e) \cdot \prod_{e \in E \setminus E_g}(1 - p(e))$ and the influence spread of S is calculated by:

$$\mathbb{I}(S) = \sum_{g \sim G} \Pr[g \sim G]|R(g, S)| \tag{1}$$

where $R(g, S)$ denotes the set of reachable nodes from S in g. In CTVM, each node $u \in V$ has a cost $c(u) > 0$ if it is selected into the seed set S and a benefit $b(u) \geq 0$ if it is activated. The total benefit over all influenced nodes (benefit function) of seed set S is defined as follows:

$$\mathbb{B}(S) = \sum_{g \sim G} \Pr[g \sim G] \sum_{u \in R(g, S)} b(u) \tag{2}$$

CTVM problem is formally defined as follows.

Definition 1 (CTVM). *Given a social network $G = (V, E, w)$ with a node set V and a directed edge set E under a IC model. Each node $u \in V$ has a selecting cost $c(u) \geq 0$ and a benefit $b(u)$ if u is active. Given a budget $B > 0$, find a seed set $S \subset V$ with the total cost $c(S) \leq B$ to maximize $\mathbb{B}(S)$.*

3   Importance Benefit Sampling

In this section, we first recap the Benefit Sampling Algorithm (BSA) to estimate the benefit function [10,14]. We then introduce our novel Importance Benefit Sample (IBS) concept along with the algorithm to generate these samples.

Benefit Sampling Algorithm (BSA) [10] generates Benefit Sample according to the following steps: (1) picking a node u as a source node with probability $\frac{b(u)}{\Gamma}$, (2) generating a sample graph g from G and (3) returning R_j as the set of nodes that can reach v in g. Denote $\mathcal{R}$ as a collection of benefit samples generated by BSA and define a random variable $Y_j = \min\{|R_j \cap A|, 1\}$. Nguyen *et al.* [10] prove the following Lemma to estimate the benefit function:

Lemma 1. *For any set of nodes $S \subset V$, we have: $\mathbb{B}(S) = \Gamma \cdot \mathbb{E}[Y_j]$*

Let Ω be a set of all benefit samples and $R_j(u)$ be a benefit sample with source node u, the probability of generating $R_j(u)$ is

$$\Pr[R_j(u) \sim \Omega] = \frac{b(u)}{\Gamma} \sum_{g \in G: u \in R(g,S)} \Pr[g \sim G] \tag{3}$$

We now describe the IBS and algorithm that generates IBS. The main idea of this method is based on the observation that benefit samples containing only one node contributes insignificantly in calculating the benefit function. For a source node u, assume Ω_u is set of all benefit samples that has source node u. We divide Ω_u into two components: Ω_u^0 - singular benefit samples which contain only node u, and Ω_u^n - importance benefit samples which contain at least two nodes. Let $N_{in}(u) = \{v_1, v_2, \ldots, v_l\}$, denote E_0 as the event that none of nodes in $N_{in}(u)$ is selected, we have $\Pr[E_0] = \prod_{v \in N_{in}(u)}(1 - p(v,u))$. The probability of generating an IBS with source node u is equal to $\gamma(u) = 1 - \Pr[E_0]$. Denote E_i as the event that v_i is the first selected node, we have:

$$\Pr[E_i] = p(v_i, u) \cdot \prod_{j=1}^{i-1}(1 - p(v_j, u)) \tag{4}$$

Events $E_0, E_1, \ldots, E_l$ are disjoint sets and $\sum_{i=0}^{l} \Pr[E_i] = 1$. The probability of generating an IBS that has source node u with v_i is the first selected node is

$$\Pr[E_i | R_j(u) \in \Omega_u^n] = \Pr[E_i]/\gamma(u) \tag{5}$$

Denote Ω^n as the probability spaces of all IBSs, we have:

$$\Pr[R_j(u) \sim \Omega^n] = \frac{1}{\gamma(u)} \Pr[R_j(u) \sim \Omega] \tag{6}$$

The probability that u is a source node of an IBS R_j in Ω is $\frac{b(u)}{\Gamma}\gamma(u)$. By normalizing factor to fulfill a probability distribution of a sample space, the probability that u is a source node of an IBS R_j in Ω^n is calculated as follows:

$$\Pr[src(R_j) = u] = \frac{\gamma(u)b(u)}{\sum_{u \in V} \gamma(u)b(u)} = \frac{\gamma(u)b(u)}{\Phi} \tag{7}$$

Lemma 2. *For any IBS R_j, we have* $\Pr[R_j \sim \Omega] = \frac{\Phi}{\Gamma} \cdot \Pr[R_j \sim \Omega^n]$

Based on the above analysis, we propose IBA, an algorithm to generate an IBS, which is depicted in Algorithm 1. The algorithm first selects a source node u with a probability according to Eq. (7) (line 1). It next picks the first incoming node to u (line 2). The rest algorithm is similar to the Importance Influence Sampling Algorithm [12]. For any IBS R_j is generated by IBA, we define random variables $X_j(S) = \min\{1, |S \cap R_j|\}$, and

$$Z_j(S) = \frac{\Phi}{\Gamma} \cdot X_j(S) + \sum_{v \in S}(1 - \gamma(v))\frac{b(u)}{\Gamma} \tag{8}$$

Algorithm 1: IBA for IC model

Input: Graph $G = (V, E)$ under IC model
Output: A Benefit Important Samples R_j
1. Pick a source node u with probability in eq. (7)
2. Select an in-neighbour $v_i \in N_{in}(u)$ of u with probability $\Pr[E_i]/\gamma(u)$
3. Initialize a queue $Q = \{v_i\}$ and $R_j = i, v_i$
4. **for** $t = i + 1$ *to* l **do**
5. $\quad$ | $\quad$ With probability $p(v_t, u)$: $Q.push(v_t)$ and $R_j \leftarrow R_j \cup \{v_t\}$
6. **end**
7. **while** Q *is not empty* **do**
8. $\quad$ | $\quad$ $v \leftarrow Q.pop()$
9. $\quad$ | $\quad$ **foreach** $u \in N_{in}(v) \setminus (R_j \cup Q)$ **do**
10. $\quad$ | $\quad$ | $\quad$ $Q.push(u)$, $R_j \leftarrow R_j \cup \{u\}$
11. $\quad$ | $\quad$ **end**
12. **end**
13. **return** R_j

We have $Z_j(S) \in [\mu_{min}, \mu_{max}]$, with $\mu_{min} = \sum_{v \in S}(1 - \gamma(v))\frac{b(u)}{\Gamma}, \mu_{max} = \frac{\Phi}{\Gamma} + \sum_{v \in S}(1 - \gamma(v))\frac{b(u)}{\Gamma}$.

Lemma 3. *For any set of nodes $A \subseteq V$, we have:*

$$\mathbb{B}(S) = \Phi \cdot \mathbb{E}[X_j(S)] + \sum_{v \in S}(1 - \gamma(v))b(u) = \Gamma \cdot \mathbb{E}[Z_j(S)] \qquad (9)$$

Proof. Let $\mathsf{Cov}(S, R_j) = \min\{1, |R_j \cap A|\}$ and $\Omega^0 = \Omega \setminus \Omega^n$. From Lemma 1, we have $\mathbb{B}(S) = \Gamma \cdot \sum_{R_j \in \Omega} \Pr[R_j \sim \Omega]\mathsf{Cov}(S, R_j)$

$$= \Gamma \cdot \left(\sum_{R_j \in \Omega^0} \Pr[R_j \sim \Omega]\mathsf{Cov}(S, R_j) + \sum_{R_j \in \Omega^n} \Pr[R_j \sim \Omega]\mathsf{Cov}(S, R_j) \right) \qquad (10)$$

Since each $R_j \in \Omega \setminus \Omega^n$ contains only source node, $X_j(S) = 1$ if $R_j \in S$. In this case, we have $\Pr[R_j \sim \Omega] = \frac{b(u)}{\Gamma}(1 - \gamma(u))$, with $u = src(R_j)$. Put it into (10), we have:

$$\mathbb{B}(S) = \Gamma \sum_{u \in S} \frac{b(u)}{\Gamma}(1 - \gamma(u)) + \Gamma \sum_{R_j \in \Omega^n} \Pr[R_j \sim \Omega]\mathsf{Cov}(S, R_j) \qquad (11)$$

$$= \sum_{u \in S} b(u)(1 - \gamma(u)) + \Gamma \sum_{R_j \in \Omega^n} \frac{\Phi}{\Gamma} \Pr[R_j \sim \Omega^n]\mathsf{Cov}(S, R_j) \qquad (12)$$

$$= \sum_{u \in S} b(u)(1 - \gamma(u)) + \Phi\mathbb{E}[Z_j(S)] \qquad (13)$$

This completes the proof.

Basically, Lemma 3 generalizes the result of Lemma 3 in [12] in which important reverse reachable sets (sketches) can be used to estimate the influence spread. Therefore, an estimation $\mathbb{B}(S)$ over a collection of IBS $\mathcal{R}$ is:

$$\hat{\mathbb{B}}(S) = \frac{\Phi}{|\mathcal{R}|} \sum_{R_j \in \mathcal{R}} \mathsf{Cov}(S, R_j) + \sum_{v \in S}(1 - \gamma(v))b(u) = \frac{\Gamma}{|\mathcal{R}|} \sum_{i=1}^{|\mathcal{R}|} Z_j(S) \qquad (14)$$

4   Importance Sample-Based Viral Marketing Algorithm

We present Importance Sample-based Viral Marketing (IVM), an $(1 - 1/\sqrt{e} - \epsilon)$-approximation algorithm for CTVM. IVM includes two components: generating IBS to estimate the benefit function and new strategy to find candidate solution and checks its approximation guarantee condition by developing two *lower* and *upper bound* functions.

Algorithm Description. Our IVM algorithm is depicted in Algorithm 2. At first glance, the IVM maintains one stream of samples similar to BCT. However, it has changed checking solution quality and limiting the maximum required samples. It first calculates the maximum number of IBSs $N_{max} = N(\epsilon, \frac{\delta}{3}) \cdot \frac{OPT}{lOPT}$ (line 1), where $lOPT$ is a lower-bound of OPT, which significantly reduces the number of required samples while still ensuring total samples. IVM then generates a set of IBSs $\mathcal{R}_1$ contains N_1 samples (line 2). The main phrase consists of at most $t_{max} = \left\lceil \log_2 \frac{N_{max}}{N_1} \right\rceil$ iterations (line 4–14). In each iterator t, the algorithm maintains a set R_t consists $N_1 \cdot 2^{t-1}$ and finds a candidate solution S_t by using Improve Greedy Algorithm (IGA) for Budgeted Maximum Coverage (BMC) problem [6]. IGA finds solution for instance $(\mathcal{R}_t, b(u), B)$ in which $\mathcal{R}_t$ is a set of samples, V is the universal set and B is the budget. This algorithm returns $(1 - 1/\sqrt{e})$-approximation solution [6] (due to limitation of space, we put IGA and alg. for calculating $lOPT$ in Appendix). The main algorithm then calculates: $f_l(R_t, \delta_1)$ - a lower bound of $\mathbb{B}(S_t)$ and $f_u(\mathcal{R}_t, \delta_1)$ - an upper bound of optimal value OPT (line 7). We show that $\Pr[f_l(R_t, \delta_1) \geq \mathbb{B}(S_t)] \geq 1 - \delta_1$ (Lemma 6) and $\Pr[f_u(R_t, \delta_1) \geq OPT] \geq 1 - \delta_1$ (Lemma 7). The algorithm checks approximation guarantee condition: $\frac{f_l(\mathcal{R}_t, \delta_1)}{f_u(\mathcal{R}_t, \delta_1)} \geq 1 - 1/\sqrt{e} - \epsilon$ (line 8). If this condition is true, it returns S_t as a solution and terminates. If not, it doubles number of samples (line 12) and moves onto the next iterator $t + 1$.

Theoretical Analysis. We observe that $Z_j(S) \in [0, 1]$. Let randomly variable $M_i = \sum_{j=1}^{i}(Z_j(S) - \mu), \forall i \geq 1$, where $\mu = \mathbb{E}[Z_j]$. For a sequence random variables $M_1, M_2, \ldots$ we have $\mathbb{E}[M_i | M_1, \ldots, M_{j-1}] = \mathbb{E}[M_{i-1}] + \mathbb{E}[Z_i(S) - \mu] = \mathbb{E}[M_{i-1}]$. Hence, $M_1, M_2, \ldots$ be a form of martingale [2]. We have following result from [2]

Lemma 4. *If $M_1, M_2, \ldots$ be a form of martingale, $|M_1| \leq a$, $|M_j - M_{j-1}| \leq a$ for $j \in [1, i]$, and*

$$\mathsf{Var}[M_1] + \sum_{j=2}^{i} \mathsf{Var}[M_j | M_1, M_2, \ldots, M_{j-1}] = b \qquad (15)$$

Algorithm 2: IVM algorithm

Input: Graph $G = (V, E)$, budget $B > 0$, and $\epsilon, \delta \in (0, 1)$
Output: seed S

1. $N_{max} \leftarrow N(\epsilon, \frac{\delta}{3}) \cdot \frac{\text{OPT}}{\text{IOPT}}$.
2. $N_1 \leftarrow \frac{1}{\epsilon^2} \ln \frac{1}{\delta}$, $t \leftarrow 1$, $N_0 \leftarrow 0$
3. $t_{max} \leftarrow \left\lceil \log_2 \frac{N_{max}}{N_1} \right\rceil$, $\delta_1 \leftarrow \frac{\delta}{3t_{max}}$
4. **repeat**
5. $\quad$ Generate more $N_t - N_{t-1}$ IBSs and add them into $\mathcal{R}_t$
6. $\quad < S_t, \hat{\mathbb{B}}(S_t) > \leftarrow \text{IGA}(\mathcal{R}_t, B)$
7. $\quad$ Calculate $f_l(\mathcal{R}_t, \delta_1)$ by Lemma 6 and calculate $f_u(\mathcal{R}_t, \delta_1)$ by Lemma 7.
8. $\quad$ **if** $\frac{f_l(\mathcal{R}_t, \delta_1)}{f_u(\mathcal{R}_t, \delta_1)} \geq 1 - 1/\sqrt{e} - \epsilon$ **then**
9. $\quad\quad$ **return** S_t
10. $\quad$ **else**
11. $\quad\quad$ $t \leftarrow t + 1$, $R_t \leftarrow R_{t-1}$, $N_t \leftarrow 2N_{t-1}$
12. $\quad$ **end**
13. **until** $|\mathcal{R}_t| \geq N_{max}$;
14. **return** S_t;

---

where $\mathsf{Var}[\cdot]$ *denotes the variance of a random variable. Then, for any* λ, *we have:*

$$\Pr[M_i - \mathbb{E}[M_i] \geq \lambda] \geq \exp\left(-\frac{\lambda^2}{\frac{2}{3}a\lambda + 2b}\right) \qquad (16)$$

Apply Martingale theory [2], we have the following Lemma:

Lemma 5. *For any* $T > 0, \lambda > 0$, μ *is the mean of* $Z_j(S)$, *and an estimation of* μ *is* $\hat{\mu} = \frac{\sum_{i=1}^{T} Z_i(S)}{T}$, *we have:*

$$\Pr\left[\sum_{j=1}^{T} Z_j(S) - T \cdot \mu \geq \lambda\right] \leq \exp\left(-\frac{\lambda^2}{\frac{2}{3}(\mu_{max} - \mu_{min})\lambda + 2p\mu T}\right) \qquad (17)$$

$$\Pr\left[\sum_{j=1}^{T} Z_j(S) - T \cdot \mu \geq -\lambda\right] \leq \exp\left(-\frac{\lambda^2}{2p\mu T}\right) \qquad (18)$$

Assume that S is a feasible solution of CTVM. Since we do not known the size of S, we can observe that the number of possible solutions is less than $\sum_{k=1}^{k_{max}} \binom{k}{n} \leq k_{max}\binom{k_0}{n}$, where $k_0 = \arg\max_{k=1...k_{max}} \binom{k}{n}$.

Theorem 1. *For* $\epsilon > 0$, $\delta \in (0, 1)$. *If the number of samples* $|\mathcal{R}| \geq N(\epsilon, \delta) = \frac{2\rho\Gamma\epsilon^{-2}}{\text{OPT}}(\alpha(\delta) + \beta(\delta))^2$, *IGA returns a* $(1 - 1/\sqrt{e} - \epsilon)$-*approximation solution with probability at least* $1 - \delta$.

We can apply Theorem 1 to obtain the following Corollary:

Corollary 1. *At iterator t, $\Pr[(N_t \geq N_{max}) \wedge (\mathbb{B}(S_t) < (1 - \frac{1}{\sqrt{e}} - \epsilon)\mathsf{OPT})] \geq 1 - \delta_1$*

Due to the space constraint, we omit some proofs and presented our full version [17]. By using Lemma 5, we give two lower-bound and upper-bound functions in Lemma 6 and Lemma 7. They help the main algorithm check the approximate condition of the candidate based on statistical evidence.

Lemma 6 (Lower-bound). *For any $\delta \in (0,1)$, a set of IBSs $\mathcal{R}$ and $\hat{\mathbb{B}}(S)$ is an estimation of $\mathbb{B}(S)$ over $\mathcal{R}$ by (14). Let $c = \ln(\frac{1}{\delta})$ and*

$$f_l(\mathcal{R}, \delta) = \min\left\{ \hat{\mathbb{B}}(S) - \frac{\rho c \Gamma}{3T}, \hat{\mathbb{B}}(S) - \frac{\Gamma}{T}\left(\frac{\rho c}{3} - cp + \sqrt{\left(\frac{\rho c}{3} - cp\right)^2 + 2Tpc\frac{\hat{\mathbb{B}}(S)}{\Gamma}} \right) \right\}$$

we have $\Pr[\mathbb{B}(S) \geq \hat{\mathbb{B}}(S)] \geq 1 - \delta$.

Lemma 7 (Upper-bound). *For any $\delta \in (0,1)$, a set of IBSs $\mathcal{R}$, S_G is a solution return by IGA for input data $(\mathcal{R}, B)$, and $\hat{\mathbb{B}}(S_G)$ is an estimation of $\mathbb{B}(S)$ over $\mathcal{R}$ by (14). Let*

$$f_u(\mathcal{R}, \delta) = \frac{\hat{\mathbb{B}}(S_G)}{1 - 1/\sqrt{e}} + \frac{\Gamma}{T}\left(-cp + \sqrt{c^2 p^2 + 2Tcp\frac{\hat{\mathbb{B}}(S_G)}{(1 - 1/\sqrt{e})\Gamma}} \right) \qquad (19)$$

we have $\Pr[\mathsf{OPT} \leq f_u(\mathcal{R}, \delta)] \geq 1 - \delta$.

Theorem 2 (Main Theorem). *IVM returns $(1 - 1/\sqrt{e} - \epsilon)$-approximation solution algorithm with probability at least $1 - \delta$.*

Proof. We consider following events. $E_1(t)$: $f_l(\mathcal{R}_t, \delta_1) > \mathbb{B}(S_t)$, $E_2(t)$: $f_u(\mathcal{R}_t, \delta_1) < \mathsf{OPT}$ and E_3 : $(|\mathcal{R}_t| \geq N_{max}) \wedge (\mathbb{B}(S_{t_{max}}) < (1 - \frac{1}{\sqrt{e}} - \epsilon)\mathsf{OPT})$. According to Lemmas 6, 7, and Corollary 1, we have: $\Pr[E_1(t)] \leq \delta_1, \Pr[E_2(t)] \leq \delta_1$ and $\Pr[E_3] \leq \delta/t_{max}$. Apply the union bound the probability that none of events $E_1(t), E_e(t), E_3, \forall t = 1, \ldots, t_{max}$ at least $1 - \left(\delta_1 \cdot t_{max} + \delta_1 \cdot t_{max} + \frac{\delta}{3}\right) = 1 - \delta$. Under this assumption, we will show that IVM returns a solution satisfying $\mathbb{B}(S_t) \geq (1 - 1/\sqrt{e} - \epsilon)\mathsf{OPT}$. If the algorithm stops with condition $|\mathcal{R}_t| \geq N_{max}$, the solution S_t satisfies approximation guarantee due to Corollary 1. Otherwise, if IVM stops at some iterator $t, t = 1, 2, \ldots, t_{max}$. At this iterator, the condition in line 8 is satisfied, i.e. $\frac{\mathbb{B}(S_t)}{\mathsf{OPT}} \geq \frac{f_l(\mathcal{R}_t, \epsilon_1)}{f_u(\mathcal{R}_t, \epsilon_1)} \geq 1 - 1/\sqrt{e} - \epsilon$. This completes the proof. $\square$

From Corollary 1, IVM needs at most $N_{max} = N(\epsilon, \delta/3)\frac{\mathsf{OPT}}{l\mathsf{OPT}} = \frac{2\rho\Gamma\epsilon^{-2}}{l\mathsf{OPT}}(\alpha(\delta/3) + \beta(\delta/3))^2$ samples. We have $(\alpha(\delta/3) + \beta(\delta/3))^2 \leq 2(\alpha^2(\delta/3) + \beta^2(\delta/3)) = 2(1 - \frac{1}{\sqrt{e}})(\ln\frac{1}{\delta} + \ln(k_{max}\binom{n}{k_0}/\delta) + \ln 18)$. Combine with $\Gamma \leq b_{max}n$, we have $N_{max} \in O(\rho n \ln(k_{max}\binom{n}{k_0}/\delta)\epsilon^{-2})$.

5   Experiment

In this section, we briefly conduct experiments to compare the performance of our algorithm IVM to other algorithms for CTVM on for aspects: the solution quality, running time, number of required samples and used memory.

5.1   Experimental Settings

Datasets. We select a diverse set of 4 datasets including Gnutella, Epinion Amazon and DBLP. The description used datasets is provided in Table 2.

Table 2. Dataset

Dataset	#Node	#Edge	Type	Avg. degree	Source
Gnutella	6.301	20.777	Directed	3.3	[8]
Epinion	75.879	508.837	Directed	6.7	[19]
Amazon	262.111	1.234.877	Directed	4.7	[7]
DBLP	317.080	1.049.866	Undirected	3.21	[23]

Algorithms Compared. We compare the IVM algorithm against the BCT algorithm [10], the state-of-the-art algorithm for CTVM with the same approximation ratio, and two baseline algorithms: Random and Degree.
Parameter Setting. We follow previous works on CTVM and IM [10,14,21] to set up parameters. The transmission probability $p(u, v)$ is randomly selected in $\{0.001, 0.01, 0.1\}$ according to the Trivalency model. The cost of a node proportional to the out-degree [10]: $c(u) = n|N_{out}(u)| / \sum_{v \in V} |N_{out}(v)|$. In all the experiments, we choose a random $p = 20\%$ of all the nodes to be the target set and assign benefit 1 and we set $\epsilon = 0.1$ and $\delta = 1/n$ as a default setting. The budget B varies from 1 to 1000.

5.2   Experiment Results

IVM outperforms other algorithms and gives the best result on Amazon network. It provides up to 5.4 times better than BCT on Amazon. For Gnutella, Epinions and DBLP networks gives similar result to BCT. This is because these two algorithms give the same approximation ratio for CTVM. Figure 1 shows the benefit value provided by algorithms. IVM outperforms other algorithms and gives the best result on Amazon network. It provides up to 5.4 times better than BCT on Amazon. For Gnutella, Epinions and DBLP networks gives similar result to BCT. This is because these two algorithms give the same approximation ratio for CTVM.

The running time of algorithms is shown in Table 3. The running time of our algorithm in all networks are significantly lower than that of BCT. IVM is up to

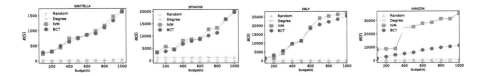

Fig. 1. The benefit function achieved by algorithms

Table 3. Running time between IVM and BCT (sec.) for CTVM

Network		Budget B									
		100	200	300	400	500	600	700	800	900	1000
Gnutella	IVM	4.10^{-3}	6.10^{-3}	2.10^{-3}	3.10^{-3}	2.10^{-3}	3.10^{-3}	0.01	7.10^{-3}	9.10^{-3}	7.10^{-3}
	BCT	0.02	0.015	0.02	0.016	0.018	0.02	0.022	0.021	0.01	0.01
Epinion	IVM	1.09	1.4	0.9	1	1.1	1	1	0.9	0.87	0.9
	BCT	7.8	0.95	6.7	3.1	3.6	3.4	3.4	3.5	1.1	1
Amazon	IVM	0.01	0.01	0.01	0.01	0.012	0.012	0.01	0.03	0.04	0.03
	BCT	1.73	0.31	0.89	0.50	0.49	0.49	0.31	0.27	0.32	0.4
DBLP	IVM	1.7	0.14	0.8	0.4	0.2	0.23	0.13	0.13	0.14	0.14
	BCT	2.6	0.4	1.7	1.9	1.1	1.2	0.7	0.6	0.5	0.4

6.4, 7.1, 153 and 4.8 times faster than BCT on Gnutella, Epinion, Amazon and DBLP networks.

Table 4 displays the memory usage and the number of required samples of IVM and BCT when the budget $B = 1000$. The number of samples generated by IVM is up to more 112 times smaller than that of BCT. However, the memory usage of IVM is only 1.5 to 4.6 times smaller than those of BCT because of the memory for storing the graph is counted into the memory usage of each algorithm. This results also confirm our theoretical establishment in Sect. 4 that IVM requires much less number of samples needed.

Table 4. Number of samples and total memory between IVM and BCT for $B = 1000$

Algorithm	Total samples ($\times 10^3$)				Memory usage (M)			
	Gnutella	Epinion	Amazon	DBLP	Gnutella	Epinion	Amazon	DBLP
IVM	0.99	1.12	1.25	1.27	5.9	46	53	66
BCT	10	10	270	140	22	67	95	102

6   Conclusion

In this paper, we propose IVM, an efficient approximation algorithm for CTVM, which has an approximation ratio of $1 - \frac{1}{\sqrt{e}} - \epsilon$ and the number of required samples is $O(\rho n \log(k_{max} \binom{n}{k_0})/\delta)\epsilon^{-2})$, which is significantly lower than that of the state-of-the-art BCT. Experiments show that IVM is up to 153 times faster and requires up to 112 times fewer total samples than the BCT algorithm. For the future work, we plan to implement this importance sampling concept on the exact approach TIPTOP to evaluate potential benefits of the importance sampling in terms of running time and number of required samples.

Acknowledgements. This work is partially supported by NSF CNS-1443905, NSF EFRI 1441231, and NSF NSF CNS-1814614 grants.

References

1. Borgs, C., Brautbar, M., Chayes, J.T., Lucier, B.: Maximizing social influence in nearly optimal time. In: Proceedings of the 25th Annual ACM-SIAM Symposium on Discrete Algorithms, SODA 2014, pp. 946–957 (2014)
2. Chung, F.R.K., Lu, L.: Survey: concentration inequalities and martingale inequalities: a survey. Internet Math. **3**(1), 79–127 (2006)
3. Dinh, T.N., Nguyen, D.T., Thai, M.T.: Cheap, easy, and massively effective viral marketing in social networks: truth or fiction? In: 23rd ACM Conference on Hypertext and Social Media, HT 2012, pp. 165–174 (2012)
4. Dinh, T.N., Shen, Y., Nguyen, D.T., Thai, M.T.: On the approximability of positive influence dominating set in social networks. J. Comb. Optim. **27**(3), 487–503 (2014)
5. Kempe, D., Kleinberg, J.M., Tardos, É.: Maximizing the spread of influence through a social network. In: Proceedings of the Ninth ACM International Conference on Knowledge Discovery and Data Mining SIGKDD, pp. 137–146 (2003)
6. Khuller, S., Moss, A., Naor, J.: The budgeted maximum coverage problem. Inf. Process. Lett. **70**(1), 39–45 (1999)
7. Leskovec, J., Adamic, L.A., Huberman, B.A.: The dynamics of viral marketing. ACM TWEB **1**(1), 5 (2007)
8. Leskovec, J., Kleinberg, J.M., Faloutsos, C.: Graph evolution: densification and shrinking diameters. TKDD **1**(1), 2 (2007)
9. Li, X., Smith, J.D., Dinh, T.N., Thai, M.T.: Why approximate when you can get the exact? Optimal targeted viral marketing at scale. In: 2017 IEEE Conference on Computer Communications, INFOCOM 2017, pp. 1–9 (2017)
10. Nguyen, H.T., Dinh, T.N., Thai, M.T.: Cost-aware targeted viral marketing in billion-scale networks. In: 35th Annual IEEE International Conference on Computer Communications, INFOCOM, pp. 1–9 (2016)
11. Nguyen, H.T., Dinh, T.N., Thai, M.T.: Revisiting of 'revisiting the stop-and-stare algorithms for influence maximization'. In: 7th International Conference on Computational Data and Social Networks, CSoNet 2018, pp. 273–285 (2018)
12. Nguyen, H.T., Nguyen, T.P., Phan, N.H., Dinh, T.N.: Importance sketching of influence dynamics in billion-scale networks. In: 2017 IEEE International Conference on Data Mining, ICDM 2017, pp. 337–346 (2017)
13. Nguyen, H.T., Thai, M.T., Dinh, T.N.: Stop-and-stare: optimal sampling algorithms for viral marketing in billion-scale networks. In: Proceedings of the 2016 International Conference on Management of Data, SIGMOD, pp. 695–710 (2016)
14. Nguyen, H.T., Thai, M.T., Dinh, T.N.: A billion-scale approximation algorithm for maximizing benefit in viral marketing. IEEE/ACM Trans. Netw. **25**(4), 2419–2429 (2017)
15. Nguyen, N.P., Yan, G., Thai, M.T.: Analysis of misinformation containment in online social networks. Comput. Netw. **57**(10), 2133–2146 (2013)

16. Pham, C.V., Duong, H.V., Hoang, H.X., Thai, M.T.: Competitive influence maximization within time and budget constraints in online social networks: an algorithmic approach. Appl. Sci. **9**(11), 2274 (2019)
17. Pham, C.V., Duong, H.V., Thai, M.T.: Importance sample-based approximation algorithm for cost-aware targeted viral marketing. https://arxiv.org/abs/1910.04134
18. Pham, C.V., Thai, M.T., Duong, H.V., Bui, B.Q., Hoang, H.X.: Maximizing misinformation restriction within time and budget constraints. J. Comb. Optim. **35**(4), 1202–1240 (2018). https://doi.org/10.1007/s10878-018-0252-3
19. Richardson, M., Agrawal, R., Domingos, P.: Trust management for the semantic web. In: Fensel, D., Sycara, K., Mylopoulos, J. (eds.) ISWC 2003. LNCS, vol. 2870, pp. 351–368. Springer, Heidelberg (2003). https://doi.org/10.1007/978-3-540-39718-2_23
20. Shen, Y., Dinh, T.N., Zhang, H., Thai, M.T.: Interest-matching information propagation in multiple online social networks. In: 21st ACM International Conference on Information and Knowledge Management, CIKM 2012, pp. 1824–1828 (2012)
21. Tang, Y., Shi, Y., Xiao, X.: Influence maximization in near-linear time: a martingale approach. In: Proceedings of the 2015 ACM International Conference on Management of Data (SIGMOD), pp. 1539–1554 (2015)
22. Tang, Y., Xiao, X., Shi, Y.: Influence maximization: near-optimal time complexity meets practical efficiency. In: International Conference on Management of Data, SIGMOD 2014, pp. 75–86 (2014)
23. Yang, J., Leskovec, J.: Defining and evaluating network communities based on ground-truth. In: 12th IEEE International Conference on Data Mining, ICDM 2012, Brussels, Belgium, 10–13 December 2012, pp. 745–754 (2012)
24. Zhang, H., Nguyen, D.T., Zhang, H., Thai, M.T.: Least cost influence maximization across multiple social networks. IEEE/ACM Trans. Netw. **24**(2), 929–939 (2016)
25. Zhang, H., Zhang, H., Kuhnle, A., Thai, M.T.: Profit maximization for multiple products in online social networks. In: 35th Annual IEEE International Conference on Computer Communications, INFOCOM 2016, San Francisco, CA, USA, 10–14 April 2016, pp. 1–9 (2016)
26. Zhang, H., Zhang, H., Li, X., Thai, M.T.: Limiting the spread of misinformation while effectively raising awareness in social networks. In: Thai, M.T., Nguyen, N.P., Shen, H. (eds.) CSoNet 2015. LNCS, vol. 9197, pp. 35–47. Springer, Cham (2015). https://doi.org/10.1007/978-3-319-21786-4_4

Location-Based Competitive Influence Maximization in Social Networks

Manh M. Vu[1,2] and Huan X. Hoang[1(✉)]

[1] University of Engineering and Technology, Vietnam National University,
Hanoi, Viet Nam
vuminhmanh@gmail.com, huanhx@vnu.edu.vn

[2] Faculty of Information and Security, People's Security Academy, Hanoi, Viet Nam

Abstract. Although the competitive influence maximization (CIM) problem has been extensively studies, existing works ignore the fact that location information can play an important role in influence propagation. In this paper, we study the location-based competitive influence maximization (LCIM) problem, which aims to select an optimal set of users of a player or a company to maximize the influence for given query region, while at the same time their competitors are conducting a similar strategy. We propose a greedy algorithm with $(1 - 1/e - \epsilon)$ approximation ratio and a heuristic algorithm LCIM-MIA based on MIA structure. Experimental results on real-world datasets show that our methods often better than several baseline algorithms.

Keywords: Location-based · Competitive influence maximization · Diffusion model · Social networks

1 Introduction

The study of influence propagation in OSNs has attracted a great deal of attention in recent years. One the fundamental problems in this area is influence maximization (IM) which is first formulated by Kempe et al. [1]. To solve the IM problem, different algorithms are proposed [1,4,8,9,11].

Apart from improving the efficiency of IM solutions, some other works have extended IM problem by incorporating more realistic aspects. Li et al. [5] is the first to study the problem of location-aware influence maximization (LIM) problem, with a focus on region queries: given a geographical region R, it aims to find a k-sized seed set S that maximizes the influence over R. Wang et al. [6] studied the location-aware promotion problem, but focused on distance-aware query. Li et al. [7] considered the LIM problem and suggested a community based seeds selection algorithm based on community detection and the MIA structure.

In reality, it is often the case that many different opinions, products and innovations are spreading concurrently in a social network. Bharathi et al. [2] is the first to propose the competition influence maximization (CIM) problem. The goal of the CIM problem is to find an optimal seed set of size at most k for

© Springer Nature Switzerland AG 2019
A. Tagarelli and H. Tong (Eds.): CSoNet 2019, LNCS 11917, pp. 133–140, 2019.
https://doi.org/10.1007/978-3-030-34980-6_15

the competitors in a social network such that one's own influence is maximized while his opponents carry out the same strategy. Zhu et al. [10] proposed a generalized competitive IC model and considered a node can serve as the seed for multiple diffusions. He et al. [3] studied the problem that one entity tries to block the influence propagation of its competing entity as much as possible by strategically selecting a number of seed nodes. They introduced the competitive linear threshold (CLT) model as an extension to the LT model.

Most existing work on the IM problem consider only either location aspect [5–7] or competitive cenarios [2–4, 10]. Therefore, in this paper, we consider both geographical region constraint and competitive situation for the influence maximization task. We introduce the problem named *Location-Based Competitive Influence Maximization* (LCIM). Our contributions in this paper are summarized as follows:

- Our work is the first to study the LCIM problem under the competitive independent cascade model. We show that the problem is NP-hard and the objective function is *monotone* and *submodular*.
- We propose a greedy algorithm to solve the LCIM problem guarantees an approximation ratio of $(1 - 1/e - \epsilon)$. To scalabe for large-scale network, we design an efficient heuristic algorithm based on MIA structure called LCIM-MIA. Due to difference between classic IC model and CIC model, we redesign suitable influence computation in MIA structure under CIC model.
- We conduct experiments with several real-world social network datasets. The results demonstrate the effectiveness and efficiency of our algorithms.

2   Model and Problem Definition

2.1   Diffusion Model

In this paper, we use the homogeneous CIC model proposed in [4] with proportional probability tie-breaking rule to simulate information propagation.

2.2   Problem Definition

In a location-based social network, each node $v \in V$ has a geographical location (x, y), where x and y denote the longitude and latitude of v respectively.

Assume that the initial seed set of competitor B is known. Given a query $Q = (R, k)$, where R is a geographical region, k is the size of the initial seed set of competitor A. We formulate the location-based competitive influence maximization (LCIM) problem as follows:

Definition 1. *(Location-Based Competitive Influence Maximization) Given a location-based social network $G = (V, E)$, a competitive influence diffusion model on G for two competitors A and B, a B-seed set $S_0^B \subseteq V$, and a query $Q = (R, k)$, the location-based competitive influence maximization problem is to find a A-seed set $S_0^A \subseteq V \setminus S_0^B$ of size k, such as the influence spread of S_0^A in R is maximized.*

Given a A-seed set S_0^A and a B-seed set S_0^B, let $\sigma(S_0^A, S_0^B, R)$ denote the expected number of A-*active* nodes which are located in R after the diffusion ends. Then, the LICM problem is the problem of finding a A-seed set S_0^A of size k such that $\sigma(S_0^A, S_0^B, R)$ is maximized.

Theorem 1. *The LICM problem is NP-hard under the homogeneous CIC model and computing the objective function $\sigma(S_0^A, S_0^B, R)$ is #P-hard.*

Theorem 2. *The objective function $\sigma(S_0^A, S_0^B, R)$ is submodular and monotone.*

3   Proposed Algorithms

3.1   Greedy Algorithm

We have shown that the objective function of the LICM problem is submodular and monotone. Therefore, we can use the greedy algorithm to find a good enough solution. By the famous result in [1,4], the greedy algorithm can achieve a $(1 - 1/e)$-approximate solution.

The greedy algorithm simply selects seed nodes one by one, and each round i, one element u is added into the candidate set S_0^A, such that u provides the largest marginal contribution to objective function σ. However, the greedy algorithm requires repeated evaluations of $\sigma(S_0^A, S_0^B, R)$, which as shown in Theorem 1, is #P-hard. Thus, we address this efficiency issue in the next section with our new algorithm LICM-MIA.

3.2   LCIM-MIA Algorithm for the LICM Problem

Due to the low efficiency of the greedy algorithm, we use the maximum influence arborescence (MIA) structure [8] to compute objective function $\sigma(S_0^A, S_0^B, R)$.

Given a seed set $S \subseteq G$, the activation probability of any node v in $MIIA(u, \theta)$, denoted as $ap(v, S, MIIA(u, \theta))$, can be calculated by Algorithm 2 in [8]. However, difference from classic IC model in [8], influence of two competitors A and B propagate concurrently and interfere with each other under CIC model. Thus, the influence computation in MIA structure should be redesigned under CIC model. Inspired by [3] which addresses the influence blocking maximization in CLT model, we propose a method to compute the A-activation probability of the node v in $MIIA(u, \theta)$ under A-seed set S_0^A and B-seed set S_0^B, denoted as $ap^A(v, S_0^A, S_0^B, MIIA(u, \theta))$. However, our method is different from that in [3].

Let $p^A(v,t)$ and $p^B(v,t)$ be the probabilities that v is activated by A and activated by B exactly at time t in $MIIA(u,\theta)$, respectively. Let $ap^A(v,t)$ and $ap^B(v,t)$ be the probabilities that v is activated by A and activated by B after time t in $MIIA(u,\theta)$, respectively. Assume that the propagation of A in $MIIA(u,\theta)$ stops at time T. According to the definition of homogeneous CIC model, we have following equations for any $v \in MIIA(u,\theta) \setminus (S_0^A \cup S_0^B)$:

$$P_1 = \prod_{w \in N^{in}(v)} (1 - p^B(w,t-1)p(w,v))(1 - \prod_{w \in N^{in}(v)} (1 - p^A(w,t-1)p(w,v)))$$
$$(1 - ap^B(v,t-1))(1 - ap^A(v,t-1)) \tag{1}$$

$$P_2 = \prod_{w \in N^{in}(v)} (1 - p^A(w,t-1)p(w,v))(1 - \prod_{w \in N^{in}(v)} (1 - p^B(w,t-1)p(w,v)))$$
$$(1 - ap^B(v,t-1))(1 - ap^A(v,t-1)) \tag{2}$$

$$P_3 = (1 - \prod_{w \in N^{in}(v)} (1 - p^A(w,t-1)p(w,v)))$$
$$(1 - \prod_{w \in N^{in}(v)} (1 - p^B(w,t-1)p(w,v)))(1 - ap^B(v,t-1))(1 - ap^A(v,t-1)) \tag{3}$$

$$p^A(v,t) = P_1 + \frac{|A_t(v)|}{|A_t(v)| + |B_t(v)|} P_3 \tag{4}$$

$$p^B(v,t) = P_2 + \frac{|B_t(v)|}{|A_t(v)| + |B_t(v)|} P_3 \tag{5}$$

$$ap^A(v,t) = ap^A(v,t-1) + p^A(v,t) \tag{6}$$

$$ap^B(v,t) = ap^B(v,t-1) + p^B(v,t) \tag{7}$$

Equation (4) comes from the fact that node v becomes A-$active$ at time t if and only if: Case-1, at least one neighbor of v becomes A-$active$ at time $t - 1$ and successfully activates v, further no neighbor of v can successfully B-$active$ activate v at time t, while v is neither A-$active$ nor B-$active$ after time $t - 1$. Case-2, v is successfully activated by both A-$active$ node and B-$active$ node, then tie-$breaking$ $rule$ is applied, v becomes A-$active$ with probability $\frac{|A_t(v)|}{|A_t(v)|+|B_t(v)|}$. Further, v is neither A-$active$ nor B-$active$ after time $t - 1$. Equation (5) is similar. Equations (6) and (7) are derived from their meaning that the activation probability after time t equals to the activation probability after $t - 1$ plus the activation probability at time t.

The boundary conditions of the above equations are as follows: For any $v \in S_0^A$, $p^A(v,0) = 1$, $p^A(v,t) = 0$ $\forall t \geq 1$, $ap^A(v,t) = 1$ $\forall t \geq 0$, $p^B(v,t) = ap^B(v,t) = 0$ $\forall t \geq 0$. For any $v \in S_0^B$, $p^B(v,0) = 1$, $p^B(v,t) = 0$ $\forall t \geq 1$, $ap^B(v,t) = 1$ $\forall t \geq 0$, $p^A(v,t) = ap^A(v,t) = 0$ $\forall t \geq 0$. For any $v \notin S_0^A \cup S_0^B$, $p^A(v,0) = ap^A(v,0) = p^B(v,0) = ap^B(v,0)$.

Based on Eqs. (4)–(7) and the corresponding boundary conditions, for each node $v \in MIIA(u,\theta)$, $ap^A(v, S_0^A, S_0^B, MIIA(u,\theta))$ can be computed easily by a dynamic programming method.

Let $Gain(w,v)$ be the marginal gain of influence of node w to node v after adding w to the seed set S_0^A, we have:

$$Gain(w,v) = ap^A(v, S_0^A \cup \{w\}, S_0^B, MIIA(v,\theta)) - ap^A(v, S_0^A, S_0^B, MIIA(v,\theta)) \tag{8}$$

Given a query $Q = (R,k)$, let V_R denote the set of nodes in region R. We use $Gain(w,R)$ to represent the sum the marginal gain of influence of node w to region R, then we have:

$$Gain(w,R) = \sum_{v \in V_R \backslash (S_0^A \cup S_0^B)} Gain(w,v) \tag{9}$$

Based on function $Gain(w,R)$, we can apply a greedy algorithm framework to find k nodes which have the largest marginal value. We propose LICM-MIA algorithm given in Algorithm 1 for the LICM problem.

Let $n = |V|$, $n_R = |V_R|$, $m_\theta = max_v\{|MIIA(v,\theta)|, |MIOA(v,\theta)|\}$, t_θ be the maximum time of construction of $MIIA(v,\theta)$ or $MIOA(v,\theta)$. The complexity of LCIM-MIA algorithm is $O(kt_\theta^3 + n_R t_\theta^2 + nt_\theta + kn)$.

Algorithm 1: LCIM-MIA Algorithm

Data: $G = (V, E)$: a geo-social network, S_0^B: a seed set of competitor B, $Q = (R, k)$: a query, θ: a threshold

Result: S_0^A: a seed set of A with size k

1   $S_0^A = \emptyset$; Set $Gain(v) = 0$ for all $v \in V$;

2   **foreach** $v \in V$ **do**

3 | Compute $MIIA(v, \theta)$;

4   **end**

5   Compute the set V_R include all nodes which are located in R;

6   **foreach** $v \in V_R \setminus S_0^B$ **do**

7 | **foreach** $u \in MIIA(v, \theta) \setminus S_0^B$ **do**

8 | | $Gain(u) = Gain(u) + ap^A(v, S_0^A \cup \{u\}, S_0^B, MIIA(v, \theta))$;

9 | **end**

10   **end**

11   **for** $i = 1$ *to* k **do**

12 | $u = \arg\max_{v \in V \setminus (S_0^A \cup S_0^B)}(Gain(v))$;

13 | Compute $MIOA(u, \theta)$;

14 | **foreach** $v \in MIOA(u, \theta) \setminus (S_0^A \cup S_0^B)$ **do**

15 | | **if** $v \in V_R$ **then**

16 | | | **foreach** $w \in MIIA(v, \theta) \setminus (S_0^A \cup S_0^B)$ **do**

17 | | | | $Gain(w) = Gain(w) - (ap^A(v, S_0^A \cup \{w\}, S_0^B, MIIA(v, \theta)) - ap^A(v, S_0^A, S_0^B, MIIA(v, \theta)))$;

18 | | | **end**

19 | | **end**

20 | **end**

21 | $S_0^A = S_0^A \cup \{u\}$;

22 | **foreach** $v \in MIOA(u, \theta) \setminus (S_0^A \cup S_0^B)$ **do**

23 | | Compute $MIIA(v, \theta)$;

24 | | **if** $v \in V_R$ **then**

25 | | | **foreach** $w \in MIIA(v, \theta) \setminus (S_0^A \cup S_0^B)$ **do**

26 | | | | $Gain(w) = Gain(w) + (ap^A(v, S_0^A \cup \{w\}, S_0^B, MIIA(v, \theta)) - ap^A(v, S_0^A, S_0^B, MIIA(v, \theta)))$;

27 | | | **end**

28 | | **end**

29 | **end**

30   **end**

31   **return** S_0^A;

---

4   Experiment and Evaluation

4.1   Experiment Setup

Datasets. To evaluate the algorithms, we use two real-world datasets Ego-Facebook, Brightkite. The two datasets are obtained from website http://snap.st-anford.edu/data.

Evaluated Algorithms. In our experiments, we compare the performance of the following algorithms: LCIM-MIA (our algorithms with $\theta = 0.015$), Greedy (our algorithms with 10000 simulations), Random (randomly select k nodes in the query region as A-seeds), MaxDegree (select top-k nodes with highest degrees located in the query region as A-seeds), Degree Discount (a degree discount heuristic algorithm proposed in [11]).

4.2   Experiment Results

Effectiveness Evaluation. Since the greedy algorithm cannot return result within 48 h on Ego-Facebook and Brightkite dataset, it is not shown in following experiment. The results are shown in Figs. 1 and 2 by varying size of A-seed set. In most cases, the influence spread returned by LCIM-MIA is the best. In contrast, random algorithm has the worst performance.

Efficiency Evaluation. To evaluate the efficiency of the proposed algorithms, we report the response time in datasets with different size. The greedy algorithm takes more than 48 h, whereas LCIM-MIA takes from about 74 s to nearly 375 s on Ego-Facebook network and from about 1312 s to around 2316 s on Brightkite network.

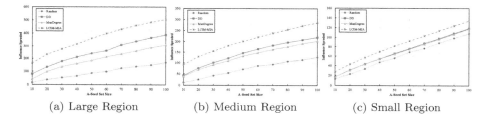

(a) Large Region   (b) Medium Region   (c) Small Region

Fig. 1. Influence spread on Ego-Facebook network

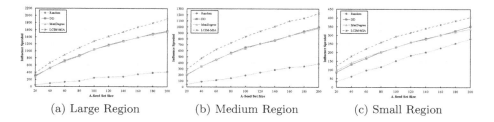

(a) Large Region   (b) Medium Region   (c) Small Region

Fig. 2. Influence spread on Brightkite network

5   Conclusions

In this paper, we is the first to investigate the LCIM problem under the CIC model. We show that the problem is NP-hard and the objective function is *monotone* and *submodular*. We propose greedy algorithm and heuristic algorithm based on MIA structure. Experimental results demonstrate the effectiveness and efficiency of our algorithms on several datasets.

Acknowledgements. This work is supported by VNU University of Engineering and Technology under project number CN 18.07.

References

1. Kempe, D., Kleinberg, J., Tardos, E.: Maximizing the spread of influence through a social network. In: Proceedings of the Ninth ACM SIGKDD International Conference on Knowledge Discovery and Data Mining, pp. 137–146 (2003)
2. Bharathi, S., Kempe, D., Salek, M.: Competitive influence maximization in social networks. In: Proceedings of the 3rd International Conference on Internet and Network Economics, pp. 306–311 (2007)
3. He, X., Song, G., Chen, W., Jiang, Q.: Influence blocking maximization in social networks under the competitive linear threshold model. In: Proceedings of the 2012 SIAM International Conference on Data Mining, pp. 463–474 (2012)
4. Chen, W., Lakshmanan, L.V.S., Castillo, C.: Information and influence propagation in social networks. Synth. Lect. Data Manage. **5**, 1–177 (2013)
5. Li, G., Chen, S., Feng, J., Tan, K., Li, W.: Efficient location-aware influence maximization. In: Proceedings of the 2014 ACM SIGMOD International Conference on Management of Data, pp. 87–98 (2014)
6. Wang, X., Zhang, Y., Zhang, W., Lin, X.: Distance-aware influence maximization in geo-social network. In: Proceedings of IEEE 32nd International Conference on Data Engineering, pp. 1–12 (2016)
7. Li, X., Cheng, X., Su, S., Sun, C.: Community-based seeds selection algorithm for location aware influence maximization. Neurocomputing **275**, 1601–1613 (2018)
8. Wang, C., Chen, W., Wang, Y.: Scalable influence maximization for independent cascade model in large-scale social networks. Data Mining Know. Discov. **25**(3), 545–576 (2012)
9. Nguyen, H.T., Nguyen, T.P., Phan, N., Dinh, T.N.: Importance sketching of influence dynamics in billion-scale networks. In: Proceedings of IEEE International Conference on Data Mining, pp. 337–346 (2017)
10. Zhu, Y., Li, D., Zhang, Z.: Minimum cost seed set for competitive social influence. In: Proceedings of the 35th Annual IEEE International Conference on Computer Communications, pp. 1–9 (2016)
11. Chen, W., Wang, Y., Yang, S.: Efficient influence maximization in social networks. In: Proceedings of the 15th ACM SIGKDD International Conference on Knowledge Discovery Data Mining, pp. 199–208 (2009)

Cascade of Edge Activation in Networks

Gabriel Lopez Zenarosa[1(✉)] [iD], Alexander Veremyev[2],
and Eduardo L. Pasiliao[3] [iD]

[1] National Academies of Sciences, Engineering, and Medicine,
Washington, DC 20001, USA
zenarosa@caa.columbia.edu
[2] Department of Industrial Engineering and Management Systems,
University of Central Florida, Orlando, FL 32816, USA
[3] Munitions Directorate, Air Force Research Laboratory,
Eglin AFB, FL 32542, USA

Abstract. We consider models for inducing a maximum cascade of activating connections in social networks over a finite horizon subject to budget constraints. These models reflect problems of choosing an initial set of pairs of individuals to connect or engage in order to maximize the cascade of new connections or engagements over time. We assume connections activate as a result of past activation of neighboring connections. We show that the optimization problem is NP-hard, and we provide a method for improving computations.

Keywords: Social networks · Edge activation · Cascade · Diffusion

1 Introduction

Edges in social networks represent the connections, relationships, and interactions among individuals through which information and influence propagate. Over time, connections between individuals emerge and dissolve, typically driven by how much the individuals have in common and their thresholds for establishing and keeping connections. Interactions among connected individuals may arise and dissipate over time, as well. Connection and interaction propagation can be viewed as the edge-based analogue to influence propagation among nodes.

Research on the spread of influence in networks focuses on the cascade of node activation [10,11], which can represent individual adoptions of innovation through viral marketing [2–5,8] and chains of power-system failures [1], among others. Influence, however, propagates to nodes through their edges, which change over time. Connections and interactions between nodes may activate or deactivate as a result of node activation (e.g., the individual's adoption of innovation may create or destroy relationships with others) and/or the activity

Supported by NRC Research Associateship Programs and the US Air Force Research Laboratory (AFRL) Mathematical Modeling and Optimization Institute and sponsored by AFRL/RW under agreement number FA8651-14-2-0002.

© Springer Nature Switzerland AG 2019
A. Tagarelli and H. Tong (Eds.): CSoNet 2019, LNCS 11917, pp. 141–147, 2019.
https://doi.org/10.1007/978-3-030-34980-6_16

changes among neighboring edges (e.g., changes in similarity of circle of friends may initiate or sever social ties).

In this paper, we study the cascade of edge activation in networks. We focus on the progressive linear-threshold activation model for its generality in mapping to other activation paradigms for influence networks [10,11]. We present our model in Sect. 2. We show our model to be NP-hard and provide a method for improving computations in Sect. 3. We conclude with a discussion in Sect. 4.

2   Model

Let $\hat{G} = (\hat{V}, \hat{E})$ be a given finite undirected graph having $|\hat{V}|$ vertices and $|\hat{E}|$ edges, and define $\check{E} \equiv \{\{i, j\} \notin \hat{E} : i \neq j\}$. Assume edges in $E^\circ \subseteq \hat{E}$ are pre-activated and a subset of (non-)edges $E^+ \subseteq \check{E} \cup (\hat{E} \setminus E^\circ)$ are candidates for activation. For example, $E^\circ = \hat{E}$ represents existing friendships and $E^\circ \subset \hat{E}$ represents only the actively engaged friendships; also, $E^+ = \check{E}$ represents candidate friendships and $E^+ \subset \hat{E} \setminus E^\circ$ represents candidate engagements among inactive friendships. We are thus interested in studying the cascade of edge activation using linear thresholds for graph $G = (V, E)$, where $V = \hat{V}$ and $E = E^\circ \cup E^+$.

Let $H \in \mathbb{Z}_{++}$ be the cascade horizon and define $T \equiv \{0, \ldots, H\}$. Let $\beta \in \mathbb{Z}_{++}$ be the budget on the number of candidate edges activated at time $t = 0$, and let $\varphi_{i,j} \in (0, 1)$ be the threshold factor for activating edge $\{i, j\} \in E$. Define the edge-activation variables by:

$$x_{i,j}^t \in \{0, 1\}, \qquad \forall \{i, j\} \subseteq V, i \neq j, \forall t \in T, \qquad (1)$$

where

$$x_{i,j}^0 = 1, \qquad \forall \{i, j\} \in E^\circ, \qquad (2)$$

$$x_{i,j}^t = 0, \qquad \forall \{i, j\} \notin E, \forall t \in T, \qquad (3)$$

and $x_{i,j}^0 \in \{0, 1\}$, for all $\{i, j\} \in E^+$ are the control variables for initiating the activation cascade at $t = 0$ subject to the budget constraint:

$$\sum_{\{i,j\} \in E^+} x_{i,j}^0 \leq \beta. \qquad (4)$$

We assume activated edges do not subsequently deactivate:

$$x_{i,j}^t \geq x_{i,j}^{t-1}, \qquad \forall \{i, j\} \in E, \forall t \in T \setminus \{0\}, \qquad (5)$$

and that each edge $\{i, j\} \in E$ is activated at $t > 0$ whenever the number of vertices with active edges to both i and j matches or exceeds a fraction ($\varphi_{i,j}$) of the number of (unique) vertices with an active edge to i or j (or both):

$$(1 - \varphi_{i,j}) M_{i,j} x_{i,j}^t \geq \sum_{k \in V \setminus \{i,j\}} x_{i,k}^{t-1} \cdot x_{k,j}^{t-1} - \varphi_{i,j} \sum_{k \in V \setminus \{i,j\}} \left(x_{i,k}^{t-1} + x_{k,j}^{t-1} - x_{i,k}^{t-1} \cdot x_{k,j}^{t-1} \right) \qquad (6)$$

$$> \varphi_{i,j} \left(M_{i,j} + 1 \right) \left(x_{i,j}^t - x_{i,j}^{t-1} - 1 \right), \qquad (7)$$

where $M_{i,j} \equiv |\{k \in V \setminus \{i,j\} : \{\{i,k\},\{k,j\}\} \cap E \neq \emptyset\}|$ is the number of vertices adjacent to i or j (or both) regardless of the edges being active or inactive.

Remark 1. Letting $A^t(i)$ denote the set of vertices adjacent to $i \in V$ whose edges with i are active at $t < H$, then:

$$|A^t(i) \cap A^t(j)| = \sum_{k \in V \setminus \{i,j\}} x_{i,k}^t \cdot x_{k,j}^t,$$

$$|A^t(i) \cup A^t(j)| = \sum_{k \in V \setminus \{i,j\}} \left(x_{i,k}^t + x_{k,j}^t - x_{i,k}^t \cdot x_{k,j}^t\right),$$

for all $\{i,j\} \in E$, so that whenever $A^t(i) \cup A^t(j) \neq \emptyset$, $\varphi_{i,j}$ can be interpreted as the activation threshold of edge $\{i,j\} \in E$ with respect to the ratio of the number of neighbors with which both i and j are actively engaged to the number of neighbors with which either i, j, or both are actively engaged:

$$\frac{|A^t(i) \cap A^t(j)|}{|A^t(i) \cup A^t(j)|} - \varphi_{i,j} \in [-\varphi_{i,j}, 1 - \varphi_{i,j}], \qquad \text{if } A^t(i) \cup A^t(j) \neq \emptyset,$$

since $0 \leq |A^t(i) \cap A^t(j)| \leq |A^t(i) \cup A^t(j)| \leq M_{i,j}$.

To relax the strict inequality in Constraint (7) to afford implementation, we make the following assumption, which is not restrictive for finite graphs [7]:

(A1) *Edge-activation threshold factors are rational numbers between 0 and 1:*

$$\varphi_{i,j} = \frac{q_{i,j}}{r_{i,j}}, \qquad \forall \{i,j\} \in E,$$

where $q_{i,j} \in \mathbb{Z}_{++}$, $r_{i,j} \in \mathbb{Z}_{++}$, and $q_{i,j} < r_{i,j}$.

Using Assumption **(A1)** on Constraint (6), for all $\{i,j\} \in E$ and $t \in T \setminus \{H\}$:

$$q_{i,j} \left(M_{i,j} + 1\right) \left(x_{i,j}^t - x_{i,j}^t - 1\right)$$

$$\leq r_{i,j} \sum_{k \in V \setminus \{i,j\}} x_{i,k}^t \cdot x_{k,j}^t - q_{i,j} \sum_{k \in V \setminus \{i,j\}} \left(x_{i,k}^t + x_{k,j}^t - x_{i,k}^t \cdot x_{k,j}^t\right) - 1,$$

$$< r_{i,j} \sum_{k \in V \setminus \{i,j\}} x_{i,k}^t \cdot x_{k,j}^t - q_{i,j} \sum_{k \in V \setminus \{i,j\}} \left(x_{i,k}^t + x_{k,j}^t - x_{i,k}^t \cdot x_{k,j}^t\right),$$

since all terms are integral. Thus, Constraint (7), for all $\{i,j\} \in E$ and $t \in T \setminus \{0\}$ can be reformulated with $\varepsilon_{i,j} = 1/r_{i,j}$ as:

$$\sum_{k \in V \setminus \{i,j\}} x_{i,k}^{t-1} \cdot x_{k,j}^{t-1} - \varphi_{i,j} \sum_{k \in V \setminus \{i,j\}} \left(x_{i,k}^{t-1} + x_{k,j}^{t-1} - x_{i,k}^{t-1} \cdot x_{k,j}^{t-1}\right) - \varepsilon_{i,j}$$

$$\geq \varphi_{i,j} \left(M_{i,j} + 1\right) \left(x_{i,j}^t - x_{i,j}^{t-1} - 1\right). \tag{8}$$

For this paper, we set our objective function as the total number of active edges in G at $t = H$, although other objectives may be used (e.g., graph diameter or total edge betweenness centrality, assuming unit edge weights). A mathematical program for maximizing our set objective is given by:

$$(\textbf{MAXCONN}) \qquad \max \left\{ \sum_{\{i,j\} \in E} x_{i,j}^H : (1), (2), (3), (4), (5), (6), (8) \right\}.$$

We denote **MAXCONN** instances by their graph and parameters: $\langle G, \varphi, \beta, H \rangle$.

3   Results

Theorem 1. *The **MAXCONN** problem is NP-hard.*

Proof. Consider an instance of the NP-complete **SET COVER** problem [6], defined by a set of $n \in \mathbb{Z}_{++}$ elements $U \equiv \{u_1, \ldots, u_n\}$, a collection of $m \in \mathbb{Z}_{++}$ subsets $S \equiv \{S_i \subseteq U : i \in \{1, \ldots, m\}\}$, and an integer $k \in \mathbb{Z}_{++}$, for which we seek to determine if there exists a collection $C \subseteq S$ such that $|C| \le k$ and $\bigcup_{S_i \in C} S_i = U$. We show that this represents a special case of **MAXCONN**.

We construct a corresponding **MAXCONN** instance with $G = (V, E^\circ \cup E^+)$, where $V = S \cup U \cup \{r\}$, $E^\circ = \{\{S_i, u_j\} \subseteq V : u_j \in S_i, S_i \in S\}$, and $E^+ = \{\{r, S_i\} \subseteq V : S_i \in S\} \cup \{\{r, u_j\} \subseteq V : u_j \in U\}$. Let $H = 1$, $\beta = k$, φ_{S_i, u_j} be arbitrary, for all $\{S_i, u_j\} \in E^\circ$, and, for sufficiently small $\delta > 0$, $\varphi_{r, S_i} \in (1 - \delta, 1)$ and $\varphi_{r, u_j} \in (0, \delta)$, for all $S_i \in S$ and $u_j \in U$. See Fig. 1.

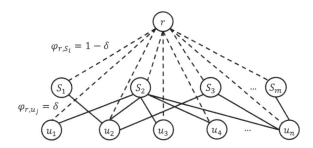

Fig. 1. Illustrated above is an example instance of **SET COVER** reduced to an instance of **MAXCONN**. Solid-line edges (in E°) are pre-activated and have arbitrary activation threshold factors. Dashed-line edges (in E^+) may be chosen to activate at $t = 0$ or activate through a cascading process at $t > 0$; activation threshold factors between r and S_is are sufficiently large while those between r and u_js are sufficiently small. The reduction uses cascade horizon $H = 1$, activation budget $\beta = k$, and target number of activated edges $|E^\circ| + \beta + n$.

If there is a set cover C of size k, then the maximum number of $|E^\circ| + k + n$ edges are activated at $t = H$. Conversely, the only way to get the maximum number of $|E^\circ| + \beta + n$ edges activated at $t = H$ is to choose to activate at $t = 0$ a set of $\beta = k$ edges with high threshold factors $\{\{r, S_i\} \in E^+ : S_i \in C\}$, where $C \subseteq S$ such that $|C| = \beta$ and $\bigcup_{S_i \in C} S_i = U$, to induce subsequent activation of all n edges with low threshold factors $\{r, u_j\} \in E^+$, for all $u_j \in U$, at $H = 1$. $\square$

We found that optimal solutions to a **MAXCONN** instance $\langle G, \varphi, \beta, H \rangle$, where $H > 1$, specifically the edges activated at $t = 0$ to induce the edge-activation cascade, may not coincide with those for instance $\langle G, \varphi, \beta, H - 1 \rangle$. Thus, myopic decision-making may be suboptimal as exemplified in Fig. 2.

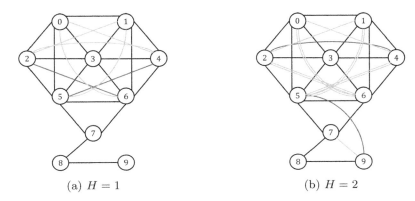

(a) $H = 1$ (b) $H = 2$

Fig. 2. The Krackhardt Kite social network [12] $\hat{G} = (\hat{V}, \hat{E})$ shown in black, annotated with the cascade of edge activation on $G = (V, E)$, where $V = \hat{V}$, $E = E^\circ \cup E^+$, $E^\circ = \hat{E}$, and $E^+ = \check{E}$, solved using **MAXCONN** for budget $\beta = 2$, threshold factors $\varphi_{i,j} = 1/2$, for all $\{i, j\} \in E$, and cascade horizons (a) $H = 1$ and (b) $H = 2$ are illustrated above. Shown in black are 18 pre-activated edges, red are $\beta = 2$ edges chosen for activation at $t = 0$, single-line orange are edges activated at $t = 1$, and double-line orange are edges activated at $t = 2$. At $t = H$, (a) $18 + 2 + 5$ and (b) $18 + 2 + 3 + 4$ edges are activated.

On a positive note, a lower bound for the objective function and a feasible partial solution to a **MAXCONN** instance with $H > 1$ can be derived from solutions to the same instance at $H - 1$. The following result follows immediately and affords an algorithm for solving H instances sequentially for increasing cascade horizons $\eta \in \{1, \ldots, H\}$.

Theorem 2. *Let $H > 1$ and let $\acute{x}^{[H-1]} \in \{0, 1\}^{|E| \cdot (H-1)}$ solve* **MAXCONN** *instance $\langle G, \varphi, \beta, H - 1 \rangle$, where $G = (V, E)$ and $E = E^\circ \cup E^+$. Then:*

$$\sum_{\{i,j\} \in E} x_{i,j}^H \geq \sum_{\{i,j\} \in E} \acute{x}_{i,j}^{H-1}$$

is a valid inequality for **MAXCONN** *instance $\langle G, \varphi, \beta, H \rangle$. Moreover, the partial solution (MIP-start) $x_{i,j}^t = \acute{x}_{i,j}^t$, for all $\{i, j\} \in E^+$ and $t \in T \setminus \{H\}$, along with its induced decisions $x^H \in \{0, 1\}^{|E|}$ is feasible to $\langle G, \varphi, \beta, H \rangle$.*

4 Discussion

We defined **MAXCONN** problem as a mathematical program that maximizes the total number of active edges on a graph G at horizon H by selecting at most β edges to activate at $t = 0$ to induce a cascade of edge activation using linear thresholds φ. We showed **MAXCONN** is NP-hard, but its computation may be improved by sequentially solving H instances for increasing cascade horizons that use valid inequalities and MIP-starts defined by previous solutions.

MAXCONN has similarities to the *influence maximization* (**MAXINF**) problem [10] but primarily differs from it in that activation of edges is supported or contradicted by their adjacent active edges depending on their adjacency structure. We are investigating heuristics with performance guaranties for solving **MAXCONN** that exploit similarities to **MAXINF**. We also seek to determine if progressive linear-threshold activation maps to other activation paradigms.

Other research directions include defining edge-based analogues to the *minimum target set selection* (**MINTSS**), *perfect target set selection* (**PTSS**), and *minimum time* (**MINTIME**) problems [9]; capturing asymmetric relationships using directed graphs; and modeling other causes for (de)activating social ties.

Acknowledgements. The US Government is authorized to reproduce and distribute reprints for Governmental purposes notwithstanding any copyright notation thereon. The views and conclusions contained herein are those of the authors and should not be interpreted as necessarily representing the official policies or endorsements, either expressed or implied, of AFRL/RW or the US Government.

References

1. Asavathiratham, C., Roy, S., Lesieutre, B.C., Verghese, G.C.: The influence model. IEEE Control Syst. Mag. **21**(6), 52–64 (2001)
2. Ashokan, R., Zenarosa, G.L., He, X.: Diffusion model for the adoption of smartphone brands under competitive pricing. Int. J. Trade Econ. Finan. **9**(3), 96–99 (2018)
3. Bass, F.M.: A new product growth for model consumer durables. Manag. Sci. **15**(5), 215–227 (1969)
4. Brown, J.J., Reingen, P.H.: Social ties and word-of-mouth referral behavior. J. Consum. Res. **14**(3), 350–362 (1987)
5. Domingos, P., Richardson, M.: Mining the network value of customers. In: Proceedings of the Seventh ACM SIGKDD International Conference on Knowledge Discovery and Data Mining, KDD 2001, pp. 57–66 (2001)
6. Garey, M.R., Johnson, D.S.: Computers and Intractability: A Guide to the Theory of NP-Completeness. W. H. Freeman & Co., New York (1979)
7. Gillen, C.P., Veremyev, A., Prokopyev, O.A., Pasiliao, E.L.: Critical arcs detection in influence networks. Networks **71**(4), 412–431 (2018)
8. Goldenberg, J., Libai, B., Muller, E.: Talk of the network: a complex systems look at the underlying process of word-of-mouth. Mark. Lett. **12**(3), 211–223 (2001)
9. Goyal, A., Bonchi, F., Lakshmanan, L.V.S., Venkatasubramanian, S.: On minimizing budget and time in influence propagation over social networks. Soc. Netw. Anal. Min. **3**(2), 179–192 (2013)

10. Kempe, D., Kleinberg, J., Tardos, É.: Maximizing the spread of influence through a social network. In: Proceedings of the Ninth ACM SIGKDD International Conference on Knowledge Discovery and Data Mining, KDD 2003, pp. 137–146. ACM, New York (2003)
11. Kempe, D., Kleinberg, J., Tardos, É.: Maximizing the spread of influence through a social network. Theory Comput. **11**(4), 105–147 (2015)
12. Krackhardt, D.: Assessing the political landscape: structure, cognition, and power in organizations. Adm. Sci. Q. **35**(2), 342–369 (1990)

Reinforcement Learning in Information Cascades Based on Dynamic User Behavior

Mengnan Chen[1], Qipeng P. Zheng[1(✉)], Vladimir Boginski[1], and Eduardo L. Pasiliao[2]

[1] University of Central Florida, Orlando, FL 32816, USA
qipeng.zheng@ucf.edu
[2] Air Force Research Laboratory, Eglin AFB, Valparaiso, FL 32542, USA

Abstract. This paper studies the Influence Maximization problem based on information cascading within a random graph, where the network structure is dynamically changing according to users' uncertain behaviors. The Discrete Choice Model is used to define the probability distribution of the directed arcs between any two nodes in the random graph. The discrete choice model provides a good description and prediction of user behavior following/unfollowing their neighbor node. To find the maximal influence at the end of the finite time horizon, this paper proposed Multi-Stage Stochastic Programming models, which can help the decision maker to select the optimal seed nodes to broadcast messages efficiently. To approximate the optimal decisions, the paper discuss two approaches, i.e., the Myopic Two-Stage Stochastic Programming at each time period, and Reinforcement Learning for Markov Decision Process. Computational experiments show that the Reinforcement Learning method exhibits better performance than the Myopic method in large-scale networks.

Keywords: Markov Decision Process · Discrete choice model · Influence maximization

1 Introduction

Cascading phenomena are typically characterized by a dynamic process of information propagation between nodes in a network, where nodes can rebroadcast or re-post information from and to their neighbors. Moreover, the content and value of information may affect not only the reach (or depth) of a cascade, but also the topology of the underlying network due to the effects that nodes may either sever their ties with neighboring nodes whose transmitted information is deemed unreliable and/or malicious or form new ties with nodes transmitting

This material is based on work supported by the AFRL Mathematical Modeling and Optimization Institute.

© Springer Nature Switzerland AG 2019
A. Tagarelli and H. Tong (Eds.): CSoNet 2019, LNCS 11917, pp. 148–154, 2019.
https://doi.org/10.1007/978-3-030-34980-6_17

"reliable" information. In an information cascade, people observe the choices of others and make their own decisions based on observations while considering their personal preferences. This phenomenon is also considered in the fields of behavioral economics and social sciences. A recent study of social networks suggested that such processes may occur in a "bursty" fashion, that is, the patterns of network links change abruptly as a result of significant information cascades. Thus, new information may create a burst of node activations and edge activations/deactivations in a network. In a decentralized autonomous network, agents or nodes act independently and behave according to their own utility functions. To model their autonomous behaviors, we will implement the concepts of discrete choice models from behavioral economics.

Our study is based on the assumptions of the Independent Cascade model [1,2,5,6]. Different from previous research on Independent Cascade model, we consider the information diffusion probabilities or the network topology probabilities are dynamically changing according to the users' behaviors. Oinas-Kukkonen [3] has introduced the concept of behavior change support systems. Based on the behavior change support systems, Ploderer et al. [4] found there is ample evidence of the strong influence exerted by social interaction on people's behaviors. For large scale real data, an extensive statistical analysis conducted by Yu et al. [7] shows that the general form of Exponential and Rayleigh, Weibull distribution can be used to preserve the characteristics of behavioral dynamics, where they also found the Networked Weibull Regression model for behavioral dynamics modeling have better result on improvement of interpretability and generality.

In this paper, we propose an influence maximization model through independent cascading with random graphs. For the network properties, the network size and the node preference is given and fixed, while the friendships between any two user (arc connection) are dynamic changed. Our model can help the decision maker choose the optimal action when facing the uncertain network topology. The stochastic formulation considers endogenous uncertainty, which is represented by the binary choice probability distribution of arc connection between any two nodes. To address this problem, we design two approaches: one is based on two-stage stochastic programming with myopic policy, and the other one uses reinforcement learning with Markov Decision Processes (MDP).

2   Mathematical Models

In social network, information is transmitted between users. At the beginning, some nodes act as the seed nodes who start broadcasting message in the network. During the information cascade, each nodes may have two roles, i.e., message receiver who is activated of certain messages by their neighbor, and message sender who repost the received message to neighbors. While the users of the network may have different preferences on different messages, selecting the seed nodes is critical to maximize the influence of the information provider.

For each time period, the information provider will select a seed node to post a certain message in the social network. Once the source user posts the message, the followers of the source user automatically receive the information. The followers have their own decisions on reposting this message, based on their own preference. As users have multiple roles in the social network, the followers act as followees of other users. The information flows are always from followee to follower. The dynamics of information transmission has great impacts on the network topology, which means that the user relationships (or the arc connections) dynamically change. We model this problem by multistage stochastic programming and the objective is to maximize the total influence within a finite time horizon. Influence is measured by seed costs and node activation.

2.1 Problem Description

Consider a simple example of viral marketing on a random network $G(n, p)$, where a company promotes two products in the social network with a random topology. To maximize the influence, the company selects certain nodes as seeds to post the promotion messages. Figure 1 gives us an information cascade example within a 4-node network. Before the seeds' selection, we know the nodal preference with respect to the message type. During the information cascade, the network topology is dynamically changing depending on the decisions. Assume there are two types of messages, blue and green, and the initial arc existence probability $p = 0.5$. Some nodes may already heard/know the messages before the information cascade.

Our model assumes that within one time period the information cascade usually includes four steps: seed selection, message transmission (nodes send messages), node activation (nodes receive messages), network topology probability update. The message is broadcast by the seed node in the network, while it cannot guarantee all other nodes will receive the message. Only direct followers will receive the message from the sender. After the information diffusion process, the network topology may change due to influences received by nodes. There is a high chance for a message receiver to disconnect the link from its followee if the received message and the follower's (also the receiver) preference mismatch. It means that some directed arcs will break up even if they existed in the previous time period. The uncertain topology is modeled by a series of Bernoulli random variables denoting the existence of directed arcs, and the probabilities are defined by the discrete choice theory. Figure 1 shows information cascade of 2 messages in a 4-node network within a time horizon $T = 2$.

At time $t = 0$, node $i = 1$ is selected as the seed node of message BLUE and node $i = 2$ is selected as a seed node of message GREEN. Then these two nodes will broadcast messages in the network. The initially guessed probability of the existence of the directed arc between any two nodes is set at 0.5. Since node 1 and node 2 are seed node, they are assumed to be activated. Node 2 is activated of message BLUE by node 1. Since node 2 dislikes message BLUE, it will break the friendship from node 1 to node 2. We use the utility function to measure the friendship. When a node receives a message for the first time, we assume there a doubled impact on the utility (i.e., +2 or −2) as the message is fresh. We reduce the utility by 2 from node 1 to node 2, because it is the first time

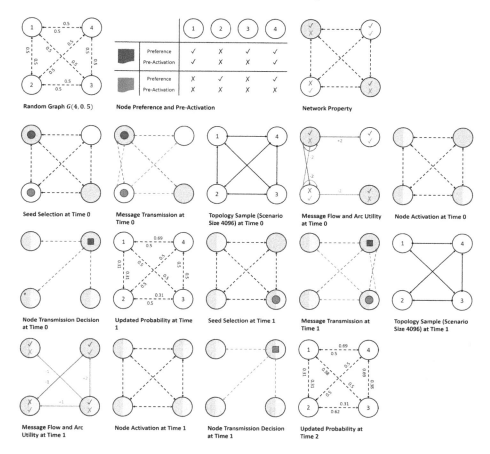

Fig. 1. Given network properties (Color figure online)

for node 1 to receive this message. Node 4 is also activated of message BLUE by node 1. Since node 4 like this message and first receiving, node 4 will decide to repost this message in the network. The utility from node 1 to node 4 will be increased by 2. The Bernoulli probabilities of directed arcs are updated due to the changing utility. For example, the probability of directed arc from note 1 to node 2 is updated as below:

$$\text{Prob}(a_{12}^{t=1} = 1) = \text{Prob}(a_{12}^{t=1} = 1 | a_{12}^{t=0} = 1) = \frac{1}{1 + exp(-u_{12}^{t=0})} = 0.1192$$

2.2 Mathematical Formulation

We formulate the Independent Cascade with Random Graph (ICRG) as a stochastic programming model. The independent cascade includes 3 decision variables, i.e., seed selection x, node activation y, message transmission z. In the objective function (1a), i.e., the total influence, has two parts: seed cost $Q(x)$, and the activation reward $R(y)$. Constraint (1b) shows the probability of scenario s depends on the probability of arcs. The directed arc a_{ij} from node i to node j is a random variable, which is following logit binary choice model with utility U_{ij}.

$$[\text{SP}] \max_{x,y,z} \mathbb{E}\left(Q(x), R(y); \varepsilon\right) = \sum_{s \in \mathcal{S}} P^s(a) \cdot (R^s(y) - Q^s(x)) \tag{1a}$$

$$s.t. P^s(a_{ij}) = \prod_{t \in \mathcal{T}} \prod_{i \in \mathcal{I}} \prod_{j \in \mathcal{I} \setminus \{i\}} \text{Prob}(a_{ij}^{t,s} = 1) \qquad \forall s \in \mathcal{S} \tag{1b}$$

$$R^s(y) = \sum_{k \in \mathcal{K}} \sum_{i \in \mathcal{I}} w_k \cdot (2b_{ki} - 1) \cdot (y_{ki}^{t=|\mathcal{T}|,s} - c_{ki}) \qquad \forall s \in \mathcal{S} \tag{1c}$$

$$Q^s(x) = \sum_{t \in \mathcal{T}} \sum_{k \in \mathcal{K}} \sum_{i \in \mathcal{I}} x_{ki}^{t,s} \qquad \forall s \in \mathcal{S} \tag{1d}$$

Utility U_{ij} is a function to measure the user friendship or the strength of arc connection, which includes two term: observed utility u_{ij} and unobserved utility ε_{ij}. The observed utility $u_{ij}^{t,s}$ at time t and scenario s is cumulative impact from node i to node j with all kinds of message type. The current direct arc $a_{ij}^{t,s}$ from node i to node j decide the impact happen or not, the impact sign is decided by the preference b_{kj} of message k and node j, and the impact amount is decided by the transmission decision $z_{ki}^{t-1,s}$ of message k and node i at last moment. The unobserved utility $\varepsilon_{ij}^{t,s}$ is assumed to have a logistic distribution.

3   Solution Approaches and Results

As uncertain directed arc connection is modeled by Bernoulli random variable, the total number of scenarios is an exponential function of the network size $|I|$ and time horizon $|T|$. It can easily grow into sizes which are not manageable. To handle the large number of scenarios, we propose two approaches to solve the information cascade in the random graph:

- Myopic Policy: It does not explicitly use any forecast network topology and separate the multi-stage into several two-stage problems (MYSP) by discrete time.
- Reinforcement Learning: It reformulates the Stochastic Programming model to Markov Decision Process (MDP).

3.1   Two-Stage Stochastic Programming with Myopic Policy

Unlike the original model, the myopic model focuses on current network topology and ignore the future changes. The seed selection(x^t) is only based on current user connection (a^t) and aims to find the local maximal influence on node activation of next time period (y^{t+1}).

$$x^t = \arg\max R(y^{t+1}, a^t)$$

By using the myopic method, the multi-stage problem is decomposed into several two-stage problems. The first stage variable is seed selection, and the second stage variable is node activation and node repost decision. Since we select seed to find the maximal expected influence at current time period, the decision only happens within one time period, eliminating the time indices. For time $t > 0$, some known parameters are given by the previous myopic model.

3.2 Reinforcement Learning with Markov Decision Process

The problem can also be defined as a Markov Decision Process (MDP), where information provider choose source users when facing the given information activation status of all users in the network. We use the Reinforcement Learning to learn the policy based on state-action pairs (s, a). In general, the MDP is described by a 4-tuple (S, A, P, R), which are the states, actions, transitions, and reward, where S is the finite set of states, i.e., activation status; A is the finite set of action, i.e., source user selection; P is the probability of transition from s to s' through action a, $P_a(s, s')$; R is the expected reward of transition from s to s' through action a, i.e., weighted information influence, $R_a(s, s')$. The reward function is shown below:

$$R(s, s') = \sum_{k \in K} \sum_{i \in I} w_K \cdot (s'_{ki} - s_{ki}) \tag{2a}$$

Policy Evaluation. If we have a policy, the probability of actions taken at each state are known. Then the MDP is turned into a Markov chain (with rewards). We can compute the expected total reward collected over time using this policy. For given policy $\pi(s)$, the state-value function $Q^\pi(s, a)$ is used to evaluate the policy value.

$$Q^\pi(s, a) = \mathbb{E}^\pi \left(R(s, s') + \gamma \cdot \sum_{a' \in A} \pi(s', a') \cdot Q^\pi(s', a') \right) \forall\ s \in S, a \in A \tag{2b}$$

where γ is the discount factor and $\pi(s, a)$ is the probability to take action a at state s.

Policy Improvement. Based on simulation results, we create a final reward (weighted total influence) list $Q(s, a)$ by state and action, which is used to improve the policy. $\pi(s, a)$ and $\pi'(s, a)$ are old policy and new policy. The action set A is split into two subsets. A^1 is the set of all occurred actions, and A^0 is the set of all actions that have not occurred. With λ being the step size, the policies is updated as follows,

$$\pi'(s, a) = \begin{cases} \left(1 - \sum_{a \in A^0} \pi(s, a) \right) \cdot \dfrac{Q(s, a) - \hat{Q}(s, a)}{\sum_{a \in A^1} Q^\pi(s, a) - \hat{Q}^\pi(s, a)}, & \forall\ a \in A^1,\ s \in S \\ \pi(s, a), & \forall\ a \in A^0,\ s \in S \end{cases}$$

$$\hat{Q}(s, a) = \lambda \cdot \min_{a \in A^1} Q(s, a)$$

3.3   Computational Results

We randomly generate three data sets, small size (2 messages, 4 nodes), medium size (2 messages, 7 nodes), and large size (3 messages, 7 nodes). The algorithms are coded in C++ linked with CPLEX 12.9. In Fig. 2, we compare the algorithm of Two-Stage Stochastic Programming with Myopic Policy (SP-MYOPIC) and the algorithm of Reinforcement Learning with Markov Decision Process (RL-MDP) using different data sets. RL-MDP method can provide better performance for the influence maximization problem.

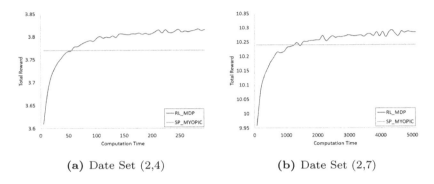

(a) Date Set (2,4)   (b) Date Set (2,7)

Fig. 2. Algorithm comparison, sample size 1000000

References

1. Chen, W., Wang, C., Wang, Y.: Scalable influence maximization for prevalent viral marketing in large-scale social networks. In: Proceedings of the 16th ACM SIGKDD International Conference on Knowledge Discovery and Data Mining, pp. 1029–1038. ACM (2010)
2. Kempe, D., Kleinberg, J., Tardos, É.: Maximizing the spread of influence through a social network. In: Proceedings of the Ninth ACM SIGKDD International Conference on Knowledge Discovery and Data Mining, pp. 137–146. ACM (2003)
3. Oinas-Kukkonen, H.: A foundation for the study of behavior change support systems. Pers. Ubiquit. Comput. **17**(6), 1223–1235 (2013)
4. Ploderer, B., Reitberger, W., Oinas-Kukkonen, H., Gemert-Pijnen, J.: Social interaction and reflection for behaviour change. Pers. Ubiquit. Comput. **18**(7), 1667–1676 (2014)
5. Saito, K., Nakano, R., Kimura, M.: Prediction of information diffusion probabilities for independent cascade model. In: Lovrek, I., Howlett, R.J., Jain, L.C. (eds.) KES 2008. LNCS (LNAI), vol. 5179, pp. 67–75. Springer, Heidelberg (2008). https://doi.org/10.1007/978-3-540-85567-5_9
6. Wang, C., Chen, W., Wang, Y.: Scalable influence maximization for independent cascade model in large-scale social networks. Data Min. Knowl. Disc. **25**(3), 545–576 (2012)
7. Yu, L., Cui, P., Wang, F., Song, C., Yang, S.: From micro to macro: uncovering and predicting information cascading process with behavioral dynamics. arXiv preprint arXiv:1505.07193 (2015)

Predicting New Adopters
via Socially-Aware Neural Graph
Collaborative Filtering

Yu-Che Tsai[1,3], Muzhi Guan[2,3], Cheng-Te Li[1], Meeyoung Cha[3,4(✉)], Yong Li[2], and Yue Wang[2]

[1] Department of Statistics, National Cheng Kong University, Tainan, Taiwan
[2] Department of Electronic Engineering, Tsinghua University, Beijing, China
[3] Data Science Group, IBS, Daejeon, South Korea
mcha@ibs.re.kr
[4] School of Computing, KAIST, Daejeon, South Korea

Abstract. We predict new adopters of specific items by proposing S-NGCF, a socially-aware neural graph collaborative filtering model. This model uses information about social influence and item adoptions; then it learns the representation of user-item relationships via a graph convolutional network. Experiments show that social influence is essential for adopter prediction. S-NGCF outperforms the prediction of new adopters compared to state-of-the-art methods by 18%.

Keywords: Graph convolutional network · Collaborative filtering · Representation learning

1 Introduction

Social activities are essential to human life. Early studies have found that individuals' opinions can be affected by others in terms of decision making as well as behavioral changes [5]. For example, product reviews or promotions get shared via social networks. Such patterns are critical to viral marketing research [9]. Scholars have found that popularity is a different kind of power from the capability to propagate actions (i.e., retweets on Twitter) [1], revealing the complexity of influence measurement. The influence of a single user may reach beyond one social hop and affect the more extensive social network. The problem of influence maximization focuses on identifying the set of adopters who can maximize the spread of influence [6]. Another method for predicting influence propagation is to utilize recommendations. For example, top-K ranking is a standard method in recommendation systems, where the goal is to return K highest ranked list of items by learning from the relationship between users and items.

Y.-C. Tsai and M. Guan—contributed equally to this paper.

A. Tagarelli and H. Tong (Eds.): CSoNet 2019, LNCS 11917, pp. 155–162, 2019.
https://doi.org/10.1007/978-3-030-34980-6_18

The current paper considers the problem of the inverse recommendation problem. *Given a specific item for promotion and users who had adopted the item previously, the goal is to identify a set of new adopters who had never viewed or adopted the same item before.* This classic problem has been studied via learning representations of users and items from historical records such as click logs or check-in data [4]. Collaborative filtering [3] aims to recommend users who had adopted similar items previously. Matrix factorization methods [11] learn the embedding vector of users and items. These methods are limited first because they only consider co-adopted behaviors and can not capture the "shared" interests of users. Secondly, their representations embed users who adopted the same item into a similar vector space, yet it cannot model the high-order connectivity from user-item interactions.

This paper addresses a new adopter prediction problem. For every item, we predict whether a user would be influenced by his friends and then become a new adopter, based on the social network-based recommendation. The user-item interactions and social relationships are combined into a heterogeneous graph. We utilize the state-of-the-art graph convolutional networks (GCN) approach to learn the representations of users and items. Based on the collaborative filtering methodology, we predict potential adopters of all items through the representations. The main contributions are:

1. This paper brings new insight into the adopter prediction task on a social graph by treating it as an inverse recommendation problem.
2. We evaluate social influence based on a socially-aware recommendation, which outperforms the state-of-the-art method.
3. The proposed model can mitigate the negative effect of "missed" check-ins and thereby gain advantage in predictions.

2   Dataset and Problem

We use data collected from the Gowalla location-based service [10]. To reduce the computation cost, we applied the Louvain community detection algorithm [2] and identified a relatively small community of 3,000 users and their check-in records. We removed all location items that appear fewer than ten times, as suggested in a previous research [12]. This leads to 5,000 valid locations. After splitting the check-in logs into the training set and testing set chronologically, for each user, we filter out those check-in locations in the testing set by two rules. First, the location must not have appeared in the previous log by the user and, second, the location has been checked-in by at least one friend of the user. This preprocessing step excludes the user's self-effect of repeated visiting.

This paper focuses on the problem of adopter prediction in viral marketing. Given a target item for promotion (e.g., a hotspot in location-based services or a product in a shopping mall) and the set of users who have already adopted the item, the goal is to predict a set of users who will adopt the target item afterward. We develop a novel graph-based neural network model to (*a*) learn the feature representation of users and items from past user-item interactions and the social connections among users and (*b*) use the learned embedding to find potential adopters in an end-to-end prediction. We run experiments to test whether there will be social propagation among friends (e.g., will Alice buy the new video game since her friends had already bought it?).

3   Methodology

Given a graph structure $G(V, E)$ and the feature vector h_{v_i} for each node v_i. A graph convolution networks (GCN) aims to learn the representation of each node by aggregating the feature vectors of itself and its neighbors through the layer-wise message passing mechanism [8]. Stacking GCN layers k times allows to learn the node representation from k-hop neighbors.

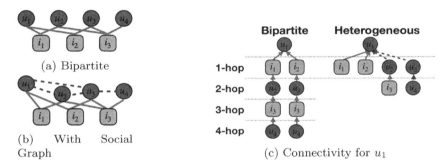

(a) Bipartite

(b)   With   Social Graph

(c) Connectivity for u_1

Fig. 1. Illustrations of (a) the bipartite interaction graph without social connections, (b) the heterogeneous graph with social connections, and (c) the user connectivity. Note that the dotted lines in (b) and (c) indicates social connections.

The Neural Graph Collaborative Filtering (NGCF) method captures the high-order connectivity based on user-item interactions well [12], by utilizing a bipartite graph to model user-item interactions. An example is shown in Fig. 1a. Here, features of different users (or items) can propagate via a co-visited item (or a co-visiting user), by applying the standard GCN structure in [8].

This work assumes the social network of users can boost product recommendations via making items more easily visible (e.g., friends sharing reviews or promotions). Figure 1b shows an example, where a user u_4 is more likely to adopt item i_2 than item i_1 because his friend u_3 had adopted it. Figure 1a then shows an example, where the likelihood of user u_4 adopting item i_2 and item i_1 is exactly the same. Such an example indicates that social relationships can be essential to item adoption. We utilize the bipartite structure of NGCF and newly create edges between users in the original bipartite graph to reveal user-user social connections. Recall what we are addressing is predicting future adopters of a target item, which is an inverse problem of item recommendations.

Since the MF-based framework is *symmetric* for users and items, we may recommend each item to a list of potential adopters by switching the position of users and items. To this end, the Laplacian matrix is updated as $\mathcal{L}_{\text{S-NGCF}}$,

$$\mathcal{L}_{\text{S-NGCF}} = D_{\text{S-NGCF}}^{-1/2} A_{\text{S-NGCF}} D_{\text{S-NGCF}}^{-1/2}, A_{\text{S-NGCF}} = \begin{bmatrix} \mathbf{0} & R^{\mathsf{T}} \\ R & S \end{bmatrix} \quad (1)$$

where S is the adjacency matrix depicting user-user social connections. Through the layer-wise message passing mechanism [8], the output of the lth layer of socially-aware NGCF is,

$$H_{\text{S-NGCF}}^{(l+1)} = \sigma(\hat{D}_{\text{S-NGCF}}^{-1/2} \hat{A}_{\text{S-NGCF}} \hat{D}_{\text{S-NGCF}}^{-1/2} H_{\text{S-NGCF}}^{(l)} W_{\text{S-NGCF}}^{(l)}) \quad (2)$$

where $\hat{A}_{\text{S-NGCF}}$ and $\hat{D}_{\text{S-NGCF}}$ follow the definition in [8]. The input of the first layer is the output of initialized user and item embedding layer. For each user and item, we then concatenate the output embedding of each layers as the ultimate embedding of user and item. Finally, we utilize the MF training method to learning the parameters of this end-to-end deep networks. For each item i in the testing set, we compute the inner product estimation $\hat{y}_s$ of all users $u_j \in U$, i.e. $\hat{y}_s(i, u_j) = \mathbf{e}_i^{(o)\mathsf{T}} \mathbf{e}_{u_j}^{(o)}$, where $\mathbf{e}_i^{(o)}$ and $\mathbf{e}_{u_j}^{(o)}$ respectively denote the ultimate item i's embedding and user u_j's embedding. We output the list of top-K $\hat{y}_s$ of each item as the predicted adopters. Such a method is also able to propagate information in a shorter path. For example in Fig. 1c, it takes two hops to propagate features of a co-visitor (e.g., u_2) of u_1 without a social link, and it takes only one hop with social links. Thus, more nodes are aggregated with the same number of GCN layers.

To summarize, this section introduced a new approach toward the adopter prediction problem with social networks, which effectively incorporates the state-of-the-art NGCF model. The benefit is to allow the social links to model the influence between users and flexibly aggregate features from more multi-hop neighboring users and items.

4   Experiments

4.1   Settings

The embedding dimensions for both users and items are set to 64 following with [12], and the batch size is fixed to 256. We randomly sample 10 negative users to train our model with BPR loss [11]. We use RMSprop optimizer for BPR-MF. For NGCF and Social-NGCF, we use Adam [7] to optimize due to its effectiveness with $\beta_1 = 0.9$ and $\beta_2 = 0.999$. The initial learning rate is set to 0.0001 uniformly. We cross-validated the number of GCN layers in NGCF and the performance plateaued with 2 hidden layers. Each of the layers has 64 neurons. We evaluate all models with three widely used ranking-based metrics: Recall@k, Precision@k, and Normalized Discounted Cumulative Gain (NDCG). We report the average values among all items in our test set.

We deploy three approaches on the adopter prediction task.

- **BPR-MF** [11]: one of the most widely used approach for recommendation model.
- **NGCF** [12]: the state-of-the-art approach for graph-based recommendation model.
- **Social-NGCF**: the proposed approach in this paper.

Table 1. Overall performance of adopter prediction. We highlight that the Social-NGCF outperforms the other competitors among all evaluation metrics.

	Recall@10	Recall@20	Precision@10	Precision@20	NDCG@10	NDCG@20
BPR-MF	0.0695	0.1087	0.0126	0.0104	0.0523	0.0678
NGCF	0.0805	0.1216	0.0136	0.0111	0.0576	0.0743
S-NGCF	**0.0948**	**0.1290**	**0.0154**	**0.0116**	**0.0656**	**0.0799**

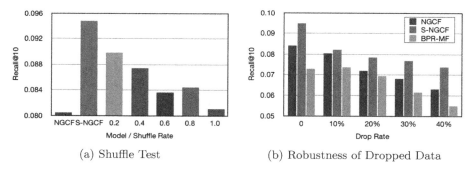

(a) Shuffle Test   (b) Robustness of Dropped Data

Fig. 2. Experiment results on (a) shuffle test and (b) robustness analysis.

4.2 Performance Evaluation

The performance of these approaches is summarized in Table 1. The socially-aware neural graph collaborative filtering (S-NGCF) model outperforms the other two competing methods across all evaluation metrics. Quantitatively, this method reaches 9.48% of recall@10, which is 18% higher than NGCF and 37% higher than BPR-MF, relatively. Similar results are reported in the precision@10, where the actual adopters receive higher rankings from our model than the other approaches. These results indicate that the social connections are not only beneficial but critical for product recommendations and that algorithms can effectively guess adopters in higher priority via ranking. Meanwhile, without considering the high-order co-adopted items, BPR-MF performs more poorly than graph-based approaches.

Shuffle Test on Social Graph. To evaluate the impact of social networks, we deploy a shuffle test experiment on NGCF with the social graph. The key idea behind the shuffle test is that, if social links were important, predictions under randomly assigned links (i.e., shuffled with a higher rate) should produce a worse result. Specifically, given a shuffle rate p_{sr}, we randomly pick $p_{sr}N(E_{social})$ edges in the social graph ($N(E_{social})$ denotes the total number of social edges). To these picked edges, we then randomly pick one of the two associated nodes and randomly change it to another node.

The result is shown in Fig. 2a, reported by recall@10. We observe that the prediction performance of S-NGCF decreases as more edges are shuffled and the original user-user relationships are lost. With 20% of shuffled edges, the performance decrease from 9.48% to 8.98%, which are 18% and 12% relatively higher than NGCF (8.05% recall@10), respectively. Such a decrease is smaller when the shuffle rate increases linearly. We also observe that even all of the social connections are shuffled, S-NGCF still performs no worse than NGCF. Such a result indicates that even a small amount of true social links between users can increase the performance of recommendation, and S-NGCF works well on preventing noisy data. To summarize, the shuffle test proves that users are likely to go to the places checked-in by their friends, and such a phenomenon is essential for designing the recommendation system.

Robustness Analysis. In real applications, user-item interactions may sometimes not be revealed due to privacy issues or forgetting to check-in. In such situation, we are unable to observe the visit. Therefore, it is essential to analyze how the model performs under noisy observational data. To address this challenge, we deploy a test that drops some check-in logs in the training set and monitor how this affects the prediction performance. We randomly drop 10% to 40% records of user-item interactions from the training set. The results are shown in Fig. 2b. Among the dropped datasets, the performance of BPR-MF drops dramatically because the dropped records are regarded as the negative ones which would have negative effect with the objective function. In contrast, graph-based models maintain reasonable performance since it captures the high-order connectivity within the user-item interactions.

Comparing the two graph-based methods, the proposed S-NGCF outperforms the baseline at different drop rates. The robustness of this method is due to the social relationships between users. Since the edges in a social network are static (over some time period), the graph is much denser in connectivity. Since the "missed" check-ins would not affect the edges between users, this method can contain high connectivity and gain robustness. To summarize, adding social connections in graphs leads to higher robustness against the negative impact of dropped data.

5   Discussion and Conclusion

This paper examined the adopter prediction problem with the check-in data from Gowalla. Our contributions lie at evaluating the impact of social connection in recommendation problems. First, this work showed that social relationships are critical in computing the rank of positive users. The shuffle test experiment showed that users are more likely to visit places that had been checked-in by their friends. The drop test experiment showed that graph-based algorithms perform better even when a considerable portion of edges are removed. This is because graph models can maintain high-order connectivity of users. Finally, the static social connection achieves robustness since it enriches the graph connectivity. These findings have implications for both academia and industry. This work brings insights into the social recommendation problem and shows the stability of the training process by adding social edges in graphs. Being able to predict potential adopters, market places and online stores may advertise products better (e.g., pushing advertisements of nearby stores to future visitors).

There are several limitations of this paper. Firstly, users' check-in behavior has a time order. This sequential data can be considered better since the items that the user adopted recently may contribute more to predicting the future adopting behavior. Also, the descriptive information of users and items such as coordinate or location type could be used in learning representation vectors. Next, the computation cost of the GCN-based model grows exponentially with the number of layers. Hence, it is crucial to set up an efficient algorithm for large-scale networks for learning to embed without losing essential information. Finally, the graph convolution network architecture applied in NGCF treats each neighbor equivalently while aggregating the feature through a message-passing algorithm. We leave these limitations as future works.

Acknowledgement. This research was partly supported by Basic Science Research Program through the National Research Foundation of Korea (NRF) funded by the Ministry of Science and ICT (No. NRF-2017R1E1A1A01076400), and the National Natural Science Foundation of China (Grant No. 61673237).

References

1. Cha, M., Haddadi, H., Benevenuto, F., Gummadi, K.P.: Measuring user influence in Twitter: the million follower fallacy. In: Proceedings of the ICWSM (2010)
2. De Meo, P., Ferrara, E., Fiumara, G., Provetti, A.: Generalized Louvain method for community detection in large networks. In: Proceedings of the ISDA (2011)
3. He, X., Liao, L., Zhang, H., Nie, L., Hu, X., Chua, T.S.: Neural collaborative filtering. In: Proceedings of the WWW (2017)
4. Kang, Z., Peng, C., Cheng, Q.: Top-N recommender system via matrix completion. In: Proceedings of the AAAI (2016)
5. Kelman, H.C.: Compliance, identification, and internalization three processes of attitude change. J. Confl. Resolut. **2**(1), 51–60 (1958)
6. Kempe, D., Kleinberg, J., Tardos, E.: Maximizing the spread of influence through a social network. In: Proceedings of the KDD (2003)

7. Kingma, D.P., Ba, J.: Adam: a method for stochastic optimization. arXiv preprint arXiv:1412.6980 (2014)
8. Kipf, T.N., Welling, M.: Semi-supervised classification with graph convolutional networks. In: Proceedings of the ICLR (2017)
9. Leskovec, J., Adamic, L.A., Huberman, B.A.: The dynamics of viral marketing. ACM Trans. Web **1**(1), 5 (2007)
10. Liu, Y., Wei, W., Sun, A., Miao, C.: Exploiting geographical neighborhood characteristics for location recommendation. In: Proceedings of the CIKM (2014)
11. Rendle, S., Freudenthaler, C., Gantner, Z., Schmidt-Thieme, L.: BPR: Bayesian personalized ranking from implicit feedback. In: Proceedings of the UAI (2009)
12. Wang, X., He, X., Wang, M., Feng, F., Chua, T.S.: Neural graph collaborative filtering. In: Proceedings of the SIGIR (2019)

Who Watches What: Forecasting Viewership for the Top 100 TV Networks

Denis Khryashchev[1]($\boxtimes$), Alexandru Papiu[2], Jiamin Xuan[2], Olivia Dinica[2],
Kyle Hubert[2], and Huy Vo[3]

[1] The Graduate Center, City University of New York,
365 5th Ave, New York, NY 10016, USA
`dkhryashchev@gradcenter.cuny.edu`
[2] Simulmedia, 11th Floor, 401 Park Ave S, New York, NY 10016, USA
`{apapiu,jxuan,odinica,khubert}@simulmedia.com`
[3] The City College of New York, City University of New York,
160 Convent Ave, New York, NY 10031, USA
`hvo@cs.ccny.cuny.edu`

Abstract. TV advertising makes up more than one third of total ad spending, and is transacted based on forecast ratings and viewership. Over time, forecast accuracy has decreased due to fragmentation of consumer behavior. Through a comprehensive study we find that an assortment of models combined with an ensemble method leads to better accuracy than any single method. This results in an 11% improvement over a naive baseline method, across 100 of the largest networks.

Keywords: TV networks · Time series · Forecasting · XGboost · Fourier · Facebooks Prophet · Seasonal averaging

1 Introduction

In this paper we examine the properties of 100 largest TV networks in US in terms of aggregated hourly viewership (impressions), and evaluate the performance of several forecasting models against a simple seasonal averaging. Understanding of the behavior of such viewership time series is vital for accurate targeted advertising for even with the rise of digital media, TV advertising spending makes up more than a third of total ad spending. It was estimated by Adweek [1] that the total TV ad spending in the US for 2018 adds up to over 68 billion dollars. The majority of it is bought and sold based on forecast ratings and impressions. Previous research [3] has found that TV forecasts have become less accurate over time due to the fragmentation of audiences and increasing number of networks. Inaccurate forecasts can lead to disruptions in the media planning process and financial losses. Thus, developing models and ways to measure forecasted performance can have a big impact on advertisers' bottom line.

The purchase of television advertisement time is mostly influenced by a television program's predicted performance. Consequently, the prediction and analysis

© Springer Nature Switzerland AG 2019
A. Tagarelli and H. Tong (Eds.): CSoNet 2019, LNCS 11917, pp. 163–174, 2019.
https://doi.org/10.1007/978-3-030-34980-6_19

of television audience sizes has been covered extensively. This analysis has shown that forecasting errors are increasing over time. This trend has been attributed to a series of causes such as the fragmentation of TV audiences due to changing ethnic diversity and increasing education levels in the American population [7]. At the program level, the increased choice of programs and networks for TV viewers has been a large cause of the reduction in forecasting accuracy [3,7]. Measurements of program quality itself are a high predictor of the error [8].

Yet another level of complexity to viewership forecasting is due to Digital Video Recording (DVR) services that allow viewers to create their own schedules and break the established viewing patterns. Zigmond et al. [9] discovered that although up to 70% of ads are skipped in the households with DVR, some of the niche ads appear to have a much higher audience retention.

1.1 Related Work

Nevertheless, numerous models have been tried to improve these forecasts, mainly at the aggregate level. Most models focus on major networks and only prime-time viewing. Arvidsson [2] studied short-term forecasting of on-demand video viewership comparing the performance of a neural network predictor against a simple seasonal averaging with the latter being slightly more accurate. Weber [10] reported that Neural Networks and general linear models provided the most accurate short- and long-term forecasts for the viewership data of the 8 major German TV networks with the SMAPE errors ranging from 15% to 28%.

Linear Holt-Winters and ARIMA models were used by Neagu [11] for long-term forecasting of Nielsen data with the latter model being less accurate. Pagano et al. [12] applied autoregressive models (AR, ARX, and STAT) for short-term forecasting of TV ratings in terms of mean viewing time per household per network. The reported normalized RMSE ranged from 0.80 to 0.87.

Meyer et al. [13] studied how forecast aggregation affects accuracy of predictors on 3 levels: population, segment, and individual. They reported regression models to slightly outperform decision trees and neural networks on all levels of aggregation, and the population level to have the most accurate forecasts.

Nikolopoulos et al. [14] compared the performance of Multiple Linear Regression, Simple Bivariate Regression, several Neural Networks, and predictors based on the nearest neighbor analysis and human judgment on the Greek TV audience ratings in terms of mean absolute error. Top two models to achieve the highest accuracy of around 9.0 were the models based on 5-nearest neighbors and simple linear regression.

Many recent research works are focused on the effects of exogenous variables on TV viewership due to the overall growth of data collection. Wang et al. [15] showed the influence of Belgian Pro League soccer games schedule (kickoff time, month, and opponents) on TV viewership and stadium attendance. Gambaro et al. [16] discovered that news content is a strong predictor of viewership: soft news turn viewers off and vice versa. Belo et al. [17] concluded that the presence of Time-Shift TV that allows to watch live programs recorded on average has increased TV viewership per household by 4 min a day.

1.2   Contributions

Motivated by the increase of the forecasting errors, earlier works predicting TV viewership at the aggregate level, and having the domain expertise of TV advertising at Simulmedia, we make the following contributions in this paper:

- we aggregate set-top box data collected from individual households into hourly viewership time series for the top 100 TV networks in US and determine their periodicity, seasonality, and presence of trends that helps us select better parameters for our predictive models;
- we examine individual performances of 4 forecasting models: seasonal averaging that we use as a baseline predictor, Facebook's prophet, Fourier extrapolation, and XGboost;
- we build an ensemble predictor that reduces the negative effects of overfitting of the 4 individual models. It benefits from the diversity of the models that results in uncorrelated errors between each pair of the models.

2   Viewership Data

2.1   Set-Top Box Data Aggregation

To accurately measure TV viewing, data scientists at Simulmedia collected viewership data from the set-top boxes of over 5 million US households using different cable providers. These data were weighed and projected to match the national Census measurements using demographic information such as age, gender, income, and presence of children. This census-weighed panel is called Simul-Panel. While historically most ratings have been done on the Nielsen panel, we used Simulmedia's panel since the larger sample size allows us to achieve more precise results by minimizing the measurement noise.

The original data were comprised of viewing sequences of individual households at a minute level. We standardized the data in two steps: 1. weighed aggregation of the viewership of all the households at a minute level; 2. averaging the viewership to the hourly level. As a result, we obtained hourly level viewership time series for each of the top 100 networks. One can think of these aggregated time series as the series of the expected counts of the households that will be reached by an ad that was shown at random during that hour. For a given minute m the computations are as follows:

$$x_m = \sum_{i \in H} w_i a_{i,m} \tag{1}$$

where the sum is over the entire household set H, w_i is the household weight, and $a_{i,m}$ is a binary indicator of whether household i watched minute m. The hourly values are acquired from the minute level ones with

$$x_{hour} = \sum_{m \in hour} x_m/60. \tag{2}$$

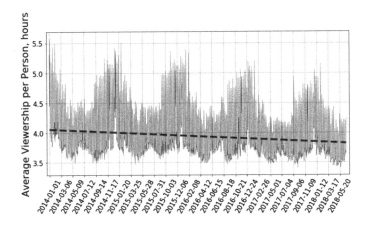

Fig. 1. Long-term trend in average daily viewership

2.2   Periodicity, Seasonality, and Trend

Aggregated viewership data have a great property: random individual viewing habits are averaged out allowing the global periodic patterns to emerge. Figure 2 displays the aggregated and normalized viewership data at an hourly level for 100 most viewed TV networks in US as of March, 2018. Visually we can notice that although there are certain differences among the networks, they tend to have a strong hourly and daily periodicity (darker areas where the points overlap).

To measure the strongest periods, we applied Fast Fourier Transform (FFT) [4] with Blackman window [5] to the network viewership time series. Figure 3 demonstrates the resulting superimposed frequency spectra for the periods within the range of 4 and 744 h (1 month). The spectra of the top 100 networks strongly overlap and have the largest common magnitudes for the periods of 24, 12, 8, 6, and 168 h.

TV Viewership has historically been fairly stable in the long term; however, there are certain global trends present. With the advent of digital media and streaming platforms, TV ratings have been undergoing a steady decline for the majority of networks that we forecast. We observed a 5% decrease in individual daily viewership during the period of about 4.5 years as seen in Fig. 1. It is reasonable to consider the trend to serve as a proxy for a decrease in national TV viewership. On the other hand, certain networks might follow different local trends. Overall, these trends have been analyzed in depth by Hubert [6].

3   Viewership Forecasting

Based on the domain knowledge, we have selected 5 better performing predictors to forecast aggregate viewership: Baseline predictor that implements simple seasonal averaging, Facebook's Prophet that being an additive regression model extracts local trends, seasonality, and blends in important days and holidays,

Fourier extrapolation that deploys prior rigorous mean averaging, XGBoost that performs gradient tree boosting, and Ensemble model that combines the predictions of the 4 individual models.

3.1   Baseline Predictor

Aggregated viewership data are known to have a strong seasonality and to be relatively stable. Therefore, our Baseline model relies on a simple arithmetic averaging of 8 time periods separated by a week (168 h) from each other. Every t^{th} element in the model's forecast $\hat{y}_{bt}$ is calculated as

$$\hat{y}_{bt} = \frac{1}{8} \sum_{i=1}^{8} x_{t-168i} \tag{3}$$

3.2   Facebook's Prophet

TV viewership follows various periodic patterns that include yearly, weekly, monthly or bimonthly seasonality as we have shown in Sect. 2.2. However, such patterns are interfered with holidays and various local trends.

Taylor and Letham of Facebook introduced the Prophet [18], a decomposable time series model that incorporates a seasonal component, trends, customizable holidays, and an error term:

$$\hat{y}_{pt} = g(t) + s(t) + h(t) + \epsilon_t \tag{4}$$

where $g(t)$ models non-periodic changes in time series. Assuming that our data do not have non-linear saturating trends, we employed linear trend with changepoints

$$g(t) = \left(k + a(t)^T \delta\right) t + \left(m + a(t)^T \gamma\right) \tag{5}$$

where k is the growth rate, δ stands for rate adjustments, m is the offset parameter, $a(t)$ is a vector of binary values with ones corresponding to the locations of certain changepoints, and γ is included to make $g(t)$ continuous.

Seasonal component $s(t)$ is evaluated with standard Fourier series

$$s(t) = \sum_{n=1}^{N} \left[a_n \cos\left(\frac{2\pi nt}{P}\right) + b_n \sin\left(\frac{2\pi nt}{P}\right) \right] \tag{6}$$

where P stands for the period and parameters a_n, b_n are estimated. We extract weekly and yearly seasonality with $P = 7$ and $P = 365.25$ correspondingly.

Holidays and special events term, $h(t)$ contains supplementary regressors initially intended to be used for holidays. However, knowing detailed TV program schedule in advance and assuming that more popular shows are to gain higher viewership than less popular ones, we incorporate both: the information on holidays and program schedules one-hot encoded into $h(t)$.

Last term, ϵ_t represents the errors introduced by any unusual changes not accounted for by the model.

The model as a whole is optimized maximizing a posteriori probability.

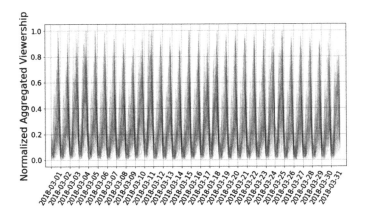

Fig. 2. Normalized aggregated hourly viewership for 100 largest networks during the March of 2018 superimposed

3.3   Fourier Extrapolation

Analyzing Figs. 2 and 3 we notice a very strong periodic pattern in viewing behavior: on a large scale network viewership has a strong autocorrelation at time lags of 24, 168, and about 1344 h which correspond to a daily, weekly and bimonthly periodicity in the time series. Strong periodic patterns assume that a Fourier-based extrapolation might be able to capture the repetitions in the signal and efficiently extrapolate it into the future.

However, due to the constant gradual change in the set-top box data: households join and leave the panel with their weights being adjusted; there might appear certain unexpected jumps in the aggregated viewership (not to mention rare hardly predictable events like Super Bowl).

In order to decrease the negative effects of such viewership jumps, we replace the original historical hourly viewership data with robust location values calculated with Huber's M-estimator [19] which is equivalent to an application of a low-pass filter. We use 7 previous values that are 168 h apart (weekly seasonality) and minimize the objective function of robust location and scale:

$$\operatorname*{argmin}_{\mu_h, \sigma_h} \sum_{i=1}^{7} \psi\left(\left[\frac{x_{t-168i} - \mu_h}{\sigma_h}\right]^2\right) \tag{7}$$

$$\psi(z) = \min\left(\max(z, -c), c\right) \tag{8}$$

where c is the threshold that limits the range of ψ, μ_h and σ_h stand for the robust estimation of location and scale. In our experiments we found that $c = 1.25$ provides the most accurate seasonal averaging.

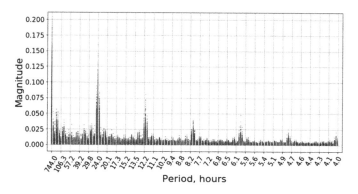

Fig. 3. Spectra of FFT with Blackman window for the viewership of 100 largest networks during the March of 2018 superimposed

After filtering of the original time series we extrapolate it with the use of the standard Fast Fourier Transform [4]. First, the magnitudes are calculated

$$M_k = \sum_{t=1}^{N} x_t e^{-\frac{2\pi i}{N} kt} \tag{9}$$

Then the extrapolation is evaluated with cosine for every t^{th} value

$$\hat{y}_{ft} = \sum_{k=1}^{N} \frac{\Re(M_k)}{N} \cos\left(2\pi \omega_k t + \arg(M_k)\right) \tag{10}$$

where ω_k is the kth frequency corresponding to the magnitude M_k.

Experiments with various windows including Blackman, Hamming, and Parzen [5] as well as zero-padding and detrending did not result in any significant improvement in the overall accuracy of the extrapolation.

3.4   XGBoost

XGBoost [20] is a tree boosting method that incorporates regularization and a 2nd order approximation of the objective function to prevent overfitting and reduce computation time. It allows for the use of an arbitrary objective function.

We combine the viewership data $x = \{x_1, \ldots, x_N\}$, $x_t \in \mathbb{R}$ with m features $X = \{X_1, \ldots, X_N\}$, $X_t \in \mathbb{R}^m$ that correspond to a specific network to obtain a data set $\mathcal{D} = \{(X_t, x_{t+\tau})\}_1^{N-\tau}$ in which some of the features X_t contain lagged viewership x_t with the maximal lag of τ, and the target is the viewership starting at time period τ. A tree ensemble model is composed of K additive functions

$$\hat{x}_{t+\tau} = \phi(X_t) = \sum_{k=1}^{K} f_k(X_t), f_k \in \mathcal{F} \tag{11}$$

where $\mathcal{F} = \{f(X) = w_{q(X)}\}$ stands for the space of regression trees with f_k representing independent tree structure q with leaf weights w. The functions f_k are found through the regularized minimization of

$$\mathcal{L}(\phi) = \sum_j l\left(\hat{x}_j, x_j\right) + \sum_k \Omega(f_k) \tag{12}$$

where $\Omega(f) = \gamma T + \frac{1}{2}\lambda||w||^2$, T is the number of leaves in a tree, and l denotes a convex differentiable loss function. The gradient boosting is performed through the iterative additive optimization. Denoting the model's prediction of the viewership on the training set at t^{th} time period at step i as $\hat{x}_t^{(i)}$ we minimize

$$\mathcal{L}^{(i)} = \sum_{t=\tau}^{N} l\left[x_t, \hat{x}_t^{(i-1)} + f_i(X_{t-\tau})\right] + \Omega(f_i) \tag{13}$$

Finally, the model's forecast is performed as

$$\hat{y}_x = \phi^*(Y) \tag{14}$$

where Y stands for the features of the testing set and ϕ^* is the trained tree ensemble. The features we used included:

- Lagged viewership at time periods that represent the same Weekday and Hour for different number of weeks in the past based on the seasonality of the series calculated with Fourier Transform;
- Seasonally Averaged Lagged Viewership: averages over the past k weeks for the same NDH (Network, Weekday, Hour). Since some NDHs are relatively volatile, looking at the seasonal average decreases the variance and gives a better prediction for the baseline trend. We also introduced the standard deviation as a feature which prevented the model from overfitting caused by outliers present throughout the 8-week period.
- Program Level Features. Since we were dealing with over 20000 programs, this categorical variable posed many challenges. To solve this problem we looked at the average number of impressions for the program and the network in the past 8 weeks, and used that as a numeric feature. We can think of this as an averaged lagged viewership feature for the programs. For certain future programs we did not have actual program names so we also used features like genre, and whether the program was live or repeated.
- Calendar Features: one-hot encoded important calendar days like Christmas.

Among the model's limitations we identified that while the model did pick certain special programs it did not perform well on extreme outliers (e.g. the Superbowl). It is rather expected of the tree-based models, since the prediction they make is an average of the prior predictions. More specialized models able to automatically detect and remove outliers might provide better accuracy.

Furthermore, the tree-based models are known to be unable to capture trends. As explored earlier, the viewership data seem to have a slowly decreasing trend but this did not pose an issue with the XGBoost model: detrending of the time series before training the XGBoost model did not offer significant improvements.

Table 1. Correlation matrix of forecast errors

	Prophet	XGBoost	Fourier
Prophet	1	0.18166874	0.51658387
XGBoost	0.18166874	1	0.13299841
Fourier	0.51658387	0.13299841	1

3.5   Ensemble Model

Quite a few researchers have demonstrated that ensemble models generate forecasts more accurate than individual models participating in the ensemble. Shen et al. [21] used an ensemble of 5 clustering techniques for electricity demand forecasting. Taylor et al. [22] combined various modifications of ARMA and GARCH models to improve the accuracy of wind power density forecasts. Kourentzes et al. [23] concluded that an ensemble of neural networks outperforms the best individual neural network model.

In our experiments we noticed that the errors produced by any two individual models have a very weak correlation (see Table 1) which could be explained by the diversity of the models. Taking it into account, our ensemble model is in essence a convex combination of the forecasts made by individual models:

$$\hat{y}_e = w_b \hat{y}_b + w_x \hat{y}_x + w_p \hat{y}_p + w_f \hat{y}_f \tag{15}$$

where $w_b + w_x + w_p + w_f = 1$, $w. > 0$ are the weights assigned to the models.

4   Evaluation

TV viewership data used in real business applications are characterized with a slight processing delay which prohibits running next-day forecasting. Set-top box data become available two weeks after the actual viewership. To take that into account we separate training and testing data sets with a 2-week window.

In order to reduce bias in our models' parameters we performed yearly cross-validation training and testing. We selected 13 testing periods of 30 days from March 1, 2017 to March 1, 2018 each starting in the beginning of the month. The corresponding training sets were constructed from the viewership data collected in a period within 1 year to 2 weeks prior the beginning of each testing period.

TV networks naturally have different sizes of their audiences and total hourly viewership. To accurately measure average performance of our models on the networks of different size, we used Symmetric Mean Absolute Percentage Error (SMAPE). It is a common metric for relative forecasting accuracy evaluation [24, 25], and for every model's forecast $\hat{y}.$ it is defined as

$$SMAPE(\hat{y}.) = \frac{1}{N} \sum_{t=1}^{N} \frac{2\,|\hat{y}_{.t} - y_t|}{\hat{y}_{.t} + y_t} \tag{16}$$

where y_t stands for actual values observed in the test set and $\hat{y}_{.t}$ is the forecast made by either of the models: $\hat{y}_b$, $\hat{y}_x$, $\hat{y}_p$, $\hat{y}_f$, or $\hat{y}_e$. The metric fits naturally for our task because the viewership time series have values $x_t, y_t > 0$ and we restrict our model's forecasts to $\hat{y}_{.t} > 0$.

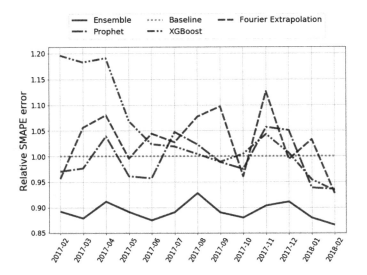

Fig. 4. Mean SMAPE errors normalized with the baseline

Table 2. Mean SMAPE errors normalized with the baseline

Period	Ensemble	Prophet	XGBoost	Fourier
Mar 2017	0.8922	0.9704	1.1961	0.9561
Apr 2017	0.8787	0.9764	1.1829	1.0561
May 2017	0.9115	1.0392	1.1910	1.0800
Jun 2017	0.8911	0.9610	1.0685	0.9955
Jul 2017	0.8748	0.9570	1.0235	1.0441
Aug 2017	0.8905	1.0473	1.0190	1.0274
Sep 2017	0.9278	1.0230	1.0042	1.0772
Oct 2017	0.8900	0.9886	0.9889	1.0968
Nov 2017	0.8798	0.9749	1.0045	0.9606
Dec 2017	0.9033	1.0567	1.0430	1.1260
Jan 2018	0.9110	1.0505	1.0062	0.9941
Feb 2018	0.8795	0.9383	0.9542	1.0328
Mar 2018	0.8653	0.9356	0.9326	0.9268
Mean, Deviation	0.89, 0.02	0.99, 0.04	1.05, 0.09	1.03, 0.06

In Table 2 we report the mean SMAPE errors for 100 top networks per testing period per model normalized with the errors made by the Baseline model. The errors are also visualized on Fig. 4.

The results of our experiments indicate that due to the presence of a very dominant seasonal signal that has a period of about 8 weeks, the simple Baseline model is on par with more complex predictors. XGBoost and Fourier Extrapolation produced slightly less accurate forecasts with the mean SMAPE errors of 5% and 3% higher correspondingly. While Prophet performed marginally better being 1% more accurate than the Baseline.

On the other hand, the Ensemble model demonstrated a significant improvement in overall accuracy being about 11% better than the Baseline which can be explained by a very weak correlation between the models' forecasts.

5   Conclusion

As discussed in the introduction, US TV viewing is undergoing a change, as more fragmentation occurs due to consumer choice. This places a focus on having a robust forecast that can handle smaller network feeds or streams with higher variation. We have undergone a study to pull together these methodologies, and have found that ensemble is a powerful way of reducing the overfitting of individual models.

While we have predicted ratings based solely on the viewing behavior exhibited prior to the broadcast, further research should focus on additional externalities that may impact movement of viewers through content. Indeed, as found in [6], individual networks have differing trends, this combined with people watching fewer networks consistently means correlative effects may be observed. Another potential direction could include bias reduction in the models' forecasts.

Acknowledgment. This work was supported in part by Pitney Bowes 3100041700, Alfred P. Sloan Foundation G-2018-11069, and NSF award 1827505.

References

1. Oster, E.: TVs share of ad spend expected to continue its decline this year. https://www.adweek.com/agencies/tvs-share-of-ad-spend-expected-to-continue-its-decline-this-year (2018)
2. Arvidsson, J.: Forecasting on-demand video viewership ratings using neural networks (2014)
3. Napoli, P.M.: The unpredictable audience: an exploratory analysis of forecasting error for new prime-time network television programs. J. Advert. **30**(2), 53–60 (2001)
4. Cooley, J.W., Tukey, J.W.: An algorithm for the machine calculation of complex fourier series. Math. Comput. **19**(90), 297–301 (1965)
5. Oppenheim, A., Schafer, R., Buck, J.: Discrete-Time Signal Processing. Prentice Hall, Upper Saddle River (1999)

6. Hubert, K.: The hidden story behind TV's ratings decline. https://www.simulmedia. com/assets/media/Hidden-Story-Behind-TV-Ratings-Decline.pdf (2017)
7. Hindman, D.B., Wiegand, K.: The big three's prime time decline: a technological and social context. J. Broadcast. Electron. Media **52**(1), 119–135 (2008)
8. Hunter III, S.D., Chinta, R., Smith, S., Shamim, A., Bawazir, A.: Moneyball for TV: a model for forecasting the audience of new dramatic television series. Stud. Media Commun. **4**(2), 13–22 (2016)
9. Zigmond, D., et al.: When viewers control the schedule: measuring the impact of digital video recording on TV viewership. In: Key Issues Forums at ARF Audience Measurement Conference (2009)
10. Weber, R.: Methods to forecast television viewing patterns for target audiences. In: Communication Research in Europe and Abroad Challenges of the First Decade. De-Gruyter, Berlin (2002)
11. Neagu, R.: Forecasting television viewership: a case study. GE Global Research, 2003GRC039 (2003)
12. Pagano, R., Quadrana, M., Cremonesi, P., Bittanti, S., Formwentin, S., Mosconi, A.: Prediction of TV ratings with dynamic models. In: ACM Workshop on Recommendation Systems for Television and Online Video, RecSysTV (2015)
13. Meyer, D., Hyndman, R.J.: The accuracy of television network rating forecasts: the effects of data aggregation and alternative models. Model Assist. Stat. Appl. **1**(3), 147–155 (2005)
14. Nikolopoulos, K., Goodwin, P., Patelis, A., Assimakopoulos, V.: Forecasting with cue information: a comparison of multiple regression with alternative forecasting approaches. Eur. J. Oper. Res. **180**(1), 354–368 (2007)
15. Wang, C., Goossens, D., Vandebroek, M.: The impact of the soccer schedule on TV viewership and stadium attendance: evidence from the Belgian Pro League. J. Sports Econ. **19**(1), 82–112 (2018)
16. Gambaro, M., Larcinese, V., Puglisi, R., Snyder Jr., J.M.: Is soft news a turn-off? Evidence from Italian TV news viewership (2017)
17. Belo, R., Ferreira, P., de Matos, M., Reis, F.: The impact of time-shift TV on TV viewership and on ad consumption: results from both natural and randomized experiments. A theory of the economics of time. Econ. J. **81**(324), 828–846 (2016)
18. Taylor, S.J., Letham, B.: Forecasting at scale. Am. Stat. **72**(1), 37–45 (2018)
19. Huber, P.J.: Robust statistics. In: Lovric, M. (ed.) International Encyclopedia of Statistical Science. Springer, Heidelberg (2011). https://doi.org/10.1007/978-3-642-04898-2
20. Chen, T., Guestrin, C.: XGBoost: a scalable tree boosting system. In: Proceedings of the 22nd ACM SIGKDD International Conference on Knowledge Discovery and Data Mining, pp. 785–794. ACM (2016)
21. Shen, W., Babushkin, V., Aung, Z., Woon, W.L.: An ensemble model for day-ahead electricity demand time series forecasting. In: Proceedings of the Fourth International Conference on Future Energy Systems, pp. 51–62. ACM (2013)
22. Taylor, J.W., McSharry, P.E., Buizza, R., et al.: Wind power density forecasting using ensemble predictions and time series models. IEEE Trans. Energy Convers. **24**(3), 775 (2009)
23. Kourentzes, N., Barrow, D.K., Crone, S.F.: Neural network ensemble operators for time series forecasting. Expert Syst. Appl. **41**(9), 4235–4244 (2014)
24. Makridakis, S., Hibon, M.: The M3-competition: results, conclusions and implications. Int. J. Forecast. **16**(4), 451–476 (2000)
25. Makridakis, S., Spiliotis, E., Assimakopoulos, V.: The M4 competition: results, findings, conclusion and way forward. Int. J. Forecast. **34**(4), 802–808 (2018)

NLP and Affective Computing

PhonSenticNet: A Cognitive Approach to Microtext Normalization for Concept-Level Sentiment Analysis

Ranjan Satapathy[1], Aalind Singh[2], and Erik Cambria[1(✉)]

[1] Nanyang Technological University, Singapore, Singapore
{satapathy.ranjan,cambria}@ntu.edu.sg
[2] Vellore Institute of Technology, Vellore, India
aalind.singh2015@vit.ac.in

Abstract. With the current upsurge in the usage of social media platforms, the trend of using short text (microtext) in place of text with standard words has seen a significant rise. The usage of microtext poses a considerable performance issue to sentiment analysis, since models are trained on standard words. This paper discusses the impact of coupling sub-symbolic (phonetics) with symbolic (machine learning) Artificial Intelligence to transform the out-of-vocabulary (OOV) concepts into their standard in-vocabulary (IV) form. We develop binary classifier to detect OOV sentences and then they are transformed to phoneme subspace using grapheme to phoneme converter. We compare the phonetic and string distance using the Sorensen similarity algorithm. The phonetically similar IV concepts thus obtained are then used to compute the correct polarity value, which was previously being miscalculated because of the presence of microtext. Our proposed framework improves the accuracy of polarity detection by 6% as compared to the earlier model. In conclusion, we apply a grapheme to phoneme converter for microtext normalization and show its application on sentiment analysis.

Keywords: Microtext normalization · Phonetics · Concept level sentiment analysis · G2P · IPA

1 Introduction

Given that most data today is mined from the web, microtext analysis is vital for many natural language processing (NLP) tasks. In the context of sentiment analysis, microtext normalization is a necessary step for the pre-processing text before polarity detection is performed [9]. The two main features of microtext are relaxed spelling and reliance on emoticons and out-of-vocabulary (OOV) words involving phonetic substitutions (e.g., 'b4' for 'before'), emotional emphasis (e.g., 'goooooood' for 'good') and popular acronyms (e.g., 'otw' for 'on the way') [32,33,40]. It could be thought that microtext normalization is as simple as performing find-and-replace pre-processing [18].

© Springer Nature Switzerland AG 2019
A. Tagarelli and H. Tong (Eds.): CSoNet 2019, LNCS 11917, pp. 177–188, 2019.
https://doi.org/10.1007/978-3-030-34980-6_20

The challenge arises when trying to automatically rectify and replace them with the correct in-vocabulary (IV) words [23]. However, the wide-ranging diversity of spellings makes this solution impractical (e.g., the spelling of the word "tomorrow" is generally written as "tomorow, 2moro, tmr" among others). Furthermore, given the productivity of users, novel forms which are not bound to orthographic norms in spelling can emerge. For instance, a sampling of Twitter study [23] found over 4 million OOV words where new spellings were created regularly, both voluntarily and accidentally.

Concept-based approaches to sentiment analysis focus on a semantic analysis of text through the use of web ontologies or semantic networks, which allow the aggregation of conceptual and affective information associated with natural language opinions. The analysis at concept-level is intended to infer the semantic and affective information associated with natural language opinions and hence, to enable a comparative fine-grained feature based sentiment analysis. In this work, we propose PhonSenticNet, a concept based lexicon which advantages from phonetic features to normalize the OOV concepts to IV concepts. The International Phonetic Alphabet (IPA)[1] is used as the phonetic feature in the proposed framework. We use Epitran [24] to transform concepts to their IPA encodings. The proposed framework can deal with the texts which are phonemic variants of their IV concepts. The results are discussed at three different levels:

1. information loss.
2. normalization of OOV concepts.
3. polarity detection.

The proposed system only works for the text with their phonetic substitutions. Though, the acronyms still rely on the lexicon built in [34]. The rest of the paper is organized as follows: Sect. 2 discusses the literature survey in microtext, Sect. 3 discusses the Framework, Sect. 4 discusses the datasets used, Sect. 5 discusses the experiments performed and Sect. 6 concludes the work done with future directions for this work.

2   Related Work

This section discusses the work done in the domain of microtext normalization and grapheme to phoneme converters.

2.1   Microtext Analysis

Microtext has become ubiquitous in today's communication. This is partly a consequence of Zipf's law, or principle of least effort (for which people tend to minimize energy cost at both individual and collective levels when communicating with one another), and it poses new challenges for NLP tools which are usually designed for well-written text [16]. Normalization is the task of transforming unconventional words or concepts to their respective standard counterpart.

---

[1] https://www.internationalphoneticassociation.org/content/full-ipa-chart.

Authors in [34] use Soundex algorithm to transform OOV to IV and demonstrates the increase in sentiment analysis accuracy due to normalization. In [22], authors present a novel unsupervised method to translate Chinese abbreviations. It automatically extracts the relation between a full-form phrase and its abbreviation from monolingual corpora, and induces translation entries for the abbreviation by using its full-form as a bridge. [14] uses a classifier to detect OOV words, and generates correction candidates based on morpho-phonemic similarity. The types and features of microtext are reliant on the nature of the technological support that makes them possible. This means that microtext will vary as new communication technologies emerge. In our related work, we categorized normalization into three well-known NLP tasks: spelling correction, statistical machine translation (SMT), and automatic speech recognition (ASR).

Spelling Correction. Correction is executed on a word-per-word basis which is also seen as a spell checking task. This model gained extensive attention in the past and a diversity of correction practices have been endorsed by [4,12,21, 25,36]. Instead, [13] and [35] proposed a categorization of abbreviation, stylistic variation, prefix-clipping, which was then used to estimate the probability of occurrence of the characters. Thus far, the spell corrector became widely popular in the context of SMS, where [11] advanced the hidden Markov model whose topology takes into account both "graphemic" variants (e.g., typos, omissions of repeated letters, etc.) and "phonemic" variants. All of the above, however, only focused on the normalization of words without considering their context.

Statistical Machine Translation. When compared to the previous task, this method appears to be rather straightforward and better since it has the possibility to model (context-dependent) one-to-many relationships which were out-of-reach previously [19]. Some examples of works include [1,17,26]. However, the SMT still overlooks some features of the task, particularly the fact that lexical creativity verified in social media messages is barely captured in a stationary sentence board.

Automatic Speech Recognition. ASR considers that microtext tends to be a closer approximation of the word's phonemic representation rather than its standard spelling. As follows, the key to microtext normalization becomes very similar to speech recognition which consists of decoding a word sequence in a (weighted) phonetic framework. For example, [19] proposed to handle normalization based on the observation that text messages present a lot of phonetic spellings, while more recently [18] proposed an algorithm to determine the probable pronunciation of English words based on their spelling. Although the computation of a phonemic representation of the message is extremely valuable, it does not solve entirely all the microtext normalization challenges (e.g., acronyms and misspellings do not resemble their respective IV words' phonemic representation). Authors in [2] have merged the advantages of SMT and the spelling corrector model.

2.2   Grapheme-to-Phoneme Converter

Grapheme-to-Phoneme (G2P) conversion is a method of predicting the utterance of a word or concept given its graphemic or written form. Many Speech and NLP tasks require a G2P step to convert the orthographic representations to phonemic or phonetic representations [3, 20, 31]. Such tasks include Text-to-speech (TTS), ASR, the training of polyglot phonetic models for (non-speech) NLP tasks, and the implementation of approximate phonetic matching. G2P research focusses on some of the most challenging scenarios in different languages. Though less attention is paid to provide G2P coverage for the full range of languages with a more direct relationship between orthography and phonology. Many such languages require more than merely a mapping table for G2P but can be handled satisfactorily by a more complex rule-based system and certainly do not require a machine learning approach. This is fortunate because many of these are also low resource languages in which sufficient training data are not available but adequate linguistic descriptions do exist. There are a few tools that already occupy this niche. Unitran is a tool that converts orthographic text to WorldBet and X-SAMPA [28]. It is limited, though, in that it does not support Roman scripts and it does not have a mechanism for specifying different behavior for different languages that use the same script.

3   Framework

Limitation of microtext normalization research is that it is considered either a find-and-replace pre-processing [18] or a phonetic substitution [34] which does not take standard IPA into consideration. We propose a framework which considers microtext as an area closely related to ASR and transforms the text to their phonemic forms.

The architecture of the proposed model is depicted in Fig. 1. The framework classifies a sentence as OOV or IV using binary classifier. Following this, the OOV sentence is passed through a concept parser, and then the concepts are transformed to IPA using Epitran. One persistent advantage of Epitran (over lexical resources) is its ability to produce consistent and accurate pronunciations for all words that a system encounters, not just thus listed in the lexicon. The IPA of OOV concepts are matched to the PhonSenticNet, and then the IV concept is fetched. The corresponding polarity of the IV concept is retrieved using sentic computing [8].

3.1   Classification of Microtext

In this subsection, we employ various binary classifiers to detect OOV sentences so as to reduce the execution time of the overall algorithm. OOV sentence are those which contain at least on of the OOV terms. We observed that the execution time of the framework was reduced by 20%. We use the term frequency-inverse document frequency (TF-IDF) [30] approach for the task of feature extraction from a given text.

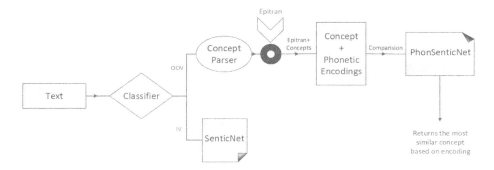

Fig. 1. Architecture of the framework

We first split the document into tokens assigning weights to them based on the frequency with which it shows up in the document along with how repetitive that term occurs in the entire corpora. We used this approach to train four different classifiers. The evaluation metrics such as Precision, Recall, F-measure and Accuracy have been enlisted in the Table 3.

3.2 Polarity Detection

The polarity detection module utilizes SenticNet lexicon [10]. While SenticNet can be used as any other sentiment lexicon, e.g., concept matching or bag-of-concepts model, the right way to use the knowledge base for the task of polarity detection is in conjunction with sentic patterns, sentiment-specific linguistic patterns that infer polarity by allowing affective information to flow from concept to concept based on the dependency relation between clauses. The sentiment sources of such affective information are extracted from SenticNet by firstly generalizing multiword expressions and words by means of conceptual primitives and, secondly, by extracting their polarity. The lexicon has polarity values associated with concepts. For a given sentence, we average the polarity over all concepts and output the polarity either as positive, or negative.

4 Datasets

This section introduces to datasets used. The twitter dataset is available on request. The concept-level lexicon SenticNet[2] and NUS SMS Data[3] are publically available.

4.1 NUS SMS Corpus

This corpus has been created from the NUS English SMS corpus, where [38] randomly selected 2,000 messages. The messages were first normalized into standard

---

[2] http://sentic.net/senticnet-5.0.zip.
[3] http://github.com/kite1988/nus-sms-corpus.

English and then translated into standard Chinese. For our training and testing purposes, we only used the actual messages and their normalized English version. It also contains Singaporean colloquial terms (Singlish). Singlish is an English-based creole that is lexically and syntactically influenced by Hokkien, Cantonese, Mandarin, Malay and Tamil [5]. It is primarily a spoken variety in Singapore, to emerge as a means of online communication for Singaporeans [39].

4.2   SenticNet

Sentic API provides the semantics and sentics (i.e., the denotative and connotative information) associated with the concepts of SenticNet, a semantic network of commonsense knowledge that contains 100,000 nodes (words and multiword expressions) and thousands of connections (relationships between nodes). We used a concept parser [29] in order to break sentences to concepts and analyze them. The concepts in the SenticNet contains their corresponding polarities.

Table 1. Sample soundex and IPA encodings with polarities for SenticNet5

Concepts	Polarity	Soundex encoding	IPA encoding
a_little	Negative	A000_L340	æ_lɪtæl
abandon	Negative	A153	æbəndæn
absolutely_fantastic	Positive	A124_F532	əbsəlutlɪ_fəntəstɪk

4.3   Normalized Tweets

The authors in [34], built a dataset which consists of tweets and their transformed IV counterparts. We demonstrate our results by extracting concepts from unconventionally written sentences and then passing them through our proposed module to convert them to standard format concepts' and their corresponding polarities from SenticNet (Table 2).

5   Results

This section dives into experiments performed to develop a concept-level microtext normalization module. The experiments performed help in deciding the best set of parameters to achieve state of the art accuracy. We name the lexicon which we built from SenticNet as PhonSenticNet. It contains concepts and their phonetic encoding which is extracted from Epitran. The detailed procedure is explained in the following subsections:

Table 2. Sample sentences with their detected polarity before and after microtext normalization

Text	Sentence Polarity before microtext normalization	Sentence Polarity after microtext normalization
I wil kil u	Neutral	Negative
m so hapy	Neutral	Positive
i dnt lyk reading	Positive	Negative
it is awesum 2 ride byk	Neutral	Positive

Table 3. Precision, Recall, F1 and Accuracy for each algorithm on different datasets

	NUS SMS dataset								Twitter dataset							
	LR		SGDC		SVC		MNB		LR		SGDC		SVC		MNB	
	IV	OOV	IV	OOV	IV	OOV	IV	OOV	IV	OOV	IV	OOV	IV	OOV	IV	OOV
Precision	0.91	0.95	0.84	0.98	0.87	0.97	0.89	0.97	0.71	0.69	0.63	0.72	0.74	0.67	0.81	0.68
Recall	0.95	0.90	0.99	0.81	0.98	0.85	0.97	0.87	0.68	0.71	0.80	0.52	0.64	0.77	0.61	0.85
F1	0.93	0.92	0.91	0.89	0.92	0.91	0.93	0.92	0.69	0.70	0.70	0.60	0.68	0.72	0.69	0.76
Accuracy	**0.9275**		0.89875		0.915		0.9225		0.6962		0.6605		0.7013		**0.7288**	

5.1 Classification of Microtext

Different classifiers were trained on the two datasets namely NUS SMS data and Twitter dataset as shown in Table 3. The datasets were divided into training, validation and test as 70:20:10. As shown in the Table 3, the best performing classifiers for NUS SMS dataset and Twitter dataset are Logistic Regression (LR) and Multinomial Naïve Bayes (MNB). SMS writing is very orthodox, whereas Tweets are dynamic. The difference in accuracy on both the datasets is due to the writing style used on Twitter.

5.2 Comparision of IPA with Phonetic Algorithm

We compare our proposed IPA based method to Soundex [34] since only [34] have incorporated phonetic features to improve sentiment analysis. Soundex gives a lot of duplicate encoding, whereas IPA gives no duplicate encoding. Each concept is unique in phonetic subspace, thereby increasing the efficiency for microtext normalization at concept-level. The number of concepts present in the lexicon is 100000. The duplicates[4] due to Soundex encoding are 46080. This shows that using Soundex for microtext normalization has some information loss at the concept-level. As a result of Soundex encoding, we have 46080 ambiguous concepts which affect the microtext normalization in real time. Hence, we propose to use IPA for all the phonetic based microtext normalization methods. The IPA based encoding has no redundancy, and thereby no information loss occurs during microtext normalization.

---

[4] Repetition of a soundex encoding for greater than one.

5.3   Microtext Normalization of Concepts Using IPA

The analysis at concept-level is intended to infer the semantic and affective information associated with natural language opinions and, hence, to enable a comparative fine-grained feature-based sentiment analysis [15,27]. Concept-based approaches to sentiment analysis focus on a semantic analysis of text through the use of web ontologies or semantic networks, which allow the aggregation of conceptual and affective information associated with natural language opinions [6,7]. In order to normalize concepts found on social media, we built a resource for concept-level phonetic encodings by using concepts from SenticNet. We used a concept parser to extract concepts from the input text. The concepts are then transformed to a subspace where they are represented by their phonetic encodings. Table 1 shows sample concepts with their respective Soundex encodings and IPA from SenticNet.

Phonetic encoding transforms concepts from the string subspace into their phonetic subspace. This transformation eliminates the redundant concept encoding produced by Soundex. The input concept is then passed through this phonetic subspace (IPA used in PhonSenticnet) to find the most phonetically similar concept and then returns it. The Algorithms 1 and 2 describe the procedures in detail.

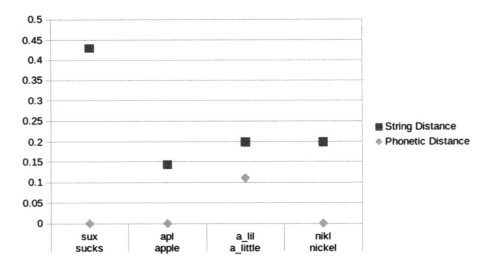

Fig. 2. Visualization of string and phonetic distance

Algorithm 1. Algorithm for microtext normalization using phonetic features

Sentence (S) $= s_1, s_2, \cdots, s_n$
c_i = concept-parser(S)
For each concept c_i in Sn
closest-match-concept = PhonSenticNet(c_i)
if closest_ match(C_i, SenticNet) **then**
  return concept polarity
else
  return sentence polarity
end if
average over polarity of concepts for sentence polarity **EndFor**
return   sentence polarity

Algorithm 2. Closest Match Algorithm

Concept (C) $= c_1, c_2, \cdots, c_m$
For each concept c_i in C
Sorensen (c_i,Senticnet)
EndFor
return phonetically closest matching concept

5.4   Polarity Detection with SenticNet

We compare accuracies of our framework with that of [34] for polarity detection[5]. The accuracy increases significantly by 6% as shown in Fig. 3. The application of

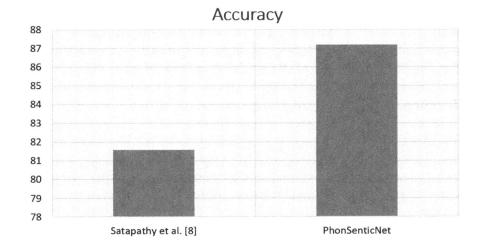

Fig. 3. Accuracy for polarity detection

---

[5] https://sentic.net/demos/#polarity.

microtext normalization to sentiment analysis shows the importance of microtext normalization module for the texting data.

6   Discussion and Future Work

The proposed framework contains concepts from SenticNet and their phonetics which is calculated using Epitran which we name as PhonSenticNet. This resource is used as a lexicon for microtext normalization. The input sentence is broken down into concepts and then transformed into their phonetic encoding. The phonetic encoding is matched with the PhonSenticNet, the resource built in this work. Then the most similar matching concept and its corresponding polarity is returned as shown in the Algorithms 1 and 2. Microtext is language-dependent: the same set of characters could have completely different meaning in different languages, e.g., '555' is negative in Chinese language because the number '5' is pronounced as 'wu' and 'wuwuwu' resembles a crying sound but positive in Thai since the number 5 is pronounced as 'ha' and three consecutive 5s correspond to the expression 'hahaha'. Hence, we are working on a multilingual version [37]. In conclusion:

1. We have taken Sorensen similarity to measure the distance. The Sorensen similarity shows how similar the two input texts are to one another, where 0 means similar and 1 means dissimilar as shown in Fig. 2.
2. Figure 2 shows distance between some of the non-standard and their standard concepts. The similarity is shown at both string and phonetic level.
3. Previous paper [34] shows sentence-level sentiment analysis, whereas in this work we focus on concept-level microtext normalization.
4. It can be observed from Table 3 that the twitter dataset does not perform as good as the NUS SMS data. The reason behind it is, the twitter dataset contains acronyms like lol, rofl, etc. instead of phonetic substitution. This also suggests how the way of writing differs in both messages and tweets.

References

1. Aw, A., Zhang, M., Xiao, J., Su, J.: A phrase-based statistical model for SMS text normalization. In: ACL, pp. 33–40 (2006)
2. Beaufort, R., Roekhaut, S., Cougnon, L.A.l., Fairon, C.d.: A hybrid rule/model-based finite-state framework for normalizing SMS messages. In: ACL, pp. 770–779. Association for Computational Linguistics (2010)
3. Bisani, M., Ney, H.: Joint-sequence models for grapheme-to-phoneme conversion. Speech Commun. **50**(5), 434–451 (2008)
4. Brill, E., Moore, R.C.: An improved error model for noisy channel spelling correction. In: Proceedings of the 38th Annual Meeting on Association for Computational Linguistics, pp. 286–293 (2000)
5. Brown, A.: Singapore English in a Nutshell: An Alphabetical Description of its Features. Federal Publications, Singapore (1999)

6. Cambria, E., Benson, T., Eckl, C., Hussain, A.: Sentic PROMs: application of sentic computing to the development of a novel unified framework for measuring health-care quality. Expert Syst. Appl. **39**(12), 10533–10543 (2012)
7. Cambria, E., Hussain, A., Durrani, T., Havasi, C., Eckl, C., Munro, J.: Sentic computing for patient centered applications. In: IEEE ICSP, pp. 1279–1282 (2010)
8. Cambria, E., Hussain, A., Havasi, C., Eckl, C.: Sentic computing: exploitation of common sense for the development of emotion-sensitive systems. In: Esposito, A., Campbell, N., Vogel, C., Hussain, A., Nijholt, A. (eds.) Development of Multimodal Interfaces: Active Listening and Synchrony. LNCS, vol. 5967, pp. 148–156. Springer, Heidelberg (2010). https://doi.org/10.1007/978-3-642-12397-9_12
9. Cambria, E., Poria, S., Gelbukh, A., Thelwall, M.: Sentiment analysis is a big suitcase. IEEE Intell. Syst. **32**(6), 74–80 (2017)
10. Cambria, E., Poria, S., Hazarika, D., Kwok, K.: SenticNet 5: discovering conceptual primitives for sentiment analysis by means of context embeddings. In: Thirty-Second AAAI Conference on Artificial Intelligence, pp. 1795–1802 (2018)
11. Choudhury, M., Saraf, R., Jain, V., Sarkar, S., Basu, A.: Investigation and modeling of the structure of texting language. Int. J. Doc. Anal. Recogn. **10**(3–4), 157–174 (2007)
12. Church, K.W., Gale, W.A.: Probability scoring for spelling correction. Stat. Comput. **1**(2), 93–103 (1991)
13. Cook, P., Stevenson, S.: An unsupervised model for text message normalization. In: Proceedings of the Workshop on Computational Approaches to Linguistic Creativity, pp. 71–78 (2009)
14. Han, B., Baldwin, T.: Lexical normalisation of short text messages: Makn sens a# Twitter. In: ACL, pp. 368–378 (2011)
15. Howard, N., Cambria, E.: Intention awareness: improving upon situation awareness in human-centric environments. Human-centric Comput. Inf. Sci. **3**(9), 1–17 (2013)
16. Hutto, C.J., Gilbert, E.: VADER: a parsimonious rule-based model for sentiment analysis of social media text. In: Eighth International AAAI Conference on Weblogs and Social Media, pp. 216–225 (2014)
17. Kaufmann, M., Kalita, J.: Syntactic normalization of Twitter messages. natural language processing, Kharagpur, India (2010)
18. Khoury, R.: Microtext normalization using probably-phonetically-similar word discovery. In: 2015 IEEE 11th International Conference on Wireless and Mobile Computing, Networking and Communications (WiMob), pp. 392–399 (2015)
19. Kobus, C., Yvon, F., Damnati, G.é.: Normalizing SMS: are two metaphors better than one? In: Proceedings of the 22nd International Conference on Computational Linguistics, vol. 1, pp. 441–448. Association for Computational Linguistics (2008)
20. Laurent, A., Deléglise, P., Meignier, S.: Grapheme to phoneme conversion using an SMT system. In: Tenth Annual Conference of the International Speech Communication Association, pp. 708–711 (2009)
21. Li, M., Zhang, Y., Zhu, M., Zhou, M.: Exploring distributional similarity based models for query spelling correction. In: ACL, pp. 1025–1032 (2006)
22. Li, Z., Yarowsky, D.: Unsupervised translation induction for Chinese abbreviations using monolingual corpora. In: Proceedings of ACL-08: HLT, pp. 425–433 (2008)
23. Liu, F., Weng, F., Wang, B., Liu, Y.: Insertion, deletion, or substitution? normalizing text messages without pre-categorization nor supervision. ACL-HLT 2011 - Proceedings of the 49th Annual Meeting of the Association for Computational Linguistics: Human Language Technologies 2, pp. 71–76 (2011)

24. Mortensen, D.R., Dalmia, S., Littell, P.: Epitran: precision G2P for many languages. In: Proceedings of the Eleventh International Conference on Language Resources and Evaluation (LREC 2018), pp. 7–12. European Language Resources Association (ELRA), Paris, France, May 2018
25. Pennell, D.L., Liu, Y.: A character-level machine translation approach for normalization of SMS abbreviations. In: IJCNLP, pp. 974–982 (2011)
26. Pennell, D.L., Liu, Y.: Normalization of informal text. Comput. Speech Lang. **28**(1), 256–277 (2014)
27. Qazi, A., Syed, K., Raj, R., Cambria, E., Tahir, M., Alghazzawi, D.: A concept-level approach to the analysis of online review helpfulness. Comput. Hum. Behav. **58**, 75–81 (2016)
28. Qian, T., Hollingshead, K., Yoon, S.Y., Kim, K.Y., Sproat, R.: A python toolkit for universal transliteration. In: Proceedings of the Seventh Conference on International Language Resources and Evaluation (LREC 2010), pp. 2897–2901 (2010)
29. Rajagopal, D., Cambria, E., Olsher, D., Kwok, K.: A graph-based approach to commonsense concept extraction and semantic similarity detection. In: WWW, pp. 565–570 (2013)
30. Ramos, J., et al.: Using TF-IDF to determine word relevance in document queries. Proceedings of the first instructional conference on machine learning. **242**, 133–142 (2003)
31. Rao, K., Peng, F., Sak, H., Beaufays, F.: Grapheme-to-phoneme conversion using long short-term memory recurrent neural networks. In: 2015 IEEE International Conference on Acoustics, Speech and Signal Processing (ICASSP), pp. 4225–4229. IEEE (2015)
32. Read, J.: Using emoticons to reduce dependency in machine learning techniques for sentiment classification. In: Proceedings of the ACL Student Research Workshop, pp. 43–48. Association for Computational Linguistics (2005)
33. Rosa, K.D., Ellen, J.: Text classification methodologies applied to micro-text in military chat. In: Proceedings of the Eight International Conference on Machine Learning and Applications, Miami, pp. 710–714 (2009)
34. Satapathy, R., Guerreiro, C., Chaturvedi, I., Cambria, E.: Phonetic-based micro-text normalization for twitter sentiment analysis. In: 2017 IEEE International Conference on Data Mining Workshops (ICDMW), pp. 407–413. IEEE (2017)
35. Sproat, R., Black, A.W., Chen, S., Kumar, S., Ostendorf, M., Richards, C.: Normalization of non-standard words. Comput. Speech Lang. **15**(3), 287–333 (2001)
36. Toutanova, K., Moore, R.C.: Pronunciation modeling for improved spelling correction. In: ACL, pp. 144–151 (2002)
37. Vilares, D., Peng, H., Satapathy, R., Cambria, E.: Babelsenticnet: a commonsense reasoning framework for multilingual sentiment analysis. In: 2018 IEEE Symposium Series on Computational Intelligence (SSCI), pp. 1292–1298. IEEE (2018)
38. Wang, P., Ng, H.T.: A beam-search decoder for normalization of social media text with application to machine translation. In: HLT-NAACL, pp. 471–481 (2013)
39. Warschauer, M.: The internet and linguistic pluralism. Silicon literacies: Communication, innovation and education in the electronic age, pp. 62–74 (2002)
40. Xue, Z., Yin, D., Davison, B.D.: Normalizing Microtext. Analyzing Microtext, pp. 74–79 (2011)

One-Document Training for Vietnamese Sentiment Analysis

Dang-Khoa Nguyen-Nhat and Huu-Thanh Duong[(✉)]

Faculty of Information Technology, Ho Chi Minh City Open University,
97 Vo Van Tan, Ward 6, District 3, Ho Chi Minh City, Vietnam
{1651010082khoa,thanh.dh}@ou.edu.vn

Abstract. The traditional studies which have based on machine learning are usually supervised learning for sentiment analysis problem, this is costly time and money to build pre-labeled dataset, not domain adaptation and hard to handle unseen data. In this paper, we have approached semi-supervised learning for Vietnamese sentiment analysis, training data is only one document. Many preprocessing techniques have been performed to clean and normalize data, complemented semantic lexicons such as negation handling, intensification handling, also augmented training data from one-document training. In experiments, we have performed various aspects and obtained competitive results which may motivate next propositions.

Keywords: Semi-supervised · Vietnamese sentiment analysis · Preprocessing techniques · Data augmentation · One-document training

1 Introduction

Sentiment analysis is an essential task to detect the sentiment polarities in the text applied widely in e-commerce system, blogs and social media. It imagines that it needs many employees following the customers' replies about a product, read and analyze the hundreds or thousands of those replies to evaluate the degree of customers' satisfaction for making next strategies about the products or take a direction in development. This is costly both human resources and money a lot, reaches the customers' expectation is slow and easy to miss ones. Sentiment analysis is a perfect solution for this problem, its main task groups the document into various polarities. Based on automatic prediction, the traders can make decision easier, and also plan the direction to develop their business.

There are three main approaches for sentiment analysis: lexicon-based approach, machine learning approach, hybrid approach [1]. Lexicon-based approach replies on the emotional lexicons to detect customers' emotions, its main drawbacks are to depend on the context and languages. Actually, sentiment analysis is text classification problem which can apply machine learning classifiers in emotional polarities, Soleymani et al. [2] makes a survey summarized sentiment analysis methods, including in text, it shows many previous researches in supervised and unsupervised learning. The traditional approach is usually

© Springer Nature Switzerland AG 2019
A. Tagarelli and H. Tong (Eds.): CSoNet 2019, LNCS 11917, pp. 189–200, 2019.
https://doi.org/10.1007/978-3-030-34980-6_21

supervised learning, supervised classifiers are used such as Naive Bayes, SVM, Random forest, Logistic Regression, ensemble of voting classifiers, also investigating on feature selection for retaining useful features and ignoring redundant features to improve the performing approach. However, the pre-labeled datasets are scarce and unavailable for a certain application, they are costly so much time to build, depend on domain adaptation and ineffectively handle unseen data. So unsupervised-learning approaches have also investigated and various propositions have also mentioned in [2] such as linguistic inquiry and word count which count positive and negative affecting terms in text, or affective norms of words measures sentiment as happiness expressed through text, or improve sentence-level classification through conceptual dependencies. Fernández-Gavilanes et al. [3] used sentiment lexicon to create by means of an automatic polarity expansion algorithm and some natural language processing techniques such as detecting of polarity conflicts or concessive subordinate clauses. In recent years, emoji icons have boomed in e-commerce system, blogs and social media, these ones express so much sentiment, Fernández-Gavilanes et al. [4] also constructed a novel emoji sentiment lexicon using an unsupervised sentiment analysis based on the definitions given by emoji creators Emojipedia and created lexicon variants based on the sentiment distribution of the informal texts.

AL-Sharuee et al. [5] used SentiWordNet 3.0 to prepare the underlying text for further processing and handle common linguistic forms such as intensifiers, negation, contrast. Next phase, they proposed binary ensemble clustering by assembling the results of a modified k-means algorithm, where the selected features are the adjectives and adverbs in all the documents.

Furthermore, data augmentation is a trend in recent years, from a limited data training will automatically generate more data training as considered semi-supervised learning. Kobayashi [6] proposed a novel data augmentation for labeled sentences called contextual augmentation. They stochastically replace words with other words predicting by a bi-directional language model at word positions, language models improved with a label-conditional architecture which allows the model to augment sentences without breaking the label-compatibility.

Preprocessing techniques are frequently used in natural language processing to prepare text that is going to be classified. Especially, reviews in e-commerce system, blogs and social media are informal, so they contain so much noise information, unnecessary in detecting the sentiment. Those ones will clean text, normalize text and only keep useful information, Symeonidis et al. [7] summarized the preprocessing techniques and performed experiments to prove they improve significantly the accuracy of classifiers.

Our approach has based on semi-supervised learning, incorporated the preprocessing techniques to increase the semantic in text and applied easy data augmentation techniques to generate training data automatically.

In the rest of this paper is organized as follows: Sect. 2 presents our background and approach, the experiments is presented in Sects. 3, and 4 is the conclusions and future works.

2   The Approach

In the paper, machine learning is main approach based semi-supervised learning with only one-document training for every polarity. Preprocessing techniques have applied to clean and normalize text, the useful lexicons is complemented or merged, and training data is enhanced with augmentation data techniques from only one-document training. In order to prove our approach, we have applied the well-known classifers such as Naive Bayes, Logistic Regression, Support Vector Machine, and ensembles of classifiers such as One-vs-One, One-vs-All.

2.1   Preprocessing Techniques

Almost of recent studies in sentiment analysis focus on the user-generated texts which have based on a habit and informal ones are necessary to clean, normalize language, also remove noise information is going to be classified.

Vietnamese segmentation this is always an essential step to work with Vietnamese, for example "đây là điện thoại tuyệt vời" (this is a wonderful phone) is tokenized "đây là điện_thoại tuyệt_vời" (using pyvi[1] library). Unlike English, words are separated by whitespaces and punctuations, Vietnamese words may contain many tokens and they must be processed, if not the meaning of the sentence can be much different from original expectation.

Lowercase the same words are merged and the dimensionality is reduced, for example tốt (good) and Tốt (Good) is the same dimensionality.

Stopwords removal stopwords which are less meaning words are removed, list of stopwords is determined manually based on the frequency of terms in datasets.

Emotional icons replacement the positive and negative icons are respectively replaced by pos and neg lexicons. In order to do that, it has also prepared a list of emotional icons manually. For example: :) is replaced by pos lexicon or :(is replaced by neg lexicon.

Punctuation removal some punctuations (excluding underscore _ is used for Vietnamese segmentation) usually do not affect the sentiment, it should be removed to reduce noise information, for example: "quá đẹp!!!, yêu điện_thoại này!!!" (so beautiful!!!, love this phone!!!) will be "quá đẹp yêu điện_thoại này". However, some punctuations contain sentiment, so it might decrease the accuracy of classification in those cases such as :), :D, ;), <3 are positive icons which affect sentiment in reviews. In our works, this one will be applied after emotional icons replacement.

---

[1] https://pypi.org/project/pyvi/ .

Replicated characters removal some characters are replicated one or more times in a lexicon to emphasize sentiment, this can lead to increase unnecessary dimensionality, so it removes the replicated characters to transform the word to the source word to merge them. For example quáaaaa is replaced by quá (so), tuyệt_vờiiiii is replaced by tuyệt_vời (wonderful).

Abbreviations or wrong-spelling lexicons replacement abbreviations and wrong-spelling words become a habit and are usually used in reviews of social media or e-commerce system, they should also merge into the source word, for example dth -> dễ_thương (cute); iu, êu -> yêu (lovely); omg -> oh my god; k -> không (not); sd -> sử dụng (use); ote, okay, oki, uki, oke -> ok; tệc vời, tẹt zời, tẹc zời, toẹt vời -> tuyệt_vời (wonderful); sức sắc, xức sắc, xúc sắc, xs -> xuất_sắc (excellent); wá, qá -> quá (so). Currently, a list of abbreviation and wrong-spelling lexicons have prepared manually for our experiments based on observing the reviews in social media and our collected datasets.

Numbers removal normally, numbers do not contain any sentiment, it is necessary to remove them, but this should be performed after emotional icon replacement, wrong-spelling replacement because any of them contain numbers such as :3, <3, 8|, 8-), etc.

Part of Speech (POS) handling POS tagging is an essential problem in natural language processing to assign part of speech to each words in a sentence as noun, verb, adjective, pronoun. This is helpful to increase semantic in text. In our works, POS tagging is used to retain words containing the sentiment, namely noun, adjective, verb, adverb. For example "điện_thoại đó đẹp quá, tôirất hài_lòng" (that phone is so beautiful, I am so pleased), the part of speech for each words is "điện_thoại/N đó/P đẹp/A quá/R, tôi/P rất/R hài_lòng/A" (N: noun, P: pronoun, A: adjective, R: adverb), the sentence becomes "điện_thoại đẹp quá, rất hài_lòng". To do this, we also used pyvi(see Footnote 1) library for POS tagging.

Other techniques relate to morpheme of word not using such as stemming, lemmatizing since Vietnamese is an inflexionless language, words are only one form.

2.2   Lexicon Complementation

Negation handling is a challenge in sentiment analysis, for example "sản_phẩm không tốt" (the product is not good) used terms to vectorize, if not considering "không" (not) term, it might evaluate this is a positive sentence instead of a negative one. Normally, when it detects a negation lexicon (không (not), chẳng (not), chưa (not yet), etc) following by a positive or negative lexicons, those phrases should be replaced by antonyms of next lexicon, for example the phrase "không tốt" (not good) is replaced by "xấu" (bad) as an antonym of "tốt" (good) based on a certain wordnet.

Our works have not a Vietnamese wordnet being strong enough for negation replacement, so if it detects the negation following by a positive lexicon, then replacing by not_pos lexicon, it also detects the negation following be a negative lexicon, then replace by not_neg lexicon. After that, in order to show affectation of lexicons, we append pos and neg lexicons when appearing a positive and negative lexicon respectively. In order to detect the negation, we have prepared a list of negation terms (không (not), chẳng (not), chưa (not yet)), also a list of positive and negative lexicons. In the experiments, this improves significantly accuracy of classifiers.

Pseudocode 1.1. Negation Handling

```
Input: document (D)
Output: D handled
Steps:
for term in D
   if term is negation lexicon
      if next of term is positive
         term = not_pos
         next of term = empty
      else next of term is negative
         term = not_neg
         next of term = empty
   else if term is positive
      D.append(pos)
   else if term is negative
      D.append(neg)
```

Intensification handling intensifier lexicons such as rất (very), quá (too), hơi (a bit), khá (pretty)(pretty) emphasize, increase or decrease the semantic meanings of the lexicons which precede or follow them. This also is so necessary to detect the degree of customers' satisfaction and handled as below. For intensification handling, we have also prepared a list of intensifier lexicons used frequently in Vietnamese, grouped into increasing (rất, quá, lắm) and decreasing (tạm, khá,hơi, cũng được) semantic.

Pseudocode 1.2. Intensification Handling

```
Input: document (D)
Output: D handled
Steps:
for term in D
   if term is increasing intensifier
      if next of term is positive
         D.append(strong_pos)
      else if next of term is negative
         D.append(strong_neg)
   else if term is decreasing intensifier
      if next of term is is positive
         D.append(pos)
```

```
else if next of term is negative
    D.append(neg)
```

2.3 Data Augmentation

The original data augmentation used in image classification by increasing image data such as rotate, translate, scale, add noise, etc. Similarly, data augmentation has also applied for text classification by increasing text data based on various techniques, Wei and Zou [12] applied some easy techniques such as synonym words, random swap, random insert, random delete to improve the performance of classifier algorithms. In limited resources of Vietnamese processing, we have tried to apply synonym replacement and random swap, it shows promising performance in experiments.

Synonym Replacement for words are not stopwords, their synonym words have gotten randomly and replaced them to compose a new review for data training. This process has repeated many times which depend on the dataset size, data augmentation is useful for a small dataset instead of a large dataset, however so many augmented data can lead to overfitting issue. In addition, lexicons in the same intensification have also consider for replacement, for example rất (very) may be replaced by cực_kỳ (extremely) for a new review.

Random Swap swapping many times two terms which are different from stopwords in random, this might lead to the meaningless sentences, but actually it can improve the accuracy of classifiers.

2.4 Classifiers

Naive Bayes applied on Bayes and probability theory to predict the label of a data point based on a predefined dataset. The probability of data point x belongs to polarity c computed as the following formula and needs to find c so that it obtains maximum value.

$$P(c|x) = \frac{P(x|c)P(c)}{P(x)} \qquad (1)$$

Because $P(c|x)$ does not depend on $P(x)$ and Naive Bayes assumes that the dimensions of vector x is independent, the problem becomes

$$c = argmax(\prod_{k=1}^{d} P(x_k|c) \times P(c)) \qquad (2)$$

where $P(c)$ which is probability of a data point belongs to polarity c is easy to calculate, and $P(x_k|c)$ is calculated by Multivariate Bernoulli and Multinomial Naïve Bayes approach, our experiments use the second one as follows:

$$P(x_k|c) = \frac{N_k + \alpha}{N + d \times \alpha} \qquad (3)$$

α is Laplace smoothing, d is number of dimensions of $\boldsymbol{x}$, N is number of terms in reviews of polarity c, and N_k is frequency of k-th term appearing in reviews of polarity c.

Logistic Regression is a statistical approach to determine relationship between the dependent variable y and a set of independent variables $\boldsymbol{x}$. In order to predict the label of a data point, this one based on the probability of logistic function and a predefined threshold belongs to $[0, 1]$. The logistic function has forms:

$$y = \phi\left(\boldsymbol{w}^T \boldsymbol{x} + b\right) \tag{4}$$

This model needs to estimate the coefficients $\boldsymbol{w}$ and b from training data, the logistic function is often used as sigmod function.

Support Vector Machine (SVM) is a strong classifier to find the hyperland which divides the dataset into various groups in multi-dimensional space, this one must be the same distance between it and two hyperlands which contains the nearest data points belongs to two groups respectively. The cost function of linear SVM:

$$y = \boldsymbol{w}^T \boldsymbol{x} + b \tag{5}$$

it also estimates $\boldsymbol{w}$ and b which have satisfied $y_k(\boldsymbol{w}^T + b) \geq 1, \forall k = 1, 2, 3, ..., N$ (N is the number of data points) and:

$$(\boldsymbol{w}, b) = argmin_{\boldsymbol{w},b} \frac{\|\boldsymbol{w}\|_2^2}{2} \tag{6}$$

For non-linearly separable dataset, SVM used kernel functions to transform the data points from non-linearly separable space into linearly separable space. Our experiments use RBF (Radial Basis Function Kernel) kernel as follows:

$$k(x, x') = exp(-\gamma \|x - x'\|_2^2), \gamma > 0 \tag{7}$$

where γ indicates how far the influence of a data point in calculation of a certain hyperland. Data points, which are low γ values are far from or high γ values which close to a separation hyperland, are considered in calculation.

One-vs-One (OVO) and One-vs-All (OVA) are ensemble of binary classifiers for multi-class problem. Each iteration of OVO takes a pairwise of classes and applies the binary classifier to indicate the label of a data point, the final label is determined based on majority voting of iterations. For OVR, the computational cost is lower, if having c classes then OVO needs to execute $c(c - 1)/2$ iterations, about OVR takes only c iterations. Every iterations, the binary classifier determines whether a data point is assigned that label, the final label is determined based on a probability. These ones affect problems having more than two classes, and mainly performed on Dataset 2 (see Table 1) with three polarities in experiments.

3   The Experiments

3.1   Data Preparation and Feature Extraction

We have prepared four Vietnamese datasets as reviews on watch, phone, food collecting from the internet and previous studies. Dataset 1 got from a contest of Vietnamese sentiment analysis prediction in comments[2], dataset 2 was built by Nguyen-Thi [11], dataset 3 and dataset 4 are food reviews collecting by streetcodevn.com (Table 1 shows the size of each dataset).

Table 1. Datasets are used for the experiments

No.	Datasets	Polarities	Size
1	Dataset 1	Positive	9280
		Negative	6870
2	Dataset 2	Strong Positive	2380
		Positive	2440
		Negative	2380
3	Dataset 3	Positive	15000
		Negative	15000
4	Dataset 4	Positive	5000
		Negative	5000

Positive and negative list contain Vietnamese positive and negative lexicons respectively, including english lexicons used usually in Vietnamese sentences such as happy, nice, good, bad, etc. Negation list is to detect negation in the sentence such as không (not), chưa (not yet). And intensification list has grouped into increasing intensifiers (rất (very), quá (so), lắm, cực kỳ (extremely)) and decreasing intensifiers (tạm (pretty), khá (pretty), cũng (also)).

To extract features for classifiers, we used $tf \times idf$ weight which is widely used in natural language processing and got high score in text classification. The number of dimensions of a review is determined by unigram and bigram models.

3.2   The Experiments

As earlier mentioned, the approach has based on semi-supervised learning with a limited training data to reduce efforts to build a pre-labeled dataset. Moreover, to show the effectiveness of data augmentation techniques and more challenges, we have used only one document for training phase. We perform one hundred of iterations, for each one, it gets only one document for training in random, the remaining ones are used for testing. In order to prove our approach,

---

we have performed various experiments with the well-known classifiers. Table 2 shows the results of original dataset without any processes, Table 3 shows the results with preprocessing techniques, negation handling, intensification handling, and Table 4 shows the results with preprocessing techniques, negation handling, intensification handling, data augmentation for training. F1 score is used to evaluate the performance of the approaches, this is the weighted average of precision and recall metrics which reaches the best score at 1 and worst score at 0.

In results (Figs. 1, 2, 3 and 4), looking at max of F1 scores which apply preprocessing techniques, lexicons complementation via negation handling, intensification handling, most of them also significantly increase the scores. And these ones incorporate with data augmentation, mainly based on synonym lexicons, the scores also improve in most of datasets, excluding the dataset 3 decreases a little bit, it may depend on the way to get the synonym words, any of them are not suitable in a certain domain context, for example "tôi hài_lòng điện_thoại" (I am pleased the phone), "hài_lòng" (pleased) word has many Vietnamese synonym words such as ["mãn_nguyện", "thoả_mãn" "bằng_lòng", "ứng_ý"], replacing "hài_lòng" by "ứng_ý" (contented) is better than "thoả_mãn" (satisfied) in this context. However, these scores prove that data augmentation is a reasonable approach which promises to improve the accuracies based on semi-supervised learning in text.

Table 2. The results of original dataset without any processes.

Datasets	Classifiers	Max of F1 score	Min of F1 score
Dataset 1	Naive Bayes	0.692	0.307
	Logistic Regression	0.697	0.307
	SVM	0.677	**0.409**
	OVO	0.677	**0.409**
	OVR	**0.697**	0.307
Dataset 2	Naive Bayes	0.521	0.311
	Logistic Regression	0.527	0.320
	SVM	**0.530**	0.315
	OVO	**0.530**	0.315
	OVR	0.521	**0.327**
Dataset 3	Naive Bayes	**0.654**	0.344
	Logistic Regression	0.651	**0.356**
	SVM	0.651	**0.356**
	OVO	0.651	**0.356**
	OVR	0.648	0.344
Dataset 4	Naive Bayes	**0.624**	0.359
	Logistic Regression	0.613	0.373
	SVM	0.613	0.374
	OVO	0.613	0.374
	OVR	0.612	**0.375**

Table 3. The results with preprocessing techniques, negation handling, intensification handling.

Datasets	Classifiers	Max of F1 score	Min of F1 score
Dataset 1	Naive Bayes	**0.800**	0.297
	Logistic Regression	0.783	0.311
	SVM	0.783	**0.300**
	OVO	0.783	**0.300**
	OVR	0.785	0.298
Dataset 2	Naive Bayes	0.632	0.235
	Logistic Regression	0.645	0.236
	SVM	0.624	0.232
	OVO	0.625	0.232
	OVR	**0.654**	**0.239**
Dataset 3	Naive Bayes	0.751	**0.342**
	Logistic Regression	0.788	0.335
	SVM	**0.789**	0.337
	OVO	**0.789**	0.337
	OVR	0.788	0.335
Dataset 4	Naive Bayes	0.709	**0.328**
	Logistic Regression	**0.764**	0.287
	SVM	**0.764**	0.287
	OVO	**0.764**	0.287
	OVR	**0.764**	0.283

Table 4. The results with preprocessing techniques, negation handling, intensification handling, augmenting data for training.

Datasets	Classifiers	Max of F1 score	Min of F1 score
Dataset 1	Naive Bayes	0.767	**0.301**
	Logistic Regression	0.809	0.270
	SVM	**0.810**	0.263
	OVO	**0.810**	0.263
	OVR	**0.810**	0.263
Dataset 2	Naive Bayes	0.615	**0.245**
	Logistic Regression	0.673	0.206
	SVM	0.670	0.195
	OVO	0.670	0.195
	OVR	**0.680**	0.202
Dataset 3	Naive Bayes	0.675	0.338
	Logistic Regression	0.759	0.341
	SVM	**0.769**	**0.343**
	OVO	**0.769**	**0.343**
	OVR	**0.769**	**0.343**
Dataset 4	Naive Bayes	0.655	**0.344**
	Logistic Regression	0.761	0.329
	SVM	**0.768**	0.317
	OVO	**0.768**	0.317
	OVR	**0.768**	0.317

Although this approach is helpful to reduce the time and money in building the pre-labeled dataset and reaches domain independence, but it has any risks. The result depends on the selected one-document training in random. For any documents might increase so high score gradually reaching to the results of supervised learning approach, but any others might decrease the result so bad. So, when performing for real-time application in any domains, it should carefully be experimented to choose the best training documents as possible.

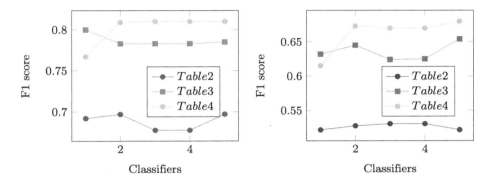

Fig. 1. Max F1 score of Dataset 1   **Fig. 2.** Max F1 score of Dataset 2

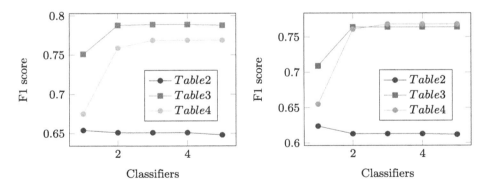

Fig. 3. Max F1 score of Dataset 3   **Fig. 4.** Max F1 score of Dataset 4

4   Conclusions and Future Works

In this paper, we have based on semi-supervised learning for Vietnamese sentiment analysis with only one-document training and taken various experiments including many preprocessing techniques, semantic lexicon complementation, also data augmentation techniques to improve the accuracies of classifiers. For almost of experimented datasets, the accuracies of classifiers are improved based on our solutions, this shows the approaches are reasonable, this saves the cost and time to build a pre-labeled dataset. In short, these results are competitive scores, it can motivate our team and other propositions to improve the score for this attractive problem in future.

In future works, we have investigated data augmentation solutions to auto-generate the useful training data from the limited training, also build a Vietnamese synonym wordnet. Studying the approaches choose the one-document training and the synonym words more effectively instead of in random.

References

1. Medhat, W., Hassan, A., Korashy, H.: Sentiment analysis algorithms and applications: a survey. Ain Shams Eng. J. **5**(4), 1093–1113 (2014)
2. Soleymani, M., Garcia, D., Jou, B., Schuller, B., Chang, S.-F., Pantic, M.: A survey of multimodal sentiment analysis. Image Vis. Comput. **65**, 3–14 (2017)
3. Fernández-Gavilanes, M., Àlvarez-López, T., Juncal-Martínez, J., Costa-Montenegro, E., González-Castaño, F.J.: GTI: an unsupervised approach for sentiment analysis in Twitter. In: Proceedings of the 9th International Workshop on Semantic Evaluation (SemEval 2015), Denver, Colorado, pp. 533–538 (2015)
4. Fernández-Gavilanes, M., Juncal-Martínez, J., García-Méndez, S., Costa-Montenegro, E., González-Castaño, F.J.: Creating emoji lexica from unsupervised sentiment analysis of their descriptions. Expert Syst. Appl. **103**, 74–91 (2018)
5. AL-Sharuee, M.T., Liu, F., Pratama, M.: Sentiment analysis: an automatic contextual analysis and ensemble clustering approach and comparison. Data Knowl. Eng. **115**, 194–213 (2018)
6. Kobayashi, S.: Contextual augmentation: data augmentation by words with paradigmatic relations. In: Proceedings of the 2018 Conference of the North American Chapter of the Association for Computational Linguistics: Human Language Technologies, Volume 2 (Short Papers), New Orleans, Louisiana, pp. 452–457 (2018)
7. Symeonidis, S., Effrosynidis, D., Arampatzis, A.: A comparative evaluation of preprocessing techniques and their interactions for twitter sentiment analysis. Expert Syst. Appl. **110**, 298–310 (2018)
8. Kim, K.: An improved semi-supervised dimensionality reduction using feature weighting: application to sentiment analysis. Expert Syst. Appl. **109**, 49–65 (2018)
9. Yoo, S., Song, J., Jeong, O.: Social media contents based sentiment analysis and prediction system. Expert Syst. Appl. **105**, 102–111 (2018)
10. Hussein, D.M.E.-D.M.: A survey on sentiment analysis challenges. J. King Saud Univ.- Eng. Sci. **30**(4), 330–338 (2018)
11. Nguyen-Thi, B.-T., Duong, H.-T.: A Vietnamese sentiment analysis system based on multiple classifiers with enhancing lexicon features. In: Duong, T.Q., Vo, N.-S., Nguyen, L.K., Vien, Q.-T., Nguyen, V.-D. (eds.) INISCOM 2019. LNICST, vol. 293, pp. 240–249. Springer, Cham (2019). https://doi.org/10.1007/978-3-030-30149-1_20
12. Wei, J., Zou, K.: EDA: easy data augmentation techniques for boosting performance on text classification. In: ICLR 2019–7th International Conference on Learning Representations (2019)

Assessing the Readability of Vietnamese Texts Through Comparison (*Extended Abstract*)

An-Vinh Luong[1] and Phuoc Tran[2](✉)

[1] University of Science, VNU-HCM, Ho Chi Minh City, Vietnam
anvinhluong@gmail.com
[2] NPL-KD Lab, Faculty of Information Technology, Ton Duc Thang University,
Ho Chi Minh City, Vietnam
tranthanhphuoc@tdtu.edu.vn

Abstract. Text readability is a measure of how easy/difficult a text is to read. Studies on readability have been noticed for a long time in English and other popular languages. In Vietnamese, studies on the text readability are still quite limited, mainly because of the lack of corpora with capacity large enough to carry out the examination. In this paper, we present a method for assessing the readability of Vietnamese texts that does not need too much cost to develop a training corpus, based on comparing the correlation difficulty between texts but still achieving positive results.

Keywords: Text readability · Text comparison · Vietnamese language

Text readability—as the definition of Bailin and Grafstein [1]—is a measure of how easy/difficult a text is to read. Studies on readability have been noticed for a long time in English and other popular languages, such as the work of Chen and Meurers [2], Jiang et al. [3]. In Vietnamese, research on the readability of texts is still quite limited, the main reason is the lack of corpora that was graded according to the difficulty level (often with the participation of language experts and at a high cost). In this study, we present a method for assessing the Vietnamese texts readability, using a small number of standard texts (texts that was graded according to the difficulty level), through comparing the correlate readability of the texts.

We collected 100 texts in the field of literature: children's stories, short stories, novels. We randomly selected some texts and gave them to the language experts to read. Each document is given to 2 experts to assess the readability according to 3 levels: Very easy (texts for children at the Elementary School); Easy (texts for people at the Middle School); and Medium (texts for people at the High School). If the evaluation results of both experts are the same, the text will be selected as a standard text. We conduct the such choice and evaluation process until each level has enough 10 texts (the total of 3 levels is 30 documents). These 30 texts are standard texts which will be used to evaluate the remaining texts.

All documents collected are extracted features for training models: Average sentence length calculated on word and syllable; Average word length calculated on syllable; Ratio

A. Tagarelli and H. Tong (Eds.): CSoNet 2019, LNCS 11917, pp. 201–202, 2019.
https://doi.org/10.1007/978-3-030-34980-6_22

of difficult words and Ratio of difficult syllables; Ratio of Sino-Vietnamese words; Ration of local words; Ratio of proper nouns and Ratio of distinct proper nouns. With standard texts, we construct vectors of text pairs by taking all 2-permutations, totally we have 870 text pairs. The feature vectors of each pair is created by vectors subtraction. For example, with 2 texts a and b, v_a and v_b are 2 feature vectors of a and b; the feature vector of text pairs (a, b), denoted as v_{ab}; calculated as $v_{ab} = v_a - v_b$. The vector v_{ab} are labeled as follows: if a is more difficult than b then $v_{ab} = 1$; if b is more difficult than a then $v_{ab} = -1$; otherwise $v_{ab} = 0$. All these vectors will be used for training a text comparative model using SVM. Using k-fold cross validation, we have checked the accuracy of the model achieved 74.94%.

For the remaining texts, we compare the readability with the standard texts: for each remaining text x, we create all feature vectors of text pairs (x, a), with a is a text in standard texts, by $v_x - v_a$. These feature vectors will, in turn, be evaluated by the trained comparison model. Finally, we classify the remaining texts through the comparison results: A text x will be classified as: (1) Medium if it is more difficult than minimum k% Easy and Very easy texts and it is easier than maximum t% Medium texts; (2) Very easy if it is easier than minimum k% Easy and Medium texts and it is more difficult than maximum t% Very easy texts; (3) Easy it is more difficult than minimum k% Very easy texts and easier than minimum k% Medium texts and it is more difficult than maximum t% Easy texts and it is easier than maximum t% Easy texts; (4) otherwise, it will be labeled as unclassifiable. k and t are classification thresholds, obtained through experiments: the higher the value of k and t, the larger the number of unclassified documents, but the precision of the classification results is higher. In this study, we used $k = 60$% and $t = 50$%.

Finally, we selected 30 newly classified documents for re-testing by experts. Each text will be read by an expert to decide if the classification results are proper. The classification results are presented in Table 1. The Precision, Recall and F1 score are 78.13%, 35.71% and 49.02% accordingly.

Table 1. Classification results.

No. of texts	Very easy	Easy	Medium	Unclassifiable
	18	9	5	38

For conclusion, with only a few pre-classified documents, we can build a model to assess the correlate readability between Vietnamese texts with an acceptable accuracy. Based on that assessment model, we have classified the texts by readability with an accuracy of over 78%.

References

1. Bailin, A., Grafstein, A.: Readability: Text and Context. Palgrave Macmillan, UK (2016)
2. Chen, X., Meurers, D.: Word frequency and readability: Predicting the text-level readability with a lexical-level attribute. J. Res. Reading (2018)
3. Jiang, Z., et al.: Enriching word embeddings with domain knowledge for readability assessment. In: Proceedings of the 27th International Conference on Computational Linguistics, Santa Fe, New Mexico, USA (2018)

Learning Representations for Vietnamese Sentence Classification (*Extended Abstract*)

Phuc H. Duong[1] and Hien T. Nguyen[2(✉)]

[1] Artificial Intelligence Laboratory, Faculty of Information Technology,
Ton Duc Thang University, Ho Chi Minh City, Vietnam
`duonghuuphuc@tdtu.edu.vn`
[2] Faculty of Information Technology, Ho Chi Minh City University of Food Industry,
Ho Chi Minh City, Vietnam
`hien@hufi.edu.vn`

Abstract. In this study, we propose a new deep language model that taking the advantage of Transformer model towards the task of Vietnamese sentence classification. We construct a new Vietnamese dataset for evaluating the model. We also conduct experiments on English corpora to evaluate our proposed model.

Keywords: Natural language processing · Sentence classification

In recent years, the evolution of artificial intelligence, especially deep learning, has opened many new opportunities for research communities to achieve better performances on natural language processing (NLP) tasks. In deep learning for NLP, the important component that can significantly affect the performance of NLP applications is language models. We can use language models to represent given words or texts as vectors of real numbers to make them mathematically computable. Bengio et al. [1] propose an approach to train a language model by employing neural networks, and then becomes a widely adopted idea. Following the success of [1], many breakthrough approaches have been recently proposed to train language models [2–8]. In our viewpoint, we categorize those approaches as context-free or contextual language models. The main difference between them is whether they consider the context of a given word. For example of "bat", according to Cambridge Dictionary[1], it has two meanings which are a stick to hit a ball or an animal. In case of context-free language models [2,3], representation vector of a given word is independent of its surrounding context, it means that no matter what the context of "bat" is, there is one representation corresponding to it. In order to overcome this problem, contextual language models do take into account the surrounding context of a given word, and this approach can significantly improve the quality of representations [4–8]. There is another

---

[1] https://dictionary.cambridge.org/dictionary/english/bat.

© Springer Nature Switzerland AG 2019
A. Tagarelli and H. Tong (Eds.): CSoNet 2019, LNCS 11917, pp. 203–204, 2019.
https://doi.org/10.1007/978-3-030-34980-6_23

noteworthy point in [4–8] that fine-tuning the pre-trained language models for downstream tasks can achieve state-of-the-art performances.

Motivated from the success of [4–6] in training a language model, we propose a neural architecture based on the Transformer model [9], which is a powerful and state-of-the-art model, to learn the representations towards the task of Vietnamese sentence classification. Our work can be summarized as follows:

- Propose and train a deep language model on Vietnamese corpora.
- Then, fine-tune our pre-trained language model towards the Vietnamese sentence classification task. (We construct a new dataset for evaluating this task.)
- We also conduct experiments on English corpora to evaluate our proposed model.

References

1. Bengio, Y., Ducharme, R., Vincent, P., Jauvin, C.: A neural probabilistic language model. J. Mach. Learn. Res. **3**, 1137–1155 (2003)
2. Mikolov, T., Sutskever, I., Chen, K., Corrado, G.S., Dean, J.: Distributed representations of words and phrases and their compositionality. In: Burges, C.J.C., Bottou, L., Ghahramani, Z., Weinberger, K.Q. (eds.) Advances in Neural Information Processing Systems 26: 27th Annual Conference on Neural Information Processing Systems 2013. Proceedings of a Meeting Held Lake Tahoe, Nevada, United States, 5–8 December 2013, pp. 3111–3119 (2013)
3. Pennington, J., Socher, R., Manning, C.D.: GloVe: global vectors for word representation. In: Empirical Methods in Natural Language Processing (EMNLP). pp. 1532–1543 (2014)
4. Peters, M.E., et al.: Deep contextualized word representations. arXiv preprint arXiv:1802.05365 (2018)
5. Radford, A., Narasimhan, K., Salimans, T., Sutskever, I.: Improving language understanding by generative pre-training (2018)
6. Devlin, J., Chang, M.W., Lee, K., Toutanova, K.: BERT: pre-training of deep bidirectional transformers for language understanding. In: Burstein, J., Doran, C., Solorio, T. (eds.) Proceedings of the 2019 Conference of the North American Chapter of the Association for Computational Linguistics: Human Language Technologies, NAACL-HLT 2019, Minneapolis, MN, USA, 2–7 June 2019, Long and Short Papers, Association for Computational Linguistics , vol. 1, pp. 4171–4186 (2019)
7. Yang, Z., Dai, Z., Yang, Y., Carbonell, J., Salakhutdinov, R., Le, Q.V.: XLNet: generalized autoregressive pretraining for language understanding (2019)
8. Liu, Y., et al.: RoBERTa: a robustly optimized BERT pretraining approach. CoRR abs/1907.11692 (2019)
9. Vaswani, A., et al.: Attention is all you need. In: Guyon, I., et al. (eds.) NIPS, pp. 6000–6010 (2017)

Exploring Machine Translation
on the Chinese-Vietnamese Language Pair
(*Extended Abstract*)

Huu-Anh Tran[1], Phuoc Tran[2(✉)], Phuong-Thuy Dao[1] and Thi-Mien Pham[1]

[1] Department of Information Technology, Thai-Binh University, Thái Bình, Vietnam
anhuni1006@gmail.com, thuy.vdc@gmail.com, phammien09@gmail.com
[2] NLP-KD Lab, Faculty of Information Technology, Ton Duc Thang University,
Ho Chi Minh City, Vietnam
tranthanhphuoc@tdtu.edu.vn

Abstract. In the machine translation field, a common approach for more than two decades has been phrase-based statistical machine translation (PSMT). However, deep learning-based machine translation, also called neural machine translation (NMT), has emerged as a potential new approach to machine translation. Initial findings show that NMT yields better results than PSMT in some language pairs, while NMT results for some language pairs are less than or equal to PSMT results. In this paper, we initially studied and performed machine translation-based NMT for the Chinese-Vietnamese language pair. In addition, we performed machine translation-based PSMT on the same Chinese-Vietnamese bilingual corpus. The experimental results showed that NMT yielded better results (indicated by Bilingual Evaluation Understudy (BLEU) scores) than PSMT, although in some specific cases, NMT translation results were lower than those of PSMT.

Keywords: Chinese-Vietnamese machine translation · Neural machine translation · Phrase-based statistical machine translation

In [1], Kinoshita et al. examined Chinese-Japanese machine translation and English-Japanese machine translation on pattern corpora. These corpora were tested in both PSMT and NTM, and the experimental results showed that NMT and PSMT gave the same results (indicated by Bilingual Evaluation Understudy (BLEU) scores) for automatic evaluation and that NMT gave superior results for human evaluation.

Dowmunt et al. [2] evaluated translation quality between PSMT and NMT for a total of thirty translation directions in the United Nations Parallel Corpus v1.0. The experiment results indicated that NMT achieved BLEU scores greater than or equal to the BLEU scores of PSMT. The authors also found that the BLEU scores of language pairs in which Chinese is the source or the target language increased significantly. This is an interesting discovery related to our work (Chinese-Vietnamese NMT).

However, some experiments have illustrated that the NMT approach does not give better results or gives results that are even lower than those of PSMT. Typical cases are the English-Malay low-resource language pair [3] and the Arabic-English language pair [4]. For the Arabic-English language pair, Menacer et al. [4] discovered that PSMT

© Springer Nature Switzerland AG 2019
A. Tagarelli and H. Tong (Eds.): CSoNet 2019, LNCS 11917, pp. 205–206, 2019.
https://doi.org/10.1007/978-3-030-34980-6_24

archived better translation results than the results of NMT. Specifically, the translated quality of PSMT is better than baseline NMT and better than NMT with incorporation of advanced techniques by values of 0.19 and 0.017 BLEU, respectively. Experimenting in the English-Malay low-resource language pair, Yeong et al. [3] found that SMT achieved a higher BLEU score than NMT for the general domain, while for a specific domain, NMT yielded better results.

In terms of language type, both Chinese and Vietnamese are language isolates. The two languages have a close linguistic relationship, and therefore, the translation results between Chinese and Vietnamese based on PSMT are better than other language pairs of different language types with no close linguistic relationship. Thus we worked within the same PSMT corpora to use the NMT approach for translations from Chinese to Vietnamese herein. While NMT yielded better final results than PSMT, in some specific cases, NMT results were lower than the results of PSMT. Table 1 shows the BLEU scores and number of UNK of four translation systems.

Table 1. BLEU scores and number of UNK of the four translation systems.

	NoTok-NMT	NoTok-PSMT	Tok-NMT	Tok-PSMT
BLEU scores	36.92	35.25	36.22	35.85

In this paper, we do not elaborate on BLEU score differences between Token and No-Token cases. Instead, we only carefully analyze the good and bad sides of NMT versus PSMT for both Token and No-Token cases, as follows:

Short Sentence Translation: Both NMT and PSMT give nearly the same results.
Long Sentence Translation and Reodering: NMT is still more correct than the reordering of PSMT.
General Errors: Both NMT and PSMT still cannot overcome the common errors of machine translation, including erroneous translation of word meaning, incorrect word order, and errors due to the ambiguous nature of languages. Specifically, NMT and PSMT still mistranslate named entity and Sino-Vietnamese in Chinese-Vietnamese machine translation.

References

1. Kinoshita, S., Oshio, T., Mitsuhashi, T.: Comparison of SMT and NMT trained with large Patent Corpora: Japio at WAT2017. In: Proceedings of the WAT2017, Taipei, Taiwan, pp. 140–145 (2017)
2. Dowmunt, M.J., Dwojak, T., Hoang, H.: Is neural machine translation ready for deployment? A case study on 30 translation directions. In: Proceedings of the IWSLT, Seattle, DC, USA (2016)
3. Yeong, Y.L., Tan, T.P., Lim, C.K., Gan, K.H., Mohammad, S.K.: Parallel text acquisition and comparison of SMT and NMT with low resources in English-Malay machine translation. In: Proceedings of the ONA, Phnom Penh, Cambodia (2017)
4. Menacer, M.A., Langlois, D., Mella, O., Fohr, D., Jouvet, D., Smaïli, K.: Is statistical machine translation approach dead? In: Proceedings of the ICNLSSP, Casablanca, Morocco, pp. 1–5 (2017)

Computational Methods for Social Good

Towards an Aspect-Based Ranking Model for Clinical Trial Search

Soumyadeep Roy[1(✉)], Koustav Rudra[2], Nikhil Agrawal[1], Shamik Sural[1], and Niloy Ganguly[1]

[1] Indian Institute of Technology Kharagpur, Kharagpur, India
soumyadeep.roy9@iitkgp.ac.in, nikhilagrawal741@gmail.com,
{shamik,niloy}@cse.iitkgp.ac.in
[2] L3S Research Center, Hannover, Lower Saxony, Germany
rudra@l3s.de

Abstract. Clinical Trials are crucial for the practice of evidence-based medicine. It provides updated and essential health-related information for the patients. Sometimes, Clinical trials are the first source of information about new drugs and treatments. Different stakeholders, such as trial volunteers, trial investigators, and meta-analyses researchers often need to search for trials. In this paper, we propose an automated method to retrieve relevant trials based on the overlap of UMLS concepts between the user query and clinical trials. However, different stakeholders may have different information needs, and accordingly, we rank the retrieved clinical trials based on the following four aspects – **Relevancy**, **Adversity**, **Recency**, and **Popularity**. We aim to develop a clinical trial search system which covers multiple disease classes, instead of only focusing on retrieval of oncology-based clinical trials. We follow a rigorous annotation scheme and create an annotated retrieval set for 25 queries, across five disease categories. Our proposed method performs better than the baseline model in almost 90% cases. We also measure the correlation between the different aspect-based ranking lists and observe a high negative Spearman rank's correlation coefficient between popularity and recency.

Keywords: Clinical trial search · Aspect-based ranking · Biomedical information retrieval

1 Introduction

In recent years, the internet is being increasingly used as a source of health information by both medical (professionals, practitioners) and non-medical (consumers) users. Nowadays, various clinical database sources such as ClinicalTrials.gov, PubMed, Embase and Cochrane are publicly accessible, which makes health information search easier for the end-users. In this paper, we focus on the retrieval of clinical trials because clinical trials are crucial for the practice of Evidence-Based Medicine and are used for establishing the efficacy of new drugs

© Springer Nature Switzerland AG 2019
A. Tagarelli and H. Tong (Eds.): CSoNet 2019, LNCS 11917, pp. 209–222, 2019.
https://doi.org/10.1007/978-3-030-34980-6_25

and treatments. Apart from that, the need for different stakeholders varies a lot. For example, medical practitioners may be interested in trials containing important information about new medicines and drugs. Users who want to participate in a clinical trial may look for the adversity score of a clinical trial (to judge the consequences of participation). It reveals that different users have various perspectives or aspects. The objective of this aspect-based trial search is two-fold. Firstly, it helps users in satisfying specific information needs, and secondly, it prevents users from taking wrong decisions. For example, it may be the case that a trial with a high number of adverse events, is ranked as highly relevant. However, it is not suitable from a participant point of view. If the user intends to participate in a trial, such results are disastrous. Based on the analysis of the data, we identify the following four essential aspects of the clinical trial search: (1) Relevancy, (2) Recency, (3) Adversity, and (4) Popularity. Goodwin et al. [8] have used aspect-based approaches (on a query) to improve the retrieval and ranking performance of clinical trials. In this work, we explore different notions of ranking aspects or relevance criteria for clinical trials search.

In this paper, we develop a novel and straightforward two-step method to retrieve and rank clinical trials. First, clinical trials are retrieved based on free-form text query given by ordinary users having less familiarity with medical terms. In the second phase, retrieved trials are ranked based on four aspects, as mentioned earlier (relevancy, recency, adversity, and popularity).

We develop a Synset Term Match-based Clinical Trial Retrieval model (STM) to retrieve relevant trials for the user given queries. For a given query, we first extract the UMLS concepts present in a query using *QuickUMLS* [26]. We are considering UMLS concepts instead of raw text to handle two issues. Firstly, users may give different variations of a single term, and secondly, users having limited knowledge of medical terminology may make spelling mistakes. Quick-UMLS tool takes care of these issues. Next, we retrieve concepts from the clinical trials and retrieve the trials based on their match with the query related concepts. Finally, we rank the trials based on four different aspects. We evaluate our proposed method over 25 queries taken from five different disease classes - *Pathological Conditions Signs and Symptoms, Cardiovascular Diseases, Nervous System Diseases, Nutritional and Metabolic Diseases, Immune System Diseases*. However, we do not have any annotated set of ground truth labels for the queries of these disease classes. Hence, in this paper, we put extensive effort to prepare the ground truth set for these 25 queries (explained in Sect. 5.1). The complete set of data (queries and the set of annotated relevant trials for each query) and code files are publicly available in Github[1].

Detailed experiment over five different disease classes reveals the efficacy of our proposed *Synset based term match* model (STM) over the baseline. For *relevancy* aspect, STM is performing better than the baseline in 90% cases and achieves a precision@5 value of 0.56 as compared to 0.12 by the baseline model. Extracting concepts from the queries and trials help in improving the coverage because users provide different variations of text as input. Side by side, we

---

[1] https://github.com/nikhil741/COCTR_multidimensional_ranking.

observe high statistically significant negative correlation exists between *recency* and *popularity*. This result is quite evident since a paper published earlier is likely to get a higher number of citations.

The rest of the paper is organized as follows. We perform the literature review in Sect. 2. Section 3 provides details about the clinical trial dataset. We discuss our proposed method in Sect. 4. Experimental results are elaborated in Sect. 5. Finally, we discuss the limitations of this work, future directions and conclude the paper in Sect. 6.

2 Related Work

Health-related information mining has gained much attention nowadays. Researchers focused on different kinds of tasks, such as biomedical information retrieval, clinical trial search, and query formulation strategies. In this section, we provide a brief overview of these tasks.

Biomedical Information Retrieval and Health Information Search: Nowadays, an abundant source of clinical repositories such as PubMed, Embase, ClinicalTrials.gov are publicly available to satisfy user requirements. Clinical trials are crucial for the practice of Evidence-Based Medicine and are used to establish the effectiveness of new drugs and treatments. Systematic reviews are time-consuming and usually take 9 to 12 months to complete. Hence, results are often outdated, and it is necessary to develop automated techniques to generate such reviews [30]. This field of research is greatly enhanced by the introduction of new datasets like MeSH-based retrieval set [13] and biomedical retrieval challenges such as bioCADDIE [1], BioASQ [2], and BioCreative Precision Medicine Track [5]. Recently, TREC [22] started a precision medicine track to deal with clinical trial retrieval challenges.

Previous works have explored and provided a taxonomy of the type of consumer health questions asked [20] and the complaints made by patients [12]. Patel et al. [19] cover the kind of clinical trial information a user searched. Generally, ordinary users face difficulty in formulating effective queries because it may involve complicated medical terminologies.

Aspect Based Information Extraction in Medical Domain: Felix et al. [9] explored two different aspects (effectiveness and side–effects) of the drug reviews. Cavalcanti et al. [7] proposed a syntactic tree based review analysis to classify reviews into four different aspects - *Condition, Side Effects, Dosage, Effectiveness*. Prior works used eligibility criteria to develop information management systems [11,15], correlate adverse events [25], and cluster trials [27].

Clinical Trial Search Systems: Several recent studies focus on searching clinical trials to improve the automation strategies for the generation of systematic review [30]. Online trial search interfaces such as ClinicalTrials.gov, WHO ICTRP, EmergingMed.com, SearchClinicalTrials.org, and UK Clinical Trials Gateway, provide users with an option to search for their requirements.

Most of the commercial trial search engines such as eTACTS [17], Antidote[2] are disease-specific and allow users to search for trials related to specific disease types [10]. In the context of consumer health search, Zuccon et al. [31] recently provided certain empirical insights to aid the development of future knowledge base based health information retrieval framework.

Aspect Based Approaches in Clinical Trial Search: Goodwin et al. [8] used six aspects – disease, genetic, demographic, precision medicine, treatment and other medical problem aspects, for developing an information retrieval system for PubMed and clinical trials. For TREC 2017, MedIER team used query expansion strategies and leveraged medical ontologies [29], while in TREC 2018, they developed a system based on query generation and document re-ranking [4].

3 Dataset

We collected the dump of clinical trials from ClinicalTrials.gov on 12/01/2019. The total number of clinical trials present in XML format was $294,679$. However, all the trials do not have a corresponding PubMed entry and Medical Subject Headings (MeSH) terms [14]. MeSH is *"the National Library of Medicine's controlled vocabulary thesaurus, used for indexing articles for the MEDLINE or PubMed database."* Hence, we only consider trials for which have an associated PubMed entry and at least one MeSH term. After this step, we are left with $35,204$ trials. Next, we map these trials into 26 disease categories as reported in the MeSH database.

Mapping Trials to Diseases. For mapping a clinical trial into disease classes, we perform the following steps. Firstly, we extract the MeSH terms from a trial. Finally, we map the MeSH terms to different diseases using the disease trees of MeSH thesaurus. In general, we find out that all the diseases are present at the root of the trees. The clinical trials are mapped into 26 different disease classes, and a clinical trial may be mapped to more than one disease class. For example, we observe that a clinical trial ($NCT00000106$) is mapped to *Musculoskeletal Diseases* and *Skin and Connective Tissue Diseases* because the trial consists of MeSH terms about both *Rheumatic Diseases* and *Collagen Diseases*. We rank the diseases based on the number of trials they contain. Finally, we consider the top five diseases for this study – (1) Pathological Conditions, Signs and Symptoms (12826 trials); (2) Cardiovascular Diseases (7293 trials); (3) Nervous System Diseases (6172 trials); (4) Nutritional and Metabolic Diseases (5240 trials); (5) Immune System Diseases (5016 trials).

4 Method

As mentioned in Sect. 1, the objective of this work is to retrieve and rank the trials across four different aspects—(1) Relevancy, (2) Adversity, (3) Recency, and (4) Popularity. In this section, we describe our ranking method in details.

---

[2] https://www.antidote.me.

4.1 Clinical Trial Retrieval

In this section, we describe our clinical trial retrieval framework. There are two components in the retrieval framework – (1) Concept extraction, and (2) Match based retrieval. After retrieving relevant trials, we rank them across four different aspects (described in the next part).

1. Concept extraction: We extract UMLS medical concepts from a trial's *brief title* and *brief summary* using an unsupervised, scalable medical concept extraction tool, *QuickUMLS* [26]. We also represent a query in terms of its extracted UMLS medical concepts, following the same methodology.

2. Match based retrieval: After the concept extraction step, each query is represented by a set of UMLS concepts. For a given query q, we retrieve all the clinical trials whose brief title contain all the UMLS concept ids which are present in the query q.

4.2 Aspect Based Ranking of Clinical Trials

Ranking Based on Relevancy. After retrieving clinical trials, we rank the clinical trials based on relevancy. We derive three different relevancy based ranking measures, as explained below.

PageRank (PGR): For ranking, we first create an undirected graph $G(V, E)$ where vertices are the clinical trials that we have retrieved for a given query. For providing edge weights between (V_i, V_j) vertices, we measure Simpson similarity between clinical trials in terms of UMLS concepts extracted from *brief title* and *brief summary* fields of a clinical trial. '*Simpson similarity*' between 2 sets, is defined as the ratio of their cardinality of intersection and the cardinality of the smaller set. Next, we apply PageRank [18] algorithm on the graph G to compute the importance of each trial. Finally, the clinical trials are ranked based on their PageRank score.

Exact Term Match (ETM): In the retrieval phase, we only focus on the UMLS concepts present in the query or the title of a trial. However, we observe that sometimes other important terms are also present in the query for which is not mapped to any UMLS concept. We analyze a lexicon containing 1440 commonly used queries by patients and observe that for 15% of the queries, QuickUMLS is unable to extract medical concepts. We also focus on such terms for ranking along with our concept based retrieval and ranking. First, we remove stopwords and perform stemming of the remaining words present in the query. The similar preprocessing technique is also applied to the *brief summary, brief title* and *official title* fields of a given clinical trial. We compute the count of such processed query words present in the three fields of a clinical trial. Finally, we rank the trials based on term frequency instead of the standard TF-IDF, because we assume each of the remaining terms of the query to be of equal importance. We observe that most of these terms are either a part of the extracted UMLS concept or strongly affect the meaning of the query (the length of a query is four words on average). We rank the trials in the following manner – (1) trials are ranked based on the frequency of those terms in the brief summary, (2) trials for which terms are not present in the brief summary, we measure their frequency in the official title field of those trials, (3) in case of mismatch in both brief summary and official title, trials are ranked based on the count in brief title, (4) trials for which terms are absent in all the three fields, they are ranked based on their PageRank score.

Synset Based Term Match (STM): We directly match the terms in case of our previous model, ETM. However, we observe that lots of variations are present in the given query and the retrieved clinical trials. Instead of performing exactly term-wise mapping, for a given query, we extract synset of those terms from WordNet [16] before matching. Therefore, we now compute the total count of the presence of all the terms (present in a synset) in the brief summary, official title and brief title fields of a trial. Finally, we rank the trials in the decreasing order of brief summary count, official title count, brief title count, and PageRank score, as explained in the previous part.

Ranking Based on Adversity. As mentioned in Sect. 1, *adversity* is another important aspect of the clinical trial search system. This aspect may be mapped to the '*safety events*' category of patient complaints, where 'adverse events' is one of its sub-categories [20], which helps them to decide whether to participate in the trial. According to ClinicalTrials.gov, an adverse event is defined as "*any unfavourable change in the health of a participant, including abnormal laboratory findings that took place immediately or within a certain point of time after the study has completed.*" The adversity report of clinical trials is accessible in a publicly available database called Aggregate Analysis of ClinicalTrials.gov (downloaded on 03/02/2019). For this analysis, we mainly consider information present in the 'Reported events' table, which contains the adverse event information (for example, the number of participants affected) of each arm of a clinical trial. A clinical trial may have multiple arms who are given different or no treatment (an arm represents a specific group of trial participants).

After extracting relevant trials (discussed in Sect. 4.1), trials are ranked in the following manner – (1) trials are ranked in decreasing order based on *Subjects Affected* field. (2) the zero value of *Subjects Affected* field indicates that the trial does not have any adverse reported events. We place such trials at the end of the list in random order.

Ranking Based on Recency. Users may have different objectives. Some may want to get enrolled in a clinical trial, and some are looking for new treatments or information. Sometimes, existing drugs or treatment methods do not work well for some patients. New inventions may help medical practitioners to handle such critical patients. Depending upon the study, the length of a clinical trial may vary; as a result, the information present may become outdated. A systematic review is a very time-consuming process and on average, takes 9–12 months. Hence, by ranking clinical trials based on completion date users can get information about new updated information about drugs, treatment, and therapies.

Completion date is reported for trials which are already completed; otherwise, the future date on which it is going to be completed is provided. The trials for which date information is missing, we consider the first day of the corresponding month. We observe that most of the trials which are going to be completed in future did not report any tested information or drugs. Hence, such trials are not useful for medical practitioners and discarded. We only consider completed trials for recency-based ranking.

Ranking Based on Popularity. From July 2005, each of the completed trials has to make an entry in the PubMed article database to increase its visibility. This also, in turn, helps to improve the readability. It also provides an opportunity for researchers to cite past related trials. In this section, we try to measure the success of a clinical trial based on the *popularity* of its corresponding PubMed article. In general, the citation count of a paper may be considered as a proxy to determine the importance of it in the community [6]. Hence, we map the clinical trials with a PubMed entry to measure its popularity. After the mapping, we find out the number of PubMed articles that cited a given article. We use the rest API [24] service provided by '*NCBI E-utilities*' to find out the citing articles. Finally, we rank the retrieved clinical trials based on decreasing popularity value (citation count). We break all ties based on the relevancy score (Sect. 4.2).

5 Experimental Setup and Results

We now describe our experimental setup and then evaluate our proposed retrieval and ranking technique for clinical trial search. We further compare the different aspect-based ranking and discuss the results. The source code and the data are available in Github[3].

5.1 Experimental Setting

Here, we explain the formation of the queries, the evaluation metrics and baseline systems used for our experimental setup.

Query Preparation: To evaluate the performance of our proposed method, we prepare a set of five queries for each of the five disease classes. We follow the semantic-based query templates proposed by Patel et al. [19] to prepare the queries, the most frequent template being *disease or syndrome + research activity*. We prepare the queries based on the following templates - (1) (disease or syndrome) + (symptom or treatment), (2) disease + age group, (3) disease + safety information. We specifically do not consider location and gene information, which are also popular consumer query variants. We consult multiple patient or

---

[3] https://github.com/nikhil741/COCTR_multidimensional_ranking.

health-related lexicons such as MedDRA[4], CLEF Consumer Health track [3], Reddit etc. to formulate the query terms.

Evaluation Metric: We have evaluated results based on two standard IR metrics, i.e. Precision and nDCG score. However, we can not measure recall due to unavailability of ground truth set of clinical trials for each query. Three annotators[5] manually annotated all the retrieved trials for each of the 25 queries. On average, 80 trials are annotated per query. They followed the 'Definitely relevant' annotation scheme for TREC Precision Medicine 2018 task [23].

Table 1. Mean precision values for different relevancy based ranking methodologies across 25 queries

Method	P@5	P@10	P@15	P@20
Baseline	0.12	0.08	0.08	0.08
PGR	0.38	0.35	0.35	0.33
ETM	0.53	0.48	0.45	0.42
STM	**0.56**	**0.52**	**0.47**	**0.46**

Baseline: Most of the existing clinical trial retrieval systems focused only on a particular class of disease. Text REtrieval Conference Precision Medicine Track (TREC-PM) has a similar task of retrieving relevant clinical trials but focus only on oncology trials. However, the state-of-the-art systems of the "TREC-PM 2017 Task B" (clinical trial retrieval) have either not published their codebases, or have used cancer-specific medical ontologies. This makes it very difficult for applying to other disease classes. We aim to develop a clinical trial retrieval model, which we may apply to multiple disease classes. Hence, we consider the system proposed by Ajinkya Throve [28] in the TREC 2017 Precision Medicine Track [21]. To the best of our knowledge, this is the only system which does not use any disease-specific knowledge bases and has made their codebase publicly available.

5.2 Performance Evaluation

We report the performance of our three relevancy based ranking methods (PGR, ETM, STM) and baseline in Table 1. We compute the mean precision values at 5, 10, 15 and 20 for all the 25 queries. We observe that **STM** outperforms all the other methods.

We now provide a detailed comparison between STM and the baseline method (BAS). We observe that STM shows significant improvement for 10 such queries. However, STM achieves precision@10 value of less than 0.31 for 28% of cases,

---

[4] https://www.meddra.org/patient-friendly-term-list.
[5] None of them is an author of this paper and has good knowledge of English.

Table 2. Performance evaluation of STM and Baseline (BAS). "–" indicates model fails to retrieve any trials. We represent the 5 disease classes—(1) PAT: Pathological Conditions, Signs and Symptoms; (2) CVD: Cardiovascular Disease; (3) NER: Nervous System Disease; (4) NMT: Nutritional and Metabolic Diseases; (5) IM: Immune System Diseases

Disease	Query	P@5		P@10		P@15		P@20	
		BAS	STM	BAS	STM	BAS	STM	BAS	STM
PAT	Q1	–	1.0	–	0.8	–	–	–	–
	Q2	–	0.2	–	0.4	–	0.4	–	0.35
	Q3	–	1.0	–	0.5	–	0.33	–	0.3
	Q4	1.0	1.0	1.0	1.0	1.0	1.0	1.0	0.9
	Q5	–	0.6	–	0.7	–	0.6	–	0.45
CVD	Q1	–	0.6	–	0.6	–	0.53	–	0.65
	Q2	–	0.0	–	0.0	–	0.07	–	0.1
	Q3	–	0.2	–	0.3	–	0.33	–	0.25
	Q4	1.0	0.6	1.0	0.8	1.0	0.8	1.0	0.8
	Q5	1.0	0.2	–	0.1	–	0.13	–	0.15
NER	Q1	–	0.2	–	–	–	–	–	–
	Q2	–	0.8	–	0.6	–	0.53	–	–
	Q3	–	0.6	–	0.5	–	0.4	–	0.4
	Q4	–	0.4	–	0.4	–	0.27	–	0.25
	Q5	–	0.8	–	0.4	–	0.27	–	0.2
NMT	Q1	–	0.4	–	0.3	–	0.2	–	0.35
	Q2	–	0.2	–	0.3	–	0.2	–	–
	Q3	–	0.0	–	0.2	–	0.4	–	–
	Q4	–	1.0	–	1.0	–	0.93	–	0.95
	Q5	–	0.6	–	0.7	–	0.67	–	–
IM	Q1	–	0.4	–	0.4	–	0.33	–	0.35
	Q2	–	1.0	–	0.8	–	0.73	–	0.6
	Q3	–	1.0	–	1.0	–	1.0	–	1.0
	Q4	–	0.6	–	0.4	–	–	–	–
	Q5	–	0.6	–	0.3	–	0.2	–	0.25

which may be due to limitation during the retrieval stage. Next, we study the queries having precision@10 $\leq$ 0.3, with no or marginal improvement across PGR, ETM and STM. We observe that it may be because our model does not consider the prior history or eligibility criteria of trials into account. For example, in certain trials, we need users who already have a specific disease, like *treating people already having hypertension (CVD), already having Celiac disease (NMT)*. Users may also search for trials with safety information, i.e. without having

Table 3. nCDG scores for STM across 25 queries

Query no.	PAT	CVD	NER	NMT	IM
Q1	0.97	0.88	0.5	0.64	0.8
Q2	0.77	0.65	0.92	0.62	0.95
Q3	0.96	0.66	0.72	0.54	0.96
Q4	1.0	0.88	0.66	0.99	0.71
Q5	0.84	0.52	0.98	0.91	0.8

any subjects affected with any form of adverse effects, like *safe treatment for Alzheimer's disease (NER), hypercholesterolemia safe treatments (NMT)*.

We also report the nDCG scores of STM model in Table 3. We observe from Table 2 that BAS is only able to retrieve at least five trials, for 3 out of 25 queries and has all precision values as 1.0, outperforming STM is such cases. BAS is based on exact lexical matching between a query and brief title of a clinical trial, and therefore will always be relevant when retrieved. However, there is much variation in the query terms, and direct matching is not possible. In such cases, dealing with a UMLS concept is a useful option.

5.3 Comparison of Different Aspect-Based Rankings

In the previous section, we measure the performance of our relevancy based ranked search results. However, as mentioned in Sect. 1, the primary objective of this work is to provide users with a multi-dimensional ranked list of clinical trials. In this section, we compare the different list of trials based on different aspects and try to understand whether any form of relationship exists among them. Table 4 shows overlap score and Spearman's rank correlation (SR) among different list pairs. Overlap score (OV) is computed as the total number of trials which intersect between the ranked list of two aspects (up to first 20 ranks). It is clear from Table 4 that high statistically significant negative correlation exists between 'recency' and 'popularity', which is quite obvious. We study the queries (Q3, Q12, Q17, Q18, Q20) which have an overlap@20 score of *greater than 15* (out of 20), among most aspect-based ranked list pairs. This is because on average, they retrieve only 18 trials.

Application in a Real-Life Setting: Instead of four separate ranked lists, a single ranked list that considers all the aspects proves to be more useful in a real-life setting. A simple ranking scheme for combining them may be as follows – (1) rank them using STM model and fix the top-K (top 20, in our case) trials. (2) sort using popularity (higher the popularity score, higher up the list). (3) Perform stable sorting in non-decreasing order of adversity (lower the number of 'subjects affected', higher up the list) because only a few trials have a positive adversity score.

Table 4. Comparison of different aspect based rankings in terms of overlap (OV) and Spearman rank correlation(SR)

Aspects	Relevancy		Adversity		Recency		Popularity	
	OV	SR	OV	SR	OV	SR	OV	SR
Relevancy	20	1.0	11	0.14	8	−0.04	10	0.11
Adversity	11	0.14	20	1.0	9	0.03	10	0.12
Recency	8	−0.04	9	0.03	20	1.0	7	−0.41
Popularity	10	0.11	10	0.12	7	−0.41	20	1.0

6   Concluding Discussions

In this paper, we introduce the concept of the multi-dimensional ranking of clinical trials in terms of **adversity, popularity** and **recency**, along with **relevancy**, with the idea of addressing the different information needs of various stakeholders associated with clinical trial search. We follow a rigorous annotation scheme and create an annotated retrieval set for 25 queries, belonging to 5 different disease categories. Our proposed multi-dimensional ranking model, Synset based term matching model achieves a precision@5 value of 0.56 and outperforms the baseline in more than 90% cases. Further, we explore the limitations of our model by testing it over an oncology-related benchmark gold standard data and report those limitations with proper justifications.

Limitations: In this paper, we have analyzed the ranked result for five different diseases. However, in all these cases, we only rely on the search term given by the user. Currently, we test our approach using only 25 queries across 5 disease classes, which does not capture all acronyms and microtext variations of a query. In some cases (e.g., cancer-related diseases), users also provide criteria along with the search terms. For example, in CLEF task, we have found that queries contain gender and age information along with the search terms to find out relevant clinical trials for a patient. We also observe that in specific topics, a description is provided instead of the specific disease. In this paper, we only focus on the brief title and brief summary of trials. It is also necessary to look into the eligibility criteria of a trial which is composed of two parts. One is *inclusion criteria*, which specifies the requirements for a person to be eligible for a trial. The second one is *exclusion criteria*, which prevents a person from participating in the study. This may significantly improve the performance of our model.

Future Work: We observe that Synset based term matching (STM) performs retrieval and ranking well at a lexical level but performs poorly when significant semantic information is required. We can leverage the publicly available generic knowledge bases like PreMedKB, PharmaGKB, LifeMap Integrated Knowledgebase, NCBI Human Gene Database and MalaCards Human Disease Database. In this paper, we propose different aspect based ranking lists. However, in a real-life setting, we require a single ranked list. In future, we will apply more sophisticated aspect fusion techniques [8] to produce a single combined ranked list or may model it as a multiple-criteria decision-making problem.

Acknowledgements. The work is supported in part by the SERB-funded project titled "IoTDiff: Service Differentiation for Personal Hubs", the IMPRINT-funded project titled "Development of a Remote Healthcare Delivery System: Early Diagnosis, Therapy, Follow-up and Preventive Care for Non-communicable Diseases (Cardiopulmonary)", and the European Union's Horizon 2020 research and innovation programme under Grant Agreement No. 832921.

References

1. Gururaj, A.E., et al.: A publicly available benchmark for biomedical dataset retrieval: the reference standard for the 2016 bioCADDIE dataset retrieval challenge. Database 2017 (2017). https://doi.org/10.1093/database/bax061
2. Tsatsaronis, G., et al.: An overview of the BIOASQ large-scale biomedical semantic indexing and question answering competition. BMC Bioinform. **16**(1), 138 (2015). https://doi.org/10.1186/s12859-015-0564-6
3. Suominen, H., et al.: Overview of the CLEF ehealth evaluation lab 2018. In: Experimental IR Meets Multilinguality, Multimodality, and Interaction, pp. 286–301 (2018). https://doi.org/10.1007/978-3-319-98932-7_26
4. Liu, J.L., et al.: Retrieving scientific abstracts iteratively: medier at TREC 2018 precision medicine track (2018). https://trec.nist.gov/pubs/trec27/papers/MedIER-PM.pdf
5. Islamaj Doğan, R., et al.: Overview of the biocreative VI precision medicine track: mining protein interactions and mutations for precision medicine. Database 2019 (2019). https://doi.org/10.1093/database/bay147
6. Bornmann, L., Daniel, H.D.: What do citation counts measure? A review of studies on citing behavior. J. Documentation **64**(1), 45–80 (2008). https://doi.org/10.1108/00220410810844150
7. Cavalcanti, D., Prudêncio, R.: Aspect-based opinion mining in drug reviews. In: Oliveira, E., Gama, J., Vale, Z., Lopes Cardoso, H. (eds.) EPIA 2017. LNCS (LNAI), vol. 10423, pp. 815–827. Springer, Cham (2017). https://doi.org/10.1007/978-3-319-65340-2_66
8. Goodwin, T.R., Skinner, M.A., Harabagiu, S.M.: UTD HLTRI at TREC 2017: precision medicine track. In: National Institute of Standards and Technology (NIST) (2017). https://trec.nist.gov/pubs/trec26/papers/UTDHLTRI-PM.pdf
9. Gräßer, F., Kallumadi, S., Malberg, H., Zaunseder, S.: Aspect-based sentiment analysis of drug reviews applying cross-domain and cross-data learning. In: Proceedings of the 2018 International Conference on Digital Health, pp. 121–125. ACM (2018). https://doi.org/10.1145/3194658.3194677
10. Jiang, S.Y., Weng, C.: Cross-system evaluation of clinical trial search engines. AMIA Jt. Summits Transl. Sci. Proc. **2014**, 223–229 (2014). https://www.ncbi.nlm.nih.gov/pmc/articles/PMC4419768/
11. Kang, T., Zhang, S., et al.: EliiE: an open-source information extraction system for clinical trial eligibility criteria. J. Am. Med. Inform. Assoc. **24**(6), 1062–1071 (2017). https://doi.org/10.1093/jamia/ocx019
12. Kilicoglu, H., Abacha, A.B., et al.: Semantic annotation of consumer health questions. BMC Bioinform. **19**(1), 34 (2018). https://doi.org/10.1186/s12859-018-2045-1

13. Kim, W., Yeganova, L., et al.: Mesh-based dataset for measuring the relevance of text retrieval. In: Proceedings of the BioNLP 2018 workshop, pp. 161–165 (2018). https://doi.org/10.18653/v1/W18-2320
14. Lipscomb, C.E.: Medical subject headings (MeSH). Bull. Med. Library Assoc. **88**(3), 265 (2000). https://www.ncbi.nlm.nih.gov/pmc/articles/PMC35238
15. MacKellar, B., Schweikert, C.: Patterns for conflict identification in clinical trial eligibility criteria. In: 2016 IEEE Healthcom, pp. 1–6, September 2016. https://doi.org/10.1109/HealthCom.2016.7749519
16. Miller, G.A.: WordNet: a lexical database for english. Commun. ACM **38**(11), 39–41 (1995). https://doi.org/10.1145/219717.219748
17. Miotto, R., Jiang, S., Weng, C.: eTACTS: a method for dynamically filtering clinical trial search results. J. Biomed. Inform. **46**(6), 1060–1067 (2013). https://doi.org/10.1016/j.jbi.2013.07.014
18. Page, L., Brin, S., et al.: The pagerank citation ranking: bringing order to the web. Technical Report 1999–66, Stanford InfoLab, November 1999. http://ilpubs.stanford.edu:8090/422/
19. Patel, C.O., Garg, V., Khan, S.A.: What do patients search for when seeking clinical trial information online? In: AMIA Annual Symposium Proceedings, vol. 2010, p. 597. American Medical Informatics Association (2010). https://www.ncbi.nlm.nih.gov/pmc/articles/PMC3041375
20. Reader, T.W., Gillespie, A., Roberts, J.: Patient complaints in healthcare systems: a systematic review and coding taxonomy. BMJ Qual. Saf. **23**(8), 678–689 (2014). https://doi.org/10.1136/bmjqs-2013-002437
21. Roberts, K., Demner-Fushman, D., et al.: Overview of the TREC 2017 precision medicine track. NIST Special Publication 500–324 (2017). https://trec.nist.gov/pubs/trec26/papers/Overview-PM.pdf
22. Roberts, K., Simpson, M., et al.: State-of-the-art in biomedical literature retrieval for clinical cases: a survey of the TREC 2014 CDS track. Inf. Retrieval J. **19**(1), 113–148 (2016). https://doi.org/10.1007/s10791-015-9259-x
23. Roberts, K., et al.: TREC precision medicine 2018 track (2018). http://www.trec-cds.org/2018.html
24. Sayers, E.: A general introduction to the e-utilities. In: Entrez Programming Utilities Help [Internet]. Bethesda (MD): National Center for Biotechnology Information (US) (2010). https://www.ncbi.nlm.nih.gov/books/NBK25497/
25. Sen, A., Ryan, P.B., et al.: Correlating eligibility criteria generalizability and adverse events using big data for patients and clinical trials. Ann. New York Acad. Sci. **1387**(1), 34–43 (2017). https://doi.org/10.1111/nyas.13195
26. Soldaini, L., Goharian, N.: QuickUMLS: a fast, unsupervised approach for medical concept extraction. In: MedIR Workshop, SIGIR (2016)
27. Surian, D., Dunn, A.G., et al.: A shared latent space matrix factorisation method for recommending new trial evidence for systematic review updates. J. Biomed. Inform. **79**, 32–40 (2018). https://doi.org/10.1016/j.jbi.2018.01.008
28. Thorve, A.: Team Ajinkya Throve at TREC 2017 precision medicine track (2017). https://github.com/ajinkyathorve/TREC-2017-PM-CDS-Track
29. Tong Yin, Danny Wu, V.V.: Retrieving documents based on gene name variations: MedIER at TREC 2017 precision medicine track (2017). https://trec.nist.gov/pubs/trec26/papers/MedIER-PM.pdf

30. Tsafnat, G., Glasziou, P., et al.: Systematic review automation technologies. Syst. Rev. **3**(1), 74 (2014). https://doi.org/10.1186/2046-4053-3-74
31. Zuccon, G., Koopman, B., et al.: Choices in knowledge-base retrieval for consumer health search. In: Pasi, G., Piwowarski, B., Azzopardi, L., Hanbury, A. (eds.) European Conference on Information Retrieval, pp. 72–85. Springer, Cham (2018). https://doi.org/10.1007/978-3-319-76941-7_6

Scalable Self-taught Deep-Embedded Learning Framework for Drug Abuse Spatial Behaviors Detection

Wuji Liu[1], Xinyue Ye[2(✉)], Hai Phan[2], and Han Hu[2]

[1] Department of Computer Science, New Jersey Institute of Technology,
Newark, NJ 07102, USA
wl87@njit.edu
[2] Department of Informatics, New Jersey Institute of Technology,
Newark, NJ 07102, USA
{xinyue.ye,phan,hh255}@njit.edu

Abstract. Drug abuse has become an increasingly challenging issue national wide in the United States, while each state has its own legislation regarding such behavior which further stimulates different semantic representations of such behavior over space. To build an accurate and robust classifier to detect such behaviors with spatial variance remains challenging due to the existence of large noise in tweets and limited number of labeled data. Most efforts have utilized humans to label tweets for the base classifier training. The randomness of human labeled data would limit the generalization of base model trained. We propose a deep learning-based centroid-attention framework to consider the spatial variance. We further explore the effect of state-based exemplars on the base model. The performance of the base classifier is thus enhanced.

Keywords: Deep learning · Drug abuse · Spatial effects

1 Introduction

Deep learning for computational social science has attracted growing attentions because of the data availability associated with pressing policy challenges [1–6, 8]. In 2018, DEA (Drug Enforcement Administration) reported the increasing number of deaths caused by abuse heroin, cocaine and other dangerous drugs since 2009. For people aged 12 or above, over 18.6 million misused medical drug, while about 1.7 million misused prescription drugs [7]. This paper builds a scalable self-taught framework to detect potential drug abuse behaviors in the tweets. Most efforts [9, 10] used specified keyword to collect data. The vague expression of drug abuse activity was also examined [3]. However, little work considered the spatiality. For example, the sampled training tweets might mainly come from one region, so the trained classifier tend to perform poorly in another region with different law and social environments. Thus, our contributions are: (1) build a document-level spatially explicit clustering framework; (2) analyze the different expression manner of same semantic meaning across states and reveal the effectiveness of exemplars to classification accuracy of the base model; (3) conduct a series of experiments and prove the significant improvement of accuracy to the base model after correcting data bias.

© Springer Nature Switzerland AG 2019
A. Tagarelli and H. Tong (Eds.): CSoNet 2019, LNCS 11917, pp. 223–228, 2019.
https://doi.org/10.1007/978-3-030-34980-6_26

2 Related Work

Social media provides prominent data resources for public health studies. [14] sampled social media posts related to six prescription opioid compounds to design an evaluation metric, the Endorsement Ratio (ERo), to verify the trustiness of the performance of multinomial logistic regression on the task of quantifying the sentiment expressed by opioid abusers. Holding the hypothesis that labeled data and unlabeled data could come from different distributions, self-taught learning method has been developed and well-studied [5, 13]. [1] sampled 9,000 tweets potentially related to the wildfire during the wildfire seasons from 2015 to 2016 in California. They trained a SVM classifier as the baseline model, and then trained a robust SVM model to outperform the baseline mode. [3] trained a deep learning model with a merged dataset containing both training dataset and testing dataset, outperforming the model solely based on the training set. We will take this model as the base model in the next section. Although the self-taught approach can improve the model, another problem arises: how many testing data is needed in order to reach such objectives? A number can be manually set to control the self-taught cycle [3], but it can also be achieved by considering the spatiality of tweets. To minimize the side impact of bias in the training data, we propose a self-taught learning framework to correct the potential bias. Instead of blindly using self-taught learning, the semantic exemplars across space are adopted.

3 Data Ad Method

Our goal is to build a bias reduced classifier that can label the unlabeled tweets as drug abuse related or not. We use a list of illegal drug and medical legal drug that have been abused [3]. Combining it with other terms such as high, blunt, and barbs, we build a keyword based filter to eliminate the unrelated tweets. Adopting such method, we collected over 3 million raw tweets over four years. 1,794 tweets are randomly picked and manually labeled by a professional team. We further train a basic SVM model to help label other unlabeled 4,985 raw tweets. We then deliver them to Amazon Mechanical Turk for verification. We then successfully generated a set of high-quality data as the initial training data set. Insufficient training data is a common issue for NLP tasks. The training data seeds we use are manually labeled by several domain experts and further verified by Amazon Mechanical Turk. It is worthy of notice that the semantic expression in the tweets regarding Drug Abuse varies across regions especially when some come from marijuana prohibited states while others are from permitted states. In such a scenario, our model would need more representative data to improve the performance of model. Motivated by such observation, we cluster the states by marijuana legality across three scales: Macro, Meso, and Micro.

At the macro level, we cluster the states into three regions: (i) Fully legal: ME, MA, VT, MI, WA, OR, NV, CA, AK. (ii) Mixed: ND, MN, OH, NY, NH, CT, RI, MD, NM, DE, MT, UT, AZ, TX, OK, AR, MO, IA, IL, IN, PA, WV, NJ, VA, GA, FL, HI, NE, NC, MS. (iii) Fully illegal: ID, WY, SD, KS, WI, KY, TN, AL, LA, SC. At the Meso scale, we cluster the states into five regions: (i) Legalized: ME, MA, VT, MI, WA, OR, NV,

CA, AK. (ii) Medical and Decriminalized: ND, MN, OH, NY, NH, CT, RI, MD, NM, DE. (iii) Medical: MT, UT, AZ, TX, OK, AR, MO, IA, IL, IN, PA, WV, NJ, VA, GA, FL, HI. (iv): Medical: MT, UT, AZ, TX, OK, AR, MO, IA, IL, IN, PA, WV, NJ, VA, GA, FL, HI. (v): Decriminalized: NE, NC, MS. (vi) Fully illegal: ID, WY, SD, KS, WI, KY, TN, AL, LA, SC. At the Micro level, each state will be treated as an observation unit and explored based on the similarity.

To demonstrate the semantic expression difference among states, we sampled two relevant exemplar tweets. "Beer and bluegrass were all set USER_MENTION drink it up check out" was from a Fully Illegal State, while "Come on over and #smoke #weed with those who #love it as much as you do" appeared in a Fully Legal State. In the fully illegal state, the user would be careful in the wording, while in the fully legal state, the user tends to be bold. To explore the influence of different semantic exemplars to the performance of pre-trained base model, we develop a deep-embedded clustering method to find the exemplars and further train the base model with exemplars that has high confidence level. Embedding is a vectorization method that cast the text documents into another vector space. The goal is to learn the robust short text embedding representation. Word2vec [11] is used to vectorize word. After vectorization, each word will be represented as 300 dimensional vectors. Doc2vec [12] is an unsupervised learning algorithm that can give a vector representations of documents and texts. Semantic meaning of same words varies largely across states. Many possible drug abuse tweets contain "weed" in Illinois, but referring to the weed river. Hence, we propose a pipeline clustering method to filter out these exemplars. Tweets stream will be stored into cache and separately stored into a cache based on geo location. After the number of tweets of state reach the pre-defined threshold, we embedded the tweets into Euclidean space using Doc2vec [12] embedding and then calculate the similarities between each tweet to get the distance matrix for the Affinity propagation algorithm to retrieve the exemplars. We further explored the similarities between different exemplars of each state as shown in Fig. 1, showing semantic representation of different states on the same topic could be significantly different. The lighter the color, the more difference. Traditional models like SVM, Naive bayes and deep learning model like MLP, CNN, and LSTM can both used to perform classification task. In this work we select a Convolution Neural Network model as our base model. Table 1 shows the parameter setting.

In summary, we develop a deep learning framework to understand the different semantic representations across states. Unlabeled twitter streams are fed into a cache and then processed and further embedded into vectors to extract the exemplars. We label the exemplars with deep learning model. Based on the confidence score of the exemplars, we merge the exemplars retrieved for each state and then put them together with previous human labeled data to further train a new model. This can be done by setting a predefined confidence threshold. In our proposed method, combining the machine labeled data along with human labeled data to train a new model will further improve the performance of basic model.

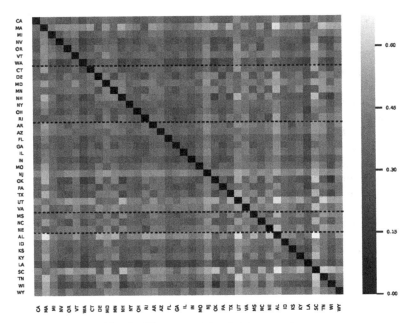

Fig. 1. Distance matrix of state exemplars.

Table 1. CNN base model.

Base model	Layers	Params
CNN model	Embedding	Size, 300, length: 30
	Dropout	Dropout rate: 0.1
	Convolutional layer	Kernel sizes: 2, Number of kernels: 128, Activation function: Relu
	Max pooling	Pool size: 2
	Flatten	None
	Concatenate	None
	Dropout	Dropout rate: 0.5
	Two dense layers	Size: 768 × 1024 1024×2

4   Experimental Results

In this research, 1,794 tweets are collected and manually labeled by two professors and three students with the rich experience in drug abuse research as initial data set. We further select 5,000 tweets from 3 million unlabeled data, and then use SVM to classify them. Finally, we send the machine labeled data to Mechanical Turk to verify. After such preprocessing procedure, we have 6,794 labeled tweets as the seed data, and use another 3 million tweets to extract exemplars.

All of the experiments have been conducted on a 12 GB NVIDIA GTX TITAN X GPU. Among 6,794 seed data, we sample out 1,000 data as the validation data set. Inspired by k-fold cross validation, we sample 1,000 data from 6,794 as the validation set to test the performance of our model and then divide the remaining 5,794 data into $K = 6$ part. We conduct six experiments. For each experiment, we select five parts of k part as the training and one part of k part as the testing to build the model. Our experiment results confirm the data bias exists in the training data set, and further prove the conclusion that combining exemplars with training data set would increase the performance of the base model.

5 Future Work

In the next step, we will focus on predicting the time and scale of the burst of drug abuse behaviors. We also plan to study the spatial diffusion pattern of such behaviors in social networks to help identify the spread of drug abuse activities.

Acknowledgement. This material is partially based upon work supported by the National Science Foundation under Grant No. 1416509. Any opinions, findings, and conclusions or recommendations expressed in this material are those of the author and do not necessarily reflect the views of NSF.

References

1. Shi, X., et al.: Detecting events from the social media through exemplar-enhanced supervised learning. Int. J. Digital Earth **12**(9), 1083–1097 (2018). https://doi.org/10.1080/17538947. 2018.1502369
2. DISA. https://disa.com/
3. Hu, H., et al.: Deep self-taught learning for detecting drug abuse risk behavior in tweets. In: Chen, X., Sen, A., Li, W.W., Thai, M.T. (eds.) CSoNet 2018. LNCS, vol. 11280, pp. 330–342. Springer, Cham (2018). https://doi.org/10.1007/978-3-030-04648-4_28
4. Huang, A.: Similarity measures for text document clustering. In: Proceedings of NZCSRSC 2008, pp. 49—56 (2008)
5. Raina, R., Battle, A., Lee, H., Packer, B., Ng, A.Y.: Self-taught learning: transfer learning from unlabeled data. In: ICML (2007)
6. Barocas, S., Selbst, A.D.: Big data's disparate impact. Calif. Law Rev. **104**(3), 671–732 (2016)
7. Drug Enforcement Administration (DEA): 2018 National drug threat assessment (2018). https://www.dea.gov/documents/2018/10/02/2018-national-drug-threat-assessment-ndta
8. Ex-DEA Agent: Opioid crisis fueled by drug industry and congress. CBS 60 Minutes (2017)
9. McNaughton, E.C., Black, R.A., Zulueta, M.G., Budman, S.H., Butler, S.F.: Measuring online endorsement of prescription opioids abuse: an integrative methodology. Pharmacoepidemiol. Drug Saf. **21**(10), 1081–1092 (2012)
10. Sarker, A., et al.: Social media mining for toxicovigilance: automatic monitoring of prescription medication abuse from Twitter. Drug Saf. **39**(3), 231–240 (2016)

11. Mikolov, T., Chen, K., Corrado, G., Dean, J.: Efficient estimation of word representations in vector space. CoRR abs/1301.3781(2013)
12. Mikolov, T., Sutskever, I., Chen, K., Corrado, G., Dean, J.: Distributed representations of words and phrases and their compositionality. In: Proceedings of NIPS (2013)
13. Bettge, A., Roscher, R., Wenzel, S: Deep self-taught learning for remote sensing image classification. CoRR abs/1710.07096 (2017)
14. Hochreiter, S., Schmidhuber, J.: Long short-term memory. Neural Comput. **9**(8), 1735–1780 (1997)

Limiting the Neighborhood: De-Small-World Network for Outbreak Prevention

Ruoming Jin[1], Yelong Sheng[1], Lin Liu[1], Xue-Wen Chen[2],
and NhatHai Phan[3(✉)]

[1] Department of Computer Science, Kent State University, Kent, USA
{jin,ysheng,lliu}@cs.kent.edu
[2] Department of EECS, The University of Kansas, Lawrence, USA
xwchen@ku.edu
[3] College of Computing, New Jersey Institute of Technology, Newark, USA
phan@njit.edu

Abstract. In this work, we study a basic and practically important strategy to help prevent and/or delay an outbreak in the context of network: limiting the contact between individuals. In this paper, we introduce the *average neighborhood size* as a new measure for the degree of being small-world and utilize it to formally define the *de-small-world* network problem. We also prove the NP-hardness of the general reachable pair cut problem and propose a greedy edge betweenness based approach as the benchmark in selecting the candidate edges for solving our problem. Furthermore, we transform the de-small-world network problem as an OR-AND Boolean function maximization problem, which is also an NP-hardness problem. In addition, we develop a numerical relaxation approach to solve the Boolean function maximization and the de-small-world problem. Also, we introduce the *short-betweenness*, which measures the edge importance in terms of all short paths with distance no greater than a certain threshold, and utilize it to speed up our numerical relaxation approach. The experimental evaluation demonstrates the effectiveness and efficiency of our approaches.

1 Introduction

The interconnected network structure has been recognized to play a pivotal role in many complex systems, ranging from natural (cellular system), to man-made (Internet), to the social and economical systems. Many of these networks exhibit the "small-world" phenomenon, i.e., any two vertices in the network is often connected by a small number of intermediate vertices (the shortest-path distance is small). The small-world phenomenon in the real populations was first discovered by Milgram [12]. In his study, the average distance between two Americans is around 6. Several recent studies [7,10,13] offer significant evidence to support similar observations in the online social networks and Internet itself. In addition, the power-law degree distribution (or scale-free property) which

© Springer Nature Switzerland AG 2019
A. Tagarelli and H. Tong (Eds.): CSoNet 2019, LNCS 11917, pp. 229–245, 2019.
https://doi.org/10.1007/978-3-030-34980-6_27

many of these networks also directly lead to the small average distance [1]. Clearly, the small-world property can help facilitate the communication and speed up the diffusion process and information spreading in a large network.

However, the small-world effect can be a dangerous *double-edged sword*. When a system is benefited from the efficient communication and fast information diffusion, it also makes itself more vulnerable to various attacks: diseases, (computer) virus, spams, and misinformation, etc. For instance, it has been shown that a small-world graph can have much faster disease propagation than a regular lattice or a random graph [14]. Indeed, the six degrees of separation may suggest that a highly infectious disease could spread to all six billion people living in the earth about size incubation periods of the diseases [14]. The small-word property of Internet and WWW not only enables the computer virus and spams to be much easier to spread, but also makes them hard to stop. More recently, the misinformation problem in the social networks has made several public outcry [3]. These small-world online social network potentially facilitate the spread of misinformation to reach a large number of audience in short time, which may cause public panic and have other disruptive effects.

To prevent an outbreak, the most basic strategy is to remove the affected individuals (or computers) from the network system, like quarantine. However, in many situations, the explicit quarantine may be hard to achieve: the contagious individuals are either unknown or hard to detect; or it is often impossible to detect and remove each infected individual; or there are many already being affected and it become too costly to remove all of them in a timely fashion. Thus, it is important to consider alternative strategies to help prevent and even delay the spreading where the latter can be essential in discovering and/or deploying new methods for dealing with the outbreaks.

Recently, there have been a lot of interests in understanding the network factors (such as the small-word and scale-free properties) in the epidemics and information diffusion process, and utilizing the network structures in detecting/preventing the outbreaks. Several studies have focused on modeling the disease epidemics on the small-world and/or scale-free networks [14–16]; in [11], Leskovec *et al.* study how to deploy sensors cost-effectively in a network system (sensors are assigned to vertices) to detect an outbreak; in [3], Budak *et al.* consider how to limit the misinformation by identifying a set of individuals that are needed to adopt the "good" information (being immune in epidemics) in order to minimize those being affected by the "bad" information (being infected in epidemics). In addition, we note that from a different angle (viral marketing), there have been a list of studies on the *influence maximization* problem [8,17], which aim to discover a set of most influential seeds to maximize the information spreading in the network. From the disease epidemics perspective, those seeds (assuming being selected using contagious model) may need particular protection to prevent an outbreak.

In this work, we study another basic and practically important strategy to help prevent and/or delay an outbreak in the context of network: limiting the contact between individuals. Different from the pure quarantine approach, here

individuals can still perform in the network system, though some contact relationships are forbidden. In other words, instead of removing vertices (individuals)
form a network as in the quarantine approach, this strategy focuses on removing edges so that the (potential) outbreaks can be slowed down. Intuitively, if
an individual contacts less number of other individuals, the chance for him or
her to spread or being infected from the disease (misinformation) becomes less.
From the network viewpoint, the edge-removal strategy essentially make the
underlying (social) network less small-world, or simply "de-small-world", i.e.,
the distances between individuals increase to delay the spreading process. In
many situations, such a strategy is often easily and even voluntarily adopted.
For instance, during the SARS epidemic in Beijing, 2004, there are much less
people appearing in the public places. This approach can also be deployed in
complement to the quarantine approach.

Our Contribution. Even though the edge-removal or *de-small-world* approach
seems to be conceptually easy to understand, its mathematical foundation is still
lack of study. Clearly, different edges (interactions) in the network are not being
equivalent in terms of slowing down any potential outbreak: for a given individual, a link to an individual of high degree connection can be more dangerous
than a link to another one with low degree connection. The edge importance (in
terms of distance) especially coincides with Kleighnberg's theoretical model [9]
which utilizes the *long-range edges* on top of an underlying grid for explaining
the small-world phenomenon. In this model, the long-range edges are the main
factors which help connect the otherwise long-distance pairs with a smaller number of edges. However, there are no direct studies in fitting such a model to the
real world graph to discover those long-range edges. In the mean time, additional
constraint, such as the number of edges can be removed from the network, may
exist because removing an edge can associate with certain cost. These factors
and requirements give arise to the following fundamental research problem: *how
can we maximally de-small-world a graph (making a graph to be less small-world)
by removing a fixed number of edges?*
To tackle the problem, we make the following contributions:

1. We introduce the *average neighborhood size* as a new measure for the degree of
   being small-world and utilizes it to formally define the de-small-world network
   problem. Note that the typical average distance for measuring the small-world
   effects cannot uniformly treat the connected and disconnected networks; neither does it fit well with the spreading process. We also reformulate the de-
   small-world as the *local-reachable pair cut* problem.
2. We prove the NP-hardness of the general reachable pair cut problem and propose a greedy edge betweenness based approach as the benchmark in selecting
   the candidate edges for solving the de-small-world network. We transform the
   de-small-world network problem and express it as a OR-AND Boolean function maximization problem, which is also an NP-hard problem.

3. We develop a numerical relaxation approach to solve the de-small-world problem using its OR-AND boolean format. Our approach can find a local minimum based on the iterative gradient optimization procedure. In addition, we further generalize the betweenness measure and introduces the *short betweenness*, which measures the edge importance in terms of all the paths with distance no greater than a certain threshold. Using this measure, we can speed up the numerical relaxation approach by selecting a small set of candidate edges for removal.
4. We perform a detailed experimental evaluation, which demonstrates the effectiveness and efficiency of proposed approaches.

2   Problem Definition and Preliminary

In this section, we first formally define the *de-small-world* network problem and prove its NP-hardness; then we introduce the basic greedy approaches based on edge betweenness which will serve as the basic benchmark; and finally we show the de-small-world network problem can be transformed and expressed as a OR-AND Boolean function maximization problem.

Problem Formulation. In order to model the edge-removal process and formally define the *de-small-world* network problem, a criterion is needed to precisely capture the *degree* of being small-world. Note that here the goal is to help prevent and/or delay the potential outbreak and epidemic process. The typical measure of small-world network is based on the average distance (the average length of the shortest path between any pair of vertices in the entire network). However, this measure is not able to provide unified treatment of the connected and cut network. Specifically, assuming a connected network is broken into several cut network and the average distance on the cut network is not easy to express. On the other hand, we note that the de-small-world network graph problem is different from the network decomposition (clustering) problem which tries to break the entire network into several components (connected subgraphs). From the outbreak prevention and delaying perspective, the cost of network decomposition is too high and may not be effective. This is because each individual component itself may still be small-world; and the likelihood of completely separating the contagious/infected group from the rest of populations (the other components) is often impossible.

   Given this, we introduce the *average neighborhood size* as a new measure for the degree of being small-world and utilize it to formally define the de-small-world network problem. Especially, the new measure can not only uniformly treat both connected and cut networks and aims to directly help model the spreading/diffusion process. Simply speaking, for each vertex v in a network $G = (V, E)$ where V is the vertex set and E is the edge set, we define the neighborhood of v as the number of vertices with distance no greater than k to v, denoted as $N^k(v)$. Here k is the user-specified *spreading* (or delaying) parameter which aims to measure the outbreak speed, i.e., in a specified time unit, the maximum distance between individual u (source) to another one v (destination) who can be infected if u is infected. Thus, the average neighborhood size of G, $\sum_{v \in V} N^k(v)$, can be used to measure the robustness of the network with respect to a potential outbreak in a certain time framework. Clearly, a potential problem of the small-world network is that even for a small k, the average neighborhood size can be still rather large, indicating a large (expected) number of individuals can be quickly affected (within time framework k) during an outbreak process.

Formally, the *de-small-world* network problem is defined as follows:

Definition 1 (De-Small-World Network Problem). Given the edge-removal budget $L > 0$ and the spreading parameter $k > 1$ we seek a subset of edges $E_r \subset E$, where $|E_r| = L$, such that the average neighborhood size is minimized:

$$\min_{|E_r|=L} \frac{\sum_{v \in V} N^k(v|G \backslash E_r)}{|V|}, \tag{1}$$

where $N^k(v|G \backslash E_r)$ is the neighborhood size of v in the graph G after removing all edges in E_r from the edge set E.

Note that in the above definition, we assume each vertex has the equal probability to be the source of infection. In the general setting, we may consider to associate each vertex v with a probability to indicate its likelihood to be (initially) infected. Furthermore, we may assign each edge with a weight to indicate the cost to removing such an edge. For simplicity, we do not study those extensions in this work; though our approaches can be in general extended to handle those additional parameters. In addition, we note that in our problem, we require the spreading parameter $k > 1$. This is because for $k = 1$, this problem is trivial: the average neighborhood size is equivalent to the average vertex degree; and removing any edge has the same effect. In other words, when $k = 1$, the neighborhood criterion does not capture the spreading or cascading effects of the small-world graph. Therefore, we focus on $k > 1$, though in general k is still relatively small (for instance, no higher than 3 or 4 in general).

Reachable Pair Cut Formulation: We note the de-small-world network problem can be defined in terms of the *reachable pair cut* formulation. Let a pair of two vertices whose distance is no greater than k is referred to as a *local-reachable pair* or simply *reachable pair*. Let $\mathcal{R}_G$ record the set of all local reachable pairs in G.

Definition 2 (Reachable Pair Cut Problem). For a given local (u, v), if $d(u, v|G) \leq k$ in G, but $d(u, v|G \backslash E_s) > k$, where E_s is an edge set in G, then we say (u, v) is being **local cut** (or simply cut) by E_s. Given the edge-removal budget $L > 0$ and the spreading parameter $k > 1$, the reachable pair cut problem aims to find the edge set $E_r \subseteq E$, such that the maximum number of pairs in $\mathcal{R}_G$ is cut by E_r.

Note that here the (local) cut for a pair of vertices simply refers to increase their distance; not necessarily completely disconnect them in the graph $(G \backslash E_s)$.

Also, since $\mathcal{R}_{G \setminus E_r} \subseteq \mathcal{R}_G$, i.e., every local-reachable pair in the remaining network $G \setminus E_r$ is also the local-reachable in the original graph G, the problem is equivalently to maximize $|\mathcal{R}_G| - |\mathcal{R}_{G \setminus E_r}|$ and minimize the number of local reachable pairs $|\mathcal{R}_{G \setminus E_r}|$. Finally, the correctness of such a reformulation (de-small-world problem = reachable pair cut problem) follows this simple observation: $\sum_{v \in V} N^k(v|G) = 2|\mathcal{R}_G|$ (and $\sum_{v \in V} N^k(v|G \setminus E_r) = 2|\mathcal{R}_{G \setminus E_r}|$). Basically, every reachable pair is counted twice in the neighborhood size criterion.

In the following, we study the hardness of the general reachable pair cut problem.

Theorem 1. *Given a set RS of local reachable pairs in $G = (V, E)$ with respect to k, the problem of finding L edges $E_r \subseteq E$ ($|E_r| = L$) in G such that the maximal number of pairs in RS being cut by E_r is NP-Hard.*

All the proofs of Theorems and Lemmas can be found in our Appendix[1]. Note that in the general problem, RS can be any subset of $\mathcal{R}_G$. The NP-hardness of the general reachable pair cut problem a strong indicator that the de-small-world network problem is also hard. In addition, we note that the submodularity property plays an important role in solving vertex-centered maximal influence [8], outbreak detection [11], and limiting misinformation spreading [3] problems. However, such property does not hold for the edge-centered de-small-world problem.

Lemma 1. *Let set function $f : 2^E \to Z^+$ records the number of local reachable pairs in $\mathcal{R}_G$ is cut by an edge set E_s in graph G. Function f is neither submodular (diminishing return) nor supermodular.*

Greedy Betweenness-Based Approach. Finding the optimal solution for the de-small-world problem is likely to be NP-hard. Clearly, it is computationally prohibitive to enumerate all the possible removal edge set E_r and to measure how many reachable pairs could be cut or how much the average neighborhood size is reduced. In the following, we describe a greedy approach to heuristically discover a solution edge-set. This approach also serves as the benchmark for the de-small-world problem.

The basic approach is based on the edge-betweenness, which is a useful criterion to measure the edge importance in a network. Intuitively, the edge-betweenness measures the edge important with respect to the shortest paths in the network. The high betweenness suggests that the edge is involved into many shortest paths; and thus removing them will likely increase the distance of those pairs linked by these shortest paths. Here, we consider two variants of edge-betweenness: the (global) edge-betweenness [4] and the local edge-betweenness [5]. The global edge-betweenness is the original one [4] and is defined as follows:

$$B(e) = \sum_{s \neq t \in V} \frac{\delta_{st}(e)}{\delta_{st}},$$

---

[1] https://www.dropbox.com/s/rpkqpn6y7mwconk/Appendix.pdf?dl=0.

where δ_{st} is the total number of shortest paths between vertex s and t, and $\delta_{st}(e)$ the total number of shortest paths between u and v containing edge e.

The local edge-betweenness considers only those vertex pairs whose shortest paths are no greater than k, and is defined as

$$LB(e) = \sum_{s \neq t \in V, d(s,t) \leq k} \frac{\delta_{st}(e)}{\delta_{st}},$$

The reason to use the local edge-betweenness measure is because in the de-small-world (and reachable pair cut) problem, we focus on those local reachable pairs (distance no greater than k). Thus, the contribution to the (global) betweenness from those pairs with distance greater than k can be omitted. The exact edge-betweenness can be computed in $O(nm)$ worst case time complexity [2] where $n = |V|$ (the number of vertices) and $m = |E$ (the number of edges) in a given graph, though in practical the local one can be computed much faster.

Using the edge-betweenness measure, we may consider the following *generic procedure* to select the L edges for E_r:

(1) Select the top $r < L$ edges into E_r, and remove those edges from the input graph G;
(2) Recompute the betweenness for all remaining edges in the updated graph G;
(3) Repeat the above procedure $\lceil L/r \rceil$ times until all L edges are selected.

Note that the special case $r = 1$, where we select each edge in each iteration, the procedure is very similar to the Girvan-Newman algorithm [4] in which they utilize the edge-betweenness for community discovery. Gregory [5] generalizes it to use the local-edge betweenness. Here, we only consider to pickup L edges and allow users to select the frequency to recompute the edge-betweenness (mainly for efficiency consideration). The overall time complexity of the betweenness based approach is $O(\lceil L/r \rceil nm)$ (assuming the exact betweenness computation is adopted).

2.1 OR-AND Boolean Function and Its Maximization Problem

In the following, we transform the de-small-world network problem and express it as a OR-AND Boolean function maximization problem, which forms the basis for our optimization problem in next section. First, we will utilize the OR-AND graph to help represent the de-small-world (reachable pair cut) problem. Let us denote P the set of all the short paths in G that have length at most k.

OR-AND Graph: Given a graph $G = (V, E)$, the vertex set of an *OR-AND* graph $\mathcal{G} = (\mathcal{V}, \mathcal{E})$ is comprised of three kinds of nodes $\mathcal{V}_E$, $\mathcal{V}_P$ and $\mathcal{V}_{\mathcal{R}_G}$, where each node in $\mathcal{V}_E$ corresponds to a unique edge in E, each node in $\mathcal{V}_P$ corresponds to a short path in P, and each node in $\mathcal{V}_{\mathcal{R}_G}$ corresponds to a unique reachable pair in G (with respect to k). Figure 1(b) shows those nodes for graph G in Fig. 1(a). The edge set consists of two types of edges: (1) Each short path node

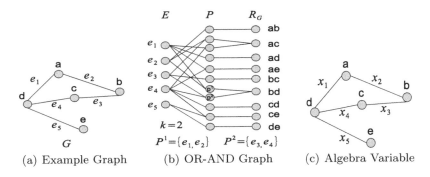

Fig. 1. *OR-AND* graph and algebra variable

in $\mathcal{V}_P$ is linked with the vertices in $\mathcal{V}_E$ corresponding to those edges in the path. For instance path node p^1 in $\mathcal{V}_P$ links to edge node e_1 and e_2 in $\mathcal{V}_E$ in Fig. 1(b). Each reachable pair node in $\mathcal{V}_{\mathcal{R}_G}$ links to those path nodes which connects the reachable pair. For instance, the reachable pair bd is connected with path node p^1 and p^2 in Fig. 1(b).

Intuitively, in the OR-AND graph, we can see that in order to cut a reachable pair, we have to cut *all* the short paths between them (AND). To cut one short path, we need to remove only one edge in that path (OR). Let $P(u, v)$ consists all the (simple) short paths between u and v whose length are no more than k. For each short path p in $P(u, v)$, let e corresponds to a Boolean variable for edge $e \in p$: if $e_i = T$, then the edge e_i is not cut; if $e_i = F$, then the edge is cut ($e_i \in E_r$). Thus, for each reachable pair $(u, v) \in \mathcal{R}_G$, we can utilize the a Boolean OR-AND expression to describe it:

$$I(u, v) = \bigvee_{p \in P(u,v)} \bigwedge_{e \in p} e \tag{2}$$

For instance, in the graph G (Fig. 1(b)),

$$I(b, d) = (e_1 \wedge e_2) \vee (e_3 \wedge e_4)$$

Here, $I(b, d) = T$ indicating the pair is being cut only if for both p^1 and p^2 are cut. For instance, if $e_1 = F$ and $e_3 = F$, then $I(b, d) = F$; and $e_1 = F$, but $e_3 = T$ and $e_4 = T$, $I(b, d) = T$. Given this, the de-small-world problem (and the reachable pair cut problem) can be expressed as the following Boolean function maximization problem.

Definition 3 (Boolean Function Maximization Problem). Given a list of Boolean functions (such as $I(u, v)$, where $(u, v) \in \mathcal{R}_G$), we seek a Boolean variable assignment where exactly L variables are assigned false ($e = F$ iff $e \in E_r$, and $|E_r| = L$), such that the maximal number of Boolean functions being false ($I(u, v) = F$ corresponding to (u, v) is cut by E_r).

Unfortunately, the Boolean function maximization problem is also NP-hard since it can directly express the general reachable pair cut problem. In the next section, we will introduce a numerical relation approach to solve this problem.

3 Path Algebra and Optimization Algorithm

In this section, we introduce a numerical relaxation approach to solve the Boolean function maximization problem (and thus the de-small-world problem). Here, the basic idea is that since the direct solution for the Boolean function maximization problem is hard, instead of working on the Boolean (binary) edge variable, we relax to it to be a numerical value. However, the challenge is that we need to define the numerical function optimization problem such that it meet the following two criteria: (1) it is rather accurately match the Boolean function maximization; and (2) it can enable numerical solvers to be applied to optimize the numerical function. In Subsect. 3.1, we introduce the numerical optimization problem based on the path algebra. In Subsect. 3.2, we discuss the optimization approach for solving this problem.

3.1 Path-Algebra and Numerical Optimization Problem

To construct a numerical optimization problem for the Boolean function maximization format of the de-small-world problem, we introduce the following path-algebra to describe all the short paths between any reachable pair in $\mathcal{R}_G$. For each edge e in the graph $G = (V, E)$, we associate it with a variable x_e. Then, for any reachable pair $(u, v) \in \mathcal{R}_G$, we define its corresponding path-algebra expression $\mathcal{P}(u, v)$ as follows:

$$\mathcal{P}(u, v) = \sum_{p \in P(u,v)} \prod_{e \in p} x_e \tag{3}$$

Taking the path-algebra for (b, d) in Fig. 1 and (c) as example, we have

$$\mathcal{P}(b, d) = x_2 x_1 + x_3 x_4$$

Basically, the path-algebra expression $\mathcal{P}(u, v)$ directly corresponds to the Boolean expression $I(u, v)$ by replacing $AND(\wedge)$ with product $(\times)$, $OR(\vee)$ with sum $(+)$, and Boolean variable e with algebraic variable x_e. Intuitively, $\mathcal{P}(u, v)$ records the weighted sum of each path in $P(u, v)$, where the weight is the product based on the edge variable x_e. Note that when $x_e = 1$ for every edge e, when $\mathcal{P}(u, v)$ simply records the number of different short paths (with length no more than k) between u and v, i.e., $\mathcal{P}(u, v) = |P(u, v)|$. Furthermore, if assuming $x_e \geq 0$, then $\mathcal{P}(u, v) = 0$ is equivalent to in each path $p \in P(u, v)$, there is at least one edge variable is equivalent to 0. In other words, assuming if variable $x_e = 0$ iff $e = T$, then $\mathcal{P}(u, v) = 0$ iff $I(u, v) = F$ and $\mathcal{P}(u, v) > 0$ iff $I(u, v) = T$.

Given this, we may be tempted to optimize the follow objective function based on the path-algebra expression to represent the Boolean function maximization problem:

$\sum_{(u,v)\in\mathcal{R}_G} \mathcal{P}(u,v)$. However, this does not accurately reflect our goal, as to minimize $\sum_{(u,v)\in\mathcal{R}_G} \mathcal{P}(u,v)$, we may not need any $\mathcal{P}(u,v) = 0$ (which shall be our main goal). This is because $\mathcal{P}(u,v)$ corresponds to the weighted sum of path products. Can we use the path-algebra to address the importance of $\mathcal{P}(u,v) = 0$ in the objective function?

We provide a positive answer to this problem by utilizing an exponential function transformation. Specifically, we introduce the following *numerical maximization* problem based on the path expression:

$$\sum_{(u,v)\in\mathcal{R}_G} e^{-\lambda\mathcal{P}(u,v)}, \text{ where}, 0 \le x_e \le 1, \sum x_e \ge X - L \quad (4)$$

Note that $0 \le e^{-\lambda\mathcal{P}(u,v)} \le 1$ (each $x_e \ge 0$), and only when $\mathcal{P}(u,v) = 0$, $e^{-\lambda\mathcal{P}(u,v)} = 1$ (the largest value for each term). When $\mathcal{P}(u,v) \approx 1$, the term $e^{-\lambda\mathcal{P}(u,v)}$ can be rather small (approach 0). The parameter λ is the adjusting parameter to help control the exponential curve and smooth the objective function. Furthermore, the summation constraint $\sum x_e \ge X - L$) is to express the budget condition that there shall have L variables with $x_i \approx 0$. Here X is the total number of variables in the objective function ($X = |E|$ if we consider every single edge variable x_e).

3.2   Gradient Optimization

Clearly, it is very hard to find the exact (or closed form) solution for maximizing function in Eq. 4 under these linear constraints. In this section, we utilize the standard *gradient* (ascent) approach together with the *active set* method [6] to discover a local maximum. The gradient ascent takes steps proportional to the positive of the gradient iteratively to approach a local minimum. The active set approach is a standard approach in optimization which deals with the *feasible regions* (represented as constraints). Here we utilize it to handle the constraint in Eq. 4.

Gradient Computation: To perform gradient ascent optimization, we need compute the gradient $g(x_e)$ for each variable x_e. Fortunately, we can derive a closed form of $g(x_e)$ in $\sum_{(u,v)\in\mathcal{R}_G} e^{-\lambda\mathcal{P}(u,v)}$ as follows:

$$g(x_e) = \frac{\partial \sum_{(u,v)\in\mathcal{R}_G} e^{-\lambda\mathcal{P}(u,v)}}{\partial x_e} = \sum_{(u,v)\in\mathcal{R}_G} -\lambda\mathcal{P}(u,v,e)e^{-\lambda\mathcal{P}(u,v)},$$

where $\mathcal{P}(u,v,e)$ is the sum of the path-product on all the paths going through e and we treat $x_e = 1$ in the path-product. More precisely, let $P(u,v,e)$ be the set of all short paths (with length no more than k) between u and v going through edge e, and then,

$$\mathcal{P}(u,v,e) = \sum_{p\in P(u,v,e)} \prod_{e'\in p\setminus\{e\}} x_{e'} \quad (5)$$

Using the example in Fig. 1 and (c), we have

$$\mathcal{P}(b, d, e_1) = x_2$$

Note that once we have all the gradients for each edge variable x_e, then we update them accordingly,

$$x_e = x_e + \beta g(x_e),$$

where β is the step size (a very small positive real value) to control the rate of convergence.

$\mathcal{P}(u, v)$ **and** $\mathcal{P}(u, v, e)$ **Computation** To compute the gradient, we need compute all $\mathcal{P}(u, v)$ and $\mathcal{P}(u, v, e)$ for $(u, v) \in \mathcal{R}_G$. Especially, the difficulty is that even compute the total number of simple short paths (with length no more than k) between u and v, denoted as $|P(u, v)|$ is known to be expensive. In the following, we describe an efficient procedure to compute $\mathcal{P}(u, v)$ and $\mathcal{P}(u, v, e)$ efficiently. The basic idea is that we perform a DFS from each vertex u with traversal depth no more than k. During the traversal form vertex u, we maintain the partial sum of both $\mathcal{P}(u, v)$ and $\mathcal{P}(u, v, e)$ for each v and e where u can reach within k steps. After each traversal, we can then compute the exact value of $\mathcal{P}(u, *)$ and $\mathcal{P}(u, *, *)$.

The DFS procedure starting from u to compute all $\mathcal{P}(u, *)$ and $\mathcal{P}(u, *, *)$ is illustrated in Algorithm 1 (Appendix D). In Algorithm 1, we maintain the current path (based on the DFS traversal procedure) in p and its corresponding product $\sum_{e \in p} x_e$ is maintained in variable w (Line 9 and 10). Then, we incrementally update $\mathcal{P}(u, v)$ assuming v is the end of the path p (Line 11). In addition, we go over each edge in the current path, and incrementally update $\mathcal{P}(u, v)$ ($w/x_e = \prod_{e' \in p \setminus \{e\}} x_{e'}$, Line 13.) Note that we need invoke this procedure for every vertex u to compute all $\mathcal{P}(u, v)$ and $\mathcal{P}(u, v, e)$. Thus, the overall time complexity can be written as $O(|V|\overline{d}^k)$ for a random graph where $\overline{d}$ is the average vertex degree.

The overall gradient optimization algorithm is depicted in Algorithm 2 (Appendix E). Here, we use $\mathcal{C}$ to describe all the edges which need be processed for optimization. At this point, we consider all the edges and thus $\mathcal{C} = E$. Later, we will consider to first select some candidate edges. The entire algorithm performs iteratively and each iteration has three major steps:

Step 1 (Lines 6–8): it calculates the gradient $g(x_e)$ of for every edge variable x_e and an average gradient $\overline{g}$;

Step 2 (Lines 9–16): only those variables are not in the active set $\mathcal{A}$ will be updated. Specifically, if the condition $(\sum_{e \in E} x_e \geq |E| - L)$ is not met, we try to adjust x_e back to the feasible region. Note that by using $g(x_e) - \overline{g}$ (Line 11) instead of $g(x_e)$ (Line 13), we are able to increase the value of those x_e whose gradient is below average. However, such adjustment can still guarantee the overall objective function is not decreased (thus will converge). Also, we make sure x_e will be between 0 and 1.

Step 3 (Lines 17–22): the active set is updated. When an edge variable reaches 0 or 1, we put them in the active set so that we will not need to update them in Step 2. However, for those edges variables in the active set, if their gradients are less (higher) than the average gradient for $x_e = 0$ ($x_e = 1$), we will release them from the active set and let them to be further updated.

Note that the gradient ascent with the active set method guarantees the convergence of the algorithm (mainly because the overall objective function is not decreased). However, we note that in Algorithm 2, the bounded condition ($\sum_{e \in E} x_e \geq |E| - L$) may not be necessarily satisfied even with the update in Line 11. Though this can be achieved through additional adjustment, we do not consider them mainly due to the goal here is not to find the exact optimization, but mainly on identifying the smallest L edges based on x_e. Finally, the overall time complexity of the optimization algorithm is $O(t(|V| * \overline{d}^k + |E|))$, given t is the maximum number of iterations before convergence.

4   Short Betweenness and Speedup Techniques

In Sect. 3, we reformulate our problem into a numerical optimization problem. We further develop an iterative *gradient* algorithm to select the top L edges in to E_r. However, the basic algorithm can not scale well to very large graphs due to the large number ($|E|$) of variables involved. In this section, we introduce a new variant of the edge-betweenness and use it to quickly reduce the variables needed in the optimization algorithm (Algorithm 2). In addition, we can further speedup the DFS procedure to compute $\mathcal{P}(u, v)$ and $\mathcal{P}(u, v, e)$ in Algorithm 1.

Short Betweenness. In this subsection, we consider the following question: *What edge importance measure can directly correlate with x_e in the objective function in Eq. 4 so that we can use it to help quickly identify a candidate edge set for the numerical optimization described in Algorithm 2?* In this work, we propose a new edge-betweenness measure, referred to as the *short betweenness* to address the this question. It is intuitively simple and has an interestingly relationship with respect to the gradient $g(x_e)$ for each edge variable. It can even be directly applied for selecting E_r using the generic procedure in Sect. 2 and is much more effective compared with the global and local edge-betweenness which measure the edge importance in terms of the shortest path (See comparison in Sect. 5).

Here we formally define $\nabla(e_i)$ as *short betweenness*.

Definition 4 (Short Betweenness). The short betweenness $SB(e)$ for edge e is as follows, $SB(e) = \sum_{(u,v) \in \mathcal{R}_G} \frac{|P(u,v,e)|}{|P(u,v)|}$.

Recall that $(u, v) \in \mathcal{R}_G$ means $d(u, v) \leq k$; $|P(u, v)|$ is the number of short paths between u and v; and $|P(u, v, e)|$ is the number of short paths between u and v which must go through edge e. The following lemma highlights the relationship between the short betweenness and the gradient of edge variable x_e:

Lemma 2. *Assuming for all edge variables $x_e = 1$, then $g(x_e) \geq -SB(e)$.*

Basically, when $x_e = 1$ for every edge variable x_e (this is also the initialization of Algorithm 2), the (negative) short betweenness serves a lower bound of the gradient $g(e)$. Especially, since the gradient is negative, the higher the gradient of $|g(e)|$ is, the more likely it can maximize the objective function (cut more reachable pairs in $\mathcal{R}_G$. Here, the short betweenness $SB(e)$ thus provide an upper bound (or approximation) on $|g(e)|$ (assuming all other edges are presented in the graph); and measures the the edge potential in removing those local reachable pairs. Finally, we note that Algorithm 1 can be utilized to compute $|P(u, v)|$ and $|P(u, v, e)|$, and thus the short betweenness (just assuming $x_e = 1$ for all edge variables).

Scaling Optimization Using Short Betweenness: First, we can directly utilize the short betweenness to help us pickup a candidate set of edge variables, and then Algorithm 2 only need to work on these edge variables (considering other edge variables are set as 1). Basically, we can choose a subset of edges E_s which has the highest short betweenness in the entire graph. The size of E_s has to be larger than L; in general, we can assume $|E_s| = \alpha L$, where $\alpha > 1$. In the experimental evaluation (Sect. 5), we found when $\alpha = 5$, the performance of using candidate set is almost as good as the original algorithm which uses the entire edge variables. Once the candidate set edge set is selected, we make the following simple observation:

Lemma 3. *Given a candidate edge set $E_s \subseteq E$, if any reachable pair $(u, v) \in \mathcal{R}_G$ can be cut by E_r where $E_r \subseteq E_s$ and $|E_r| = L$, then, each path in $P(u, v)$ must contains at least one edge in E_s.*

Clearly, if there is one path in $P(u, v)$ does not contain an edge in E_s, it will always linked no matter how we select E_r and thus cannot cut by $E_r \subseteq E_s$. In other words, (u, v) has to be cut by E_s if it can be cut by E_r. Given this, we introduce $\mathcal{R}_s = \mathcal{R}_G \subseteq \mathcal{R}_{G \backslash E_s}$. Note that $\mathcal{R}_s$ can be easily computed by the DFS traversal procedure similar to Algorithm 1. Thus, we can focus on optimizing

$$\sum_{(u,v) \in \mathcal{R}_s} e^{-\lambda \mathcal{P}(u,v)}, \text{ where}, 0 \leq x_e \leq 1, \sum x_e \geq X - L \qquad (6)$$

Furthermore, let $E_P = \bigcup_{(u,v) \in \mathcal{R}_s} \bigcup_{p \in P(u,v)} p$, which records those edges appearing in certain path linking a reachable pair cut by E_P. Clearly, for those edges in $E \backslash E_P$, we can simply prune them from the original graph G without affecting the final results. To sum, the short betweenness measure can help speed up the numerical optimization process by reducing the number of edge variables and pruning non-essential edges from the original graph.

5   Experimental Study

In this section, we report the results of the empirical study of our methods. Specifically, we are interested in the performance (in terms of reachable pair cut) and the efficiency (running time).

Table 1. Network statistics

Dataset	$|V|$	$|E|$	π
Gnutella04	10,876	39,994	9
Gnutella05	8,846	31,839	9
Gnutella06	8,717	31,525	9
Gnutella08	6,301	20,777	9
Gnutella09	8,114	26,013	9
Gnutella24	26,518	65,369	10
Gnutella25	22,687	54,705	11
Gnutella30	36,682	88,328	10
Gnutella31	62,586	147,892	11

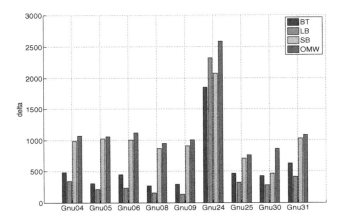

Fig. 2. δ for all real datasets

Performance: Given a set of edges E_r with budget L, the total number of reachable pairs being cut by E_r is $|\mathcal{R}_G| - |\mathcal{R}_{G \setminus E_r}|$ or simply $\Delta|\mathcal{R}_G|$. We use the average pair being cut by an edge, i.e., $\delta = \frac{\Delta|\mathcal{R}_G|}{L}$ as the performance measure.

Efficiency: The running time of different algorithms.

Methods: Here we compare the following methods:

(1) *Betweenness based method*, which is defined in terms of the shortest paths between any two vertices in the whole graph G; hereafter, we use BT to denote the method based on this criterion.
(2) *Local Betweenness based method*, which, compared with betweenness method(BT), takes only the vertex pair within certain distance into consideration; hereafter, we use LB to stand for the method based on local betweenness.

(3) *Short Betweenness based method*, the new betweenness introduced in this paper, which considers all short paths whose length is no more than certain threshold. Here we denote the method based on short betweenness as SB.

(4) *Numerical Optimization method*, which solves the de-small-world problem iteratively by calculating gradients and updating the edge variables x_e. Based on whether the method use the candidate set or not, we have two versions of optimization methods: OMW (Optimization Method With candidate set) and OMO (Optimization Method withOut candidate set). Note that we normally choose the top $5L$ edges as our candidate set.

We have a generic procedure to select L edges depending on parameter r (batch size) (Sect. 2). We found for different methods BT, LB and SB, the effects of r seem to be rather small (as illustrated in Fig. 3). Thus, in the reminder of the experiments, we choose $r = L$, i.e., we select the top L edges using the betweenness calculated for the entire (original graph).

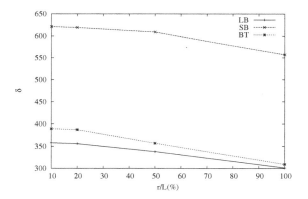

Fig. 3. Varying $\frac{r}{L}$

Table 2. Time (Seconds)   **Table 3.** δ By Varying l **Table 4.** δ By Varying k

Time	BT	LB	SB	OMW
10,876	382.27	24.82	33.75	1021.66
8,846	21346.54	496.17	8.98	110.80
62586	392.54	25.31	34.60	1092.55

l	BT	LB	SB	OMW	OMO
500	240	415	912	996	973
1000	261	372	740	803	805
2000	301	329	572	620	622

k	BT	LB	SB	OMW	OMO
2	25	32	55	58	58
3	261	372	740	803	805
4	761	976	2113	2389	-

All the algorithms are implemented using C++ and the Standard Template Library (STL), and the experiments are conducted on a 2.0 GHz Dual Core AMD Opteron CPU with 4.0 GB RAM running on Linux.

We study the performance of our algorithms on real datasets. The benchmarking datasets are listed in Table 1. All networks contain certain properties commonly observed in social networks, such as small diameter. All datasets are downloadable from Stanford Large Network Dataset Collection[2].

In Table 1, we present important characteristics of all real datasets, where π is graph diameter. All these nine networks are snapshots of the Gnutella peer to peer file sharing network starting from August 2002. Nodes stand for the hosts in the Gnutella network topology and the edges for the connections between the hosts (Table 2).

Varying L: We perform this group of experiments on dataset $Gnu05$ and we fix $k = 3$. Here we run these methods on three different edge buget L: 500, 1000 and 2000. The result is reported in Table 3. The general trend is that with smaller L, δ becomes bigger. This is because the set of reachable pairs removed by different edges could have intersection; when one edge is removed, the set of reachable pairs for other edges is also reduced. For particular methods, BT and OMO methods produces the lowest and highest δ, and the different between OMW and OMO is very small.

Varying k: In this group of experiments, we fix $L = 1000$ and we choose $Gnu04$. Here we choose three values for k: 2, 3 and 4. The result is reported in Table 4. From the result, we can see that when k becomes bigger, δ become higher. This is also reasonable: when k becomes bigger, more reachable pairs are generated and meanwhile $|E|$ is constant; therefore, each edge is potentially able to remove more reachable pairs. From the above three groups of experiments, we can see that OMO does not produce significant results compared with OMW. Therefore, in the following experiment, we do not study OMO method again.

δ on all Real Datasets: In this groups of experiment, we study the performance of each method on these nine datasets, with L being proportional to $|E|$. Specifically, $L = |E| \times 1\%$. We report the result in Fig. 2. LB generally produces the lowest δ, around half that of BT; and also the best method, is the SB and OMW methods. Specifically, OMW is always slightly better than SB.

6   Conclusion

In this paper, we introduce the *de-small-world* network problem; to solve it, we first present a greedy edge betweenness based approach as the benchmark and then provide a numerical relaxation approach to slove our problem using OR-AND boolean format, which can find a local minimum. In addition, we introduce the *short-betweenness* to speed up our algorithm. The empirical study demonstrates the efficiency and effectiveness of our approaches. In the future, we plan to utilize MapReduce framework (e.g. Hadoop) to scale our methods to handle graphs with tens of millions of vertices.

---

[2] http://snap.stanford.edu/data/index.html.

References

1. Andersen, R., Chung, F., Lu, L.: Modeling the small-world phenomenon with local network flow. Internet Math. **2**, 359–385 (2005)
2. Brandes, U.: A faster algorithm for betweenness centrality. J. Math. Sociol. **25**, 163–177 (2001)
3. Budak, C., Agrawal, D., El Abbadi, A.: Limiting the spread of misinformation in social networks. In: Proceedings of the 20th International Conference on World Wide Web, WWW 2011 (2011)
4. Girvan, M., Newman, M.E.J.: Community structure in social and biological networks. Proc. Nat. Acad. Sci. **99**(12), 7821–7826 (2002)
5. Gregory, S.: Local betweenness for finding communities in networks. Technical report, University of Bristol, February 2008
6. Hager, W.W., Zhang, H.: A new active set algorithm for box constrained optimization. SIAM J. Optim. **17**, 526–557 (2006)
7. Jin, S., Bestavros, A.: Small-world characteristics of internet topologies and implications on multicast scaling. Comput. Netw. **50**, 648–666 (2006)
8. Kempe, D., Kleinberg, J., Tardos, E.: Maximizing the spread of influence through a social network. In: Proceedings of the Ninth ACM SIGKDD International Conference on Knowledge Discovery and Data Mining, KDD 2003, pp. 137–146 (2003)
9. Kleinberg, J.: The small-world phenomenon: an algorithmic perspective. In: 32nd ACM Symposium on Theory of Computing, pp. 163–170 (2000)
10. Leskovec, J., Horvitz, E.: Planetary-scale views on a large instant-messaging network. In: Proceedings of the 17th International Conference on World Wide Web, WWW 2008 (2008)
11. Leskovec, J., Krause, A., Guestrin, C., Faloutsos, C., VanBriesen, J., Glance, N.: Cost-effective outbreak detection in networks. In: Proceedings of the 13th ACM SIGKDD International Conference on Knowledge Discovery and Data Mining, KDD 2007, pp. 420–429 (2007)
12. Milgram, S.: The small world problem. Psychol. Today **2**, 60–67 (1967)
13. Mislove, A., Marcon, M., Gummadi, K.P., Druschel, P., Bhattacharjee, B.: Measurement and analysis of online social networks. In: Proceedings of the 7th ACM SIGCOMM Conference on Internet Measurement, IMC 2007 (2007)
14. Moore, C., Newman, M.E.J.: Epidemics and percolation in small-world networks. Phys. Rev. E **61**, 5678–5682 (2000)
15. Newman, M.E.J.: Spread of epidemic disease on networks. Phys. Rev. E **66**, 016128+ (2002)
16. Pastor-Satorras, R., Vespignani, A.: Epidemic spreading in scale-free networks. Phys. Rev. Lett. **86**, 3200–3203 (2001)
17. Richardson, M., Domingos, P.: Mining knowledge-sharing sites for viral marketing. In: Proceedings of the Eighth ACM SIGKDD International Conference on Knowledge Discovery and Data Mining, KDD 2002, pp. 61–70 (2002)

Online Community Conflict Decomposition with Pseudo Spatial Permutation

Yunmo Chen[1] and Xinyue Ye[2(✉)]

[1] Department of Computer Science, The Johns Hopkins University,
Baltimore, MD 21218, USA
chanwanmok@gmail.com
[2] Department of Informatics, New Jersey Institute of Technology,
Newark, NJ 07102, USA
xye@njit.edu

Abstract. Online communities are composed of individuals sharing similar opinions or behavior in the virtual world. Facilitated by the fast development of social media platforms, the expansion of online communities have raised many attentions among the researchers, business analysts, and decision makers, leading to a growing list of literature studying the interactions especially conflicts in the online communities. A conflict is often initiated by one community which then attacks the other, leading to an adversarial relationship and worse social impacts. Many studies have examined the origins and process of online community conflict while failing to address the possible spatial effects in their models. In this paper, we explore the prediction of online community conflict by decomposing and analyzing its prediction error taking geography into accounts. Grounding on the previous natural language processing based model, we introduce pseudo spatial permutation to test the model expressiveness with geographical factors. Pseudo spatial permutation employs different geographical distributions to sample from and perturbs the model using the pseudo geographical information to examine the relationship between online community conflict and spatial distribution. Our analysis shows that the pseudo spatial permutation is an efficient approach to robustly test the conflict relation learned by the prediction model, and also reveals the necessity to incorporate geographical information into the prediction. In conclusion, this work provides a different aspect of analyzing the community conflict that does not solely rely on the textual communication.

Keywords: Online community · Spatial permutation · Text mining · Spatial social network · Neural network

1 Introduction

There has been a list of growing and extensive studies on how information diffuse and spread in an online community and across multiple communities

© Springer Nature Switzerland AG 2019
A. Tagarelli and H. Tong (Eds.): CSoNet 2019, LNCS 11917, pp. 246–255, 2019.
https://doi.org/10.1007/978-3-030-34980-6_28

[1, 11, 14, 16–19]. An online community tends to be formed by those sharing similar opinions. Within a web portal or social media platform, the inter-community interactions can reveal the behavioral patterns of multiple social groups, which facilitate the identification of potential conflicts among online communities. The open access nature of web or social media platforms allows many of these inter-community interactions observable to the public, which increases the awareness of theses conflicts while also provides big social data available for the analysis and modelling.

The conflict is considered as a scenario featured with serious disagreements or arguments, which is often in the form of quarrel in the online platform or might even lead to violence in the real world. It is challenging to capture and characterize the form of conflicts among online communities because the virtual world does not have the physical existence which is as visible as the real world. Without the appropriate definition of online community conflicts, it is difficult to model this interaction. [6] adopted Reddit, an American social news aggregation, web content rating, and discussion website, to define the inter-community interaction as the mobility of users from the source to the target community, namely subreddit, formulating the conflict between online communities as a hyperlink between two communities indicating negative opinion. Their work successfully predicted the online community conflict using the sentiment analysis [12]. However, their model did not consider potential geographical information or spatial effects to study the relationship between the geo-spatial world and online communities regarding the conflict issues.

In this paper, we adopt the same definitions for online community and conflicts of online communities as above. The main purpose of this pilot study is to investigate the prediction error of the previous model and introduce pseudo spatial permutation approach to test the latent geographical effects.

In summary, our main contributions are as below:

- A new approach that can verify whether location and geographical distribution of users matter, but are ignored in most of the current models.
- An improved prediction model for detecting online community conflict and in-depth error analysis indicating how different components contribute to the prediction accuracy.

2   Approach

The previous conflict detection models do not consider spatial effects due to the lack of geographical information, and more importantly, ignoring the geography of topics and opinions. In other words, the physical location in their modelling assumptions can be seen as within the same city, so the space and place will not play any role in the opinion conflicts. However, such assumption does not hold in the real world where users' posts actually come from different cities and regions. Hence the assumption that conflict among online communities should also be influenced by geographical distribution of users and communities. In addition,

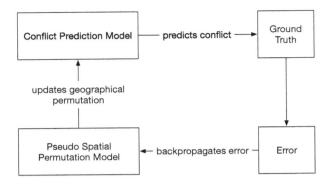

Fig. 1. The overview of models

social network is highly relevant to the spatial context. For example, most of our friends and social contacts are physically near us. At the same time, people from different cities tend to form various social and cultural systems (Fig. 1).

In order to decompose the model estimation error to analyze whether geographical information might influence the prediction, we develop a pseudo spatial permutation approach, which learns a pseudo geographical distribution based on the prediction error of the original model and then takes the learned distribution as a factor to improve the original model. The correlation between the model prediction and the learned geographical information is then passed to the permutation test [7] and significant test [4] to determine whether geographical information is probably the factor missed from the original modelling schema. In the end, we can map the learned geographical information back to the real world to see if there is any correlation between actual demographics and the learned spatial distribution.

2.1 Problem Formulation

We formalize prediction of conflict between two online communities as

$$p(C|P, S_{\text{source}}, S_{\text{target}}, G)$$

where C denotes whether there will be a conflict, P denotes the given post containing a hyperlink, S_{source} denotes the source subreddit, S_{target} denotes the target subreddit and G denotes the latent geographical variable. However, in our definition of the original model missing geographical information, the last term G is dropped from the equation.

The prediction model is basically defined as a binary classification problem, namely whether a conflict will happen. It employs negative log likelihood (NLL) as the optimization objective

$$NLL(\mathbf{y}, \hat{\mathbf{y}}) = \frac{1}{N} \sum_{i=1}^{N} y_i \log \hat{y}_i + (1 - y_i) \log(1 - \hat{y}_i)$$

where $\mathbf{y} \in \{0, 1\}^N$ is the ground truth labels indicating conflicts and $\hat{\mathbf{y}} \in [0, 1]^N$ denotes the predicted odds of conflict. By optimizing this objective, the prediction model learns to minimize prediction error, hence outputting the prediction for the conflict.

The pseudo random permutation model employs mean squared loss (MSE) as the optimization objective

$$MSE(\mathbf{y}, \hat{\mathbf{y}}) = \frac{1}{N} \sum_{i=1}^{N} (\hat{y}_i - y_i)^2$$

where $\mathbf{y}$ is used to learn embeddings that minimize the prediction error and $\hat{\mathbf{y}} \in \mathbb{R}^N$ denotes the actual prediction error.

2.2 Conflict Prediction Model

The conflict prediction model is built upon the sentiment analysis [8] of the text with additional embeddings learned from the graph structure, namely community embeddings $\mathbf{S}_{\text{source}} \in \mathbb{R}^{300}$ and $\mathbf{S}_{\text{target}} \in \mathbb{R}^{300}$, to accurately model the influence of the interaction between two communities.

The prediction model as a binary classification task has neutral and conflict labels. In addition to the original model, the improved prediction model incorporates geographical vector $\mathbf{g} = (l_{\text{latitude}}, l_{\text{longitude}})$, which is first initialized randomly and then gradually fitted into the prediction error by the pseudo spatial permutation.

According to Fig. 2, the prediction model employs a bidirectional long short-term memory network (BiLSTM) to encode the text content. The encoded text representation is then infused with community representation and geographical vector through a multi-layer perceptron (MLP). The original and improved models are defined as:

Original:

$$p(C|P, S_{\text{source}}, S_{\text{target}}) = \sigma(\text{FFNN}([\mathbf{h} \ ; \ \bar{\mathbf{h}} \ ; \ \mathbf{S}_{\text{source}} \ ; \ \mathbf{S}_{\text{target}}]))$$

Improved:

$$p(C|P, S_{\text{source}}, S_{\text{target}}, G) = \sigma(\text{FFNN}([\mathbf{h} \ ; \ \bar{\mathbf{h}} \ ; \ \mathbf{S}_{\text{source}} \ ; \ \mathbf{S}_{\text{target}} \ ; \ \mathbf{g}]))$$

where σ is the sigmoid function, a non-linearity, that produces the odds of conflict, FFNN is a MLP, $\mathbf{h}$ and $\bar{\mathbf{h}}$ are the contextual hidden states of the forward and backward LSTM, g is the geographical vector.

2.3 Pseudo Spatial Permutation

The pseudo spatial permutation approach uses a neural network to learn a geographical distribution (over a given list of geographical locations) from the original model prediction error. After the learning, the geographical representation

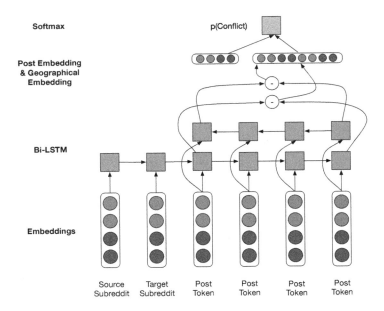

Fig. 2. Conflict prediction model

will be inserted into the prediction model to verify whether the learned decomposition actually improves the model expressiveness and will also be passed to the permutation and significance test to determine whether the learned representation is highly related to spatial demographics or other geographical distribution.

The geographical embedding is a fundamental way to embed the information from multiple sources to a low dimensional representation, which also features spatial relationship. Previous research has proven the sparse social media data can be used to obtain geographical embeddings [13]. In our model, we further employ the textual data and inter-community relationships.

The learning process can be formulated as learning a spatial embedding $\mathbf{g}$ constituted of latitude $l_{\text{latitude}} \in [-90, 90]$ and longitude $l_{\text{longitude}} \in [-180, 180]$, learned from the prediction error. This learned spatial embedding is adjusted during the learning and then is infused with other features as a feature vector at all to support the prediction.

Assuming the actual post is jointly generated from the distribution $p(P, S_{\text{source}}, S_{\text{target}}, G)$, but the previous addressed conflict prediction model can only learn $p(C|P, S_{\text{source}}, S_{\text{target}})$, which differs from the actual posterior distribution $p(C|P, S_{\text{source}}, S_{\text{target}}, G)$.

Therefore, we assume that the loss of geographical information results in the prediction error to a certain extent, and we can propose a spatial distribution to approximate its influence by fitting the geographical embedding to the prediction error. After fitting this pseudo spatial permutation, we can analyze the learned

Table 1. Feature descriptions

Feature name	Description
Title	Title of the post
Author ID	Identifier of the author
Content	Text content of the post
Published date	Date and time when the post published
Source subrredit	Subrredit where the post were posted
Target subrredit	Subrredit that post potentially points at

geography by comparing it with the actual spatial demographics. Further permutation test and significance test can thus reveal the statistical interpretability of the approach.

According to the axiom that mutually independent random variables is irrelevant to the model prediction, we assume that, when the graphical vector is randomly initialized, it does not affect the model predictions. After it gradually fits into the error, if the prediction error can be significantly reduced by the fitted distribution, we can assert with a certain amount of confidence that the model is indeed influenced by the geographical information and its expressiveness is limited because these spatial factors are excluded.

3 Experiment

3.1 Reddit

Reddit is an American online social media, where people can post social news, rate multi-media contents, and discuss various topics. Subreddit, where discussions about a specific topic happen, is a key feature of Reddit that aggregates information in a structured manner. Due to the community nature of subrredits, it is natural to employ it as the data source for the online community research.

3.2 Datasets Preparation and Pre-trained Models

We crawled about 60,000 posts from Reddit.com to construct our dataset. In the preprocessing, we tokenize the posts and extract features from both posts and their meta data. Descriptions of the features that are directly derived from the post and its meta data are shown in Table 1. The dataset is then divided into train/dev/test datasets with 70%/20%/10% portion of data respectively. In addition, we use pre-trained graphical subreddits embeddings from [6] and pre-trained ELMo embeddings (model) from [9].

Table 2. Experimental results on predicting conflict between online communities

Models	Development	Test
Ours (Single model)	74.82%	72.30%
Ours (Ensemble model)	78.33%	78.10%
Kumar et al. (Single model)	69.32%	70.10%
Kumar et al. (Ensemble model)	74.32%	73.10%

3.3 Model Setup

Our network consists of 2 BiLSTM layers (1 for forward LSTM and 1 for backward LSTM) with hidden units of dimension in 300. The ELMo embedding is in 1024 dimension, but the subreddit embedding is in 300 dimension. So we also use a feedforward network to map the subreddit embedding into 1024 dimension to be consistent with other post embeddings, whose weight is also learned during the training. In addition, there is a final softmax layer that predicts the probability the given post would lead to the conflict.

Initialization. All weights of the BiLSTM are initialized using random orthonormal matrices as described in [10].

Before being fed into the BiLSTM, the tokens are embeded using the last layer of the hidden state in the pre-trained ELMo model, and the embeddings are fixed during the training time.

Training. We use Adam [5] as our optimizer with learning rate $\eta = 1e^{-3}$ and mini-batches of size 64. The BiLSTM dropout rate is set to 0.2. All the models are trained for 50 epochs.

Ensembling. For the ensemble models, we employ product of experts method from [2]. The final prediction is thus constructed from the combination of 5 models, which are trained separately and use 80% of training data and validated on the rest of 20%.

3.4 Results

Prediction Results. In Table 2, we compare our best performed models with the models proposed by [6]. In order to fairly compare the models, we reproduce their results by using their open source code, and then train and run the models on the same datasets. According to the experiment results, we can find that our models outperform the previous models to a certain amount of improvement. The further analysis of improvements will be broken down in the following ablation tests.

Table 3. Statistical tests

Test	p-value
Permutation test	0.023
Pearson correlation test	0.043

Permutation (Randomness) Tests. The pseudo spatial permutation learns how to decompose the prediction error, and the decomposed geographical attributes need to pass the permutation tests to determine whether the error is truly due to the lack of geographical information. We run the permutation test and find that, in Table 3, the p-value is $0.023 < 0.05$, so we reject the hypothesis that the geographical information is an independent random variable, hence the geographical information indeed contributes to the conflict prediction.

Correlation Tests. The effectiveness of the learned geographical representation should also be tested with the correlation to spatial demographics, which indicates the close relationship between the online users and the offline real world life.

Using the same demographic dataset, we run the correlation test between the demographics and the learned geographical information of posts. The correlation test is Pearson correlation test. The test result shown in Table 3 indicates that the geography learned is closely related to demographics.

3.5 Ablation.

In ablation test, we perform the analysis over different components of our model so that we can discover how different part of the model contribute to the overall performance on the conflict prediction tasks.

Table 4. Ablation tests on different model components

Model component	Development	Improvement
Base model	66.8%	–
+ BiLSTM	68.02%	+1.22%
+ ELMo embedding	72.40%	+4.38%
+ Pseudo spatial permutation	74.82%	+2.42%
+ Ensembling	78.33%	+3.51%

According to Table 4, the ELMo embedding contributes most of the improvement of the model. However, the Pseudo Spatial Permutation that learns geographical information also contributes a non-trivial improvement to the overall

Table 5. Ablation tests on LSTM layers

Model (# of LSTM layers)	Development
1 Unidirectional LSTM	71.3%
2 Unidirectional LSTM	72.92%
3 Unidirectional LSTM	73.1%
4 Unidirectional LSTM	73.6%
1 Bidirectional LSTM	73.2%
2 Bidirectional LSTM	74.82%
3 Bidirectional LSTM	74.98%
4 Bidirectional LSTM	74.83%

performance, which further confirms that the previous discovery of relationship between the online community conflict and the geographical distribution.

We also test our model with different numbers of BiLSTM layers and compare their performances. Through our experiments, we discover that increasing the number of LSTM layers contributes only a minor improvement and using BiLSTM significantly improves the prediction. In Table 5, the performance gain of using more than 2 LSTM layers becomes trivial. The computational efficiency is highly related to the complexity of the neural network. In order to trade-off between better performance and computational efficiency, we select the model with 2 BiLSTM layers to ingest post and subreddit information.

4   Conclusion

We present a deep learning model for predicting the conflict among the online communities. Our improved model harnesses geographical information by learning the pseudo random permutation from the prediction error. The final ensemble model outperforms the previous model by 5.0%.

The success of the model shows that the improved semantic representation and additional geographical information are crucial in modelling the online community behaviors and interactions [3]. Furthermore, our proposed pseudo spatial permutation technique is proved to be efficient in decomposing the error and learn geographical representation.

Finally, through the ablation tests, we analyse the contribution from different model components. Despite the improvement from better understanding the semantic of the post, geographical information is indeed an important factor that should be considered in the future modelling [15].

Acknowledgement. This material is partially based upon work supported by the National Science Foundation under Grant No. 1416509. Any opinions, findings, and conclusions or recommendations expressed in this material are those of the author and do not necessarily reflect the views of the National Science Foundation.

References

1. Dang, L., Chen, Z., Lee, J., Tsou, M.H., Ye, X.: Simulating the spatial diffusion of memes on social media networks. Int. J. Geograph. Inf. Sci. **33**, 1–24 (2019)
2. Hinton, G.E.: Training products of experts by minimizing contrastive divergence. Neural Comput. **14**(8), 1771–1800 (2002)
3. Hu, Y., Ye, X., Shaw, S.L.: Extracting and analyzing semantic relatedness between cities using news articles. Int. J. Geograp. Inf. Sci. **31**(12), 2427–2451 (2017)
4. Ioannidis, J.P., Trikalinos, T.A.: An exploratory test for an excess of significant findings. Clin. Trials **4**(3), 245–253 (2007)
5. Kingma, D.P., Ba, J.: Adam: a method for stochastic optimization. arXiv preprint arXiv:1412.6980 (2014)
6. Kumar, S., Hamilton, W.L., Leskovec, J., Jurafsky, D.: Community interaction and conflict on the web. In: Proceedings of the 2018 World Wide Web Conference on World Wide Web. pp. 933–943. International World Wide Web Conferences Steering Committee (2018)
7. Odén, A., Wedel, H., et al.: Arguments for Fisher's permutation test. Ann. Stat. **3**(2), 518–520 (1975)
8. Pang, B., Lee, L.: Opinion mining and sentiment analysis. Found. Trends Inf. Retrieval **2**(1–2), 1–135 (2007). https://doi.org/10.1561/1500000011
9. Peters, M.E., et al.: Deep contextualized word representations. In: Proceedings of NAACL (2018)
10. Saxe, A.M., McClelland, J.L., Ganguli, S.: Exact solutions to the nonlinear dynamics of learning in deep linear neural networks. arXiv preprint arXiv:1312.6120 (2013)
11. Shi, X., et al.: Detecting events from the social media through exemplar-enhanced supervised learning. Int. J. Digit. Earth **12**(9), 1083–1097 (2019)
12. Tang, D., Qin, B., Liu, T.: Document modeling with gated recurrent neural network for sentiment classification. In: Proceedings of the 2015 Conference on Empirical Methods in Natural Language Processing, pp. 1422–1432 (2015)
13. Wang, F., Lu, C.-T., Qu, Y., Yu, P.S.: Collective geographical embedding for geolocating social network users. In: Kim, J., Shim, K., Cao, L., Lee, J.-G., Lin, X., Moon, Y.-S. (eds.) PAKDD 2017. LNCS (LNAI), vol. 10234, pp. 599–611. Springer, Cham (2017). https://doi.org/10.1007/978-3-319-57454-7_47
14. Wang, Y.D., Fu, X.K., Jiang, W., Wang, T., Tsou, M.H., Ye, X.Y.: Inferring urban air quality based on social media. Comput. Environ. Urban Syst. **66**, 110–116 (2017)
15. Wang, Z., Ye, X., Lee, J., Chang, X., Liu, H., Li, Q.: A spatial econometric modeling of online social interactions using microblogs. Comput. Environ. Urban Syst. **70**, 53–58 (2018)
16. Ye, X., Lee, J.: Integrating geographic activity space and social network space to promote healthy lifestyles. SIGSPATIAL Spec. **8**(1), 20–33 (2016)
17. Ye, X., Liu, X.: Integrating social networks and spatial analyses of the built environment. Environ. Plan. B Urban Anal. City Sci. **45**, 395–399 (2018)
18. Ye, X., Sharag-Eldin, A., Spitzberg, B., Wu, L.: Analyzing public opinions on death penalty abolishment. Chin. Sociol. Dialogue **3**(1), 53–75 (2018)
19. Yue, Y., Dong, K., Zhao, X., Ye, X.: Assessing wild fire risk in the united states using social media data. J. Risk Res. 1–15 (2019). https://doi.org/10.1080/13669877.2019.1569098

Attribute-Enhanced De-anonymization
of Online Social Networks

Cheng Zhang[1,2], Shang Wu[2], Honglu Jiang[1,2,3(✉)], Yawei Wang[2], Jiguo Yu[4],
and Xiuzhen Cheng[1,2]

[1] School of Computer Science and Technology, Shandong University,
Qingdao 266237, Shandong, People's Republic of China
[2] Department of Computer Science, The George Washington University,
Washington, DC 20052, USA
{zhangchengcarl,swu23,hljiang0720,yawei,cheng}@gwu.edu
[3] School of Information Science and Engineering, Qufu Normal University,
Rizhao 276826, Shandong, People's Republic of China
[4] School of Computer Science and Technology,
Qilu University of Technology (Shandong Academy of Sciences),
Jinan 250353, Shandong, People's Republic of China
jiguoyu@sina.com

Abstract. Online Social Networks (OSNs) have transformed the way
that people socialize. However, when OSNs bring people convenience,
privacy leakages become a growing worldwide problem. Although several
anonymization approaches are proposed to protect information of user
identities and social relationships, existing de-anonymization techniques
have proved that users in the anonymized network can be re-identified
by using an external reference social network collected from the same
network or other networks with overlapping users. In this paper, we
propose a novel social network de-anonymization mechanism to explore
the impact of user attributes on the accuracy of de-anonymization.
More specifically, we propose an approach to quantify diversities of user
attribute values and select valuable attributes to generate the multipartite graph. Next, we partition this graph into communities, and then map
users on the community level and the network level respectively. Finally,
we employ a real-world dataset collected from Sina Weibo to evaluate
our approach, which demonstrates that our mechanism can achieve a
better de-anonymization accuracy compared with the most influential
de-anonymization method.

Keywords: Online social network · Privacy · De-anonymization

1 Introduction

Nowadays, Online Social Networks (OSNs), such as Twitter and Instagram, are
an integral part of daily life. According to the statistics revealed on [1], the world
population reached 7.6 billion in January 2019. Over half the population used

© Springer Nature Switzerland AG 2019
A. Tagarelli and H. Tong (Eds.): CSoNet 2019, LNCS 11917, pp. 256–267, 2019.
https://doi.org/10.1007/978-3-030-34980-6_29

online social networks via websites and mobile applications every day. These active users provide a huge amount of valuable data including personal information and relationship among them for service providers. And such data also have a broad application area on academic research [10,14], business applications [18], homeland security [7], public health care [21], and so on [2]. Therefore, to protect the sensitive information of users while preserving the value of social network data, service providers usually publish "anonymized" social network data by removing the Personally Identifiable Information (PII, which are identifiable information to uniquely identify a user) while retaining user non-personally identifiable information (non-PII, or user attributes, e.g., gender, age, address), and modifying relationships before data publishing/sharing.

However, naive anonymized techniques cannot provide good protection, which have been proved to be vulnerable to de-anonymization attacks. Various de-anonymization attacks have been proposed to re-identify users in the anonymized social network by mapping them to the users in reference social network. Reference social networks include social relationships and real identities of users that can be collected by attackers via crawling the same social network or other social networks with overlapping users. Existing de-anonymization studies consider both the social network structure and attributes associated with users in social networks. However, most studies require a large number of "seeds" and often susceptible to a high noise ratio which represents the fraction of modified edges in an anonymized network.

Based on existing research, in this paper, we explore the impact of attribute values on users' privacy, and implement the multipartite graph consisting of users and attribute values in the anonymized network and the reference network to improve the accuracy of de-anonymization. Our contributions are summarized as follows:

- To the best of our knowledge, we are the first to perform de-anonymization attacks within a multipartite graph consisting of users and user attribute values in the anonymized network and the reference network.
- We propose an approach to quantify the attribute value diversity of each user attribute. This value is used to select valuable attributes from the anonymized network and the reference network to create the multipartite graph.
- Through extensive simulations on a real-world network dataset collected from the Sina Weibo, which is a famous social media in China, we suggest that our de-anonymization algorithm without the seeding phase is more robust to noise and can provide a significant improvement of accuracy compared to the baseline algorithm.

2 Related Work

Existing de-anonymization attacks could be divided into two main types, *structure-based de-anonymization attacks* and *attribute-attached de-anonymization attacks*.

Structure-based de-anonymization attacks aim to de-anonymize the anonymized social networks leveraging different structure (topology) similarities between the anonymized network and the reference network. This kind of attack has two branches, *seed-based de-anonymization attacks* and *seed-free de-anonymization attacks*.

- Seed-based de-anonymization attacks consist of *seed identification* phase and *propagation* phase. In the first phase, some users in the anonymized network are mapped to users with real identities in the reference network, and these mapped user pairs will serve as "seeds" in the next propagation phase. In the second phase, unmapped neighbors of seeds from the anonymized social network will be iteratively mapped to unmapped neighbors of seeds in the reference network using different structural similarity measurements, and the new mapped user pair will serve as a new seed pair for the next mapping iterations. In [14], Narayanan *et al.* proposed a de-anonymization algorithm based on social network topology to map users in an anonymized Twitter dataset to users in a Flickr dataset. Nilizadeh *et al.* [16] proposed a divide-and-conquer approach to de-anonymize the network from the community level to the entire network. Ji *et al.* [10] designed a De-Anonymization (DA) framework and an Adaptive De-Anonymization (ADA) framework based on proposed structural similarity, relative distance similarity and inheritance similarity. In [4], Chiasserini *et al.* proposed a degree-driven graph matching (DDM) algorithm with considering a social network to be represented by a Chung-Lu random graph [5].
- Seed-free de-anonymization attacks do not require pre-mapped user pairs as seeds to bootstrap the de-anonymization attacks. Pedarsani *et al.* [17] proposed a Bayesian model-based probabilistic framework to de-anonymize two networks. At first, users in each network are sorted by degree (number of neighbors) in descending order. Then, starting from mapping users with the highest degree by the bipartite matching, other users are iteratively mapped based on their degrees and distance to one user mapped in the previous round, until all users are mapped. Ji *et al.* [8,9] proposed an optimization-based de-anonymization (ODA) algorithm. ODA is a single-phase cold start algorithm and aims at minimizing the neighborhood's difference between an unmapped user in the anonymized network and an unmapped user in the reference network.

Attribute-Attached De-anonymization Attacks. By considering the impacts of user attributes (non-PII), which are published with the social network structure, various stronger attribute-attached de-anonymization attacks are proposed. Zhang *et al.* introduced a de-anonymization attack to heterogeneous information networks in [22]. They utilized attribute information in user entity matching and link matching to improve the accuracy of de-anonymization. In [12], Korayem and Crandall took a machine learning approach which employs various features based on temporal activity similarity, text similarity, geographic similarity, and social connection similarity to de-anonymize users across heterogeneous social computing platforms. Li *et al.* [13] took into account the structural transformation similarity in social networks to propose an enhanced structure-based de-anonymization attack. In [19], Qian *et al.* presented that attacker's background information can be modeled by knowledge graphs to enhance the de-anonymization and attribute inference attacks. To de-anonymize Structure-Attribute Graph (SAG) data, Ji *et al.* [11] proposed a new de-anonymization framework called De-SAG which considered both the graph structure and the attribute information. In [23], Zhang *et al.* introduced an approach to quantify the significance of attributes in a social network. Then, based on the significance values of attributes, they proposed an attribute-based similarity measure to improve the social network de-anonymization performance.

3 Background

In this section, we introduce the definitions of the data model and three types of graphs as well as the attack model. Moreover, we introduce the community detection which is a crucial method for multipartite graph partition in our work. The mathematical notations used in this paper are summarized in Table 1.

3.1 Network Model

In this paper, we model the social network as an *undirected, unweighted, attributed and connected graph*. The terms "network", "user", and "link" are used interchangeably with "graph", "node", and "edge", respectively.

A graph, $G(V, E, A)$ consists of a set of users $V = \{v_1, v_2, ..., v_i, ...\}$ in social network, a set of edges $E = \{e_{i,j} = (v_i, v_j) | v_i, v_j \in V, i \neq j\}$ that represent social relationships between users, and a set of attributes (all the non-PII related to the users in V) $A = \{a_1, a_2, ..., a_i, ...\}$. Each attribute a_i has a set of attribute values denoted by $a_i = \{a_i^1, a_i^2, ..., a_i^j, ...\}$ (in order to simplify the discussion, all attribute values are discrete). $A(v_i)$ denotes the set of attribute values associated with user v_i. Given a graph G, it can be partitioned into a set of communities, which can be denoted by $C = (c_1, c_2, ..., c_i, ..)$. Furthermore, $|V|, |E|, |A|, |C|$ denote the number of users, edges, attributes and communities, respectively.

Given an original graph G, the anonymized G is denoted by $G_a = (V_a, E_a, A_a)$. In G_a, V_a is obtained by removing the PII from users ($V_a = V$, but the identities of users in V_a are indistinguishable). The edge set E_a is obtained by randomly adding and/or removing edges to/from E. The attributes (non-PII) associated with users are preserved in A_a, which means $A_a = A$ (it is also realizable to make $A \neq A_a$ by modifying attribute values from users in V during the anonymization process).

A reference graph denoted by $G_r = (V_r, E_r, A_r)$ can be obtained by crawling the same social network or different social networks with overlapping users, or by collecting from public databases.

A multipartite graph $G_m(V_m, E_m)$ is a graph whose nodes can be or are divided into several independent sets, $V_m = \{V_{m1}, V_{m2}, ..., V_{mn}\}$. E_m denotes the edge set.

Table 1. Notations

Symbol	Definition
G, G_a, G_r, G_m	Original, anonymized, reference, multipartite graphs
V, V_a, V_r	Node (user) set
E, E_a, E_r	Edge (relationship) set
A, A_a, A_r	Attribute set
$A(v_i), A_a(v_i), A_r(v_i)$	The set of attribute values associated with user v_i in G, G_a, G_r
v_i	The ith user
a_i	The ith attribute
a_i^j	The jth value of attribute a_i
C	Community set
c_i	The ith community
$|V|, |E|, |A|, |C|$	The number of users, edges, attributes and communities.
S_{a_i}	The set of users in V that possess the attribute a_i
Sa_i^j	The set of users possessing the attribute value a_i^j
$Deg(v_i)$	The degree of user v_i

3.2 Attack Model

Next, in the attack model, we assume that attackers can access two social graphs. One is the anonymized graph G_a including sensitive information associated with users in V_a. The other one is the reference graph G_r including the true identities associated with users in V_r. In these two graphs, we assume $V_r \cap V_a \neq \emptyset$, $E_a \cap E_r \neq \emptyset$, and $A_a = A_r$. Based on these assumptions, the attacker aims to map the users in G_a to those in G_r so that they can disclose the private information of users in G_a. This attack can be mathematically defined as a mapping from V_a to V_r [8,16]:

$$f : V_a \rightarrow V_r = \{(i, f(i) = j) | i \in V_a, j \in V_r\}. \tag{1}$$

3.3 Community Detection

Community structure (or clusters, groups) commonly exists in various types of networks, such as social networks, academic structures like research citations (Arxiv, Google Scholar), biological networks, etc. Members in the same community have a higher probability of being connected and are more likely to have interaction with each other than with other members from other communities. As one of the most popular research topics, community detection (or graph partitioning) has been a fundamental problem in exploring complex network structures and extracting valuable information.

Many community detection approaches have been proposed and widely used. In our work, we employ the modularity-based community detection algorithm [6] to partition the multipartite graph into small groups, since it has a good balance between speed and accuracy, and has the ability to partition the multipartite graph into a set of small and dense communities without a predefined number of communities. In community detection, *modularity* [3,15] is a quality index to assess the quality of a network partition. Networks with high modularity have dense connections among the nodes within communities but sparse connections between nodes in different communities. Given an undirected connected graph $G(V, E)$, it can be partitioned into a set of communities C which can be used to calculate modularity $M(C)$ of G by the following equation:

$$M(C) = \sum_{c_i \in C} \left[\frac{|E_{c_i}|}{|E|} - \left(\frac{|E_{c_i}| + \sum_{c_j \in C} |E_{c_i,c_j}|}{2|E|} \right)^2 \right], \tag{2}$$

where $|E_{c_i}|$ denotes the number of edges in cluster c_i, and $|E_{c_i,c_j}|$ indicates the number of inter-community edges that connect one node in community c_i with the other node in community c_j, and $c_i \neq c_j$.

4   Attribute-Enhanced De-anonymization Scheme

The motivation of our work is that attributes with diverse values could better represent a user if those values of attributes are widely distributed in a social network.

Network communities can offer an efficient way to divide and conquer the de-anonymization attack. Based on the attribute with diverse values, the anonymized graph and the reference graph could be merged into one multipartite graph which provides a fresh idea to conduct de-anonymization attacks. After dividing the multipartite graph into small communities, some users inside each community are mapped first, and then the remaining users in the anonymized graph are mapped to users in reference graph based on the global propagation which runs on the whole network.

Figure 1 illustrates our approach which has four steps: (1) multipartite graph generation, (2) multipartite graph partitioning, (3) local mapping, and (4) global propagation.

4.1   Attribute Value Diversity (AVD)

We first define $AVD(a_i)$ which indicates the diversity of attribute value for each attribute in a social network. This definition borrows the concept of information entropy. Thus, $AVD(a_i)$ is measured as follows:

$$AVD(a_i) = -\sum_{j=1}^{|a_i|} \left(\frac{|Sa_i^j|}{|S_{a_i}|} \times \ln \frac{|Sa_i^j|}{|S_{a_i}|} \right), \tag{3}$$

where a_i is the *ith* attribute in A, $|S_{a_i}|$ denotes the number of users in V that possess the attribute a_i in A, and $|Sa_i^j|$ represents the number of users possessing the value of a_i^j in a_i. $|a_i|$ denotes the number of different attribute values

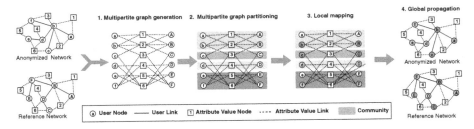

Fig. 1. An overview of our approach: (1) the anonymized network and reference network are merged into one multipartite graph; (2) the multipartite graph are divided to small communities; (3) users inside each community are mapped; and (4) the remaining users are mapped by performing a global propagation on the whole network.

a_i^j of attribute a_i. A large $AVD(a_i)$ indicates that attribute a_i has large diverse attribute values. For example, a user in a social network has two attributes: *Gender* and *Address*. For each user, gender only has two possible attribute values (male and female), while address could be different from one to the other. A fine-grained address, such as the detailed mailing address, could more precisely identify a user than the gender. Therefore, we claim that $AVD(Address)$ is larger than $AVD(Gender)$. In addition, as an important step in our de-anonymization approach. We apply the attribute value diversity to generate a multipartite graph.

4.2   Node Similarity

In mapping step and global propagation step, the node v_a in V_a is mapped to node v_r in V_r based on the node similarity $sim(v_a, v_r)$, which is defined as follows:

$$sim(v_a, v_r) = \frac{|A(v_a) \cap A(v_r)|}{|A(v_a) \cup A(v_r)|} \times (1 - \frac{|Deg(v_a) - Deg(v_r)|}{\sqrt{Deg(v_a) * Deg(v_r)}}), \quad (4)$$

where $\frac{|A(v_a) \cap A(v_r)|}{|A(v_a) \cup A(v_r)|}$ measures the similarity of attribute values between node v_a and node v_r; $Deg(v_a)$ and $Deg(v_r)$ denote the degree of v_a and v_r in G_a and G_r, respectively. As a result, the similarity between two nodes is determined by their attribute information and structural characteristics.

4.3   Algorithm Details

Multipartite Graph Generation: The first step of our approach is to create a multipartite graph G_m. As shown in Algorithm 1, given an anonymized graph $G_a(V_a, E_a, A_a)$ and a reference graph $G_r(V_r, E_r, A_r)$, their user sets V_a, V_r are added to G_m as nodes sets V_{m1} and V_{m2}, respectively (Line 1–3). For any attribute a_i, it will be removed from A_a and A_r if its diversity of attribute value $AVD(a_i)$ is smaller than a threshold (Line 4–13), because adding attributes with few attribute values into the multipartite graph would make the graph too complex to get a good graph partitioning quality. This threshold depends on the number of attributes owned by graphs. For instance, a graph with abundant attributes would select a large threshold. After that, attribute values of each user in V_a and V_r serve as a set of nodes V_{m3} and are added into G_m, respectively. Meanwhile, if a user possesses an attribute value, an edge should be added between the user and the attribute value (Line 14–25). Finally, the multipartite graph consisting of user nodes and attribute value nodes are created.

Multipartite Graph Partitioning: As mentioned in Sect. 3.3, we employ modularity-based community detection algorithm [6]. The partitioning operation will keep repeating until no community can be split further (or reaching a maximum number of iterations).

Algorithm 1: Creating a multipartite graph

Input : Two social graphs: $G_a(V_a, E_a, A_a)$ and $G_r(V_r, E_r, A_r)$
Output: A multipartite graph $G_m(V_{m1}, V_{m2}, V_{m3}, E_m)$

1 Set an undirected graph $G_m = \emptyset$
2 $G_m.add\_nodes\_from(V_a, type = V_{m1})$
3 $G_m.add\_nodes\_from(V_r, type = V_{m2})$
4 **for** *each attribute $a_i \in A_a$* **do**
5   **if** $AVD(a_i) < threshold$ **then**
6          $A_a.remove(a_i)$
7   **end**
8 **end**
9 **for** *each attribute $a_i \in A_r$* **do**
10   **if** $AVD(a_i) < threshold$ **then**
11         $A_r.remove(a_i)$
12   **end**
13 **end**
14 **for** *each user $v_i \in V_a$* **do**
15   **for** *each attribute value $a_i^j \in A_a(v_i)$* **do**
16         $G_m.add\_node(a_i^j, type = V_{m3})$
17         $G_m.add\_edge((v_i, a_i^j), type = E_m)$
18   **end**
19 **end**
20 **for** *each user $v_i \in V_r$* **do**
21   **for** *each attribute value $a_i^j \in A_r(v_i)$* **do**
22         $G_m.add\_node(a_i^j, type = V_{m3})$
23         $G_m.add\_edge((v_i, a_i^j), type = E_m)$
24   **end**
25 **end**

Local Mapping: After graph partitioning, each community $c_i \in C$ has three sets of nodes which are V'_{m1}, V'_{m2}, and V'_{m3}. These three sets are the subset of V_{m1}, V_{m2} and V_{m3}, where V_{m1} contains V_a, V_{m2} contains V_r and V_{m3} attribute values, respectively. In each community, an unmapped user v_i in V'_{m1} is mapped to a candidate user v_j in V'_{m2}, based on the node similarity calculated by Eq. (4) in Sect. 4.2. Furthermore, during the local mapping, we employ the following eccentricity [14] to measure the uniqueness of the unmapped user candidate:

$$ecc(D) = \frac{\max_1(D) - \max_2(D)}{\delta(D)}, \tag{5}$$

where D is the list of similarity scores sim between v_i and all candidate users in V_{m2}, $\max_1(D)$ and $\max_2(D)$ are the two highest similarity values in D, and $\delta(D)$ represents the standard deviation of the values in D. If the $ecc(D)$ exceeds a threshold, the users v_i is mapped to v_j with the similarity equals to $\max_1(D)$.

Algorithm 2: Local mapping

 Input : A set of communities: C
 Output: A set of mapped user pairs M
1 Initialize $M = \emptyset$
2 **for** *each community $c_i \in C$* **do**
3 $c_i = V'_{m1} \cup V'_{m2} \cup V'_{m3}$, where $V'_{m1} \subset V_{m1}, V'_{m2} \subset V_{m2}, V'_{m3} \subset V_{m3}$
4 **for** *each $v_i \in V'_{m1}$* **do**
5   Initialize $D = \emptyset$
6   **for** *each $v_j \in V'_{m2}$* **do**
7   Calculate $sim(v_i, v_j)$ based on Equation (4)
8    $D.add(sim(v_i, v_j))$
9   **end**
10   Calculate $ecc(D)$ based on Equation (5), if it is above a threshold, select the user v_j with the highest $sim(v_i, v_j)$
11   $M = M \cup \{(v_i, v_j)\}$
12 **end**
13 **end**

Global Propagation: This phase is similar to the propagation proposed in [14]. Staring from the identified users M from local mapping, each unmapped user v_a in G_a will be mapped to an unmapped user v_r in G_r. At each iteration, we randomly pick an unmapped user v_a who has a successfully mapped neighbor from anonymized social graph G_a, and use similarity measurement Eq. (4) to quantify its similarity values with all unmapped users candidates in G_r who possess at least one successfully mapped neighbor. Finally, the v_r will be selected based on the eccentricity defined in Eq. (5) to map with v_a. The new mapped pair (v_a, v_r) will be added into M to serve the next round iteration.

5   Experiments

In this section, we employ a real-world dataset collected from Sina Weibo, the most famous social media in China, to evaluate our attribute-enhanced de-anonymization approach.

5.1   Experimental Setup

We converted Weibo dataset which captures the "following" relationships among users into an undirected graph with 3859 nodes, 4992 edges and an average degree of 2.587. Each user in this dataset possesses three attributes including "gender", "city" and "province". We make a copy of the original graph and replace all user identities with random characters, then employ two edge randomization methods [20], Random Add/Del and Random Switch on this copy to generate anonymized graphs. Next, we duplicate the original graph and randomly remove 10% of nodes and their edges to generate the reference network. In our work, we used the most influential de-anonymization approach [14] as the baseline. The de-anonymization accuracy is used to evaluate the de-anonymization performance, which denotes the ratio of the number of users correctly re-identified over the number of overlapping users of G_a and G_r. The following evaluation results are the average of 30 trials.

5.2   Results

At first, we apply two edge randomization approaches to add noises into the anonymized network. The first approach is Random Add/Del, which randomly deletes a number of edges from a network and then randomly adds the same number of edges into the network. The second approach called Random Switch randomly removes two edges $e_{i,j}$ and $e_{p,q}$ from network and then add two edges $e_{i,p}$ and $e_{j,q}$ to the network. In evaluations, the *noise ratio*, which decides the number of added and deleted edges over the total number of edges in the network, is changed from 0 to 0.3 at an interval of 0.05. Based on experiences from our experiments, the threshold used in multipartite graph generation is set to the average value of AVD, and the maximum number of partitioning iterations is set to 6. The eccentricity threshold used in local mapping is set to 0.1 [16], and the number of seeds in the baseline algorithm is set to 150 [14].

Figure 2a depicts the result of de-anonymization accuracy in the anonymized network processed by Random Add/Del. As a result of using degrees of nodes to calculate a similarity between users, both de-anonymization methods are negatively affected by adding and removing edges, compared to the case without adding noise. Despite this, our algorithm has better performance than the baseline. Figure 2b presents the result in the network processed by Random Switch. As shown in the result, we can see that both our algorithm and the baseline are impacted by added noises. This is because even though the degrees of nodes are not changed by Random Switch, the inside structure of the network which both de-anonymization algorithms rely on is disturbed. In spite of this, our algorithm is still better than the baseline.

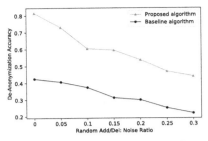
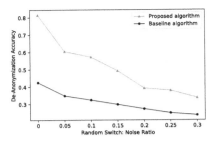

(a) Random Add/Del anonymized graph.   (b) Random Switch anonymized graph.

Fig. 2. Impact of noise on the de-anonymization accuracy in the different anonymized graphs

6   Conclusion and Future Work

In this paper, we propose a new approach to de-anonymize a social network with user attributes. Our method merges the anonymized network and reference network into a multipartite graph and employs a modularity-based community detection technique to partition the multipartite graph into small and dense communities. After that, the local mapping and global propagation are performed sequentially to de-anonymize users from the community level and the network level, respectively. We use a Sina Weibo dataset processed by two edge randomization methods to evaluate our algorithm. The evaluation results indicate that our approach is more efficient than the most influential algorithm. In the future, we would explore ways to de-anonymize the networks with modified attribute values and measure the degree of anonymity of users in an anonymized network with user attributes.

Acknowledgment. This work was partially supported by the US National Science Foundation under grant CNS-1704397, and the National Science Foundation of China under grants 61832012, 61771289, and 61672321.

References

1. The global state of digital in 2019 report, January 2019. https://hootsuite.com/pages/digital-in-2019
2. The U.S. governments open data, July 2019. https://www.data.gov
3. Brandes, U., et al.: On modularity clustering. IEEE Trans. Knowl. Data Eng. **20**(2), 172–188 (2007)
4. Chiasserini, C.F., Garetto, M., Leonardi, E.: Social network de-anonymization under scale-free user relations. IEEE/ACM Trans. Netw. **24**(6), 3756–3769 (2016)
5. Chung, F., Lu, L.: The average distance in a random graph with given expected degrees. Internet Math. **1**(1), 91–113 (2003). https://projecteuclid.org:443/euclid.im/1057768561
6. Clauset, A., Newman, M.E., Moore, C.: Finding community structure in very large networks. Phys. Rev. E **70**(6), 066111 (2004)

7. Hayes, B.: Connecting the dots. Am. Sci. **94**(5), 400–404 (2006)
8. Ji, S., Li, W., Srivatsa, M., Beyah, R.: Structural data de-anonymization: quantification, practice, and implications. In: Proceedings of the 2014 ACM SIGSAC Conference on Computer and Communications Security, pp. 1040–1053. ACM (2014)
9. Ji, S., Li, W., Srivatsa, M., Beyah, R.: Structural data de-anonymization: theory and practice. IEEE/ACM Trans. Netw. **24**(6), 3523–3536 (2016)
10. Ji, S., Li, W., Srivatsa, M., He, J.S., Beyah, R.: General graph data de-anonymization: from mobility traces to social networks. ACM Trans. Inf. Syst. Secur. (TISSEC) **18**(4), 12 (2016)
11. Ji, S., Wang, T., Chen, J., Li, W., Mittal, P., Beyah, R.: De-SAG: on the de-anonymization of structure-attribute graph data. IEEE Trans. Dependable Secure Comput. (2017)
12. Korayem, M., Crandall, D.: De-anonymizing users across heterogeneous social computing platforms. In: Seventh International AAAI Conference on Weblogs and Social Media (2013)
13. Li, H., Zhang, C., He, Y., Cheng, X., Liu, Y., Sun, L.: An enhanced structure-based de-anonymization of online social networks. In: Yang, Q., Yu, W., Challal, Y. (eds.) WASA 2016. LNCS, vol. 9798, pp. 331–342. Springer, Cham (2016). https://doi.org/10.1007/978-3-319-42836-9_30
14. Narayanan, A., Shmatikov, V.: De-anonymizing social networks. arXiv preprint arXiv:0903.3276 (2009)
15. Newman, M.E., Girvan, M.: Finding and evaluating community structure in networks. Phys. Rev. E **69**(2), 026113 (2004)
16. Nilizadeh, S., Kapadia, A., Ahn, Y.Y.: Community-enhanced de-anonymization of online social networks. In: Proceedings of the 2014 ACM SIGSAC Conference on Computer and Communications Security, pp. 537–548. ACM (2014)
17. Pedarsani, P., Figueiredo, D.R., Grossglauser, M.: A Bayesian method for matching two similar graphs without seeds. In: 51st Annual Allerton Conference on Communication, Control, and Computing (Allerton), pp. 1598–1607. IEEE (2013)
18. Perez, S.: Twitter partners with IBM to bring social data to the enterprise. Tech Crunch (2014)
19. Qian, J., Li, X.Y., Zhang, C., Chen, L.: De-anonymizing social networks and inferring private attributes using knowledge graphs. In: The 35th Annual IEEE International Conference on Computer Communications, INFOCOM 2016, pp. 1–9. IEEE (2016)
20. Ying, X., Wu, X.: Randomizing social networks: a spectrum preserving approach. In: Proceedings of the 2008 SIAM International Conference on Data Mining, pp. 739–750. SIAM (2008)
21. Young, S.D.: A big data approach to HIV epidemiology and prevention. Prev. Med. **70**, 17–18 (2015)
22. Zhang, A., Xie, X., Chang, K.C.C., Gunter, C.A., Han, J., Wang, X.: Privacy risk in anonymized heterogeneous information networks. In: EDBT, pp. 595–606. Citeseer (2014)
23. Zhang, C., Jiang, H., Wang, Y., Hu, Q., Yu, J., Cheng, X.: User identity de-anonymization based on attributes. In: Biagioni, E.S., Zheng, Y., Cheng, S. (eds.) WASA 2019. LNCS, vol. 11604, pp. 458–469. Springer, Cham (2019). https://doi.org/10.1007/978-3-030-23597-0_37

Subgraph-Based Adversarial Examples Against Graph-Based IoT Malware Detection Systems

Ahmed Abusnaina[1]([⊠]), Hisham Alasmary[1], Mohammed Abuhamad[1,2], Saeed Salem[3], DaeHun Nyang[2], and Aziz Mohaisen[1]

[1] University of Central Florida, Orlando, FL 32816, USA
{ahmed.abusnaina,hisham,abuhamad}@Knights.ucf.edu, mohaisen@ucf.edu
[2] Inha University, Incheon, South Korea
nyang@inha.ac.kr
[3] North Dakota State University, Fargo, ND 58105, USA
saeed.salem@ndsu.edu

Abstract. Internet of Things (IoT) has become widely adopted in many fields, including industry, social networks, health care, and smart homes, connecting billions of IoT devices through the internet. Understanding and studying IoT malware through analysis using various approaches, such as Control Flow Graph (CFG)-based features and then applying deep learning detection, are widely explored. In this study, we investigate the robustness of such models against adversarial attacks. Our approach crafts the adversarial IoT software using the Subgraph Embedding and Augmentation (SGEA) method that reduces the embedded size required to cause misclassification. Intensive experiments are conducted to evaluate the performance of the proposed method. We observed that SGEA approach is able to misclassify all IoT malware samples as benign by embedding an average size of 6.8 nodes. This highlights that the current detection systems are prone to adversarial examples attacks; thus, there is a need to build more robust systems to detect such manipulated features generated by adversarial examples.

Keywords: IoT malware detection · Adversarial learning · Graph embedding

1 Introduction

Internet of Things (IoT) malware has emerged as one of the most challenging threats on the Internet today [1], and is expected to grow for many years to come. To cope with this threat, there has been a lot of works in the literature on the analysis, characterization and detection of IoT malware [2], falling under both static and dynamic analysis-based approaches [3]. One of the prominent static-based approaches to IoT analysis and detection uses abstract graph structures, such as the control flow graph (CFG) [4–6]. In using the CFGs for

© Springer Nature Switzerland AG 2019
A. Tagarelli and H. Tong (Eds.): CSoNet 2019, LNCS 11917, pp. 268–281, 2019.
https://doi.org/10.1007/978-3-030-34980-6_30

detecting IoT malware, defenders extract feature representations that are capable of identifying those malware, including various graph properties, such as the degree distribution, centrality measures, diameter, radius, etc. [4]. Those properties, represented as a feature vector, are used in tandem with machine learning algorithms to automate the labeling and detection of IoT malware samples.

As with other machine learning algorithms and applications, machine learning-based IoT malware detection algorithms are prone to manipulation. The rise of adversarial machine learning has highlight the fragile nature of those algorithms to perturbation attacks that would lead to misclassification: an adversary can introduce a small modification to the input sample space that would make the classifier to identify a piece of malware as a benign sample (i.e., adversarial example; or AE). Indeed, there has been a large body of work exploring the generation of AEs in general image-based classification problems [7, 8] as well as in the context of malware classification [9–11].

In this work, we optimize the Graph Embedding and Augmentation (GEA), a recent work on generating AEs in the context of CFG-based malware detection [11]. GEA aims to inject a piece of code into a target sample to alter its graph representation and the resulting feature used by the machine learning algorithm. In this work, we introduce sub-GEA (SGEA), an AE generation algorithm that mines for discriminative patterns (subgraphs) from a targeted class, and embeds such subgraphs in a sample towards generating the AE. SGEA does not only result in a high misclassification rate, but achieves the essence of AE generation: a small perturbation (as measured by the perturbation size) to the sample to result in the misclassification.

Contributions. Our contributions in this paper are as follows. First, we propose SGEA, a graph embedding technique to generate AEs with reduced injection size. Second, we show the favorable performance of SGEA by comparing it to GEA for both IoT malware detection and classification. GEA and SGEA both generate adversarial IoT software through embedding representative target sample to the original CFG representation of the targeted sample, while maintaining its practicality and functionality. We evaluate the performance of the methods via intensive experiments showing the effectiveness of the approach in producing successful AEs.

Organization. In Sect. 2, we discuss the related work. Then, the practical approach for generating practical adversarial IoT software is described in Sect. 3. The performance of the proposed approach, evaluated through intensive experiments, are in Sect. 4. Finally, we conclude our work in Sect. 5.

2 Related Work

Static analysis using various methods, including and CFGs, is well explored. Wuchner *et al.* [12] proposed a graph-based classification system that uses features generated from the quantitative data flow graphs of system calls. Moreover, Alasmary *et al.* [4] analyzed Android and IoT malware based on CFG features and built a deep learning-based detection system for IoT malware utilizing these features. Caselden *et al.* [13] proposed an attack on the program binaries using static representations of hybrid information and CFG. Alam *et al.* [14] proposed a malware detection system that matches CFGs of small malware samples and addresses changes occurred in opcodes' frequencies using two methods. Bruschi *et al.* [15] proposed a CFG-based malware detection system to compare extracted CFGs to known malware samples CFGs and then detect the malware based on these graphs. Similarly, Yan *et al.* [16] classified malware samples using CFG-based representation with deep convolutional neural networks. Machine and deep learning algorithms are widely deployed in malware detection [3,4,17]. However, deep learning-based models are vulnerable to adversarial attacks [9]. As a result, current malware detection systems can be fooled to misclassify crafted malware samples that are generated by applying small perturbation to the malware resulting in disastrous consequences. For example, DeepFool attack was proposed by Moosavi *et al.* [8] that uses iterative methods of L_2 distance-based adversarial to generate AEs with minimal perturbation. Also, Goodfellow *et al.* [7] proposed fast method attacks, FGSM, to generate AEs that fools the model. Moreover, three adversarial attacks, called C&W, were proposed by Carlini *et al.* [18] to explore the robustness of neural networks and existing defense techniques. Although AE generation approaches are well explored in image-based classifiers, limited research have been conducted on generating AE for malware samples [10,19], such as GEA [11].

3   Generating Adversarial Examples

Adversarial examples are generated by applying perturbation to the input feature space, $x' = x + \epsilon$, where x is the input vector, and ϵ is the perturbation. The adversary aims to misclassify the output of the targeted model, altering $f(x) \neq f(x')$, where f is the model's output. To reduce the detectability of the generated AEs, ϵ is minimized while preserving the adversarial behavior, $f(x) \neq f(x + \delta)$, where $\delta = \epsilon_{min}$. To do so, multiple approaches have been proposed [8,18]. In IoT malware, the process aims to generate realistic AEs that preserve the functionality of the original samples, although not maintained by the literature. Recently, Abusnaina *et al.* [11] proposed a new approach to highlight these issues, called Graph Embedding and Augmentation (GEA), in which the perturbation is applied at the code-level of the samples, ensuring the practicality of the generated AE. In this study, SGEA is an enhanced approach to generate AEs that reduces the perturbation overhead compared to GEA.

```
#include <stdio.h>
void main(){
    int a = 0;
    do{
        a++;
    }while(a < 10);

}
```

Listing 1.1. C script (original)

```
#include <stdio.h>
void main(){
    int x = 0;
    int s = 0;
    if(x!=0){
        s++;
    }
}
```

Listing 1.2. C script (original)

3.1 Graph Embedding and Augmentation (GEA)

GEA [11] generates practical AEs that maintain the functionality of the original IoT software while also achieving a high misclassification rate. This is done by combining the CFG of the original sample with a selected CFG (graph merging).

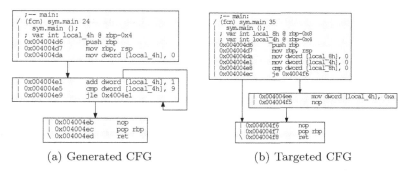

(a) Generated CFG   (b) Targeted CFG

Fig. 1. The generated CFG of the samples used for extracting graph-based features (graph size, centralities, etc.) for graph classification and malware detection.

Practical Implementation. GEA preserves the practicality of GEA by merging the original sample x_{org} with a selected target sample x_{sel}, which we highlight by an example. Listing 1.1 refers to the original sample script, while Listing 1.2 refers to the selected target sample script. The goal is to combine the two scripts while insuring that x_{sel} does not affect the functionality of x_{org}. Listing 1.3 shows the script after the combination. Note that the condition is set to execute only the functionality associated with x_{org} while preventing x_{sel} functionality from being executed. Figure 1a–b show the corresponding graphs for x_{org} and x_{sel}, respectively. It can be seen that the combined graph in Fig. 2 consists of the two aforementioned scripts sharing the same entry and exit nodes.

```
#include <stdio.h>
void main(){
    /*set a condition  variable */
    int cond=1;
    if(cond==1){
        /*script of  original  sample*/
        /*this section  will  be executed*/
        int a = 0;
        do{
            a++;
        }while(a<10);
    }
    else{
        /*script of  target sample*/
        /*this  section  will  not  be
                executed*/
        int x = 0;
        int s = 0;
        if(x!=0){
            s++;
        }
    }
}
```

Listing 1.3. C script of combining original and selected samples

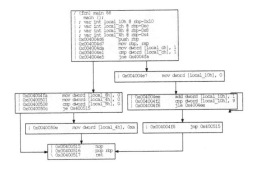

Fig. 2. The generated adversarial graph using GEA approach. Note that this graph is obtained logically by embedding the graph in Fig. 1b into the graph in Fig. 1a, although indirectly done by injecting the code listings as highlighted in Listings 1, 2, and 3.

3.2 Sub-GEA (SGEA)

While GEA combines original and selected targeted graphs of the samples to cause misclassification, this method reduces the injection size while preserving the same behavior, misclassification. To achieve that, we first convert the training samples of each class to CFGs using Radare2 [20], then, we extract discriminative subgraph patterns of each class using a correspondence-based quality criterion (CORK) [21]. This is done by extracting subgraphs that appear frequently in one class and less frequently in the other class. Let D denotes the CFGs of the training samples, $D = \{G_i\}_{i=1}^n$ and class labels $C = \{c_i\}_{i=1}^n$ where $c_i \in \{+1, -1\}$ is the class label of graph G_i; Also let D^+ and D^- denote the set of graphs in the corresponding classes. Let $D_S = \{G_i | S \subseteq G_i \text{ and } G_i \in D\}$ denote the supporting graphs of S. Moreover, let D_S^+ and D_S^-, denote the supporting graphs of the subgraph in the positive graphs and negative graphs, respectively. The CORK algorithm defines a submodular quality criterion, q, for a subgraph based on the set of supporting graphs ('hits') and non-supporting graphs ('misses') in the two classes and is calculated as follows: $q(G_s) = -(|D_S^{+\sim}| * |D_S^{+\sim}| + |D_S^+| * |D_S^-|)$. The best quality score is achieved when a subgraph appears in all the graphs of one class and not once in the graphs of the other class; the quality score is 0. Pruning strategies, proposed based on the quality criterion in the CORK algorithm, are integrated in the gSpan algorithm to directly mine discriminative subgraphs. Once the set of discriminative subgraphs are mined using the CORK algorithm, we further employ the gSpan [22], a graph-based substructure pattern mining, for mining frequent subgraphs of size five nodes or higher.

Constructing an AE. Then, we combine the original sample with the smallest extracted subgraph of the targeted class regarding nodes' number. If the generated CFG failed to be misclassified, another subgraph is selected in an ascending order with respect to the number of nodes in the collection of subgraphs. When a subgraph successfully achieves the misclassification, the operation ends. If no existing subgraph could cause misclassification, the original sample is returned and the operation fails.

Practical Implementation. The process is done by combining the x_{org} with a selected discriminative subgraph x_{sel} extracted from the targeted class. Figure 3 shows the discriminative subgraph extracted from Gafgyt IoT malicious family. Listing 1.4 is an equivalent sample of C script to generate such subgraph, which can be combined with the original sample to generate the practical AE.

4 Evaluation and Discussion

In this section, we evaluate the performance of the approaches over deep learning-based malware detection and classification systems trained over CFG-based features.

4.1 Dataset

To assess our proposed approaches, we started by gathering the dataset. To facilitate the evaluation, we gathered a dataset of binaries of two categories, IoT malicious and benign samples. Malicious samples are recent, in particular they were collected from the period of January 2018 to late February of 2019 from CyberIOCs [23]. Moreover, we assembled a dataset of benign samples from source files on GitHub [24].

```c
#include<stdio.h>
void  main(){
    int  GEAVar1 = 0; // block 0
    if (GEAVar1 == 1){ // block 1
        GEAVar1 += 1;
    }
    else  if (GEAVar1 == 2){ // block 2
        GEAVar1 += 2;
    }
    int  GEAVar2 = 0; // block 3
    if (GEAVar2 == 0){ // block 4
        GEAVar2 += 1;
    }
    else { // block 5
        GEAVar2 += 2;
    }
    int  GEAVar3 = 0; // block 6
}
```

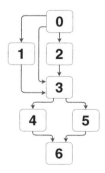

Listing 1.4. C script of an example Gafgyt extracted subgraph

Fig. 3. Sample of extracted discriminative subgraph from Gafgyt malicious family.

Dataset Creation. Our dataset consists of 3,000 IoT benign samples and 5,670 IoT malware samples gathered from CyberIOCs [23]. We reverse-engineered the datasets using Radare2 [20], a reverse engineering framework that provides various analysis and automation capabilities, including disassembly. Upon disassembling the binary of each sample, benign or malicious, we extracted the corresponding CFG of each sample.

Ground Truth Class. To validate our benign and malicious samples, we uploaded them on *VirusTotal* [25] and gathered the scan results corresponding to each sample. Then, we used AVClass [26] to classify malicious samples to their corresponding families. We summarized our dataset in Table 1.

Moving forward, we find different algorithmic features of the CFGs corresponding to individual binaries. In particular, for each sample, we extract 23 various algorithmic features categorized into seven groups, as in [4]. Table 2 represents the feature category and the number of features in each category. The five features extracted from each of the four feature categories represent minimum, maximum, median, mean, and standard deviation values for the observed parameters.

4.2   Experimental Setup

IoT Malware Detection System. The goal of our detection system is to recognize IoT malicious applications from benign. Therefore, we trained two deep learning models, Convolutional Neural Network (CNN)-based and Deep Neural Network (DNN)-based models, over the extracted CFG-based features. In this study, the input (X) of the model is a one dimensional (1D) vector of size 1×23 representing the extracted features.

Table 1. Distribution of IoT samples across the classes.

Class	# of Samples			% of Samples
	# Train	# Test	# Total	
Benign	2,400	600	3,000	34.60%
Gafgyt	2,400	600	3,000	34.60%
Mirai	1,927	481	2,408	27.68%
Tsunami	210	52	262	3.02%
Overall	6,937	1,733	8,670	100%

Table 2. Distribution of extracted features.

Feature category	# of features
Betweenness centrality	5
Closeness centrality	5
Degree centrality	5
Shortest path	5
Density	1
# of Edges	1
# of Nodes	1
Total	23

CNN-Based Design. We implemented the CNN architecture utilized in Abusnaina *et al.* [11]. Figure 4 shows the internal design of the CNN architecture and, although a standard design, more details can be found in the original paper [11].

DNN-Based Design. The DNN-based model architecture consists of two consecutive fully connected dense layers of size 1×100 connected to the input vector, followed by a dropout with a probability of 0.25. Similarly, the output of

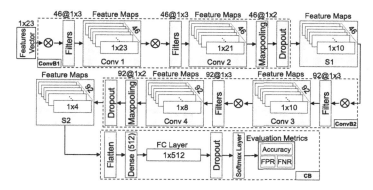

Fig. 4. The design of our CNN architecture.

the dropout function is fully connected with another two fully connected dense layers of size 1×100, followed by a dropout with a probability of 0.5. The output is then fed to the softmax layer to be evaluated based on the AR, FNR, FPR, to measure the performance of the model.

We trained both models using 100 epochs with a batch size of 32. The architecture of the CNN and DNN designs are shown in Figs. 4 and 5, respectively.

IoT Malware Classification System. In addition to recognizing IoT malicious applications, the malware classification system distinguishes and classifies the malicious samples to their corresponding families. Similar to the detection system, we utilized the aforementioned CNN- and DNN-based architectures and trained two deep learning models to classify the samples.

GEA. Due to the nature of the extracted features, the applied changes on the CFG will be reflected in the features, regardless of the effects on the functionality and practicality of the original sample. Similar to [11], we selected six different sized graphs (minimum, median and maximum) from the benign and malware samples as x_{sel}, where the size is referred to as the number of nodes in the graph.

SGEA. While GEA modifies the CFG of the sample by simply connecting the selected graph with the original sample. SGEA connects a carefully generated subgraph with the original sample to cause misclassification, reducing the injected graph size. To generate the subgraph, we extracted the

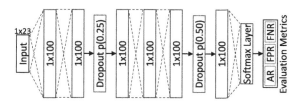

Fig. 5. The design of our DNN architecture.

discriminative subgraph patterns from each class and their subgraphs of size five nodes or higher. Then, in order to reduce the injected graph size, we connected the original sample with the subgraph of the minimum size. If the generated AE misclassifies the classifier, the process succeeds, and the AE will be returned, if not, the next subgraph is selected, in ascending order regarding the number of nodes in the subgraph. In case none of the subgraphs cause misclassification, the original sample will be returned as the process failed.

4.3   Results and Discussion

Deep Learning-Based IoT Malware Detection Systems. We designed two-class classifications, CNN- and DNN-based models, that distinguish IoT malware from IoT benign applications. The model is trained over 23 CFG-based features categorized into seven groups. More detailed information regarding the dataset is provided in Sect. 4.1. We achieved a CNN- and DNN-based model accuracy rate of 98.96% and 98.67% with a False Negative Rate (FNR) of 0.88% and 1.41% and a False Positive Rate (FPR) of 1.33% and 1.16%, respectively.

Deep Learning-Based IoT Malware Classification Systems. We designed four-class classifications, CNN- and DNN-based models, that are capable of classifying the malicious samples into their corresponding families. We achieved a CNN- and DNN-based model accuracy rate of 98.09% and 97.57%, respectively. Figure 6a and b are the confusion matrices of the trained models.

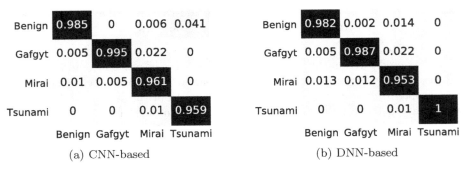

Fig. 6. Confusion matrices of IoT malware classification systems.

GEA. We investigated the impact of the size of the graph on the misclassification rate. We selected three graphs, as targets, from each of the benign and malicious IoT software, and connected each of these target graphs with a graph of the other class to understand the impact of size on misclassification with GEA. The results for the IoT detection system are shown in Table 3. It can be observed that the misclassification rate increases when the number of nodes increases. In addition, the time needed to craft the AE is proportional to the size of the

Table 3. GEA: Misclassification rate over IoT detection systems. MR refers to misclassification rate, whereas, CT refers to the crafting time in millisecond per sample.

		Malware to benign MR.					Benign to malware MR.		
Size	# Nodes	MR (%) CNN	DNN	CT (ms)	Size	# Nodes	MR (%) CNN	DNN	CT (ms)
Minimum	10	50.57	61.03	37.39	Minimum	11	45.92	19.33	34.10
Median	23	99.64	98.76	40.46	Median	43	**60.22**	59.90	56.83
Maximum	1075	**100**	**100**	6,430.66	Maximum	274	47.36	**60.89**	763.63

selected sample. In the IoT malware detection systems, we achieved a malware to benign misclassification rate of as high as 100% on both CNN- and DNN-based models, and a benign to malware misclassification rate of 60.22% and 60.89% on CNN- and DNN-based models, respectively. Table 4 shows the targeted and non-targeted misclassification rates over the IoT malware classification systems. Non-targeted misclassification indicates that after combining the original and selected samples, the original sample class changes. Moreover, if the new assigned label is the selected sample class, it is considered as targeted misclassification. Here, we achieved a targeted misclassification rate of 100% from all malicious families into benign on both CNN- and DNN-based models, highlighting the security issue in such systems.

SGEA. Similar to GEA, SGEA focuses on generating the adversarial desired output. In addition, SGEA reduces the size of injection by combining the original sample with a carefully selected subgraph. Table 5 shows the evaluation

Table 4. GEA: Misclassification rate over IoT classification systems.

Class	# Nodes	Misclassification rate				Crafting time (ms)
		Non-targeted		Targeted		
		CNN	DNN	CNN	DNN	
Benign	10	48.72%	58.87%	45.89%	48.54%	37.39
	23	99.64%	99.55%	99.64%	99.38%	40.46
	1075	**100%**	**100%**	**100%**	**100%**	6,430.66
Gafgyt	13	24.62%	41.74%	0.17%	0.35%	32.36
	64	**66.81%**	**77.40%**	**15.97%**	**16.06%**	68.77
	155	54.63%	47.13%	8.03%	0.00%	125.15
Mirai	11	41.37%	37.22%	0.32%	0.80%	34.10
	48	62.30%	52.15%	12.46%	0.96%	56.84
	274	**95.60%**	**91.05%**	**93.45%**	**53.67%**	763.63
Tsunami	15	59.54%	60.73%	**0.12%**	**0.12%**	35.25
	59	63.95%	64.06%	0.00%	0.00%	59.93
	138	**66.74%**	**64.36%**	0.00%	0.00%	201.82

Table 5. SGEA: IoT malware detection system evaluation. Here, MR refers to misclassification rate, AVG. Size refers to the overall average subgraph size used to achieve misclassification, and CT is the AEs crafting time per sample in seconds.

Benign to malware misclassification.				Malware to benign misclassification.			
Architecture	MR(%)	AVG. Size	CT (s)	Architecture	MR(%)	AVG. Size	CT (s)
CNN	22.22	10.15	2.57	CNN	100	6.80	0.23
DNN	33.88	11.09	2.23	DNN	100	6.86	0.21

of SGEA against CNN- and DNN-based IoT malware detection systems. Notice that GEA outperforms SGEA in benign to malware misclassification. However, SGEA achieves 100% malware to benign misclassification rate against CNN- and DNN-based models, with an average subgraph size of 6.8 nodes, outperforming the GEA approach.

Figures 7 and 8 show the evaluation of CNN- and DNN-based IoT malware classification systems against SGEA approach. Here, Fig. 7a–c represent the non-targeted and targeted misclassification rate over CNN-based model, respectively. Similarly, Fig. 8a–c show the non-targeted and targeted misclassification rate over DNN-based model. Figures 7b, d, and 8b,d represent the average size of the

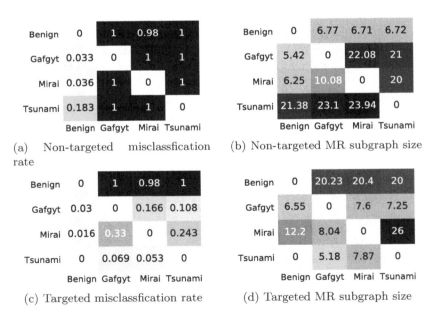

(a) Non-targeted misclassfication rate

(b) Non-targeted MR subgraph size

(c) Targeted misclassfication rate

(d) Targeted MR subgraph size

Fig. 7. SGEA: CNN-based IoT malware classification system evaluation. Here, MR refers to misclassification rate, columns represent the sample original class, whereas, rows represent the connected subgraph pattern class.

connected subgraphs to generate the AEs over the CNN- and DNN-based models. For instance, SGEA approach successfully targeted misclassifies all Gafgyt test samples into benign over CNN-based classification model with an average subgraph size of 20.23 nodes, which is significantly better than GEA. Moreover, it misclassifies all Gafgyt test samples into other classes using discriminative subgraphs extracted from benign samples with an average size of 6.77 nodes. Notice that all classes have a high targeted misclassification rate towards the benign class and a low targeted misclassification rate from benign to malicious families and among malicious families. This behavior is caused by the nature of the benign samples, as they are diverse in characteristics and functionalities. However, malicious samples within the same family tend to have the same functionalities, resulting in high level of similarity in the extracted CFGs and their corresponding features.

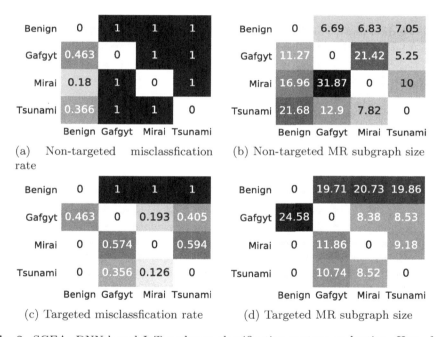

(a) Non-targeted misclassfication rate

(b) Non-targeted MR subgraph size

(c) Targeted misclassfication rate

(d) Targeted MR subgraph size

Fig. 8. SGEA: DNN-based IoT malware classification system evaluation. Here, MR refers to misclassification rate, columns represent the sample original class, whereas, rows represent the connected subgraph pattern class.

Summary. The goal of this study is to investigate the robustness of CFG-based IoT malware detection systems against targeted and non-targeted adversarial examples. The main focus of the evaluation is to misclassify the malicious samples into benign. GEA and SGEA have been evaluated over CNN- and DNN-based IoT malware detection systems. In addition, our proposed approach,

SGEA, significantly reduces the perturbation overhead of the generated samples, increasing its immunity against detection.

5   Conclusion

In this work, we study the robustness of graph-based deep learning models against adversarial machine learning attacks. To do so, we design SGEA, an approach to generate AEs corresponding to IoT software by reducing the embedded size to result in model misclassification. The performance of the method is validated through various experiments. We observed that SGEA misclassifies all malware samples as benign while only embedding a subgraph of an average size of 6.8 nodes. This highlights the need for more robust IoT malware detection and classification tools against adversarial learning, particularly those optimized to operate with a small graph perturbation.

Acknowledgement. This work is supported by NRF grant 2016K1A1A2912757, NVIDIA GPU Grant (2018 and 2019), and a Cyber Florida Seed Grant.

References

1. Antonakakis, M., et al.: Understanding the Mirai Botnet. In: Proceedings of the 26th USENIX Security Symposium, pp. 1093–1110 (2017)
2. Azmoodeh, A., Dehghantanha, A., Choo, K.-K.R.: Robust malware detection for Internet of (Battlefield) Things devices using deep eigenspace learning. IEEE Trans. Sustain. Comput. **4**, 88–95 (2019)
3. Mohaisen, A., Alrawi, O., Mohaisen, M.: AMAL: high-fidelity, behavior-based automated malware analysis and classification. Comput. Secur. **52**, 251–266 (2015)
4. Alasmary, H., et al.: Analyzing and detecting emerging Internet of Things malware: a graph-based approach. IEEE Internet Things J. (2019)
5. Mohaisen, A., Yun, A., Kim, Y.: Measuring the mixing time of social graphs. In: ACM IMC, pp. 383–389 (2010)
6. Mohaisen, A., Hopper, N., Kim, Y.: Keep your friends close: incorporating trust into social network-based Sybil defenses. In: Proceedings of the 30th IEEE International Conference on Computer Communications, INFOCOM, pp. 1943–1951 (2011)
7. Ian, C.S., Goodfellow, J., Shlens, J.: Explaining and harnessing adversarial examples. In: International Conference on Learning Representations, pp. 1–11 (2015)
8. Moosavi-Dezfooli, S., Fawzi, A., Frossard, P.: DeepFool: a simple and accurate method to fool deep neural networks. In: IEEE Conference on Computer Vision and Pattern Recognition, pp. 2574–2582 (2016)
9. Papernot, N., McDaniel, P.D., Jha, S., Fredrikson, M., Celik, Z.B., Swami, A.: The limitations of deep learning in adversarial settings. In: Proceedings of the IEEE European Symposium on Security and Privacy (EuroS&P), pp. 372–387 (2016)
10. Grosse, K., Papernot, N., Manoharan, P., Backes, M., McDaniel, P.: Adversarial examples for malware detection. In: Foley, S.N., Gollmann, D., Snekkenes, E. (eds.) ESORICS 2017. LNCS, vol. 10493, pp. 62–79. Springer, Cham (2017). https://doi.org/10.1007/978-3-319-66399-9_4

11. Abusnaina, A., Khormali, A., Alasmary, H., Park, J., Anwar, A., Mohaisen, A.: Adversarial learning attacks on graph-based IoT malware detection systems. In: 39th IEEE International Conference on Distributed Computing Systems, ICDCS (2019)

12. Wüchner, T., Ochoa, M., Pretschner, A.: Robust and effective malware detection through quantitative data flow graph metrics. In: Almgren, M., Gulisano, V., Maggi, F. (eds.) DIMVA 2015. LNCS, vol. 9148, pp. 98–118. Springer, Cham (2015). https://doi.org/10.1007/978-3-319-20550-2_6

13. Caselden, D., Bazhanyuk, A., Payer, M., McCamant, S., Song, D.: HI-CFG: construction by binary analysis and application to attack polymorphism. In: Crampton, J., Jajodia, S., Mayes, K. (eds.) ESORICS 2013. LNCS, vol. 8134, pp. 164–181. Springer, Heidelberg (2013). https://doi.org/10.1007/978-3-642-40203-6_10

14. Alam, S., Horspool, R.N., Traoré, I., Sogukpinar, I.: A framework for metamorphic malware analysis and real-time detection. Comput. Secur. **48**, 212–233 (2015)

15. Bruschi, D., Martignoni, L., Monga, M.: Detecting self-mutating malware using control-flow graph matching. In: Büschkes, R., Laskov, P. (eds.) DIMVA 2006. LNCS, vol. 4064, pp. 129–143. Springer, Heidelberg (2006). https://doi.org/10.1007/11790754_8

16. Yan, J., Jin, D., Yan, G.: Classifying malware represented as control flow graphs using deep graph convolutional neural networks. In: IEEE/IFIP DSN, pp. 1–12 (2019)

17. Antonakakis, M., et al.: From throw-away traffic to bots: Detecting the rise of DGA-based malware. In: Proceedings of the 21th USENIX Security Symposium, pp. 491–506 (2012)

18. Carlini, N., Wagner, D.A.: Towards evaluating the robustness of neural networks. In: Proceedings of the IEEE Symposium on Security and Privacy, pp. 39–57 (2017)

19. Khormali, A., Abusnaina, A., Nyang, D., Yuksel, M., Mohaisen, A.: Examining the robustness of learning-based DDoS detection in software defined networks. In: Proceedings of the IEEE Conference on Dependable and Secure Computing, IDSC (2019)

20. Developers, Radare2 (2019). http://www.radare.org/r/

21. Thoma, M., et al.: Discriminative frequent subgraph mining with optimality guarantees. Stat. Anal. Data Min. **3**(5), 302–318 (2010)

22. Yan, X., Han, J.: gSpan: graph-based substructure pattern mining. In: Proceedings of the 2002 IEEE International Conference on Data Mining, pp. 721–724 (2002)

23. Developers, Cyberiocs (2019). https://freeiocs.cyberiocs.pro/

24. Github (2019). https://github.com/

25. VirusTotal (2019). https://www.virustotal.com

26. Sebastián, M., Rivera, R., Kotzias, P., Caballero, J.: AVCLASS: a tool for massive malware labeling. In: Monrose, F., Dacier, M., Blanc, G., Garcia-Alfaro, J. (eds.) RAID 2016. LNCS, vol. 9854, pp. 230–253. Springer, Cham (2016). https://doi.org/10.1007/978-3-319-45719-2_11

Incorporating Content Beyond Text: A High Reliable Twitter-Based Disaster Information System

Qixuan Hou[1,2] and Meng Han[3(✉)]

[1] Guizhou Provincial Key Laboratory of Public Big Data, Guizhou University,
Guiyang 550025, Guizhou, China
qhou6@gatech.edu
[2] Georgia Institute of Technology, Atlanta, GA 30332, USA
[3] Data-Driven Intelligence Research (DIR) Laboratory, Kennesaw State University,
Atlanta, GA 30060, USA
mhan9@kennesaw.edu

Abstract. Social media is a valuable information source with high-volume and real-time data. It has been used in a great number of event detection applications, especially in disaster information system. However, most of the systems only extract textual content. In this paper, we present an infrastructure pipeline of disaster information system using Twitter data. Landslide is used as an example for the demonstration purpose. To further improve the quality of the detected events, the pipeline integrates both textual and imagery content from tweets in hope to fully utilize the information. The text classifier is built to remove noises, which can achieve 0.92 F1-score in classifying individual messages. The image classifier is constructed by fine-tuning pretrained VGG-F network, which can achieve 90% accuracy. The image classifier serves as a verifier in the pipeline to reject or confirm the detected events. The evaluation indicates that this verifier can significantly reduce false positive events.

Keywords: Social media · Multimodal information · Image classification

1 Introduction

Social media has become an important source for rich and real-time data in both industry and academia, as the public usage remarkably grows in recent years. Data gathered from social media is extensively used in a wide range of topics, including monitoring outdoor air pollution in London [33], modeling rumor spreading [31, 32], preventing sensitive information attacks [19–21], achieving disease surveillance [34], detecting natural disasters [29], and etc.

With high-volume and real-time data, social media can at times outperform news sources on reporting some types of events [18, 35–37]. For instance, it is quite a hot topic

Supported by the Foundation of Guizhou Provincial Key Laboratory of Public Big Data (No. 2018BDKFJJ002).

© Springer Nature Switzerland AG 2019
A. Tagarelli and H. Tong (Eds.): CSoNet 2019, LNCS 11917, pp. 282–292, 2019.
https://doi.org/10.1007/978-3-030-34980-6_31

that the Amazon rainforest now has alarming clusters of burning wildfires. The left pane of Fig. 1 shows a popular comment that the Amazon rainforest wildfire has experienced a delayed media coverage. Power from Media Matters presented the bar chart in Fig. 2 to show the number of cable news segments mentioning the Amazon rainforest fires [30]. The first report of the wildfire on cable news was on August 21, 2019. However, on the other hand, the earliest tweet I can find about this wildfire is from August 6, 2019, as shown on the right pane of Fig. 1.

Fig. 1. Tweets about the Amazon rainforest wildfires from August 21 and August 6, 2019

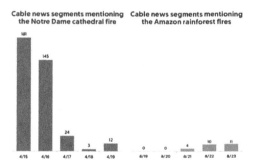

Fig. 2. Cable news coverage of Notre-Dame cathedral fire and the Amazon rainforest fires [30]

In the meantime, using social media data in event detection system raises some challenges due to high volume, noisy information, and lack of geo-tagged data. For example, if we are designing a social media-based application for landslide detection, we might face challenges as follows. As defined in Merriam Webster dictionary, "landslide" refers to "rapid downward movement of a mass of rock, earth, or artificial fill on a slop", or "a great majority of votes for one side". When collecting tweets with the keyword, "landslides", we will get tweets not only about natural disasters but also about elections, as two tweets shown in Fig. 3.

Fig. 3. Two tweets with the keyword "landslides"

There is a great amount of studies in attempting to reduce noises and improve quality of data extracted from social media. Harris et al. used geolocation to limit the number of irrelevant tweets collected [23]. Musaev et al. designed text classification to filter irrelevant tweets and took relevance ranking of Twitter users into consideration to achieve better accuracy on landslide detection [1, 29]. McGough et al. included news source in addition to social media to improve the accuracy on Zika incidence forecasting [22].

However, to the best of our knowledge, there is so far no social media-based event detection application incorporating imagery messages. Due to the nature of Twitter's design and the official limitation, tweets tend to have limited number of words. It is more than likely that imagery and textual messages of one tweet are relevant. Additionally, as shown in Fig. 3, images can carry high-quality information. Hence, we propose to integrate imagery messages into social media-based event detection systems to confirm or reject the detected events. In this paper, the landslide detection system is used as an example. We implement a pre-trained convolutional neural network to extract features from images and apply the clustering algorithm to identify potential groups. Then, we fine-tune a pre-trained CNN to classify images for our task. Finally, we compare the detected events from the system with and without imagery messages. It shows that imagery information can help the system successfully confirm 12.46% of the detected events on average and reject 6.31% of the detected events on average.

The rest of the paper is organized as follows. Section 2 includes related works. Section 3 outlines the system overview. Section 4 focuses on the image analysis, including image clustering and image classification. Section 5 shows the evaluation of the multimodal information system. Section 6 concludes the paper.

2   Related Work

Social media platforms, such as Twitter, Facebook and Instagram, generate a considerable amount of data every day due to their wide public usage. The rich source of real time information continuously attracts researchers and companies from different areas. Culnan et al. discussed how large U.S. companies use Twitter and other social media to gain business value [2]. Signorini et al. demonstrated the use of Twitter to track levels of disease activity and public concern during the influenza A H1B1 pandemic [3]. Social Media also emerged as a potential resource in the disaster management.

Yates et al. and Gao et al. presented a case study of the 2010 Haitian earthquake, where social media technologies were employed as the main knowledge sharing mechanisms among US government agencies. They studied social media as knowledge management systems, particularly for disaster and emergency management [4, 5]. Gao et al. identified several challenges when social media is used as a crowdsourcing mechanism to aggregate situational awareness, including geo-tag determination, report verification, and automated report summarization. Our system integrates multimodal information sources, including both text and images, to verify geo-tags and detected events, and can produce event summaries on a timely basis.

There are a lot of Twitter-based systems for identifying natural disasters and improving situation awareness [6–11, 18]. Unfortunately, most of the proposed systems only focus on textual messages to extract natural disaster events, and no systems have regarded images in the tweets as an information source. Textual messages of tweets in general are short. Twitter only allows 280 characters. Kokalitcheva shared some statistics about the length of English-language tweets [12]. Only about 1% tweets hit the 280-character limit, and 12% are longer than 140 characters. The brevity of the text limits the amount of extractable information. Lee stated that about 42% tweets include images [13]. Images in tweets are most likely relevant to the textual messages. As shown in Fig. 3, the 8-character long tweet includes an image of landslides. In order to fully utilize information from tweets, we propose to regard images as an additional source to confirm events. To the best of our knowledge, our system is among the first of few ones to take advantages of both textual and imagery messages to achieve better event coverage and accuracy.

3 System Overview

The basic architecture of the Twitter-based landslide detection system is shown in Fig. 4. **Downloader**: "Landslide", "mudslides", and etc. are used as search terms to retrieve data from Twitter. **Cleaner**: Stop words, including "election", "won", and etc. are used to remove noises to some extent. **Geotagger**: Name Entity Recognizer is used to extract geolocation entities (geo-terms) in text, and then Google Maps APIs converts geo-terms into geographic coordinates (geo-code) [24, 25]. **Text Classifier**: This is another filtering stage to further remove noises. Text is converted into vectors with a pre-trained model from Google and then SVM algorithm is used for classification [26, 27]. **Detector**: Geotagged tweets are grouped into cells by month and by geo-codes. A score is generated for each cell to evaluate how likely there is a landslide that happened in this cell this month. **Image Classifier Verifier**: We fine-tune a pre-trained deep network, VGG-F, to classify images from tweets. The details of our image analysis will be presented in the next section. The image classification results are used to reject or confirm events.

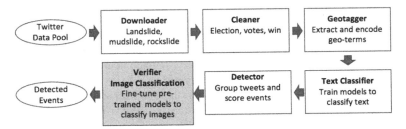

Fig. 4. The infrastructure pipeline for landslide detection

4 Image Analysis

We collect about 438,000 tweets with keywords, such as "landslides", etc., from 2018, and more than 56,000 tweets among these contain at least one image. We analyze 2,000 images from January 2018 to understand the content of the images and how textual and imagery messages are related. We manually label tweets as relevant to natural disasters or irrelevant.

4.1 Image Labeling

Image labeling service from Google Vision AI is used to help us capture the general content of the images. Most common labels of relevant tweets are geological, road, mountain, text, and terrain. By browsing images of relevant tweets, we spot three major categories, maps, terrain, and text, as shown in Fig. 5.

Fig. 5. Three major categories of tweets relevant to natural disasters

Most common labels of irrelevant tweets are text, font, photograph, and hair. By browsing images of irrelevant tweets, we spot three major categories, portrait, text, and poster, as shown in Fig. 6. As discussed above, "landslides" are also commonly used to describe elections, which explains why most of images on irrelevant tweets are portraits. There is a movie, named "landslide", released in February 2018, leading to some movie posters in irrelevant tweets.

Fig. 6. Three major categories of tweets irrelevant to natural disasters

4.2 Image Clustering

We use a Keras' pre-trained model, VGG16, for feature extraction. VGG16 is a deep convolutional network developed and trained by Oxford's Visual Geometry Group (VGG), which achieved good performance on the ImageNet Challenge 2014 submission [14]. We apply K-means clustering method on extracted features to further understand the overall content of the images. The input layer takes an image of the size of 224 * 224 * 3, and the output layer is a soft-max prediction on 1000 classes. The feature extraction part of the model is from the input layer to the last max pooling layer. The rest of the network is regarded as the classification part.

We use VGG16 to extract features from the images and use K-means clustering method to identify clusters. Figure 7 presents a sample of clustering results. The left cluster majorly contains terrain images, which mainly come from the tweets are relevant to natural disasters; the right cluster majorly includes portraits, which are from the tweets relevant to elections, and irrelevant to natural disasters.

The clustering results confirm our findings from the observation, that images with terrain are always from the tweets relevant to natural disasters, and those with portraits are always from the tweets irrelevant to natural disasters.

4.3 Image Classification

With image classification, we would like to know if an image shows terrain or portrait, in order to help the system to confirm or reject the detected events. We fine-tune a pre-trained VGG-F network to achieve our task.

Fig. 7. A sample clustering results

Table 1. Evaluation of text classifier with the annotated tweets from 2014

2014	1	2	3
Precision	0.88	0.90	0.90
Recall	0.98	0.93	0.97
F1 score	0.93	092	0.93

Donahue et al. demonstrated that features extracted from a deep convolutional network, which is trained on a large and fixed set of object recognition tasks, can be reused for novel generic tasks [15]. This is a surprising finding. It might be expected that the representations of a deep network are overfitted for one particular task, as the network is discriminatively trained to perform well at one specific task. However, pre-trained networks often surprisingly achieve better performance than that of hand-crafted features, especially when there are limited training images.

VGG-F network was proposed by Chatfield et al. and it comprises 8 learnable layers, 5 of which are convolutional, and the last 3 are fully connected [16]. The network is a simpler version of the network developed by Krizhevsky et al. [17]. We take the existing VGG-F network, replace the final layer with random weights, and train the network again with images labeled as terrain or portrait. We are able to achieve 87% accuracy with five training epochs.

5   Evaluation

Downloader collects about 438,000 tweets from 2018. Cleaner removes about 40% tweets and about 260,000 tweets remain. Geotagger is able to find geo-terms in about 114,000 tweets. Since the events should be defined by spatiotemporal features, we only analyze these 114,000 tweets with geo-terms. Among these, 17,651 tweets, about 15%, contain images.

In order to evaluate the text classifier, we use the annotated landslides dataset prepared by GRAIT-DM [28]. The dataset contains about 4,000 tweets collected based on the keywords related to landslide disasters from 2014. We use the first three months' tweets as testing set and the rest as training set. The average F1-score is about 0.92, and the detailed evaluation is shown in Table 1. The text classifier has good recall with the average as 0.96, which is the fraction of the relevant text that are successfully classified as relevant, and not promising precision with the average as 0.89, which is the fraction of the classified as relevant text that are relevant. It means, without image classifier, the pipeline can already manage to collect most of the true events but might report a number of false events. We would like to use imagery messages as a verification in order to reduce false positives.

In order to evaluate the image classifier, we label 2000 images from January 2018 as portrait, terrain, or others. The images are resized to 224 * 224; grey images are changed into RGB; images are normalized by subtracting the mean. With five training epochs, we can achieve about 86% accuracy. The detailed performance of the image classifier is shown in Fig. 8. The left pane shows the training loss and validation loss by training epochs. Whenever the network makes mistakes, a loss is calculated, and backpropagation algorithm updates the weights of the network in the direction that will decrease the loss. The middle one presents the training and validation accuracy with top 1 error (how often the highest scoring label is wrong). The right one show top 5 error.

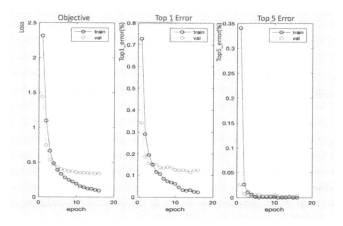

Fig. 8. The performance of image classifier

We compare the events detected by the pipeline with and without image classifier in order to confirm if image classifier can reduce false positive events. The text classifier is applied on textual messages of the tweets which have geo-terms tagged. As shown in Table 1, there are about 42,000 tweets classified as relevant to landslide disasters. The tweets are grouped into cells based on their geo-codes. The surface of the earth is considered as a grid consisting of cells. The row and the column are defined based on the formulas as shown below, where N and E are latitude and longitude of geo-codes. Each cell is roughly equal to 2.3 miles by 2.3 miles. Detector reports an event in cell (0,0) from January 2018, if there are more than 10 tweets from January 2018 grouped in cell (0,0).

$$\text{row} = \left(90^\circ + N\right)/(2.5'/60') = \left(90^\circ + N\right) * 24 \tag{1}$$

$$\text{column} = \left(180^\circ + E\right)/(2.5'/60') = \left(180^\circ + E\right) * 24 \tag{2}$$

Table 2. The events confirmed or rejected by image classifier

2018	1	2	3	4	5	6
#_events_detected_without_imagery_messages	121	43	102	96	87	89
%_events_with_images	26.45%	30.23%	27.45%	25.00%	24.14%	25.84%
%_events_rejected_by_imagery_messages	6.61%	6.98%	6.86%	5.21%	3.45%	5.62%
%_events_confirmed_by_imagery_messages	12.40%	16.28%	13.73%	10.42%	14.94%	11.24%
2018	**7**	**8**	**9**	**10**	**11**	**12**
#_events_detected_without_imagery_messages	93	68	61	78	74	59
%_events_with_images	26.88%	26.47%	39.34%	29.49%	25.68%	35.59%
%_events_rejected_by_imagery_messages	8.60%	8.82%	6.56%	3.85%	8.11%	5.08%
%_events_confirmed_by_imagery_messages	7.53%	8.82%	19.67%	11.54%	9.46%	13.56%

The number of events detected by the system is shown in Table 2. About 28% of events have at least one images. Image classifier is applied on these images. Verifier confirms the detected events if 60% images from the event are classified as terrain and verifier rejects the detected events if 60% images from the event are classified as portrait. The evaluation confirms image classifier can help the system reduce false positive events and improve the accuracy of the detected events.

6 Conclusion

The example of the Amazon rainforest wildfire shows the surprising power of social media on event reporting. In this paper, we would like to further improve the accuracy of event detection with data from social media. We propose to integrate imagery messages into Twitter-based landslide information system to confirm or reject detected events. The system overview is presented with an emphasis on building image classifier for verification purpose. We are able to fine-tune VGG-F network to classify images from tweets into portrait, terrain, and others. The network can achieve 86% accuracy with 5 training epochs and achieve about 90% accuracy within 20 training epochs. The image classifier helps the system improve the quality of the detected events by reducing false positive events.

Our future work includes to evaluating the proposed methods with more extensive data sets from different social media, such as Instagram and Facebook. We would also like to integrate imagery messages into other existing social media-based event detection platforms, such as London air pollution detection and disease surveillance, to assess how the additional information can improve the quality of detected events.

References

1. Musaev, A., Hou, Q.: Gathering high quality information on landslides from twitter by relevance ranking of users and tweets. In: 2016 IEEE 2nd International Conference on Collaboration and Internet Computing (CIC) (2016). https://doi.org/10.1109/cic.2016.045
2. Culnan, M., McHugh, P., Zubillaga, Jesus.: How Large U.S. Companies Can Use Twitter and Other Social Media to Gain Business Value. MIS Quarterly Executive (2010)
3. Signorini, A., Segre, A.M., Polgreen, P.M.: The use of Twitter to track levels of disease activity and public concern in the U.S. during the Influenza A H1N1 pandemic. PLoS ONE **6**, e19467 (2011)
4. Yates, D., Paquette, S.: Emergency knowledge management and social media technologies: a case study of the 2010 Haitian earthquake. Int. J. Inf. Manage. **31**(1), 6–13 (2011)
5. Gao, H., Barbier, G., Goolsby, R.: Harnessing the crowdsourcing power of social media for disaster relief. IEEE Intell. Syst. **26**(3), 10–14 (2011)
6. Yin, J., Karimi, S., Lampert, A., Cameron, M., Robinson, B., Power, R.: Using social media to enhance emergency situation awareness: extended abstract. In: Proceedings of the Twenty-Fourth International Joint Conference on Artificial Intelligence (2015)
7. Becker, H., Naaman, M., Gravano, L.: Beyond trending topics: real-world event identification on Twitter. In: Proceedings of the Fifth International Conference on Weblogs and Social Media (2011)
8. Fung, G., Yu, X., Yu, P., Lu, H.: Parameter free bursty events detection in text streams. In: Proceedings of the 31st International Conference on Very Large Data Bases (2005)
9. Karimi, S., Yin, J., Paris, C.: Classifying microblogs for disasters. In: Proceedings of the 2013 Australasian Document Computing Symposium (2013)
10. Li, R., Lei, K.H., Khadiwala, R., Change, K.: TEDAS: a Twitter-based event detection and analysis system. In: Proceedings of the IEEE 28th International Conference on Data Engineering (2012)
11. Yin, J.: Clustering microtext streams for event identification. In: Proceedings of the 6th International Joint Conference on Natural Language Processing (2013)
12. Kokalitcheva, K.: A Year after Tweets Doubled in Size, Brevity Still Rules (2018). https://www.axios.com
13. Lee, K.: What Analyzing 1 Million Tweets Taught Us (2015). https://thenextweb.com
14. Simonyan, K., Zisserman, A.: Very Deep Convolutional Networks for Large-Scale Image Recognition. eprint arXiv:1409.1556 (2014)
15. Donahue, J., et al.: DeCAF: A Deep Convolutional Activation Feature for Generic Visual Recognition. eprint arXiv:1310.1531 (2013)
16. Chatfield, K., Simonyan, K., Vedaldi, A., Zisserman, A.: Return of the devil in the details: delving deep into convolutional nets. In: British Machine Vision Conference (2014)
17. Krizhevsky, A., Sutskever, I., Hinton, G.: ImageNet classification with deep convolutional neural networks. In: Advances in Neural Information Processing Systems (2012)
18. He, J.S., Han, M., Ji, S., Du, T., Li, Z.: Spreading social influence with both positive and negative opinions in online networks. Big Data Mining Anal. **2**(2), 100–117 (2019)
19. Cai, Z., He, Z., Guan, X., Li, Y.: Collective data-sanitization for preventing sensitive information inference attacks in social networks. IEEE Trans. Dependable Secure Compu. **15**(4), 577–590 (2018)
20. He, Z., Cai, Z., Yu, J.: Latent-data privacy preserving with customized data utility for social network data. IEEE Trans. Veh. Technol. **67**(1), 665–673 (2018)
21. Zheng, X., Cai, Z., Yu, J., Wang, C., Li, Y.: Follow but no track: privacy preserved profile publishing in cyber-physical social systems. IEEE Internet Things **4**(6), 1868–1878 (2017)

22. McGough, S.F., Brownstein, J.S., Hawkins, J.B., Santillana, M.: Forecasting Zika incidence in the 2016 Latin America outbreak combining traditional disease surveillance with search, social media, and news report data. PLoS Neql. Trop. Dis. **11**, e0005295 (2017)

23. Harris, J., et al.: Evaluating the implementation of twitter-based foodborne illness reporting tool in the city of St. Louis Department of Health. Int. J. Environ. Res. Public Health **15**, 833 (2018)

24. Finkel, J., Grenager, T., Manning, C.: Incorporating non-local information into information extraction systems by Gibbs sampling. In: Proceedings of the 43nd Annual Meeting of the Association for Computation Linguistics (2005)

25. Google Inc.: The Google Geocoding API. https://developers.google.com/maps/documentation/geocoding/. Accessed 20 Aug 2019

26. Google Inc.: Word2Vec. https://code.google.com/archive/p/word2veca/. Accessed 20 Aug 2019

27. Hall, M., Frank, E., Holmes, G., Pfahringer, B., Reutemann, P. Witten, I.: The WEKA data mining software. ACM SIGKDD Explor. Newsl. **11**(1) (2009)

28. GRAIT-DM.: The Annotated Landslide Dataset. http://grait-dm.gatech.edu. Accessed 20 Aug 2019

29. Musaev, A., Pu, C.: Landslide information service based on composition of physical and social sensors. In: International Conference on Data Engineering (2017)

30. Power, L.: The Notre Dame fire garnered wall-to-wall cable news coverage. The Amazon fires are barely breaking through. https://www.mediamatters.org/msnbc/notre-dame-fire-garnered-wall-wall-cable-news-coverage-amazon-fires-are-barely-breaking. Accessed 20 Aug 2019

31. He, Z., Cai, Z., Wang, X.: Modeling propagation dynamics and developing optimized countermeasures for rumor spreading in online social networks. In: The 35th IEEE International Conference on Distributed Computing Systems (2015)

32. He, Z., Cai, Z., Yu, J., Wang, X., Sun, Y., Li, Y.: Cost-efficient strategies for restraining rumor spreading in mobile social networks. IEEE Trans. Veh. Technol. **66**(3), 2789–2800 (2017)

33. Hswen, Y., Qin, Q., Brownstein, J.S., Hawkins, J.B.: Feasibility of using social media to monitor outdoor air pollution in London. England. Prev. Med. **121**, 86–93 (2019)

34. Nsoesie, E.O., et al.: Social Media as a Sentinel for Disease Surveillance: What Does Sociodemographic Status Have to Do with It? PLOTS Current Outbreaks (2016)

35. Han, M., Miao, D., Wang, J., Liu, L.: Defend the clique-based attack for data privacy. In: Kim, D., Uma, R., Zelikovsky, A. (eds.) International Conference on Combinatorial Optimization and Applications, pp. 262–280. Springer, Cham (2018). https://doi.org/10.1007/978-3-030-04651-4_18

36. Albinali, H., Han, M., Wang, J., Gao, H., Li, Y.: The roles of social network mavens. In: 2016 12th International Conference on Mobile Ad-Hoc and Sensor Networks (MSN), pp. 1–8. IEEE, December 2016

37. Han, M., Yan, M., Li, J., Ji, S., Li, Y.: Neighborhood-based uncertainty generation in social networks. J. Comb. Optim. **28**(3), 561–576 (2014)

Reduced-Bias Co-trained Ensembles for Weakly Supervised Cyberbullying Detection

Elaheh Raisi$^{(\boxtimes)}$ and Bert Huang

Virginia Tech, Blacksburg, VA, USA
{elaheh,bhuang}@vt.edu

Abstract. Social media reflects many aspects of society, including social biases against individuals based on sensitive characteristics such as gender, race, religion, physical ability, and sexual orientation. Machine learning algorithms trained on social media data may therefore perpetuate or amplify discriminatory attitudes against various demographic groups, causing unfair decision-making. One important application for machine learning is the automatic detection of cyberbullying. Biases in this context could take the form of bullying detectors that make false detections more frequently on messages by or about certain identity groups. In this paper, we present an approach for training bullying detectors from weak supervision while reducing the degree to which learned models reflect or amplify discriminatory biases in the data. Our goal is to decrease the sensitivity of models to language describing particular social groups. An ideal, fair language-based detector should treat language describing subpopulations of particular social groups equitably. Building on a previously proposed weakly supervised learning algorithm, we penalize the model when discrimination is observed. By penalizing unfairness, we encourage the learning algorithm to avoid unfair behavior in its predictions and achieve equitable treatment for protected subpopulations. We introduce two unfairness penalty terms: one aimed at removal fairness and another at substitutional fairness. We quantitatively and qualitatively evaluate the resulting models' fairness on a synthetic benchmark and data from Twitter comparing against crowdsourced annotation.

Keywords: Cyberbullying detection · Social media · Weakly supervised machine learning · Co-trained ensemble · Fairness in machine learning · Embedding models

1 Introduction

As a technology to better connect individuals, social media introduces benefits that can be nullified by the detrimental behaviors it amplifies, such as online harassment, cyberbullying, hate speech, and online trolling [2]. The serious consequences of these behaviors compels the development of automated, data-driven

© Springer Nature Switzerland AG 2019
A. Tagarelli and H. Tong (Eds.): CSoNet 2019, LNCS 11917, pp. 293–306, 2019.
https://doi.org/10.1007/978-3-030-34980-6_32

techniques for detecting such behaviors. A key concern in the development and adoption of machine learning for building harassment detectors is whether the learned detectors are *fair*. Most machine learning models trained on social media data can inherit or amplify biases present in training data, or they can fabricate biases that are not present in the data. Biases in harassment detectors could be characterized as when harassment detectors are more sensitive to harassment committed by or against particular groups of individuals, such as members of ethnic, gender, sexual orientation, or age groups, which result in more false detections on protected target groups. Recent reactions to a Google Jigsaw tool for quantifying toxicity of online conversations (see e.g., a post by Sinders [23]) have highlighted such concerns. A flaw of these detectors is how differently they flag language used by or about particular groups of people.

Our goal in this paper is to address discrimination against particular groups of people in the context of cyberbullying detection. Many machine learning algorithms have been introduced to detect cyberbullying in social media. Raisi and Huang in [21] introduced a framework called *co-trained ensembles*, which uses weak supervision to significantly alleviate the need for tedious data annotation. Their weak supervision is in the form of expert-provided key phrases that are highly indicative or counter-indicative of bullying. In addition, their framework is based on consistency of two detectors that co-train one another. These detectors use two different perspectives of the data: (1) language and (2) social structure. By using different forms of evidence, the detectors train to reach the same conclusion about whether social interactions are bullying. Furthermore, they incorporate distributed word and graph-node representations by training nonlinear deep models.

With the advantages of weakly supervised training, there is also a concern that the self-training mechanism used to amplify the weak supervision may also amplify patterns of societal bias. Therefore, in this paper, we extend the co-trained ensemble model to mitigate unfair behavior in the trained model. We add unfairness penalties to the training framework introduced by Raisi and Huang [21] when we observe discrimination in predictions. We explore two unfairness penalty terms, each aiming toward a different notion of fairness. One targets *removal fairness* and the other targets *substitutional fairness*. For removal fairness, we penalize the model if the score of a message containing sensitive keywords is higher than if those keywords were removed. For substitutional fairness, for each protected group, we provide a list of sensitive keywords and appropriate substitutions. For example, for the keyword "black" describes an ethnicity, and substitutions are "asian", "american", "middle-eastern", etc. A fair model would score a message containing any sensitive keyword the same if we replace that sensitive keyword with another; otherwise, we penalize the objective function.

We measure the learned model's fairness on synthetic data and a dataset of Twitter messages. Our synthetic data is a corpus of sentences generated using the combination of some sensitive keywords describing different attributes: sexual orientation, race, gender, and religion. Mirroring the benchmark established by Raisi and Huang [20], we generated statements of identity (e.g., "black woman", "muslim middle-eastern man") that are not harassment. To assess each model's fairness, we compute the *false-positive rate* on these identity statements. Since these statements are not bullying, an ideal fair language-based detector should yield a lower false-positive rate on these examples. For evaluation on Twitter data, we measure model fairness using the equality of odds gaps [10]. Specifically, we use a criterion we call *category dispersion*, which is the standard deviation of area under the curve (AUC) of receiver operating characteristic (ROC) curves across multiple keywords in a category of substitutable keywords. A low category dispersion is more desirable since it indicates that a model treats the subpopulations equitably. A high category dispersion indicates that the model behavior is more favorable toward some subgroups; hence, it discriminates against some other subpopulations. We also test each model's fairness qualitatively by examining conversations with sensitive keywords where their score using the reduced-bias model is much lower than the default model. In another qualitative analysis, we examine the change in the bullying score of sensitive keywords when fairness imposed to the harassment detector. Together, our evaluations demonstrate the ability of our approach to reduce the biases of weakly supervised bullying detectors.

2 Related Work

This study mainly builds on two bodies of research: machine learning for detection of online harassment and cyberbullying, and fairness in machine learning. We cover only the most directly relevant literature because of limited space.

Online Harassment and Cyberbullying Detection. A variety of methods have been proposed for cyberbullying detection. These methods mostly approach the problem by treating it as a classification task, where messages are independently classified as bullying or not. Many of the research contributions in this space involve the specialized design of message features for supervised learning. Many contributions consider features based on known topics used in bullying [5,7,22], sentiment [27], topic models [17], vulgar language expansion [19], audio and video features [24], and social structure features [3,4,14,30]. Hosseinmardi et al. studied negative user behavior in the Ask.fm and Instagram [11,12]. Tomkins et al. propose a probabilistic model [25] for cyberbullying detection. Raisi and Huang [20,21] introduced a weakly supervised machine learning method for cyberbullying detection. Our work builds on their approach.

Fairness in Machine Learning. In recent years, there has been rapid progress in designing *fair* machine learning algorithms. Machine learning algorithms can exhibit discriminatory decision making in areas such as recommendation, prediction, and classification [1,15]. Various fairness measures have been introduced such as *equal opportunity* [10] and *disparate mistreatment* [28]. Zhang et al. [29] examine three fairness measures: demographic parity, equality of odds, and equality of opportunity in the context of adversarial debiasing. Garg et al. [8]

introduce counterfactual fairness in text classification by substituting individual tokens related to sensitive attributes. This approach is similar to ours in this paper, but our method is aimed toward weakly supervised learning for cyberbullying detection.

3 Review of Co-trained Ensembles for Weak Supervision

In this section, we review the co-trained ensemble framework introduced by Raisi and Huang [21] and how it is applied to train cyberbullying detectors. The approach learns from weak supervision by seeking consensus between two model families: (1) message classifiers and (2) user classifiers. Message classifiers take a message as input and output a classification score for whether the message is an example of harassment. User classifiers take an ordered pair of users as input and output a score indicating whether one user is harassing the other user. For message classifiers, the framework accommodates a generalized form of weakly supervised loss function ℓ (which could be extended to also allow full or partial supervision). Let Θ be the model parameters for the combined ensemble of both classifiers. The training objective is

$$\min_{\Theta} \underbrace{\frac{1}{2|M|} \sum_{m \in M} (f(m; \Theta) - g\left(s(m), r(m); \Theta\right))^2}_{\text{consistency loss}} + \underbrace{\frac{1}{|M|} \sum_{m \in M} \ell\left(f(m; \Theta)\right)}_{\text{weak supervision loss}} \quad (1)$$

where M is a set of all messages and $s(m)$ and $r(m)$ are the sender and receiver of message m. The first loss function is a consistency loss, and the second loss function is the weak supervision loss. The consistency loss penalizes the disagreement between the scores output by the message classifier for each message and the user classifier for the sender and receiver of the message. The weak supervision relies on annotated lists of key-phrases that are indicative or counter-indicative of harassment. Let there be a set of indicator phrases and a set of counter-indicator phrases for harassment. The weak supervision loss ℓ is based on the fraction of indicators and counter-indicators in each message, so for a message containing $n(m)$ total key-phrases, let $n^{+}(m)$ denote the number of indicator phrases in message m and $n^{-}(m)$ denote the number of counter-indicator phrases in the message. The weak supervision loss is

$$\ell(y_m) = -\log\left(\min\left\{1, 1 + (1 - \tfrac{n^{-}(m)}{n(m)}) - y_m\right\}\right) - \log\left(\min\left\{1, 1 + y_m - \tfrac{n^{+}(m)}{n(m)}\right\}\right). \quad (2)$$

Within this framework, they used classifiers built on vector representations of message and users. Vector embeddings of text are incorporated into the framework in two ways: (1) using existing word-embedding models as inputs to message classifier, (2) creating new embedding models specifically geared for analysis of cyberbullying. The user classifiers represent each user as a vector, classifying the vector pair as either a bullying or a non-bullying relationship.

Raisi and Huang [21] examined four message classifiers: (1) BoW: a randomly hashed bag of n-grams model with 1,000 hash functions [26], (2) doc2vec: a linear classifier based on the pre-trained doc2vec vector of messages trained on the dataset [16], (3) emb: a custom-trained embedding model with each word represented with 100 dimensions, (4) RNN: a recurrent neural network with two hidden layers of dimensionality 100. The emb and RNN models are trained end-to-end to optimize overall loss function, while pre-trained models (BoW, doc2vec) are used to only adjust the linear classifier weights given the fixed vector representations for each message. For the user classifiers, they use a linear classifier on concatenated vector representations of the sender and receiver nodes. To compute the user vector representations, they pre-train a node2vec [9] representation of the communication graph. The pre-trained user vectors are then the input to a linear classifier that is trained during the learning process. There are eight combinations of message and user learners (including the option to use no user learner, in which case we use the weak supervision loss to train message classifiers).

According to the quantitative experimental evaluation in [21], the top five combinations of text and user classifiers that produce the highest precision@100 **on Twitter** are: "emb_none", "emb_node2vec", "bow_none", "rnn_none", and "doc2vec_node2vec". In our experiments, we do not consider "rnn_none" because its performance was similar to "bow_none" but was much more computationally expensive. Therefore, we use four configurations of their ensemble framework for our experiments.

4   Reduced-Bias Co-trained Ensembles

In this section, we introduce our approach to reduce bias in co-trained ensemble models. Our goal is to disregard discriminatory biases in the training data and create fair models for cyberbullying detection. We add a term to the loss function to penalize the model when we observe discrimination in the predictions. We investigate the effectiveness of two such *unfairness penalty terms*.

Removal Fairness. The motivation for *removal fairness* is that, in a fair model, the score of a message containing sensitive keywords should not be higher than the same sentence without these keywords. Therefore, we penalize the model with an unfairness loss:

$$\ell(y_m) = \alpha \times - \log \left(\min \left\{ 1, 1 - (y_m - y_{m-}) \right\} \right). \tag{3}$$

where y_m is the score of message containing sensitive keywords and y_{m-} is the score of the same message when sensitive keywords are dropped. The parameter α represents to what extent we enforce fairness to the model. In our experiments, we examined three values $\alpha \in \{1, 10, 100\}$. The best value resulting better generalization and lower validation error was $\alpha = 10$.

Substitutional Fairness. In *substitutional fairness*, for each category of sensitive keyword, we provide a list of sensitive keywords and appropriate substitutions. For example, the keyword "black" describes a type of ethnicity, so substitutions are "asian", "native-american", "middle-eastern", etc. Or the keyword "gay" describes a sexual orientation, so it can be substituted with "straight", "bisexual", "bi", etc. In a fair model, the score of a message containing a sensitive keyword should not change if we replace that sensitive keyword with its substitutions. We penalize the objective function with

$$\ell(y_m) = \frac{\alpha}{|S_c| - 1} \times \sum_{i \in S_c, i \neq k} \left(y_{m(k)} - y_{m(i)}\right)^2. \qquad (4)$$

where S_c is the set of all sensitive keywords in category c, $|S_c|$ is the cardinality of set S_c, $y_{m(k)}$ is the score of original sentence containing sensitive keyword k in category c, and $y_{m(i)}$ is the score of the substitution sentence with sensitive keyword i in category c. As with removal fairness, α represents the strength of the unfairness penalty. We tested $\alpha \in \{1, 10, 100\}$, and the value 10 again led to the best validation error.

5   Experiments

Mirroring the setup initially used to evaluate the co-trained ensemble framework, we construct a weak supervision signal by collecting a dictionary of offensive key-phrases (unigrams and bigrams) [18]. For our weak supervision, we manually curated a collection of 516 high-precision bullying key phrases that do not specifically target particular groups. We augment this with a list of positive opinion words collected by Hu and Liu [13]. The offensive phrases are our weak indicators and the positive words are our counter-indicators. Out of eight combinations of message and user learners introduced in [21], we selected the top four models with the highest precision@100 on Twitter for our evaluation: "emb_none", "emb_node2vec", "bow_none", and "doc2vec_node2vec".

We consider four categories of sensitive keywords: race, gender, religion, and sexual orientation. For each category, we provide a list of keywords. Some example keywords in the race category are "white", "black", "caucasian", "asian", "indian", and "latina"; and some example keywords in religion category are "christian", "jewish", "muslim", "mormon", and "hindu". In each message, there might be many sensitive keywords. Hence, for computational purposes, we limit the number of substitutions to a randomly selected 20 substituted sentences.

Evaluation on Synthetic Data. We analyze the sensitivity of models toward some often targeted groups on a synthetic benchmark established by [20]. This benchmark is a corpus of sentences using the combination of sensitive keywords describing different attributes. These statements of identity (e.g., "I am a Black woman", "I am a Muslim middle-eastern man", etc.) are not bullying since they are simply stating one's identity. In total, there are 2,777 non-bullying statements. To assess each model's fairness, we compute the *false-positive rate* on these synthetic benchmark statements. An ideal fair language-based detector should yield a lower false-positive rate on these non-toxic statements. Table 1 shows the *false-positive rates* (at threshold 0.5) of four aforementioned co-trained

Table 1. False positive rate of models on non-bullying synthetic benchmark statements (using threshold 0.5). Both *removal* and *substitutional* fair models reduce the false positive rate compare to without bias reduction (vanilla).

Method	emb_none	emb_node2vec	bow_none	doc2vec_node2vec
Vanilla	0.8416	0.7055	0.2663	0.0000
Substitutional	0.7685	0.1439	0.0305	0.0000
Removal	0.0000	0.0418	0.0000	0.0000

ensembles with and without penalizing unfairness. Since the generated statements are not bullying, the false-positive rate of an ideal fair model should be 0.0. According to the results in Table 1, the false-positive rate of these four methods reduces when either removal or substitutional fairness constraints applied. When removal fairness is imposed to the "emb_none" and "bow_none", their false-positive rate reduced to zero. The false-positive rate of "doc2vec_node2vec" with and without enforcing fairness is zero. Since the synthetic data does not have social networks to train node2vec, we just used the message learner to give bullying score to these statements.

Evaluation on Twitter. We use the data collected by Raisi and Huang [21]. They collected data from Twitter's public API, extracting tweets containing offensive-language words posted between November 1, 2015, and December 14, 2015. They then extracted conversations and reply chains that included these tweets. They then used snowball sampling to gather tweets in a wide range of topics. After some preprocessing, the Twitter data contains 180,355 users and 296,308 tweets.

We evaluate the effectiveness of our approach using post-hoc crowdsourced annotation to analyze the score of fair-imposed model for conversations with sensitive keywords. We extract all of the conversations in Twitter data containing at least one sensitive keyword. We then asked crowdsource workers from Amazon Mechanical Turk to evaluate the interactions. We showed the annotators the anonymized conversations and asked them, "Do you think either user 1 or user 2 is harassing the other?" The annotators indicated either "yes", "no", or "uncertain". We collected three annotations per conversation. For each of the three annotators, we score a positive response as +1, a negative response as −1, and an uncertain response as 0. We sum these scores for each interaction, and we consider the interaction to be harassment if the score is 2 or greater.

To measure a model's fairness, we use an "equality of odds" criterion, which states all subpopulations in a group experience the same true- or false-positive rate [10]. We generalize a notation "accuracy equity" [6]. We compute the standard deviation of the area under the curve (AUC) of the receiver order characteristic (ROC) for messages containing keywords in a category of sensitive keywords. We refer to this measure as *category dispersion*. For example, in the "religion" category, we compute the category dispersion across different keywords in this category such as "muslim", "christian", "jewish", "protestant", etc. An ideal,

Table 2. The category dispersion of four co-trained ensemble methods for three targeted groups. A bold value means the category dispersion of the reduced-bias model is lower than the default method (vanilla). Substitutional emb_none and doc2vec_node2vec have better category dispersion than the vanilla method in all three groups.

Category	Fairness type	emb_none	emb_node2vec	bow_none	doc2vec_node2vec
Race	Vanilla	0.0937	0.0525	0.0231	0.0546
	Substitutional	**0.0531**	0.0528	0.0514	**0.0460**
	Removal	**0.0640**	0.0594	0.0665	0.0587
Religion	Vanilla	0.0858	0.0862	0.0716	0.0748
	Substitutional	**0.0657**	**0.0376**	**0.0660**	**0.0494**
	Removal	0.0902	**0.0424**	**0.0190**	**0.0661**
Sexual orientation	Vanilla	0.1096	0.0791	0.0915	0.0702
	Substitutional	**0.0629**	0.0821	**0.0666**	**0.0623**
	Removal	**0.0894**	0.0914	**0.0467**	0.0784

fair language-based detector should treat these keywords equitably, which would induce a lower category dispersion.

Table 2 shows the category dispersions of methods on each targeted group. We bold values when the category dispersion of the reduced-bias method is lower than the vanilla learner (without fairness), which indicates that the reduced-biased model treats the keywords in the protected category more equitably. Enforcing substitutional fairness on emb_none and doc2vec_node2vec leads to fairer models across all three categories. Enforcing substitutional fairness on bow_none leads to fairer models in two out of three categories; and substitutional emb_node2vec is fairer for only the religion category. Enforcing removal fairness on emb_none, doc2vec_node2vec, and bow_none leads to fairer behavior in two out of three categories, while doing so on emb_node2vec only treats keywords in the religion category more equitably. In summary, emb_none and doc2vec_node2vec, when trained with substitutional fairness terms produce lower standard deviation of AUC across keywords for all three tested categories.

An important question is whether there is accuracy degradation as our approach encourages more equitable errors within categories. In Fig. 1, we plot the ROC curve of four co-trained ensemble methods stratified by fairness type. Surprisingly, the AUC of substitutional bow_none, emb_none, and doc2vec_node2vec actually improve over the default approach. The performance of removal emb_none improves over vanilla, but other methods' performance reduce when adding removal fairness. In Fig. 2 we compare the ROC curve of emb_none method for some sensitive keywords for the categories of sexual orientation and religion. The ROC curves of sensitive keywords in each group are closer to each other in both removal and substitutional fair methods, while the AUC of most keywords in the substitutional and removal versions are higher than the vanilla approach. This trend indicates that bias-reduction successfully equalizes behavior across language describing different subpopulations of people.

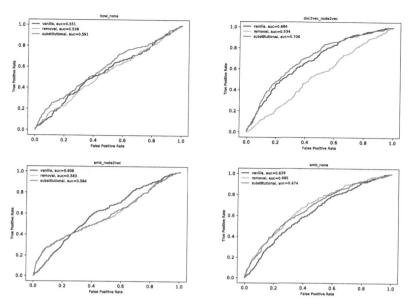

Fig. 1. ROC curve of the four co-trained ensemble methods stratified by fairness type. The performance of substitutional bow_none, doc2vec_node2vec, and emb_none improves over the vanilla method. Removal emb_none also improves over vanilla, but emb_node2vec has worse performance.

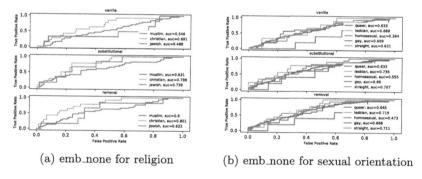

(a) emb_none for religion   (b) emb_none for sexual orientation

Fig. 2. ROC curves for the emb_none model on data containing sensitive keywords in the sexual orientation and religion categories. The gap between AUC of sensitive keywords in these two groups reduces, without degradation in performance.

Qualitative Analysis. We qualitatively test the model's fairness by analyzing the highest scoring conversations identified by the models. An ideal fair model should give a lower score to non-bullying interactions containing sensitive keywords. Figure 3 displays three non-bullying conversations highly ranked by the vanilla model, but given a low score by the reduced-bias model.

User1: all figure that you are, in fact, **gay** and theyre freaking out about it? F*CK THOSE PEOPLE. User2: I think my Uncle has figured it out, him & my cuz are always trying to out me, I feel nervous/sick every time theyre around.
User1: Alienate minorities? Why would anyone, of any color, stand w/ppl that dont believe al lives matter? User2: All Lives matter Is a gasp of a little racist mind, when Cops shot white boys at racist of **Blacks** then OK
User1: you cant really be racist against a religion... User2: i know my friend but you can be racist against followers of this religion.iam an exMuslim but refuse to be a racist against them User1: Racist is hating someone based in their skin color, not their faith. Hating someone just for their faith is just bigotry. User2: remamber the **Jewish** and the holocaust or you think it wasnt racist!!!!!!!!!!!! #ExMuslim-Because User1: **Jewish** can be a race or a religion. There is no Muslim race. Theres an Arab race, but you cant assume Arabs are Muslim.

Fig. 3. Three examples of conversations given a high score by the vanilla model and given a low score by a reduced-bias model. These conversations discuss sensitive topics but may not represent one user bullying another.

We also compare the bullying score of messages containing only one sensitive keyword with and without bias reduction. We consider the scores of embedding message classifiers since they learned a vector representation for all words in corpus. We plot the scores in Fig. 4. Our findings are as follows: The score of most sensitive keywords in the ethnicity category, such as "black", "indian", "african", "american", "asian", "hispanic", and "white" reduces when fairness is imposed on the model. The reason the keyword "white" is scored higher using the vanilla model could be the occurrence of this word in bullying interactions in our dataset. In the gender category, the score of "boy" and "man" increases when imposing substitutional fairness, but the score of "girl" and "woman" either reduces or does not change. In the religion category, the bullying score of "muslim", "protestant", "mormon", and "jewish" reduce when fairness is imposed. In the sexual orientation category, the score of "transexual", "queer", "lesbian", "bi", "heterosexual", "homosexual", and "straight" reduce using biased-reduced models.

One interesting observation is how well the score of message with sensitive keywords becomes more uniform after enforcing the fairness to the model. More particularly, in the emb_node2vec model, the score of two keywords "boy" and "girl" get closer to each other after imposing substitutional fairness. This is also true for "woman" and "man". By scrutinizing the behavior of the emb_none model, we observe a remarkable change in the score of sensitive keywords when fairness is imposed on the model. Its vanilla version gives the highest bullying score to most sensitive keywords, but the scores reduce noticeably when fairness is imposed. On the other hand, the score of some keywords using the vanilla method is significantly low, but when fairness terms are applied, their scores increase. An open question is whether this significant variation is desirable especially with considering the performance improvement of emb_none in our quantitative analysis.

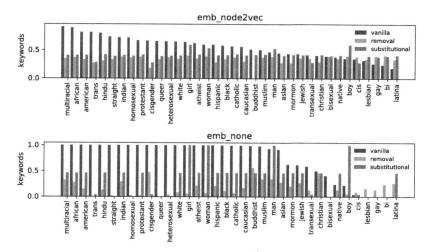

Fig. 4. Bullying scores of messages containing only one sensitive keyword as scored by emb_none and emb_node2vec with and without fairness terms. The bullying score of most sensitive keywords reduce when fairness is imposed on the model, and the scores become more uniform than without any fairness terms (vanilla).

Discussion. One question that might arise is which fairness objective best provides the desired fairness? Considering our quantitative analysis in Table 2, which follows the equality of odds criterion, substitutional constraints improve the AUC gap of more groups for each method. However, the difference is not significant. Both penalty terms reduce the false-positive rate on the synthetic benchmark. Another question is which combination of model architecture and fairness objective has better behavior? Table 2 suggests emb_none and doc2vec_node2vec with substitutional fairness a produce lower AUC gap between keywords for all three groups. One might ask about the trade-off between accuracy and fairness. As shown in Fig. 2, adding a fairness term reduces the accuracy of emb_node2vec, but emb_node2vec is also unable to produce fair predictions either. This pattern suggests that emb_node2vec is not compatible with the introduced fairness constraints. The emb_none and doc2vec_node2vec models have better fairness behavior with the substitutional objective, and their accuracy also improves. The removal objective, however, reduces the accuracy when added to most models.

6   Conclusion

Fairness is one of the most important challenges for automated cyberbullying detection. As researchers develop machine learning approaches to detect cyberbullying, it is critical to ensure these methods are not reflecting or amplifying discriminatory biases. In this paper, we introduce a method for training a less biased machine learning model for cyberbullying analysis. We add unfairness penalties to the learning objective function to penalize the model when we observe discrimination in the model's predictions. We introduce two fairness penalty terms based on removal and substitutional fairness. We use these fairness terms to augment co-trained ensembles, a weakly supervised learning framework [21]. We evaluate our approach on a synthetic benchmark and real data from Twitter. Our experiments on the synthetic benchmark show lower *false-positive rates* when fairness is imposed on the model. To quantitatively evaluate model's fairness on Twitter, we use an equality of odds measure that computes the standard deviation of AUC for messages containing sensitive keywords in a category. A fair model should treat all keywords in each category equitably, i.e., have a lower standard deviation. We observe that two ensemble learners, when augmented with substitutional fairness, reduce the gap between keywords in three groups, while their detection performance actually improves. We did not always observe such behavior when models were augmented with removal fairness. In addition, we qualitatively evaluate the framework, extracting conversations highly scored by the vanilla model but not flagged by the bias-reduced models. These conversations tended to be false-positive, non-bullying conversations that used sensitive language. We therefore demonstrate the capability to reduce unfairness in cyberbullying detectors trained with weak supervision.

References

1. Bolukbasi, T., Chang, K., Zou, J.Y., Saligrama, V., Kalai, A.: Man is to computer programmer as woman is to homemaker? Debiasing word embeddings. CoRR abs/1607.06520 (2016)
2. Boyd, D.: It's Complicated. Yale University Press, New Haven (2014)
3. Chatzakou, D., Kourtellis, N., Blackburn, J., Cristofaro, E.D., Stringhini, G., Vakali, A.: Mean birds: detecting aggression and bullying on Twitter. CoRR abs/1702.06877 (2017)
4. Chelmis, C., Zois, D.S., Yao, M.: Mining patterns of cyberbullying on Twitter. In: 2017 IEEE International Conference on Data Mining Workshops (ICDMW), pp. 126–133 (2017)
5. Chen, Y., Zhou, Y., Zhu, S., Xu, H.: Detecting offensive language in social media to protect adolescent online safety. In: International Conference on Social Computing, pp. 71–80 (2012)
6. Dieterich, W., Mendoza, C., Brennan, T.: Compas risk scales: demonstrating accuracy equity and predictive parity performance of the compas risk scales in broward county (2016)
7. Dinakar, K., Reichart, R., Lieberman, H.: Modeling the detection of textual cyberbullying. In: ICWSM Workshop on Social Mobile Web (2011)
8. Garg, S., Perot, V., Limtiaco, N., Taly, A., Chi, E.H., Beutel, A.: Counterfactual fairness in text classification through robustness. CoRR abs/1809.10610 (2018)
9. Grover, A., Leskovec, J.: node2vec: scalable feature learning for networks. CoRR abs/1607.00653 (2016)

10. Hardt, M., Price, E., Srebro, N.: Equality of opportunity in supervised learning. CoRR abs/1610.02413 (2016)
11. Hosseinmardi, H., Ghasemianlangroodi, A., Han, R., Lv, Q., Mishra, S.: Towards understanding cyberbullying behavior in a semi-anonymous social network. In: International Conference on Advances in Social Networks Analysis and Mining, pp. 244–252 (2014)
12. Hosseinmardi, H., Mattson, S.A., Rafiq, R.I., Han, R., Lv, Q., Mishra, S.: Detection of cyberbullying incidents on the Instagram social network. Association for the Advancement of Artificial Intelligence (2015)
13. Hu, M., Liu, B.: Mining and summarizing customer reviews. In: Proceedings of the ACM SIGKDD International Conference on Knowledge Discovery and Data Mining, pp. 168–177 (2004)
14. Huang, Q., Singh, V.K.: Cyber bullying detection using social and textual analysis. In: Proceedings of the International Workshop on Socially-Aware Multimedia, pp. 3–6 (2014)
15. Kim, M.P., Ghorbani, A., Zou, J.Y.: Multiaccuracy: black-box post-processing for fairness in classification. CoRR abs/1805.12317 (2018)
16. Le, Q., Mikolov, T.: Distributed representations of sentences and documents. In: Proceedings of the International Conference on Machine Learning, pp. 1188–1196 (2014)
17. Nahar, V., Li, X., Pang, C.: An effective approach for cyberbullying detection. Commun. Inf. Sci. Manag. Eng. **3**(5), 238–247 (2013)
18. noswearing.com: List of swear words & curse words (2016). http://www.noswearing.com
19. Ptaszynski, M., Dybala, P., Matsuba, T., Masui, F., Rzepka, R., Araki, K.: Machine learning and affect analysis against cyber-bullying. In: Linguistic and Cognitive Approaches to Dialog Agents Symposium, pp. 7–16 (2010)
20. Raisi, E., Huang, B.: Co-trained ensemble models for weakly supervised cyberbullying detection. In: NeurIPS Workshop on Learning with Limited Labeled Data (2017)
21. Raisi, E., Huang, B.: Weakly supervised cyberbullying detection using co-trained ensembles of embedding models. In: Proceedings of the IEEE/ACM International Conference on Social Networks Analysis and Mining, pp. 479–486 (2018)
22. Rezvan, M., Shekarpour, S., Thirunarayan, K., Shalin, V.L., Sheth, A.P.: Analyzing and learning the language for different types of harassment. CoRR abs/1811.00644 (2018)
23. Sinders, C.: Toxicity and tone are not the same thing: analyzing the new Google API on toxicity, PerspectiveAPI (2017). https://medium.com/@carolinesinders/toxicity-and-tone-are-not-the-same-thing-analyzing-the-new-google-api-on-toxicity-perspectiveapi-14abe4e728b3
24. Soni, D., Singh, V.K.: See no evil, hear no evil: audio-visual-textual cyberbullying detection. Proc. ACM Hum.-Comput. Interact. **2**, 164:1–164:26 (2018)
25. Tomkins, S., Getoor, L., Chen, Y., Zhang, Y.: A socio-linguistic model for cyberbullying detection. In: International Conference on Advances in Social Networks Analysis and Mining (2018)
26. Weinberger, K., Dasgupta, A., Langford, J., Smola, A., Attenberg, J.: Feature hashing for large scale multitask learning. In: Proceedings of the International Conference on Machine Learning, pp. 1113–1120 (2009)
27. Yin, D., Xue, Z., Hong, L., Davison, B.D., Kontostathis, A., Edwards, L.: Detection of harassment on Web 2.0. Content Analysis in the WEB 2.0 (2009)

28. Zafar, M.B., Valera, I., Gomez Rodriguez, M., Gummadi, K.P.: Fairness beyond disparate treatment & disparate impact: learning classification without disparate mistreatment. In: Proceedings of the International Conference on World Wide Web, pp. 1171–1180 (2017)
29. Zhang, B.H., Lemoine, B., Mitchell, M.: Mitigating unwanted biases with adversarial learning. CoRR abs/1801.07593 (2018)
30. Zois, D.S., Kapodistria, A., Yao, M., Chelmis, C.: Optimal online cyberbullying detection. In: 2018 IEEE International Conference on Acoustics, Speech and Signal Processing, pp. 2017–2021 (2018)

A Novel Privacy-Preserving Socio-technical Platform for Detecting Cyber Abuse (*Extended Abstract*)

Sriram Chellappan[✉] and Nathan Fisk

Department of Computer Science and Engineering and College of Education,
University of South Florida, Tampa, USA
{sriramc,fisk}@usf.edu

Abstract. In this abstract, we present perspectives on on-going work by the authors in creating a massive scale digital platform that enables youth to share content that suits their own privacy expectations, while still contributing to cyber-abuse research.

1   Design of Our Data Collection Platform

Currently, research in cyber-abuse suffers from two problems: (a) linguistic differences between younger people (i.e., victims) and adults (that flag abuse) in cyber space [1] and (b) IRB regulations that are strict in protecting vulnerable subjects (e.g., children) in research [2]. As a result, existing research in cyber-abuse lacks robust ground truth datasets, that incorporates victim perspectives.

Figure 1 illustrates our platform that aims to correct the above trend. We design a smart-phone app that allows users (in this case younger people) to download the app after their parents/guardians consent. Users will then be asked a series of questions on the app related to situations of discomfort they have faced in the past, along with a timeline of related event(s). Subsequently, meta-data of communication logs that are in the vicinity of the event(s) described are searched and retrieved within the device, and displayed to the user. The meta-data logs in our current prototype are only (a) the exact times of communication; (b) whether the communication was sent or received; (c) the sizes of the content of communication (i.e., sizes of textual or imagery or video content); (d) whether the communication was bi-directional or within a group; and (e) results of sentiment analysis algorithms applied on textual messages. For our prototype, only SMS logs are processed, but the system can be easily expanded to other content with right permissions. All user identities are anonymized. These meta-data logs (which are highly privacy preserving) are exported upon user assent to a secure cloud, where a domain expert will process user entered responses and follow up

This work was supported in part by US National Science Foundation. Findings and conclusions are those of the authors alone, and not necessarily those of the funding agency.

A. Tagarelli and H. Tong (Eds.): CSoNet 2019, LNCS 11917, pp. 307–308, 2019.
https://doi.org/10.1007/978-3-030-34980-6_33

with a subject on a need basis via the app only. Note though all user responses are filtered if any identifiable information like names, phone numbers, emails etc. are provided before uploading to the cloud.

2   Challenges

We are currently demoing our prototype, and surveying many stakeholders - young people, parents, counselors, tech developers and privacy/law experts also to assess our system from multiple angles including usability, efficacy, privacy-preservation and maintenance cost. We are already getting interesting results. While there is near unanimous agreement on the fact that perspectives of victims (in this case young people) are considered for abuse detection, there is some push back from the tech community in terms of data sharing (even meta-data). There were concerns raised on long-term privacy implications, especially on the power of longitudinal meta-data to identify individuals. Furthermore, with meta-alone, there are interesting algorithmic challenges ahead for us on identifying and modeling network topologies, especially under churn.

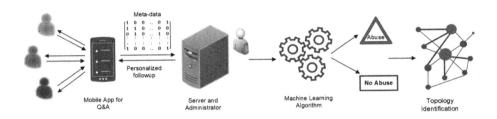

Fig. 1. Workflow of our platform

3   Insights for Future

Should we resolve all challenges (technical and social) satisfactorily, we will be piloting our system soon. With larger scale participation and massive scale meta-data, future work includes design of algorithms to (a) flag abuse at early stages; (b) classify the type of abuse; (c) detect changes in patterns of abuse at the individual level; (d) identify group dynamics during abuse; (e) model the evolution of the generated social network toplogies and so much more. Ensuring privacy, while simultaneously keeping the end users engaged on this important global problem today are the most significant aspects of our research.

References

1. Selwyn, N.: The digital native-myth and reality. In: Aslib Proceedings, vol. 61, pp. 364–379. Emerald Group Publishing Limited (2009)
2. Glantz, L.H.: Conducting research with children: legal and ethical issues. J. Am. Acad. Child Adolesc. Psychiatry **35**(20), 1283–1291 (1996)

Projection-Based Coverage Algorithms in 3D Camera Sensor Networks for Indoor Objective Tracking

Yi Hong[1], Yongcai Wang[2(✉)], Yuqing Zhu[3], Deying Li[2], Mengjie Chang[4], and Zhibo Chen[1]

[1] School of Information Science and Technology, Beijing Forestry University, Beijing 100083, People's Republic of China
[2] School of Information, Renmin University of China, Beijing 100872, People's Republic of China
ycw@ruc.edu.cn
[3] Department of Computer Science, California State University Los Angeles, Los Angeles, CA 90032, USA
[4] Information Engineering College, Beijing Institute of Petrochemical Technology, Beijing 102617, People's Republic of China

Abstract. For persistent objective tracking based on camera sensor networks, sensor deployment and scheduling are challenging problems especially in indoor environments. In this paper, we focus on the indoor objective tracking in three-dimensional (3D) camera sensor networks (CSNs) and aim to design the scheduling strategies to guarantee the coverage quality of the objective trajectory. We introduce the active-period-minimizing scheduling problem in CSNs for indoor objective tracking, with the goal of minimizing the total active durations of all the sensors. To solve the problem, we propose a pair of projection scheduling algorithms from the perspectives of the sensors and the trajectory correspondingly. To evaluate the algorithm performance on the time efficiency, we conduct extensive simulation experiments and their results indicate the proposed algorithms' advantages on time efficiency.

Keywords: Objective tracking · Camera sensor networks · Coverage quality · Projection scheduling

1 Introduction

With the requirements of accuracy and richness of supervision information, CSNs have been applied into extensive monitoring scenarios and drawn a lot of attention of researchers. The application scenarios of CSNs can be classified into outdoor monitoring like electricians patrol work monitor system, and indoor monitoring like the security monitoring of buildings, airports and hotels. Indoor monitoring has more particularities on deployment and scheduling than outdoor monitoring: the deployment of camera sensors has specific requirements

© Springer Nature Switzerland AG 2019
A. Tagarelli and H. Tong (Eds.): CSoNet 2019, LNCS 11917, pp. 309–320, 2019.
https://doi.org/10.1007/978-3-030-34980-6_34

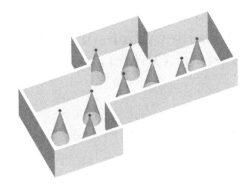

Fig. 1. An instance of indoor objective monitoring scenarios

or limitations, i.e. ceiling placement or corner placement as shown in Fig. 1. In most indoor monitoring, the trajectories of moving objectives are limited in a range depended on the structure of the building, i.e., there are enumerable and predicted routes for moving objectives. Furthermore, the monitoring scheduling of camera sensors is generally mission-driven for specific objectives or areas with special requirements of coverage quality and sustaining duration. Under these particular constraints, it is necessary and critical to design an efficient and durable coverage strategy for CSNs in indoor objective tracking.

In terms of accuracy and efficiency, the solutions to the objective tracking problem mostly depend on the sensing model of the camera sensors. Most existing related works focused on two-dimensional (2D) sensing model of directional sensors or camera sensors [1,2]. The 3D model has the peculiar coverage properties: it can be modeled as a circular cone, where its generatrix stands for the camera's working direction and its basal diameter can be viewed as the camera's working diameter. With the peculiar 3D sensing model, the judging of trajectory coverage becomes more difficult than that of target coverage: the authors in [3] summarized the existing coverage algorithms for video-based sensor networks and analyzed the difference in coverage problems between video-based sensor networks and traditional ones; the authors in [4] designed an efficient greedy heuristic algorithm to solve coverage problem considering the obstacles for the 3D environment. For a moving target in most applications, its labeled trajectory should be covered continuous and consistently under the sensing ranges of the cooperative cameras. Therefore, the effective coverage of a moving target is the first issue to design coverage strategies of camera sensor networks under 3D sensing model for indoor space scenarios.

The second issue is to make a tradeoff between the lifetime of CSNs and the quality of monitoring provided by the network. Objective tracking focuses on the monitoring of objective's trajectory, and the monitoring process is continuous and dynamic for camera sensors, i.e., they alternately enter active mode and cooperatively cover the trajectory along with the objective's movement. Most previous literatures dealt with the tradeoff by maximizing the network lifetime while satisfying the basic coverage requirement [5,8], i.e., many efforts are made to organize the sensors into disjoint subsets and activating the nodes in each subset alternatively [9]. The authors in [10] proposed a coverage algorithm for multimedia sensor networks via utilizing the redundant nodes. Guo et al. [6] proposed to maximize the number of β-view covered targets in visual sensor networks. Wang et al. [7] proposed target cover and counting by infra-red sensors. In the indoor objective tracking applications, the scheduling of camera sensors should provide durative surveillance for the target's moving, thus we aim to prolong the monitoring lifetime via minimizing the amount of active periods for the trajectory.

Considering the above two issues, we focus on the design of CSNs monitoring schedule and introduce a new scheduling problem, the active-period-minimizing scheduling problem in CSNs for indoor objective tracking (APMS Problem). The list of our contributions is as follows.

(i) We propose a new camera sensor scheduling problem, the *active-period-minimizing scheduling problem in CSNs for indoor objective tracking (APMS Problem)*, based on the sensing model of camera sensors, the movement model of the objective and the space discretization.
(ii) We design a pair of projection-based algorithms for APMS Problem from the perspectives of sensors and trajectories respectively.
(iii) We conduct the simulations and evaluate the performance of the proposed algorithms in terms of the average working duration of camera sensors.

The rest of the paper is organized as follows. Section 2 introduces some preliminaries and the definition of our problem. Section 3 introduces two projection-based algorithms for APMS Problem. Simulation results and corresponding discussions are given in Sect. 4. Section 5 concludes this paper.

2   Preliminaries and Problem Formulations

In this section, we first illustrate the 3D sensing model of camera sensors and present the judging method of effective sensing of the moving trajectory. Then we introduce the space discretization method for the deployment of sensors and the locations of targets. Based on these preliminaries, we introduce the formal definition of our problem and its NP-hardness proof.

2.1   3D Sensing Model of Camera Sensors

In most general application scenarios of CSNs, the monitoring mission has the coverage requirement of the target's facing direction, which can be modeled as full-view sensing model [11]. But in most indoor applications, the monitoring mission focuses on the capture of the target's movement rather that its facing direction. Therefore, we adopt the circular cone model as the 3D sensing model

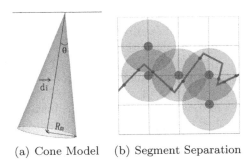

(a) Cone Model   (b) Segment Separation

Fig. 2. The illustration of 3D sensing model of camera sensors

of camera sensors, which is decided by the camera sensor node v_i's position (x_i, y_i, z_i), its orientation direction $\overrightarrow{d_i}$, the uniform Field-of-Vision θ, and the maximum sensing radius R_m, as shown in Fig. 2(a). The orientation directions of camera sensors can be adjusted in the monitoring scheduling, and the number of available directions of each sensor is set as J.

With the consideration of the limitation and dynamics of the target's movement, its moving trajectory can be model as a vector function $r(\overrightarrow{tar}) = \overrightarrow{r_0} + \int_0^t vel(\overrightarrow{tar})\, dt$, where $\overrightarrow{r_0}$ is the original vector of the target, $\overrightarrow{tar}$ is the target's current moving direction vector and $vel(\overrightarrow{tar})$ is the target's current velocity.

Note that it is assumed that the target is moving at a constant speed, i.e., $||vel(\overrightarrow{tar})||$ can be regarded as a constant vel. Thus the duration of the target's movement can be separated into several unit timeslots. Correspondingly, we can also separate the trajectory into several segments according to the growth of t, i.e., $seg_{t,t+1}$ stands for the moving segment of tar from timeslot t to timeslot $t + 1$. Based on the moving segment in each timeslot, the segment division is decided by the intersection of different camera sensors' sensing ranges which is shown by the blue points in Fig. 2(b). On the trajectory of a moving target, the timeslot points and the intersection points are divided the trajectory into several candidate monitored segments, which are the scheduling basic of target tracking. The formal definition of 3D sensing model of camera sensors is as follows.

Definition 1 (3D Sensing Model of Camera Sensors). *Consider a certain space with the ceiling and the ground modeled as planar $\mathcal{T}$ and planar $\mathcal{B}$ respectively, a camera sensor v_i located at (x_i, y_i, z_i) on $\mathcal{T}$, segment seg_k of a trajectory on $\mathcal{B}$ can be sensed/covered by v_i if seg_k is within the projection area of v_i's sensing circular cone on $\mathcal{B}$.*

2.2 3D Space Modeling and Discretization

Most monitored indoor rooms or buildings are 3D spaces with regular shape and structural characteristics, e.g., series spaces, parallel spaces, mother-and-child spaces. We model the indoor space as a continuous space $\mathcal{IR}$ with the top

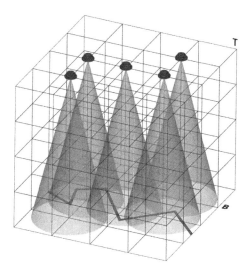

Fig. 3. The illustration of space discretization and node deployment

planar $\mathcal{T}$ and the bottom planar $\mathcal{B}$. With the structural characteristics, $\mathcal{IR}$ can be viewed as a complex space composed of several regular spaces like cuboids or cubes. Since the deployment of camera sensors may be dense and the moving trajectories are irregular, the simple regularization of the indoor space cannot benefit the scheduling for sensors to monitor the trajectories. For example, the space can be divided into three cuboids, which have no much difference in size. The sensor scheduling in each cuboid is just an equivalent problem with a smaller scale compared to the original problem, which has less benefit for the scheduling. Thus we adopt the grid discretization for the indoor space as shown in Fig. 3, in which the space is discretized by the grid with unit side length a. In other words, we can predefine and adjust a to control the discretization degree of the space based on the sensor deployment and the trajectory changes.

Based on the grid discretization of $\mathcal{IR}$, we assign each grid an ID in the order of top-to-bottom, inside-to-outside and left-to-right. The grids' IDs are beneficial for the positions of sensors and segment division of the trajectory. We assume that the candidate and available camera sensors are located at all the vertices of grids on the top layer in the space, and we can choose the optimal sensors and decide their working directions for surveillance. And for the trajectory, it can be divided by the grids on the bottom layer and these grids' ID set can be viewed as the approximate range of the trajectory curve.

2.3 Problem Definitions and Hardness Results

We propose a new surveillance scheduling problem in CSNs based on the above preliminaries, the active-period-minimizing scheduling problem for indoor objective tracking (APMS Problem), which is based on the two assumptions: **i.** the candidate camera sensors are deployed on the ceil of the indoor space; **ii.** the tracked target's trajectories are limited by the structure of the indoor space and they can be predefined into a strip or predicted. The formal definition of the problem is as follows.

Definition 2 (APMS Problem). *Given*

- *a 3D continuous space $\mathcal{IR}$ with the top planar $\mathcal{T}$ and the bottom planar $\mathcal{B}$, which can be discretized into unit grid with side length a,*
- *the camera sensor set V set on the top planar $\mathcal{T}$, $\{v_1, v_2, \cdots, v_N\}$, where each node v_i has its position (x_i, y_i, z_i), J available orientations $\{\overrightarrow{d_i}^1, \overrightarrow{d_i}^2, ..., \overrightarrow{d_i}^J\}$, the uniform Field-of-Vision θ, and the maximum sensing radius R_m,*
- *the target's moving trajectory, a vector function $r(\overrightarrow{tar}) = \overrightarrow{r_0} + \int_0^t vel(\overrightarrow{tar})\, dt$, where $\overrightarrow{r_0}$ is the original vector of the target, $\overrightarrow{tar}$ is the target's current moving direction vector and $vel(\overrightarrow{tar})$ is the target's current velocity.,*

APMS Problem is to choose the optimal camera sensors and decide their working directions for guaranteeing the full coverage of the target's movement on the trajectory and minimizing the total working duration of all the scheduled sensors, with the constraint that each sensor cannot be scheduled with more than one direction in the same timeslot.

Theorem 1. *The APMS Problem is NP-hard.*

Proof. To prove the NP-hardness of APMS problem, we consider the special case of the problem: each camera sensor has only one available working direction.

Under the assumption that the target is moving at a constant speed, the target's moving trajectory can be separated into several segments according to the growth of t, e.g., $seg_{t,t+1}$ (the moving segment of tar from timeslot t to timeslot $t + 1$). The division of the trajectory can be continued based on the intersection of different camera sensors' sensing ranges which is illustrated in Fig. 2(b). Thus the moving trajectory is composed of these dividing segments $\{seg_1, seg_2, ..., seg_M\}$ and the length of each segment stands for its necessary monitoring duration by camera sensors.

Based on the segment division, the coverage range can be decided for each camera sensor's available working direction, which can be represented as CR_i. We assign each sensor a weight as the length sum of the segments in the sensor's coverage range, $weight(v_i) = \sum_{seg_i \in CR_i} length(seg_i)$. Then the problem in this case is to choose the optimal camera sensors to continuously cover the target's movement and minimize the sum of working durations, i.e., the goal is to find an optimal subset V_{opt} of V to satisfy that $\{seg_1, seg_2, ..., seg_M\} \subset V_{opt}$ and minimize $\sum_{v_i \in V_{opt}} weight(v_i)$.

Since this special version of APMS Problem is equivalent to Minimum Weighted Set Cover Problem, which is proven to be NP-hard [12]. Therefore, APMS Problem is NP-hard in general, which completes the proof. □

3   Heuristic Algorithms Design

To schedule the camera sensors with the goal of minimizing the total working duration, we propose a pair of heuristics from two perspectives: from the perspective of camera sensors, the optimal sensor with the minimum coverage redundancy will be chose in each iteration until all the segments can be covered; from the perspective of trajectory segments, the segment covered by the sensor with the minimum working duration will be selected in each round until each segment can be considered.

3.1   Projection-Based Algorithm for APMS Problem

For the coverage of the moving target, we design a projection-based algorithm to minimize the total working duration. Here we adopt the idea of redundancy minimization and realize the process into iterations: in each iteration, we choose the sensor direction with the minimum redundant working duration as the current optimal one and the other directions which belong to the same sensor will be out of consideration in the next iteration. And the iteration will be loop until all the segments have been covered, as shown in steps 8–11 in Algorithm 1.

Algorithm 1. Projection-based Algorithm for APMS (V, Seg)

1: Set $V^* \leftarrow \emptyset$, $TotDur = 0$
2: **for** each sensor direction v_i^j in V **do**
3:     $V_i^j = \{seg_1, seg_2, ..., seg_K\}$, which is the set of segments covered by v_i^j
4:     $weight(v_i^j) = \sum_{seg_k \in V_i^j} length(seg_k)$
5:     $redweight(v_i^j) = -1$
6:     **if** $v_i^j ! = \emptyset$ **then**
7:         Find the segments in v_i^j which are covered by other directions and record them in set $OL(v_i^j)$, $redweight(v_i^j) = \sum_{seg_k \in OL(v_i^j)} length(seg_k)$

8: **while** $Seg! = \emptyset$ **do**
9:     Select the sensor direction v_i^{j*} with the minimum positive $redweight(v_i^{j*})$,
10:     $V^* \leftarrow V^* \cup \{v_i^{j*}\}$, $TotDur = TotDur + weight(v_i^{j*})$
11:     $V \leftarrow V \setminus \{v_i^1, v_i^2, ..., v_i^J\}$, $Seg \leftarrow Seg \setminus V_i^{j*}$
12: Return V^*, $TotDur$.

Note that the iteration for redundancy minimization needs preliminaries as shown in steps 3–7 in Algorithm 1: for each sensor direction v_i^j, it has two kinds of information about working duration, the effective one and the redundant one. For the effective working duration, we use the total length of the trajectory segments which are covered by v_i^j, which are recorded into set V_i^j. And for the redundant working duration, we first decide whether v_i^j can cover some segment, i.e., if it cannot cover any segment on trajectory, its redundant value is meaningless for coverage and is set to be -1. After confirming v_i^j's coverage, we continue to determine the segments which can be covered by both v_i^j and other directions, which are collected into $OL(v_i^j)$. Then the total length of all the segments in $OL(v_i^j)$ stands for v_i^j's redundant working duration. Based on $OL(v_i^j)$ and V_i^j, the direction with the minimal redundant duration can be chose in each iteration and realize the redundancy minimization.

3.2 Back-Projection-based Algorithm for APMS Problem

Different from Projection-based Algorithm, Back-Projection-based Algorithm is designed from the view of trajectory segments: for each segments seg_k, it might be in more than one sensor directions' sensing ranges, and it prefers to select the direction with minimum working duration to cover it. For this selection of each segment, the directions' working durations and the segments' covering sets should be calculated in advance as shown in steps 2–6 of Algorithm 2: we firstly calculate each direction's working duration which is represented by $weight(v_i^j)$; then we count up all the covering directions for each segment and collect them into set Seg_k. In the scheduling, seg_k can be covered if one direction v_i^{j*} in set Seg_k has been selected into the working set V^* and other segments covered by v_i^{j*} are satisfied to be covered as well.

Algorithm 2. Back-Projection-based Algorithm for APMS (V, Seg)

1: Set $V^* \leftarrow \emptyset$, $TotDur = 0$
2: **for** each sensor direction v_i^j in V **do**
3:     $V_i^j = \{seg_1, seg_2, ..., seg_K\}$, which is the set of segments covered by v_i^j
4:     $weight(v_i^j) = \sum_{seg_k \in V_i^j} length(seg_k)$
5: **for** each segment seg_k in Seg **do**
6:     $Seg_k = \{v_{i_1}^{j_1}, v_{i_2}^{j_2}, ..., v_{i_k}^{j_k}\}$, which is the set of sensor directions which cover seg_k
7: **while** $Seg! = \emptyset$ **do**
8:     Select the sensor direction v_i^{j*} with the minimum $weight(v_i^{j*})$,
9:     $V^* \leftarrow V^* \cup \{v_i^{j*}\}$, $TotDur = TotDur + weight(v_i^{j*})$
10:     $Seg \leftarrow Seg \setminus \{seg_{k'} | v_i^{j*} \in Seg_{k'}\}$
11: Return V^*, $TotDur$.

Based on the preliminaries, we execute selection cycles until all the segments have been considered: in each loop, the direction with the minimum weight will be selected and the segments in its coverage are under consideration in the current loop. Then we update the unconsidered segment set Seg by deleting the current considered segments and enter into the next loop.

4   Performance Evaluation

4.1   Simulation Plan

The simulations are performed in a cubic space with the size of $100 * 100 * 100$ and the grid for space discretization is with side length 0.01 for the location of the moving target's trajectory. There are n camera sensors deployed on the ceiling plane of the space and the moving trajectory is randomly generated within the length of L on the bottom plane. For each camera sensor, it has Field-of-Vision θ and 3 candidate working directions which have the angles with the horizontal direction as $-30°$, $0°$, $30°$.

We will check how each algorithm is affected by three important parameters: the number of camera sensors n, Field-of-Vision θ and the length of trajectory L. In particular, we will consider the following three group of settings:

(i) Group 1: n varies from 1500 to 4500 by the step of 500
    (a) $L = 200$, $\theta = 40°$; (b) $L = 200$, $\theta = 60°$; (c) $L = 200$, $\theta = 80°$;
(ii) Group 2: θ varies from $40°$ to $80°$ by the step of $10°$
    (a) $L = 200$, $n = 1600$; (b) $L = 200$, $n = 2400$; (c) $L = 200$, $n = 3200$;
(iii) Group 3: L varies from 120 to 200 by the step of 20
    (a) $n = 4000$, $\theta = 40°$; (b) $n = 4000$, $\theta = 60°$; (c) $n = 4000$, $\theta = 80°$.

To evaluate the performance of the algorithms for APMS Problem, we adopt **the average working duration** as the evaluation criterion, which is the average value of all the scheduled directions' working periods. For each parameter setting, we run 100 instances and compute their average for evaluation.

4.2 Performance of Algorithms for APMS Problem:

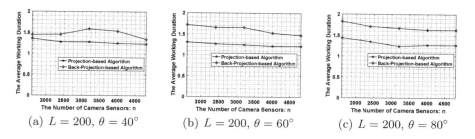

(a) $L = 200$, $\theta = 40°$ (b) $L = 200$, $\theta = 60°$ (c) $L = 200$, $\theta = 80°$

Fig. 4. Average working duration vs. number of nodes n

Based on the results in Fig. 4, it can be observed that the average working durations obtained by the two algorithms can be decreased with the growth of the number of sensors. It can be explained that the increasing of the network scale is beneficial for the cooperative sensing for the moving trajectory and the time efficiency of monitoring is also enhanced. Furthermore, from Fig. 4(a) to (c), Projection-based Algorithm outperforms Back-Projection-based one and the advantage becomes more significant when the uniform Field-of-Vision θ gets larger. That is because that the enlargement of Field-of-Vision improves the nodes' coverage capacities and Projection-based Algorithm is from the perspective of nodes. Thus Projection-based one performs better than Back-Projection-based one when Field-of-Vision can be adjusted.

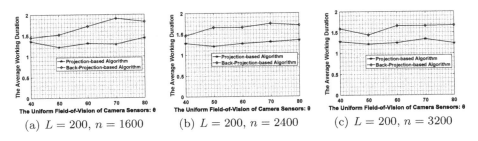

Fig. 5. Average working duration vs. Field-of-Vision of nodes θ

From Fig. 5 for the consideration of Field-of-Vision's changes, we can find that the change of θ has little influence on the algorithms' performance and the average working durations in two algorithms slightly fluctuate. Between the two algorithms, Projection-based Algorithm varies more slightly than Back-Projection-based one. With the enlargement of Field-of-Vision, the overlapped sensing ranges between each neighbor sensors will be enlarged as well, which can cause more working duration overlap or redundancy. Moreover, as shown from Fig. 5(a) to (c), it can be also concluded that the increase of network scale contributes to enhance the time efficiency.

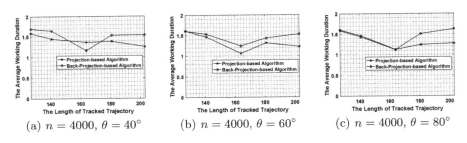

Fig. 6. Average working duration vs. length of tracked trajectory L

As shown in Fig. 6, the two algorithms' performance shows obvious variation with the changes of trajectory length. Especially when the length is near the value 160, the average working durations gotten by the two algorithms reach the lowest value. It can be explained that in a space of certain size, the trajectory with too short length or too long length causes the growth of the complexity of the route. It might infer that the trajectory which obtain the optimal monitoring has a length range related to the space scale.

Via analyzing the above three groups of simulation results, we can conclude that it is better to adopt Projection-based Algorithm in the scenarios with the changeable scale of sensor networks or the changeable Field-of-Vision, while it is preferential to apply Back-Projection-based Algorithm in the scenarios with the variable trajectory length.

5   Conclusions

In this paper, we investigated the active-period-minimizing scheduling problem in CSNs for indoor objective tracking. To exactly and effectively determine the coverage of a moving objective, we propose a segment division method to construct the projection relationship between camera sensors and the moving target. To make a tradeoff between the network lifetime and monitoring quality, we design a pair of active-period scheduling strategies to minimize the total working durations on monitoring the target's one pass on its trajectory. The simulation results showed the performance on the time efficiency of the algorithms and analyzed their suitable scenarios. In the future, we will focus on the scenarios with multiple objectives and design the cooperative scheduling strategies with the consideration of time efficiency and coverage quality.

Acknowledgment. This research was partly supported by National Natural Science Foundation of China under Grant 11671400 and 61672524, General Project of Science and Technology Plan of Beijing Municipal Education Commission (KM201910017006), Program of Beijing Excellent Talents Training for Young Scholar (2016000020124-G056).

References

1. Han, K., Xiang, L., Luo, J., Liu, Y.: Minimum-energy connected coverage in wireless sensor networks with omni-directional and directional features. In: Proceedings of ACM International Symposium on Mobile Ad Hoc Networking and Computing, pp. 85–94. ACM (2012)
2. Deif, D.S., Gadallah, Y.: Classification of wireless sensor networks deployment techniques. IEEE Commun. Surv. Tutorials **16**(2), 834–855 (2014)
3. Costa, D.G., Guedes, L.A.: The coverage problem in video-based wireless sensor networks: a survey. Sensors **10**, 8215–8247 (2010)
4. Brown, T., Wang, Z.H., Shan, T., Wang, F., Xue, J.X.: Obstacle-aware wireless video sensor network deployment for 3D indoor monitoring. In: Proceedings of IEEE Global Communications Conference (GLOBECOM), pp. 1–6 (2017)
5. Cardei, M., Thai, M.T., Li, Y.S., Wu, J.: Energy-efficient target coverage in wireless sensor networks. Proceedings of IEEE International Conference on Computer Communications (INFOCOM), pp. 1976–1982 (2005)
6. Guo, L., Li, D., Wang, Y., et al.: Maximisation of the number of β-view covered targets in visual sensor networks. IJSNet **29**(4), 226–241 (2019)
7. Wang, Y., Song, L., et al.: IntenCT: efficient multi-target counting and tracking by binary proximity sensors. In: SECON, pp. 1–9 (2016)
8. Cardei, M., Wu, J.: Energy-efficient coverage problems in wireless ad-hoc sensor networks. Comput. Commun. **29**(4), 413–420 (2006)
9. Cardei, M., Du, D.Z.: Improving wireless sensor network lifetime through power aware organization. Wireless Netw. **11**(3), 333–340 (2005)
10. Xu, S., Lyu, W., Li, H.: Optimizing coverage of 3D wireless multimedia sensor networks by means of deploying redundant sensors. Int. J. Adv. Stud. Comput. Sci. Eng. **4**(9), 28 (2015)

11. Wang, Y., Cao, G.H.: On full-view coverage in camera sensor networks. In: Proceedings of IEEE International Conference on Computer Communications (INFO-COM), pp. 1781–1789 (2011)
12. Garey, M.R., Johnson, D.S.: Strong NP-completeness results: motivation, examples, and implications. J. ACM **25**, 499–508 (1978)

User Profiling and Behavior Modeling

Enhancing Collaborative Filtering with Multi-label Classification

Yang Zhou[1]([⊠]), Ling Liu[2], Qi Zhang[3], Kisung Lee[4], and Balaji Palanisamy[5]

[1] Auburn University, Auburn, USA
yangzhou@auburn.edu
[2] Georgia Institute of Technology, Atlanta, USA
lingliu@cc.gatech.edu
[3] IBM T.J. Watson Research Center, Yorktown Heights, USA
Q.Zhang@ibm.com
[4] Louisiana State University, Baton Rouge, USA
lee@csc.lsu.edu
[5] University of Pittsburgh, Pittsburgh, USA
bpalan@pitt.edu

Abstract. This paper presents a multi-label classification based CF framework, MLCF, which improves the quality of recommendation in the presence of data sparsity by learning over a heterogeneous information network consisting of a rating bipartite graph, a user graph and an item graph. MLCF is novel by three unique features. First, we explore the latent correlations among users and items w.r.t. a given set of K semantic categories beyond user-item ratings by employing multi-label clustering of items, and multi-label classification of users and rating-based similarities on the heterogeneous network. Second, based on the user/item/similarity multi-label clustering/classification, we propose a fine-grained multi-label classification based rating similarity measure to capture the class-specific relationships between users by introducing a novel concept of vertex-edge homophily. Third but not the least, we propose to integrate two kinds of multi-label classification based CF models focusing on rating and social information into a unified prediction model.

1 Introduction

Networked data analysis has attracted active research in the last decade [1–17]. Recently, collaborative Filtering (CF) based recommendation techniques have received increasing attention in recent years, to promote the marketing efforts of many online vendors, such as Amazon and Netflix. We can broadly classify existing CF studies into two categories: conventional CF and social network enhanced CF. The conventional CF algorithms rely solely on the user-item rating matrix to make recommendations [18–28]. Thus, conventional CF methods often lead to poor recommendation quality in the presence of data sparsity. The social network enhanced CF methods attempt to integrate the rating matrix with the social networks from multiple data sources to improve prediction accuracy in the

© Springer Nature Switzerland AG 2019
A. Tagarelli and H. Tong (Eds.): CSoNet 2019, LNCS 11917, pp. 323–338, 2019.
https://doi.org/10.1007/978-3-030-34980-6_35

presence of data sparsity [34–44]. A recent study reports that social information can not always result in substantial performance gains of CF prediction, and sometimes may lead to biased prediction result [45]. Thus, simply integrating rating and social information without considering the labeling of connected nodes and associated links may introduce serious inaccuracy.

In this paper we propose a multi-label classification based CF approach, MLCF, to enhance the CF prediction by addressing the following challenges:

Utilizing Heterogeneous Types of Information of Users And Items. Many real-world rating datasets are content-rich in terms of not only the user-item rating data but also the user social network and the item information network with semantic category information. For example, the Last.fm dataset in Table 1 contains a user friendship graph and a track graph consisting of the *similar track* relationships between song tracks in addition to the user-song rating data. In MLCF, we want to strategically utilize heterogeneous types of information: rating and social information of users and items, and category information of items to enhance the recommendation performance in the presence of data sparsity.

CF Prediction With Multi-label Classification. Traditional clustering-based CF methods use the user-designated number of clusters (K) to partition users and/or items into disjoint K clusters based on the user-item rating matrix and then apply CF methods to each cluster to improve the prediction accuracy. One of serious issues with traditional clustering approach is rooted by the fact that the clusters of users/items are disjoint and that data sparsity exists in most of the real rating datasets. A large K may lead to lots of cluster outliers and deteriorates the cold start problem even if the user-item rating matrix is relatively dense. A small K may result in too many users or items in a single cluster and fail to improve the prediction quality due to the inability to differentiate rating-based neighbors at cluster level. We argue that the multi-label classification model over user-item rating graph, user social network and item information network is attractive for two reasons. First, multi-label classification of a dataset takes an input of the pre-defined set of K class labels, and computes multi-label based class membership probability for each entity w.r.t. each of K class labels. We then can utilize such multi-label clustering/classification of users, items and similarities to perform accurate prediction. Second, many real rating datasets have the specific numbers of semantic categories of items, which can be used as the pre-defined set of class labels, say Yelp with 20 business categories for posting its user-business ratings. In addition, entities in real rating datasets usually belong to multiple semantic categories. In this case, instead of performing simple aggregation of predictions (e.g., average aggregation) from all rating-based neighbors, we argue that we should perform CF prediction by incorporating multi-label classification based relations between users.

Fine-Grained Rating-Based Similarity With Multi-label Item Classification. Existing CF algorithms compute rating-based similarity scores based on the heuristic rule that two users (or items) are similar if they share similar rating

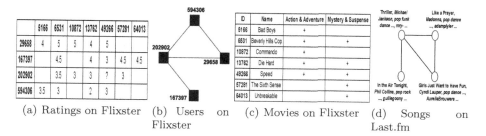

(a) Ratings on Flixster   (b) Users on Flixster   (c) Movies on Flixster   (d) Songs on Last.fm

Fig. 1. Real example of heterogeneous information

preferences. By modeling the rating-based similarity scores between users as a rating-based similarity graph where a vertex specifies a user and a link represents the similarity score between two users, the above rule is similar to the concept of vertex homophily widely used in social network analysis, i.e., the principle that similar vertices in nature are connected to each other with social links. However, users connected through such general rating-based similarity links may be similar in different ways w.r.t. a given set of semantic categories of items. For example, a Flixster user *Nancy* is connected to both *Bob* and *Alice* through similarity links in the rating-based similarity graph due to their common rating tastes. However, *Bob* and *Nancy* co-rated many *AA* movies but *Alice* and *Nancy* co-rated many *Romance* movies. Thus, relying solely on vertex homophily based similarity without considering labeling of similarity links is too coarse-grained, and may lead to poor recommendation.

This paper makes three original contributions. First, we integrate different types of entities, links and attributes from rating network and social networks into a heterogeneous information network. We enhance the user-item rating relationships by exploring the latent correlations among users and items through multi-label clustering/classification over the heterogeneous network of users and items. Second, we propose a multi-label classification based rating similarity measure by introducing a novel concept of vertex-edge homophily in terms of multi-label vertices (users/items) and multi-label edges (similarities). Third, we propose and combine two kinds of multi-label prediction models into a unified prediction model: multi-label rating similarity-based prediction and multi-label class affinity-based prediction. Finally, empirical evaluation over real datasets demonstrates the competitiveness of MLCF against the state-of-the-art CF methods.

2 The MLCF Approach

2.1 Overview

MLCF designs and implements five core functional components: (1) modeling the CF problem as a graph analysis problem over a heterogeneous information network of users and items with different types of links; (2) performing multi-label clustering of items via soft clustering; (3) executing multi-label classification of users through iterative label propagation; (4) capturing vertex-edge homophily by multi-label classification of similarities; and (5) conducting multi-label CF prediction by integrating multi-label rating similarity based prediction with multi-label class affinity based prediction.

Concretely, given a rating dataset, we first create a heterogeneous network, comprised of the user-item rating matrix as a bipartite graph, the social network of users as a user graph, and the item information network as an item graph. Formally, a *user graph* is denoted as $UG = (U, E_U)$, where U is the set of N_U user vertices and E_U is the set of edges denoting the social relationships between users. An *item graph* is denoted as $IG = (V, E_V, A)$, where V is the set of N_V item vertices, an edge in E_V represents the social relationship between items, and $A = \{a_1, ..., a_s\}$ is the set of s attributes of items in V. The second step of MLCF is to cluster items into K item semantic categories in terms of structure and/or attribute information of items. Notice that not each real rating dataset contains structure information of items. However, it is enough to do item clustering with only attribute information. A *rating bipartite graph* is denoted as $RG = (U, V, E_R)$, where U and V have the same definitions in UG and IG. An edge $(u_i, v_l) \in E_R$ $(1 \leq i \leq N_U, 1 \leq l \leq N_V)$ connecting a user $u_i \in U$ to an item $v_l \in V$, denoting the rating relationship between them.

Figure 1(a) presents a fragment of the rating matrix in Flixster, where the first column represents user ids and the first row specifies movie ids. Figure 1(b) shows the social graph of users corresponding to the rating fragment. Figure 1(c) exhibits movie attributes in Flixster. Each movie in Flixster is associated with one or more *genre*(s), such as AA and MS. The symbol + represents an association between a movie and a *genre*. Figure 1(d) is an example of item graph from Last.fm, where a vertex specifies a song and an edge represents a *similar track* relationship between two songs. Each song has three kinds of attributes: blue *artist*, red *tags* list, and green *listeners* list.

The second component of MLCF is to perform multi-label clustering of items, which consists of two tasks. (1) choose related structure and/or attribute information of items based on the specific context; and (2) cluster items into a given K categories using a soft clustering algorithm. The rational of using soft clustering over hard clustering (an item belongs to only one cluster) is based on the observation that most of items belong to more than one categories. For example, Fig. 2(b) is the bipartite graph of Fig. 1 (a), where rectangle vertices represent Flixster users, circle vertices specify Flixster movies, and links denote the rating relationships between users and movies. For the datasets containing both structure and attribute information of items, say Last.fm in Fig. 1(d), we utilize a soft-clustering method, GenClus [4], to clusters each item to each of K item categories. For the datasets only comprising item attributes, say Yelp and Flixster, we compute the Jaccard distance [46] between item attribute vectors and employ the Fuzzy C-Means method [47] to execute the soft clustering task. The multi-label item clustering results generated by two clustering methods satisfy the following condition: $0 \leq p_{lk} \leq 1$ and $\sum_{k=1}^{K} p_{lk} = 1$, where p_{lk} to represent the

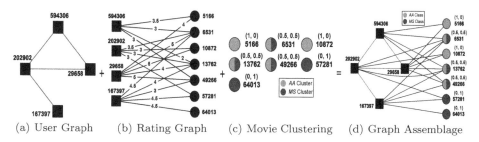

(a) User Graph   (b) Rating Graph   (c) Movie Clustering   (d) Graph Assemblage

Fig. 2. An illustrating example from Flixster

cluster membership probability of an item vertex $v_l \in V$ in IG $(1 \leq l \leq N_V)$ belonging to cluster c_k $(1 \leq k \leq K)$.

Figure 2(c) exhibits the clustering result of Flixster movies in Fig. 1(c), where green numbers or ochre numbers in the brackets denote the membership probabilities of movies on two clusters AA or MS respectively. Upon the completion of the item clustering, we assemble the user graph, the rating graph and the item clustering into a heterogeneous network. Figure 2(d) shows the heterogeneous graph by assembling Figs. 2(a)–(c).

2.2   User Multi-label Classification

In real world, one item may belong to multiple semantic categories and users often favor one category of items over another. For instance, movies *Die Hard* and *Sherlock Holmes* have two *genres* of *AA* and *MS*, attracting users with high interest in *AA* or *MS* movies. On the other hand, two Flixster users *Tom* and *Jack* may have viewed or rated both *AA* movies and *MS* movies. This motivates us to explore the latent user correlations based on multi-label classification of users over the heterogeneous network through iterative label propagation starting from multi-label clustering of items. Concretely, we perform multi-label classification of users in three steps: (1) compute the transition probability on the heterogeneous graph; (2) define a classification kernel based on the social links between users and the rating links between users and items on the heterogeneous graph; and (3) execute iterative label propagation to infer the class membership of each user.

Definition 1 *[Assembled Heterogeneous Graph]. Let $AG = (U, V, E_R, E_U)$ be an assembled heterogeneous graph where U is the set of user vertices in the user graph UG, V is the set of item vertices in the item graph IG, E_R is the set of rating edges between users and items in the rating bipartite graph RG, and E_U is the set of social edges between users in UG. The edge weights on AG can be defined below.*

$$\mathbf{W_R}(i, l) = \begin{cases} 1, & if \ u_i \in U, v_l \in V, (u_i, v_l) \in E_R, \\ 0, & otherwise. \end{cases} \tag{1}$$

where $\mathbf{W_R}(i, l)$ $(1 \leq i \leq N_U, 1 \leq l \leq N_V)$ *denotes the interest relation between user* u_i *and item* v_l *through rating.*

$$\mathbf{W_U}(i, j) = \begin{cases} 1, \text{ if } u_i, u_j \in U, (u_i, u_j) \in E_U, \\ 0, \text{ otherwise.} \end{cases} \tag{2}$$

where $\mathbf{W_U}(i, j)$ $(1 \leq i, j \leq N_U)$ *represents the social relationship between two users* u_i *and* u_j *in AG.*

Note that all edges in AG have the weight of 1. In MLCF we utilize the user-item rating graph in the multi-label classification of users and the similarity computation differently. Given that the intuition that a rating behavior shows a user's interest in a specific item category to which the rated item belongs, whichever score is given by user, we do not use the rating scores here. However, the rating scores will be utilized in computing the rating-based similarity between users, the next functional component of MLCF.

Definition 2 *[Transition Probability on Assembled Heterogeneous Graph]. Given* $\mathbf{W_R}$ *and* $\mathbf{W_U}$ *defined on the assembled heterogeneous graph* $AG = (U, V, E_R, E_U)$*, the transition probability on AG is defined as follows.*

$$\mathbf{T_R}(i, l) = \frac{\mathbf{W_R}(i, l)}{\sum_{m=1}^{N_V} \mathbf{W_R}(i, m) + \sum_{m=1}^{N_U} \mathbf{W_U}(i, m)} \tag{3}$$

where $\mathbf{T_R}(i, l)$ $(1 \leq i \leq N_U, 1 \leq l \leq N_V)$ *is the transition probability from unlabeled user* u_i *to labeled item* v_l *in AG.*

$$\mathbf{T_U}(i, j) = \frac{\mathbf{W_U}(i, j)}{\sum_{m=1}^{N_V} \mathbf{W_R}(i, m) + \sum_{m=1}^{N_U} \mathbf{W_U}(i, m)} \tag{4}$$

where $\mathbf{T_U}(i, j)$ $(1 \leq i, j \leq N_U)$ *specifies the transition probability from unlabeled user* u_i *to unlabeled user* u_j *in AG.*

Figure 3(a) presents the transition probabilities from user *594306* to its connected items and users computed over the assembled heterogeneous graph in Fig. 2(d).

Instead of decomposing the multi-label classification problem into a set of binary classification problems, we construct a multi-label classification kernel by using labeled items as the training data to iteratively infer the class membership of each user. In this work, we assume that the labels of the item vertices in V are fixed during this classification process. The classification kernel $\mathbf{K}$ is thus defined as follows.

$$\mathbf{K} = \begin{bmatrix} \mathbf{I} & \mathbf{O} \\ \mathbf{T_R} & \mathbf{T_U} \end{bmatrix} \tag{5}$$

where $\mathbf{O}$ is an $N_V \times N_U$ zero matrix representing the zero transition probabilities from labeled item vertices to unlabeled user vertices. We set the $\mathbf{I}$ to be an $N_V \times N_V$ identity matrix denoting the transition probabilities among labeled item vertices to keep the labels on the item vertices in V unchanged during the classification process.

The multi-label classification of users is performed by the iterative label propagation from items/users to users. We treat the set of items V as training data labeled with given K labels, and the set of users U as test data unlabeled. Let $\mathbf{X}_k = [\mathbf{X}_{kV}; \mathbf{X}_{kU}]$ be the class membership vector based on cluster (class) c_k $(1 \leq k \leq K)$, where $\mathbf{X}_{kV}$ specifies the probabilities of the labeled items in V belonging to c_k, and $\mathbf{X}_{kU}$ represents the probabilities of the unlabeled users in U belonging to c_k. We initialize $\mathbf{X}_k$ as follow: all $\mathbf{X}_{kV}^{(0)}$ $(1 \leq k \leq K)$ are initialized with the item clustering result, i.e., $\mathbf{X}_{kV}^{(0)}(l) = p_{lk}$ $(1 \leq l \leq N_V)$, and all $\mathbf{X}_{kU}^{(0)}$ $(1 \leq k \leq K)$ are initialized with zeros, i.e., $\mathbf{X}_{kU}^{(0)}(i) = 0$ $(1 \leq i \leq N_U)$. Let $\mathbf{X} = [\mathbf{X}_1, \mathbf{X}_2, \cdots, \mathbf{X}_K] \in \mathbb{R}^{(N_V + N_U) \times K}$ be the class membership matrix. For each class membership vector $\mathbf{X}_k$ based on class c_k $(1 \leq k \leq K)$, we use the classification kernel $\mathbf{K}$ to iteratively infer the probabilities of the user vertices on class c_k as follows.

$$\mathbf{X}_k^{(t)} = \mathbf{K}\mathbf{X}_k^{(t-1)} \tag{6}$$

Given that $\mathbf{X}_{kV}^{(t)} = \mathbf{X}_{kV}^{(t-1)} = \cdots = \mathbf{X}_{kV}^{(0)}$ for all $k \in \{1, \cdots, K\}$, we only need to compute $\mathbf{X}_{kU}^{(t)}$ in each iteration:

$$\mathbf{X}_{kU}^{(t)} = \mathbf{T_R}\mathbf{X}_{kV}^{(t-1)} + \mathbf{T_U}\mathbf{X}_{kU}^{(t-1)} \tag{7}$$

In each iteration, the label propagation process aggregates labels of social friends and labels of rated items for each user. We normalize each entry $\mathbf{X}_{kU}^{(t)}(i)$ in $\mathbf{X}_{kU}^{(t)}$ $(1 \leq k \leq K)$.

$$\mathbf{Y}_{kU}^{(t)}(i) = \frac{\mathbf{X}_{kU}^{(t)}(i)}{\sum_{l=1}^{K} \mathbf{X}_{lU}^{(t)}(i)} \tag{8}$$

where $\mathbf{Y}_{kU}^{(t)}$ represents the normalized class membership vector based on class c_k. Thus, the class membership matrix is updated as follow.

$$\mathbf{X}^{(t)} = \begin{bmatrix} \mathbf{X}_{1V}^{(0)} & \mathbf{X}_{2V}^{(0)} & \cdots & \mathbf{X}_{KV}^{(0)} \\ \mathbf{Y}_{1U}^{(t)} & \mathbf{Y}_{2U}^{(t)} & \cdots & \mathbf{Y}_{KU}^{(t)} \end{bmatrix} \tag{9}$$

$\mathbf{X}^{(t)}$ will be used to enter the next classification round. This iterative classification process continues until a certain convergence condition is met, such as $\sum_{k=1}^{K} \|\mathbf{Y}_{kU}^{(t)} - \mathbf{Y}_{kU}^{(t-1)}\| < \epsilon$, namely all entries in $\mathbf{Y}_{kU}^{(t)}$ are no longer changing for more than a system-defined ϵ. The colored numbers in the brackets in Fig. 3(b) show the normalized class membership probabilities of Flixster users in five iterations.

2.3 Similarity Multi-label Classification

The next core component of MLCF is to define the multi-label classification based rating similarity scores between users in terms of vertex-edge homophily and construct a user similarity multigraph (i.e., a graph that allows for parallel similarity edges (multiple similarity edges) between a pair of user vertices) through multi-label edge classification with multi-label vertex (item) clustering.

As mentioned in Sect. 1, existing CF methods compute rating-based similarity scores based on the existence of vertex homophily. However, relying solely on vertex homophily, without differentiating similarity scores at class level, is too coarse-grained, and may lead to poor prediction. For the Flixster dataset, suppose that the (vertex homophily based) similarity score between *Nancy* and *Bob* is the same as the similarity score between *Nancy* and *Alice* based on their common rating tastes through simple aggregation. However, *Nancy* and *Alice* co-rated many *Romance* movies but *Nancy* and *Bob* co-rated many *AA* movies. even though the similarity between *Nancy* and *Alice* is established in the context of *Romance* movies, while the similarity between *Nancy* and *Bob* is only valid in the context of *AA* movies. We argue that the recommendation by *Bob* should be more important than that by *Alice* on *AA* movies, since *Bob* is a fan (expert) of *AA* movies and the co-rating relationship between *Bob* and *Nancy* is dominated by their similar ratings on *AA* movies.

This motivates us to propose the concept of vertex-edge homophily in terms of both vertex (user) labels and edge (similarity) labels, i.e., the principle that both similarity links and their associated user vertices should be similar and likely belong to the same classes, to further improve the prediction accuracy. We first construct an augmented user similarity graph by computing the similarity between users based on each individual co-rated item.

$$\tilde{S}_m(i,j) = \frac{(R(i,m) - \bar{R}(i))(R(j,m) - \bar{R}(j))}{\sqrt{\sum_{v_l \in V_{ij}} (R(i,l) - \bar{R}(i))^2 \sum_{v_l \in V_{ij}} (R(j,l) - \bar{R}(j))^2}} \tag{10}$$

where $\tilde{S}_m(i,j)$ represents the similarity between users u_i and u_j based on a co-rated item $v_m \in V_{ij}$, V_x represents the set of items rated by user u_x, $V_{ij} = V_i \cap V_j$ is the set of items rated by both user u_i and user u_j, $R(x,l)$ is the rating score by user u_x to item v_l, and $\bar{R}(x)$ is the average rating of user u_x. It is essentially a projection of the Pearson similarity [18] on item v_m. We thus generate an augmented user similarity graph by projecting a Pearson similarity edge between any pair of user vertices into a set of parallel similarity edges based on each co-rated item. The size of each set of parallel edges is at most $|V_{ij}|$, i.e., the number of co-rated items. Figure 4(a) presents an augmented user similarity graph based on the rating bipartite graph in Fig. 2(b).

We then perform multi-label edge classification to classify and project each of the above similarity edges into K classes by utilizing the items' labels and aggregate the similarity projections with the same class labels as follow.

$$S_k(i,j) = \sum_{v_m \in V_{ij}} \mathbf{X}_{kV}^{(0)}(m)\tilde{S}_m(i,j), \ 1 \le k \le K \tag{11}$$

where $S_k(i,j)$ represents a projection of the Pearson similarity [18] (denoted by $S(i,j)$) on class c_k, i.e., the preference of $S(i,j)$ to c_k. $\mathbf{X}_{kV}^{(0)}(m)$ denotes

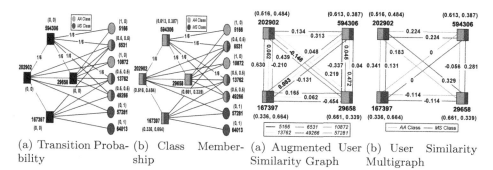

(a) Transition Proba- (b) Class Member-   (a) Augmented User (b) User Similarity
bility   ship   Similarity Graph   Multigraph

Fig. 3. User classification on Flixster   **Fig. 4.** Multigraph representation on
                                                     Flixster

the probability of item v_m belonging to class c_k. Notice that the sum of the
projections of the Pearson similarity $S(i, j)$ over K classes is still equal to itself,
i.e., $S(i, j) = \sum_{k=1}^{K} S_k(i, j)$.

After producing the projections on K classes, we reduce the augmented user
similarity multigraph with up to $|V_{ij}|$ edges (see Fig. 4(a)) to a multi-label user
similarity multigraph with up to K classified similarity edges between any pair
of users (see Fig. 4(b)). Figure 4(a) shows three similarity projections between
users *167397* and *202902* based on three co-rated items.

2.4 Unified Multi-label CF Prediction

To enhance the prediction accuracy and address the cold start problem at class
level, we propose and integrate two multi-label classification based CF models
into a unified prediction model. This allows MLCF to respond to different degrees
of contribution of two kinds of prediction models at each individual class.

(1) **Multi-label Rating Similarity-based Prediction.** We first compute
the projection of a rating score by user u_i to item v_l on class c_k, denoted by
$R_k(i, l)$.

$$R_k(i, l) = \frac{\mathbf{Y}_{kU}^{(t)}(i)\mathbf{X}_{kV}^{(0)}(l)R(i, l)}{\sum_{k=1}^{K} \mathbf{Y}_{kU}^{(t)}(i)\mathbf{X}_{kV}^{(0)}(l)} \tag{12}$$

where $R(i, l)$ is the actual rating score by u_i to v_l, $\mathbf{Y}_{kU}^{(t)}(i)$ is the probability
of user u_i belonging to c_k generated by user multi-label classification (recall
Eq. (9)), and $\mathbf{X}_{kV}^{(0)}(l)$ is the probability of item v_l belonging to c_k resulting
from item multi-label clustering (recall Sect. 2.1). Notice that the sum of the
projections of a rating score by user u_i to item v_l on all K classes is equal to the
original rating score, i.e., $\sum_{k=1}^{K} R_k(i, l) = R(i, l)$. Thus, we will predicate the
projection ($\hat{R}_k(i, l)$) of $R(i, l)$ on each class c_k and aggregate the projection on
each class to produce the total prediction $\hat{R}(i, l)$ in Eq. (15).

Thus, the average rating of u_i on c_k is computed as follow.

$$\bar{R}_k(i) = \frac{\sum_{v_l \in V_i} R_k(i,l)}{|V_i|} \tag{13}$$

where V_i represents the set of items rated by u_i.

Based on the concept of vertex-edge homophily, we compute the predicted rating score $\hat{R}_k(i,l)$ on c_k as follow.

$$\hat{R}_k(i,l) = \bar{R}_k(i) + \frac{\sum_{u_j \in U} S_k(i,j)(R_k(j,l) - \bar{R}_k(j))}{\sum_{u_j \in U} |S_k(i,j)|} \tag{14}$$

The total predicted rating $\hat{R}(i,l)$ is thus given below.

$$\hat{R}(i,l) = \sum_{k=1}^{K} \hat{R}_k(i,l) \tag{15}$$

(2) **Multi-label Class Affinity-based Prediction.** In the context of multi-label classification, two entities are similar if they have the similar distributions over K classes. We thus define the class affinity-based similarity between users u_i and u_j on class c_k based on the Jaccard similarity [46].

$$J_k(i,j) = \frac{\min(\mathbf{Y}_{kU}^{(t)}(i), \mathbf{Y}_{kU}^{(t)}(j))}{\sum_{n=1}^{K} \max(\mathbf{Y}_{nU}^{(t)}(i), \mathbf{Y}_{nU}^{(t)}(j))} \tag{16}$$

where $J_k(i,j)$ is essentially a projection of the Jaccard similarity (denoted by $J(i,j)$) on class c_k if we utilize the class membership vectors of u_i and u_j over K classes to compute their Jaccard similarity. If u_i and u_j have the similar class membership probabilities over each of K classes, i.e., $\min(\mathbf{Y}_{kU}^{(t)}(i), \mathbf{Y}_{kU}^{(t)}(j)) \approx \max(\mathbf{Y}_{kU}^{(t)}(i), \mathbf{Y}_{kU}^{(t)}(j))$, then $J(i,j)$ should be very large. Notice that $J(i,j) = \sum_{k=1}^{K} J_k(i,j)$.

In the CF context, we argue that users from the same classes often make similar ratings to the same items. We thus devise the multi-label class affinity-based prediction model as an alternative to address the cold start problem. Concretely, we make the rating prediction by user u_i to item v_l on class c_k by taking the average over the ratings by those users from the same classes as u_i to v_l.

$$\check{R}_k(i,l) = \bar{R}_k(i) + \frac{\sum_{u_j \in U} J_k(i,j)(R_k(j,l) - \bar{R}_k(j))}{\sum_{u_j \in U} J_k(i,j)} \tag{17}$$

where $\check{R}_k(i,l)$ is the predicted rating score on c_k.

(3) **Unified Prediction.** To achieve a good balance between improving the prediction accuracy and addressing the data sparsity problem, we combine two kinds of predictions into a unified prediction model through a weight function.

Concretely, the unified prediction $\tilde{R}_k(i, l)$ on class c_k is defined by incorporating Eqs. (14) and (17).

$$\tilde{R}_k(i, l) = \alpha_k \hat{R}_k(i, l) + \beta_k \check{R}_k(i, l) \qquad (18)$$

where weighting factors $\alpha_k + \beta_k = 1, \alpha_k, \beta_k \geq 0$ for all $k \in \{1, \cdots, K\}$. The total prediction $\tilde{R}_{(}i, l)$ is then computed by aggregating all K class-specific prediction results as follow.

$$\tilde{R}(i, l) = \sum_{k=1}^{K} \tilde{R}_k(i, l) \qquad (19)$$

Table 1. Experiment datasets

	Yelp	Flixster	Last.fm
#users	252,898	1,049,511	595,623
#items	42,153	66,726	1,970,137
#ratings	1,125,458	8,196,077	65,830,086
#ratings/user	4.450	7.809	110.523
#ratings/item	26.699	122.832	33.414
density	0.00011	0.00012	0.00006
#user social edges	955,999	5,897,324	6,041,319
#item social edges	0	0	72,169,251
#attributes	1	1	2
#classes	20	21	21

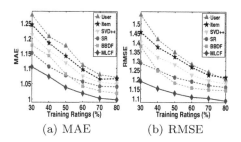

(a) MAE   (b) RMSE

Fig. 5. CF performance on Yelp

3   Experimental Evaluation

We have performed extensive experiments on several real-world graph datasets, as shown in Table 1. **Yelp**[1]: we construct a *user graph* by collecting the list of *friends* for each user and construct a *user-business rating bipartite graph* with the *stars* scores. We also choose one multivalued attribute of *categories* for each business. We classify each user/business/similarity into a subset of 20 business categories. **Flixster**[2]: It contains a *user-movie rating bipartite graph* and a *user graph*. We also collect one multivalued attribute of *genres* for each movie from the Flixster website[3]. We associate each user/movie/similarity with a subset of 21 movie genres. **Last.fm**[4]: we build a *user graph* by using the API *user.getFriends* to collect the list of friends. The *track graph* is built by invoking the API *track.getSimilar*. By using the API *track.getInfo*, we pick up two multivalued attributes for each track: *artist* and *tags*. We assign each user/track/similarity to 21 track genres.

---

[1]   http://www.yelp.com/dataset_challenge/.
[2]   http://www.cs.ubc.ca/~jamalim/datasets/.
[3]   http://www.flixster.com/.
[4]   http://www.last.fm/api/.

We compare MLCF with five representative recommendation algorithms. **SVD++** [28] is an SVD-based latent factor model integrates matrix factorization technique with implicit feedback from users. **Social Regularization (SR)** [39] is a social recommendation model incorporates social network information into the training process with social regularization terms to constrain matrix factorization objective functions. **Bordered Block Diagonal Form (BBDF)** [33] is a clustering-based method to partition rating matrix into multiple user-item communities, where each user or item belongs to only one community. NMF [23] is then applied to each rating submatrix in BBDF to make prediction. **User-based CF** [18] is a memory-based method predicts a target user's rating preference with the ratings from his/her neighbors with the similar rating preferences. **Item-based CF** [20] is a memory-based approach finds a set of similar items with the similar rating patterns to predict the unknown rating of the target item.

We use two popular measures used in existing recommendation papers to evaluate the quality of CF results generated by different methods: **mean absolute error (MAE)** and **root mean squared error (RMSE)** [28,33,39]. A smaller MAE or RMSE value indicates a better recommendation.

3.1 Prediction Quality

Figures 5, 6 and 7 exhibit the prediction quality by all six approaches on Yelp, Flixster and Last.fm respectively by varying the proportion of training ratings. Each rating dataset is divided into two disjoint pieces: the randomly chosen training data with a given proportion, say 50% of total ratings, and the rest as testing data. We make the following observations on the performance comparison.

First, among all six CF methods, MLCF achieves the best prediction accuracy on all three datasets. Compared to other algorithms, MLCF decreases MAE on average by 6.9% and RMSE by 12.2% on Yelp, reduces MAE by 10.7% and RMSE by 14.8% on Flixster, and cutbacks MAE by 13.9% and RMSE by 15.6% on Last.fm, respectively. Note that even if the proportion of training ratings is very small, such as 30% and 40%, MLCF still can achieve comparable accuracy on all datasets. This shows the importance of exploiting multi-label clustering/classification of users/items/similarities to make the accurate prediction based on vertex-edge homophily.

Second, MLCF, BBDF and SR significantly outperform User-based CF, Item-based CF and SVD++ on three datasets. However, BBDF outperforms SR on Yelp and Flixster but falls behind SR on Last.fm. A careful examination reveals that Yelp and Flixster are relatively dense but Last.fm is fairly sparse. A reasonable explanation is that BBDF puts each user and each item into one and only one community. The sparse rating matrix may lead to more community outliers and deteriorate the data sparsity issue.

3.2   Impact of Classification Strategies

Figures 8 and 9 present the prediction quality on Flixster and Last.fm by four versions of MLCF with different classification strategies: no classification, only vertex (user/item) classification, only edge (similarity) classification, and both vertex and edge classifications. We make a number of interesting observations. First, MLCF with both classifications achieves the best prediction performance. This demonstrates that it is very important for CF to differentiate the special interest of both users and items on each class, and distinguish the user similarities on each class. Second, MLCF without any classification leads to the highest quality loss in terms of both MAE and RMSE. When the training data becomes very sparse, the loss value increases quickly. Third, the performance by MLCF with only vertex classification or only edge classification stands in between.

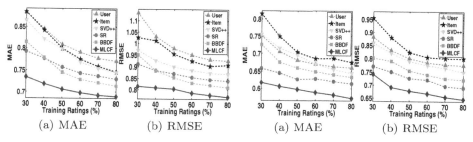

(a) MAE   (b) RMSE   (a) MAE   (b) RMSE

Fig. 6. CF performance on Flixster   **Fig. 7.** CF performance on Last.fm

4   Related Work

Research activities on conventional CF approaches can be categorized into: (1) memory-based approaches [18–21] discover the neighborhood of like-minded users for each user and predict the user's ratings on unrated items in terms of the ratings of his/her neighbors, or find the most similar items based on their ratings by all users as the recommendation source and predict the unknown rating of a user on an item by averaging the known ratings of similar items by the test user; and (2) matrix factorization approaches [22–28], which aim to reduce the dimensions of the user-item rating matrix by factorizing the rating matrix into products of low rank user-specific and item-specific matrices and minimizing the sum-squared errors between ground truth and prediction.

Three categories of clustering-based collaborative filtering methods have been proposed to improve the prediction quality: (1) user clustering method [29], which improves the scalability of recommender system by clustering the user set based on user similarity, and using clustering based neighborhood to provide comparable prediction quality; (2) item clustering algorithm [30], which partitions the item set into clusters based on rating data to improve the prediction quality and increase the system scalability; and (3) co-clustering approaches

[31–33], which simultaneously cluster users and items into the user-item groups based on rating matrix to improve the scalability of recommender systems.

The social network enhanced CF methods can be classified into two categories: (1) matrix factorization or network embedding based methods [34–41], which integrate the user friendship or user trust relationship in a social network into the basic matrix factorization or network embedding models by factorizing the social network or capturing the dependencies between feature vectors of users and their social neighbors; and (2) neighborhood based approaches [42–44], which combine the basic memory-based solutions and the social network based approaches to improve the recommendation performance.

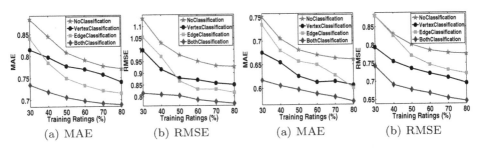

(a) MAE   (b) RMSE   (a) MAE   (b) RMSE

Fig. 8. Classification on Flixster   **Fig. 9.** Classification on Last.fm

5   Conclusion

We have presented a multi-label classification based CF method with three novel features. First, we model a rating bipartite graph, a user graph and an item graph as a heterogeneous network. We construct a rating-based similarity multi-graph with classified similarity edges. Second, we execute multi-label clustering/classification of users, items and similarities to capture latent correlations. Third, we propose and combine two kinds of multi-label prediction models into a unified prediction model.

References

1. Zhou, Y., Cheng, H., Yu, J.X.: Graph clustering based on structural/attribute similarities. In: VLDB, pp. 718–729 (2009)
2. Sun, Y., Yu, Y., Han, J.: Ranking-based clustering of heterogeneous information networks with star network schema. In: KDD (2009)
3. Zhou, Y., Cheng, H., Yu, J.X.: Clustering large attributed graphs: an efficient incremental approach. In: ICDM, pp. 689–698 (2010)
4. Sun, Y., Aggarwal, C.C., Han, J.: Relation strength-aware clustering of heterogeneous information networks with incomplete attributes. PVLDB 5(5), 394–405 (2012)

5. Kong, X., Yu, P.S., Ding, Y., Wild, D.J.: Meta path-based collective classification in heterogeneous information networks. In: CIKM (2012)

6. Gu, Q., Aggarwal, C., Liu, J., Han, J.: Selective sampling on graphs for classification. In: KDD, pp. 131–139 (2013)

7. Zhou, Y., Liu, L.: Social influence based clustering of heterogeneous information networks. In: KDD, pp. 338–346 (2013)

8. Zhou, Y., Liu, L.: Activity-edge centric multi-label classification for mining heterogeneous information networks, In: KDD, pp. 1276–1285 (2014)

9. Zhou, Y., Liu, L., Lee, K., Pu, C., Zhang, Q.: Fast iterative graph computation with resource aware graph parallel abstractions. In: HPDC, pp. 179–190 (2015)

10. Zhou, Y., Liu, L.: Social influence based clustering and optimization over heterogeneous information networks. TKDD 10, 1–53 (2015)

11. Yang, P., Zhao, P., Zheng, V.W., Li, X.: An aggressive graph-based selective sampling algorithm for classification. In: ICDM (2015)

12. Zhou, Y., Liu, L., Buttler, D.: Integrating vertex-centric clustering with edge-centric clustering for meta path graph analysis. In: KDD, pp. 1563–1572 (2015)

13. Zhou, Y., Liu, L., Lee, K., Zhang, Q.: Graphtwist: fast iterative graph computation with two-tier optimizations. In: PVLDB, vol. 8, no. 11, pp. 1262–1273 (2015)

14. Lee, K., et al.: Scaling iterative graph computations with GraphMap. In: PVLDB, vol. 8, no. 11, pp. 1262–1273 (2015)

15. Yu, W., Cheng, W., Aggarwal, C.C., Chen, H., Wang, W.: Link prediction with spatial and temporal consistency in dynamic networks. In: IJCAI, pp. 3343–3349 (2017)

16. Zhou, Y., et al.: Density-adaptive local edge representation learning with generative adversarial network multi-label edge classification. In: ICDM (2018)

17. Zhou, Y., Amimeur, A., Jiang, C., Dou, D., Jin, R., Wang, P.: Density-aware local Siamese autoencoder network embedding with autoencoder graph clustering. In: BigData (2018)

18. Resnick, P., Iacovou, N., Suchak, M., Bergstrom, P., Riedl, J.: Grouplens: an open architecture for collaborative filtering of netnews. In: CSCW (1994)

19. Herlocker, J.L., Konstan, J.A., Borchers, J.R.A., Riedl, J.: An algorithmic framework for performing collaborative filtering. In: SIGIR, pp. 230–237 (1999)

20. Sarwar, B., Karypis, G., Konstan, J., Riedl, J.: Item-based collaborative filtering recommendation algorithms. In: WWW, pp. 158–167 (2001)

21. Deshpande, M., Karypis, G.: Item-based top-n recommendation algorithms. In: TOIS, vol. 22, pp. 143–177 (2004)

22. Sarwar, B.M., Karypis, G., Konstan, J.A., Riedl, J.T.: Application of dimensionality reduction in recommender system - a case study. In: WEBKDD (2000)

23. Lee, D.D., Seung, H.S.: Algorithms for non-negative matrix factorization. In: NIPS (2000)

24. Yu, K., Zhu, S., Lafferty, J., Gong, Y.: Fast nonparametric matrix factorization for largescale collaborative filtering. In: SIGIR, pp. 211–218 (2009)

25. Chen, K., Chen, T., Zheng, G., Jin, O., Yao, E., Yu, Y.: Collaborative personalized tweet recommendation. In: SIGIR, pp. 661–670 (2012)

26. Lee, J., Bengio, S., Kim, S., Lebanon, G., Singer, Y.: Local collaborative ranking. In: WWW (2014)

27. Zhang, M., Tang, J., Zhang, X., Xue, X.: Addressing cold start in recommender systems: a semi-supervised co-training algorithm. In: SIGIR, pp. 73–82 (2014)

28. Koren, Y.: Factorization meets the neighborhood: a multifaceted collaborative filtering model. In: KDD (2008)

29. Sarwar, B.M., Karypis, G., Konstan, J., Riedl, J.: Recommender systems for large-scale e-commerce: scalable neighborhood formation using clustering. In: ICCIT (2002)
30. O'Connor, M., Herlocker, J.: Clustering items for collaborative filtering. In: SIGIR (1999)
31. George, T., Merugu, S.: A scalable collaborative filtering framework based on co-clustering. In: ICDM (2005)
32. Xu, B., Bu, J., Chen, C., Cai, D.: An exploration of improving collaborative recommender systems via user-item subgroups. In: WWW, pp. 21–30 (2012)
33. Zhang, Y., Zhang, M., Liu, Y., Ma, S.: Improve collaborative filtering through bordered block diagonal form matrices. In: SIGIR, pp. 313–322 (2013)
34. Ma, H., Yang, H., Lyu, M.R., King, I.: SoRec: social recommendation using probabilistic matrix factorization. In: CIKM, pp. 931–940 (2008)
35. Ma, H., King, I., Lyu, M.R.: Learning to recommend with social trust ensemble. In: SIGIR (2009)
36. Jamali, M., Ester, M.: A matrix factorization technique with trust propagation for recommendation in social networks. In: RecSys, pp. 135–142 (2010)
37. Noel, J., et al.: New objective functions for social collaborative filtering. In: WWW, pp. 859–868 (2012)
38. Liu, X., Aberer, K.: SoCo: a social network aided context-aware recommender system. In: WWW (2013)
39. Ma, H.: An experimental study on implicit social recommendation. In: SIGIR, pp. 73–82 (2013)
40. Zhang, C, Yu, L, Wang, Y., Shah, C., Zhang, X.: Collaborative user network embedding for social recommender systems. In: SDM, pp. 355–366 (2017)
41. Xu, L., Jiang, C., Chen, Y., Ren, Y., Liu, K.: User participation in collaborative filtering-based recommendation systems: a game theoretic approach. IEEE Trans. Cybern. vol. 49, no. 4, pp. 1339–1352 (2019)
42. Jamali, M., Ester, M.: Trustwalker: a random walk model for combining trust-based and item-based recommendation. In: KDD, pp. 397–406 (2009)
43. Jamali, M., Ester, M.: Using a trust network to improve top-n recommendation. In: RecSys (2009)
44. Wei, J., He, J., Chen, K., Zhou, Y., Tang, Z.: Collaborative filtering and deep learning based recommendation system for cold start items. ESWA **69**, 29–39 (2017)
45. Shmueli, E., Kagian, A., Koren, Y., Lempel, R.: Care to comment? recommendations for commenting on news stories. In: WWW, pp. 429–438 (2012)
46. Tan, P., Steinbach, M., Kumar, V.: Introduction to Data Mining. Addison Wesley, Boston (2005)
47. Bezdek, J.C.: Pattern Recognition with Fuzzy Objective Function Algorithms. Plenum Press, New York (1981)
48. Hillier, F.S., Lieberman, G.J.: Introduction to Operations Research. Mcgraw-Hill College, New York (1995)

Link Prediction on Dynamic Heterogeneous Information Networks

Chao Kong$^{(\boxtimes)}$, Hao Li, Liping Zhang, Haibei Zhu, and Tao Liu

School of Computer and Information, Anhui Polytechnic University, Wuhu, China
kongchao315@163.com, lhthomas@163.com, sanf9@163.com, zhb877097717@163.com,
liutao@ahpu.edu.cn

Abstract. This work develops a broad learning method for link prediction on dynamic heterogeneous information networks. While existing works have primarily focused on dynamic homogeneous networks or static heterogeneous networks. As such, the existing methods can be suboptimal for link prediction on dynamic heterogeneous information networks.

In this paper, we try to study the problem of link prediction combining dynamic networks and heterogeneous networks. However, none of the existing works has paid special attention to connect these two kinds of network data. To tackle this challenge, we propose a new broad learning-based method named HA-LSTM, short for Hierarchical Attention Long-Short Time Memory to address this problem on dynamic heterogeneous information networks. Firstly, we employ the Graph Convolutional Network (GCN) to extract the feature from Heterogeneous Information Networks (HINs). Then, we utilize a broad learning and attention based framework to fuse and extract the information among HINs broadly over timestamps. Finally, the link prediction in time-dimension by employing LSTM could be performed. We conduct extensive experiments on several real dynamic heterogeneous information networks covering the task of link prediction. Both quantitative results and qualitative analysis verify the effectiveness and rationality of our HA-LSTM method.

Keywords: Dynamic heterogeneous information network · Link prediction · Broad learning

1 Introduction

The users from Facebook, Twitter and Youtube can manifest their unique preferences from the other by following or unfollowing them. These relations sorted out by these behaviors can be abstracted as the dynamic information networks,

This work is supported by the Initial Scientific Research Fund of Introduced Talents in Anhui Polytechnic University (No. 2017YQQ015), Pre-research Project of National Natural Science Foundation of China (No. 2019yyzr03) and National Natural Science Foundation of China Youth Fund (No. 61300170 and No. 61902001).

A. Tagarelli and H. Tong (Eds.): CSoNet 2019, LNCS 11917, pp. 339–350, 2019.
https://doi.org/10.1007/978-3-030-34980-6_36

which can be represented by temporal graphs. Previous works aim at the research of dynamic homogeneous networks or static heterogeneous networks. Emerging applications requires more effective models for dynamic social network, which is one of the most popular dynamic heterogeneous information networks. The applications of dynamic social networks are evident in link prediction [1], link error and attack detection [2], user alignment [3], etc.

The users from social media platform establish the relations through following or chatting behavior. As a prevalent research problem on mining the implicit relations between users, link prediction aims at predicting the probability of new edges generated from existing nodes and edges. Due to the multi-source information from social networks, network embedding (or graph embedding) and heterogeneous data fusion can lift the accuracy of link prediction. [4] performs the graph embedding based on edge-sampling, and common practice in prior work is to make use of meta-paths from graph structures to do the link prediction [5]. These methods usually embed high-dimensional sparse node vectors to generate low-dimensional dense node vectors and then generate meta-paths through the random walk. Finally, the meta-paths are directly used as corpora for training. Despite effectiveness and prevalence, we argue that these methods can be suboptimal for embedding dynamic HINs due to two primary reasons:

- The characteristic of time-lag is not considered. Relations may change or evolve their attribute values over time. For example, people often change their status after getting bored or interested, which is known as a temporal record linkage problem in the traditional database community.
- Do not devise a model to fuse the data from heterogeneous data sources. In the era of big data, all kinds of data are available, such as spatio-temporal information, implicit associations of temporal graphs and so on, which may affect the performance of link prediction task.

To the best of our knowledge, none of the existing works has paid special attention to combine broad learning with attention mechanism simultaneously for link prediction. While this is our focus in this paper. We propose HA-LSTM, short for Hierarchical Attention-Long Short Term Memory model, which addresses the aforementioned limitations of existing link prediction solutions. Below we highlight our major contributions in this work.

- To account for both the explicit information and implicit associations, we propose a new broad learning framework. In particular, the algorithm can handle data fusion broadly and information mining temporally simultaneously.
- To explain the characteristic of time-lag, we improve the traditional LSTM and set the update gate to update new and effective data, ignore old or invalid data in the pre-processing phase. Moreover, we employ *softmax* to convert the information to score and normalize it.
- We illustrate the performance of our algorithm against comparable baselines on three real dynamic HINs. Empirical study results manifest that HA-LSTM outperforms baselines in link prediction task from multiple dynamic HINs.

The reminder of paper is organized as follows. We shortly discuss the related work in Sect. 2. We formally define the problem and describe the overview of our algorithm in Sect. 3, before delving into details of the proposed method in Sect. 4. We perform extensive empirical studies in Sect. 5 and conclude the paper in Sect. 6.

2   Related Work

Link Prediction aims at extracting the implicit relations and predicting them between users that may occur at some timestamp in the future on the current social networks. The earlier research on dynamic networks can be traced back to 2003s [6]. As a hot topic in social media, the dynamic network is one of the most popular research orientations whose solutions can be mainly divided into two categories: random walk-based methods and deep learning-based methods.

The random walking-based methods construct the meta-paths and train the models via the random walk method [7–9]. [7] discusses how nodes find their neighbors via the random walk and embed them through heterogeneous skip-gram model. [8] generates the training set through existed meta-paths, and [9] produces the node series through the random walk and learn them as sentences via Word2Vec model to generate the representation vectors. [10] predicts links based on the values of PageRank to make the meta-path similarity search. Similarly, [11] shows the searching methods via the values of SimRank. However, the latter aims at increasing the robustness of the model via the auto encoder [12–15]. [12] performs the first-order proximity and second-order proximity prediction by measuring the common link between two nodes. Cao et al. make the graph embedding via combining the random walk method and deep autoencoder [13]. Niebert et al. iteratively embed aggregation node's neighborhood, and use the embedding in previous iterations and inline function to generate new embedding [14].

It is worth pointing out that the above mentioned methods are designed for static homogeneous networks or heterogeneous networks only. In addition, they may not consider the characteristic of time-lag, such as the temporal records. To tackle this challenge, we set the update gate to update the effective data in the pre-processing phase. Moreover, to process the multi-source heterogeneous data, we design the algorithm hierarchically and employ the broad learning mechanism to make the heterogeneous data fusion. Broad learning aims at fusing all kinds of available data sources to discover more useful knowledge [16]. It has been widely used in many applications such as fraud detection [17], enterprise community detection [18], social network analysis [16], recommender systems [19] and so on. The supervised learning techniques are used to automatically predict the links between two random nodes in traditional link prediction task.

3   Link Prediction Approach

In this section, before we overview our proposed approach, we describe a formal definition of the heterogeneous data fusion and link prediction on dynamic HINs.

3.1   The Problem Definition

Definition 1. *(Heterogeneous Data Fusion) Dynamic HINs can be defined as a series of temporal directed graph G_i, where G_{it_j} represents the static graph in timestamp t_j at i-th temporal graph $(i > 1)$, and each temporal graph can be represented as $G_i = \{V_i, E_i\}$, in which V_i denotes the set of the nodes at i-th temporal graph, and E_i denotes the set of the links at i-th temporal graph. The attribute matrices of G_i in timestamp t_j can be represented as $\boldsymbol{W} = [W_{Git_j}]$. The first problem is to determine the tuples S' and D, i.e.,*

$$S' = \{W_{G_{1t_j}}, ..., W_{G_{nt_j}} | \forall G_{1t_j} \rightarrow \cdots \rightarrow G_{nt_j}\} \tag{1}$$

$$D = \{W_{G_{1t_j}}, ..., W_{G_{nt_j}} | \exists G_{1t_j} \nrightarrow G_{nt_j}\} \tag{2}$$

in tuple S', each attribute matrix in heterogeneous graph can be related with each other, while in tuple D cannot. In heterogeneous data fusion problem, the inputs are the attribute matrices of adjacent matrices $W_{G_{it_j}}$ in timestamp t_j from N data sources, the output is the fusion attribute matrix F_{t_j} in timestamp t_j.

Definition 2. *(Link Prediction) The link prediction task is to predict the possible links through the generated nodes and edges, which is essentially a prediction task. Formally, the link prediction problem can be defined as:*
Input: *The fusion attribute matrix F_{t_j} in frame t_j from N data sources.*
Output: *The top-k highest probability of $P(S_{t_k}, t_k, u, v)$ in G_t.*

3.2   Overview of HA-LSTM

Our proposed approach consists of four components as following.

Step1. Graph Features Extraction via GCN. Graph convolution network (GCN) can map adjacency graph into eigenmatrix for output and establish the mapping relations between input and output. In the process of convolution network training, the central node and its neighborhood are traversed and labeled, then feature extraction and mapping relations are established through the convolutional neural network (CNN). CNN can learn and provide the mapping between input and output, which does not require any precise mathematical expression between the input and output. The input features are converted to a two-dimensional matrix. The training phase compresses it to obtain the actual features, enabling the convolutional neural networks to map the input data into eigenvalue accurately.

Step2. Data Fusion via Bidirectional GRU. Due to the characteristic of time-lag in real-world datasets, we try to employ LSTM and its variant HA-LSTM to train. First, we set a update gate to determine what information should be updated from memory state: $f_t = \sigma(W_f \times [h_{t-1}, x_t] + b_f)$, where W_f and b_f represent weight and bias of sigmoid function respectively. Then, the sigmoid layer of the input gate layer determines which information needs to be updated by tanh layer. Finally, the LSTM cells control the output information: $o_t =$

$\sigma(W_o \times [h_{t-1}, xt] + b_o)$, $h_t = o_t \times tanh(C_t)$. For HA-LSTM model, we input the output matrix of GCN as the input layer of bidirectional GRU (Bi-GRU) to perform the feature extraction and data fusion.

Step3. Attention Mechanism. The attention mechanism aims at measuring the similarity of features between the input nodes and the target nodes. The more similar the current input is to the target, the greater the input weight will be. After the data fusion, we calculate the node relation matrix A whose elements represent the degree of correlation between the nodes, and when two nodes are given in the same network, a matching score can be calculated in the form of a dot product. Then the network incidence matrix is calculated to obtain a column of a probability distribution, and each column represents the matching probability of nodes in multiple networks. By matrix multiplication of node incidence matrix and network incidence matrix, the network relation matrix of the associated nodes in the whole fusion network can be calculated.

Step4. Temporal Link Prediction. After network relation matrix S is obtained, we generate the time series matrix $I(S_t, t, u, v)$, consider it as the input layer of the bidirectional LSTM (Bi-LSTM), then the predicted results are normalized and converged in softmax layer:

$$P(S_{t_k}, t_k, u, v) = softmax(I) \tag{3}$$

The ultimate outcomes are the top-k highest probability of the linked node pair (u, v) in G_t.

4   HA-LSTM: Hierarchical Attention Long-Short Time Memory

We now present the full HA-LSTM algorithm in Algorithm 1. In this algorithm, $P(S_{t_k}, t_k, u, v)$ maintains the probability of linking between two nodes(u, v) in timestamp t_k. The input is the adjacent matrix A_{it_j} in timestamp t_j. At lines 1–14, The algorithm sorts the nearest neighbor nodes by traversing the neighborhood of the central node, then normalizes and extracts the features by GCN. From lines 15–22, we integrate attribute feature vectors from heterogeneous data sources. At lines 23–27, we calculate network relation matrix S. Finally, at lines 28–31, The algorithm introduces the timestamp variable t_k, uses Bi-LSTM to predict the newly generated links, and employs softmax function to converge their probability. Eventually, The ultimate outcomes are returned as the top-k highest probability of the links.

4.1   Graph Features Extraction via GCN

In GCN, the spectral convolutions on graphs are defined as the multiplication of the signal matrix $X \in \mathbb{R}^N$ and the convolutional kernel K:

$$K * X = UU^T X, \tag{4}$$

Algorithm 1. HA-LSTM: Hierarchical Attention LSTM Algorithm

Require: adjacent matrix of N data sources $A_{it_j} = (V_{it_j}, E_{it_j})$ in timestamp t_j, convolutional
kernel K , receptive field k, width q, label set L and step s;
Ensure: Probability eigenvalues $P(S_{t_k}, t_k, u, v)$ of G_{it_j} ;
    //*Step 1: Graph features extraction via GCN;*
 1: $A_{q_{it_j}} =$ top q elements of A_{it_j} according to L;
 2: $N_{it_j} = [V_{it_j}], L_{it_j} = [E_{it_j}]$;
 3: **while** $N_{it_j} < k$ and $L_{it_j} > 0$ **do**
 4:     $L_{it_j} = \bigcup_{v \in L} N_1(V), N_{it_j} = N_{it_j} \cup L_{it_j}$; //*extract the attribute feature;*
 5:     **while** $j < n$ **do**
 6:        **if** $i \leq |A_{q_{it_j}}|$ **then**
 7:           $f = Receptivefield(V_{sort[i]})$; // *value reception;*
 8:        **else**
 9:           $f = ZeroReceptivefield(V_{sort[i]})$; // *zero-value reception;*
10:        **end if**
11:     **end while**
12: **end while**
13: $T_{V_{it_j}}(q, k, a_{V_{it_j}}), T_{E_{it_j}}(q, k, a_{E_{it_j}}) = Nauty(f)$;
14: $At_{it_j} = CNN(T_{V_{it_j}}(q, k, a_{V_{it_j}}), T_{E_{it_j}}(q, k, a_{E_{it_j}}), K)$; //*feature extraction*
    //*Step 2: data fusion via Bi-GRU;*
15: **for** $FeaturesF$ in At_{it_j} **do**
16:     $length =$ F.number(); //*calculate the number of features;* Layer number $= [lb\ length]$
17:     **while** $\boldsymbol{Features}$ into $\boldsymbol{InputLayer}$ and $length \neq 1$ **do**
18:        $H(F) = (\overleftarrow{GRU}(F) \otimes \overrightarrow{GRU}(F))$ //*feature fusion;*
19:        Length $/= 2$;
20:     **end while**
21: **end for**
    //*Step 3: attention mechanism;*
22: **for** $H_t(F)$ in G_{it_j} **do**
23:     $A(u_{it_j}, v_{it_j}) = softmax(H_t(u_{it_j}) \bullet H_t(v_{it_j}))$; //*node relation matrix*
24:     $B = \frac{1}{n}\Sigma softmax(H_t(u_{it_j}) \bullet H_t(v_{it_j}))$; //*attention distribution matrix*
25: **end for**
26: $S = A^T B$; //*network relation matrix*
    //*Step 4: temporal link prediction;*
27: $I(S_t, t, u, v) = Bi - LSTM(S_t, t, u, v)$
28: **for** k in length **do**
29:     $P(S_{t_k}, t_k, u, v) = softmax(I)$;
30: **end for**
31: **return** top-$k(P(S_{t_k}, t_k, u, v))$

---

where U denotes the eigenvalue matrix of the normalized Laplacian matrix $L = U\Lambda U^T$ of graph G, and the Λ represents its diagonal matrix of eigenvalue matrix. $U^T X$ is the Fourier transform of X. In order to simplify calculation, we employ the Chebyshev polynomial $T_k(\Lambda)$ to approximate the $K(\Lambda)$ [20]:

$$K(\Lambda) * X \approx \sum_{i=0}^{k} T_i(\widehat{\Lambda})X, \tag{5}$$

where $\widehat{\Lambda} = \frac{2}{\lambda_{max}}\Lambda - I_N$ represents the eigenvector matrix with self-connection I_N under the spectral radius scaling, λ_{max} is the maximum eigenvalue of L, and $U\widehat{\Lambda}^k U^T = \widehat{L}^k$. Therefore, for graph G_{it_j} and its label set, we define the normalized objective function as follows:

$$\mathbf{l}_{G_{it_j}} = \arg\min_l [|d_A(\mathbf{A}^l(G), \mathbf{A}^l(G')) - d_G(G, G')|], \tag{6}$$

where $d_\mathbf{A}$ denotes the euclidean distances between nodes in G, $d_\mathbf{G}$ denotes the euclidean distances between G and G'. Then we employ the BFS algorithm to do the traversal search to get the set of the k-th neighbor nodes V_{it_j} till the amount is k. Then we rank the neighbor nodes N_{it_j} according to the distance of each node in N_{it_j} and labeling its q neighbor subgraphs. After that, we employ the Nauty algorithm [21] to normalize the label of each node and choose top-K labels. The final output are n*j $q \times k$ matrices, in which $T_{V_{it_j}}(q, k, a_{V_{it_j}})$ and $T_{E_{it_j}}(q, k, a_{E_{it_j}})$ represents the eigenmatrix of the links and edges. After that, we use the normal 4-layer CNN model and import $T_{E_{it_j}}(q, k, a_{E_{it_j}})$ to extract the attribute eigenmatrix. The forward propagation process between hidden layers are defined as follows:

$$H^{(l+1)} = \sigma(\widehat{D_{T_E}}^{-\frac{1}{2}} \widehat{A}^l_{G_{it_j}} \widehat{D_{T_E}}^{-\frac{1}{2}} - \frac{1}{2}H^{(l)}W^{(l)}), \tag{7}$$

where $\widehat{D_{T_E}}$ denotes the degree matrix of nodes, $\widehat{A}^l_{G_{it_j}} = A^l_{G_{it_j}} + I_N$ represents the adjacent matrix with self-connection, and σ denotes the activation function. In CNN model, we choose ReLU as its activate functions. To reduce the representation cost, we use skip-connection to obtain better computational and statistical performance on the next layer. $At^l_{G_{it_j}}$ represents the attribute eigenmatrices as the final outputs.

4.2 Data Fusion via Bidirectional GRU

After we obtain the $At^l_{G_{it_j}}$, we put them into the input layer and extract the information through bidirectional GRU (Bi-GRU):

$$\overrightarrow{H}(At^l_{G_{it_j}}) = \overrightarrow{GRU}(At^l_{G_{it_j}}) \tag{8}$$
$$\overleftarrow{H}(At^l_{G_{it_j}}) = \overleftarrow{GRU}(At^l_{G_{it_j}})$$
$$H(At^l_{G_{it_j}}) = \overrightarrow{H}(At^l_{G_{it_j}}) \times \overleftarrow{H}(At^l_{G_{it_j}})),$$

where $\overleftarrow{H}(At^l_{G_{it_j}})$, $\overrightarrow{H}(At^l_{G_{it_j}})$ denotes the information extracted by forward GRU and backward GRU, $H(At^l_{G_{it_j}})$ is the cross product of the information extracted by B-GRU, and the number of layer is depended by number of feature matrices. For the next $(i+1)^{th}$ input layer, the forward transmission are defined as follows:

$$\mathbb{H}_{i+1}(At^l) = \mathbb{H}_i(At^l_{G_{it_j}}) + \mathbb{H}_{i-1}(At^l_{G_{it_j}}) \tag{9}$$

which used i^{th} and $(i-1)^{th}$ layer to perform the skip-connection [22] to simplify the number of layers. The fusion will stop when the number of matrix is 1.

4.3 Attention Mechanism

As mentioned above, we obtained the fused attribute eigenmatrix $H_t(F)$ in the last fusion layer. To extract the implicit relation between nodes, we employ the attention mechanism. First of all, the algorithm employs softmax function to calculate the node relation matrix:

$$A(u_{it_j}, v_{it_j}) = softmax(\mathbf{O}_{t_j}(u_{it_j})^T \times \mathbf{O}_{t_j}(v_{it_j})^T), \tag{10}$$

where $A(u_{it_j}, v_{it_j})$ in graph G denotes the node relation matrices. Then we calculate the effect in one network on corresponding nodes in other networks in rows and generate a attention distribution matrix$B(u_{it_j})$ and average it. Eventually, we do the dot product to A,B and get the network relation matrix S:

$$\mathbf{B}(u_{it_j}) = softmax(\mathbf{O}_t(u_{it_j}), ..., \mathbf{O}_t(u_{kt_j}))) \tag{11}$$

$$\mathbf{B} = \frac{1}{n} \sum_{i=1}^{N} \mathbf{B}(u_{it_j})$$

$$\mathbf{S} = \mathbf{A}^T \mathbf{B}$$

4.4   Temporal Link Prediction

Once the relation matrix $\mathbf{S}$ is estimated, we input the relation matrix S to the Bi-LSTM and employ the frame t as a vertices to make the link prediction:

$$I(S_t, t, u, v) = Bi - LSTM(S_t, t, u, v) \tag{12}$$

The results are more accurate due to the bidirectional temporal prediction. The final output are the matching score of nodes(u, v). We employ softmax function again to convergence the results and turn them to the probability distribution:

$$P(S_{t_j}, t_j, u, v) = softmax(I) \tag{13}$$

Finally, we rank all the probabilities and choose the top-K maximum values as the new generated edges.

5   Empirical Study

To evaluate the performance of HA-LSTM, we employ them to a representative application on three real dynamic HINs. Through empirical evaluation, we aim to answer the following research questions:

RQ1: How does HA-LSTM perform compared with state-of-the-art work methods and other representative baselines of the application?

RQ2: Is the heterogeneous data fusion model helpful to learn more implicit relations for HA-LSTM?

In what follows, we first introduce the experimental settings, and then answer the above research questions in turn to demonstrate the rationality of HA-LSTM.

5.1   Experiment Settings

Datasets. We conduct two groups of experiments to compare the proposed HA-LSTM with the baselines on three real dynamic heterogeneous network data from reddit[1], StackOverflow[2] and AskUbuntu[3]. Reddit covers the hyperlinks between the subreddits, StackOverflow represents the Q&A and comments on StackOverflow website, and the AskUbuntu dataset is similar to StackOverflow. Since link prediction is not targeted at weighted graph, the weight between links is not taken into consideration. The descriptive statistics about the datasets are shown in Table 1.

Table 1. Descriptive statistics of datasets

Name	Node (V)	Temp-Edges (TE)	Static-Edges (SE)	Timespan
Reddit	55,863	858,490	/	1,216
StackOverflow	2,601,977	63,497,050	36,233,450	2,774
AskUbuntu	159,316	964,437	596,933	2,613

Comparative Method and Evaluation Measures. We find three prevalent representation learning-based approach, named LINE, Metapath2vec, Node2vec respectively, to be the comparative baseline. These baselines consider the implicit associations in static heterogeneous networks in link prediction and two of them employ the random walk to generate the meta-path and train them directly by employing the skip-gram [23]. However, the implicit associations such as time-lag is not considered.

As mentioned above, we evaluate our proposed method using Precision@K, Recall@K and F-measure (or F1) which is equal to $2 * Precision@K * Recall@K/(Precision@K + Recall@K)$. Precision@K is the fraction of the relations in the top-K result that are correctly predict. Recall@K is the fraction of ground truth relations that appear among the top-K results. Precision and Recall interact on each other in the practical engineering, so we employ F1 as an equilibrium.

5.2   Performance Comparison (RQ1 & RQ2)

In this experiment, four different algorithms are compared to predict the Precision, Recall and F1-measure of link prediction on dynamic HINs. As the dynamic network changes, HA-LSTM predicts whether new links will be generated within a timestamp. In this paper, 75% data are selected by random sampling for training and 25% for prediction.

---

[1] http://snap.stanford.edu/data/soc-RedditHyper-links.html.

[2] http://snap.stanford.edu/data/sx-stackoverflow.html.

[3] http://snap.stanford.edu/data/sx-askubuntu.html.

We perform our method in link prediction task which is designed such that we know the complete ground truth for the nodes. We use three network data which are dynamic directed graphs. Figures 1(a)–(i) manifest the performance of HA-LSTM on three datasets by varying the rank of top-k from 100 to 600. We observe that the precision of HA-LSTM is promised. Top-100 links are chosen from the $pair(u, v)$, almost 80% matched pair can be found by HA-LSTM. Even if the number of k increases to 600, the precision in the StackOverflow and AskUbuntu is over 70%. The experimental results indicate that HA-LSTM is an effective approach to predict the links comparing to the baseline approaches in three datasets.

As shown in Figs. 2(a)–(c), we compare the normal HA-LSTM algorithm without heterogeneous data fusion variant to measure the effect of data fusion. The experimental result illustrates that HA-LSTM outperforms with data fusion significantly for link prediction on Reddit and indicates that data fusion is helpful to learn more implicit relations.

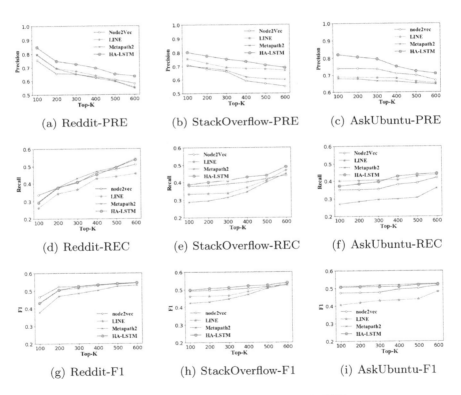

Fig. 1. Performance on three dynamic HINs

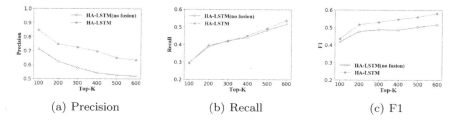

(a) Precision   (b) Recall   (c) F1

Fig. 2. Performance comparison of HA-LSTM and variant on Reddit

6   Conclusions

In this paper, we have studied the problem of link prediction on dynamic heterogeneous information networks. It is a challenging task due to temporal factors, implicit relations, and heterogeneous data fusion among multiple sources. We propose a supervised method to deal with the mentioned challenges. We have illustrated our proposed method on three real dynamic heterogeneous information networks. Experimental results indicate that HA-LSTM not only outperforms the comparable baselines but also obtains the promising performance after integrating of heterogeneous network data.

In our future work, we plan to extend our work to handle some of ground-truth tuples with semi-supervised approach, and deploy a distributed algorithm to support more efficient computation.

References

1. Zhao, A., Zhao, L., Yu, Y.: The joint framework for dynamic topic semantic link network prediction. IEEE Access **7**, 7409–7418 (2019)
2. Manzoor, E., Milajerdi, S.M., Akoglu, L.: Fast memory efficient anomaly detection in streaming heterogeneous graphs. In: Proceedings of ACM SIGKDD International Conference of Knowledge Discovery and Data Mining, pp. 1035–1044. ACM, San Francisco (2016)
3. Liu, L., et al.: ABNE: an attention-based network embedding for user alignment across social networks. IEEE Access **7**, 23595–23605 (2019)
4. Tang, J., et al.: LINE: large-scale information network embedding. In: Proceedings of ACM WWW International World Wide Web Conferences, pp. 1067–1077. ACM, Florence (2015)
5. Grover, A., Leskovec, J.: node2vec: scalable feature learning for networks. In: Proceedings of ACM SIGKDD International Conference of Knowledge Discovery and Data Mining, pp. 855–864. ACM, San Francisco (2016)
6. Liben-Nowell, D., Kleinberg, J.M.: The link prediction problem for social networks. In: Proceedings of ACM CIKM International Conference on Information and Knowledge Management, pp. 556–559. ACM, New Orleans (2003)
7. Dong, Y., Chawla, N.V., Swami, A.: metapath2vec: scalable representation learning for heterogeneous networks. In: Proceedings of ACM SIGKDD International Conference of Knowledge Discovery and Data Mining, pp. 135–144. ACM, Halifax (2017)

8. Li, J., et al.: Meta-path based heterogeneous combat network link prediction. Phys. A **482**, 507–523 (2017)
9. Perozzi, B., Al-Rfou, R., Skiena, S.: Deepwalk: online learning of social representations. In: Proceedings of ACM SIGKDD International Conference of Knowledge Discovery and Data Mining, pp. 701–710. ACM, New York (2014)
10. Richardson, M., Domingos, P.M.: The intelligent surfer: probabilistic combination of link and content information in PageRank. In: Proceedings of Annual Conference on Neural Information Processing Systems, pp. 1441–1448. MIT Press, Vancouver (2001)
11. Jeh, G., Widom, J.: SimRank: a measure of structural-context similarity. In: Proceedings of ACM SIGKDD International Conference of Knowledge Discovery and Data Mining, pp. 538–543. ACM, Edmonton (2002)
12. Wang, D., Cui, P., Zhu, W.: Structural deep network embedding. In: Proceedings of ACM SIGKDD International Conference of Knowledge Discovery and Data Mining, pp. 1225–1234. ACM, San Francisco (2016)
13. Cao, S., Lu, W., Xu, Q.: Deep neural networks for learning graph representations. In: Proceedings of AAAI Conference on Artificial Intelligence, pp. 1145–1152. AAAI, Phoenix (2016)
14. Niepert, M., Ahmed, M., Kutzkov, K.: Learning convolutional neural networks for graphs. In: Proceedings of ACM International Conference on Machine Learning, pp. 2014–2023. ACM, New York (2016)
15. Goyal, P., Ferrara, E.: Graph embedding techniques, applications, and performance: a survey. Knowl. Based Syst. **151**, 78–94 (2018)
16. Zhang, J., Yu, P.S.: Broad learning: an emerging area in social network analysis. SIGKDD Explor. **20**(1), 24–50 (2018)
17. Cao, B., Mao, M., Viidu, S., Yu, P.S.: HitFraud: a broad learning approach for collective fraud detection in heterogeneous information networks. In: Proceedings of ACM International Conference on Data Mining, pp. 769–774. New Orleans (2017)
18. Zhang, J., et al.: BL-ECD: broad learning based enterprise community detection via hierarchical structure fusion. In: Proceedings of ACM CIKM International Conference on Information and Knowledge Management, pp. 859–868. ACM, Singapore (2017)
19. Zhu, J., Zhang, J., et al.: Broad learning based multisource collaborative recommendation. In: Proceedings of ACM CIKM International Conference on Information and Knowledge Management, pp. 1409–1418. ACM, Singapore (2017)
20. Hammond, D.K., Vandergheynst, P., Gribonval, R.: Wavelets on graphs via spectral graph theory. Appl. Comput. Harmonic Anal. **30**(2), 129–150 (2011)
21. Wang, P., Niamat, M., Vemuru, S.: Majority logic synthesis based on Nauty algorithm. In: Anderson, N.G., Bhanja, S. (eds.) Field-Coupled Nanocomputing. LNCS, vol. 8280, pp. 111–132. Springer, Heidelberg (2014). https://doi.org/10.1007/978-3-662-43722-3_6
22. Tong, T., Li, G., Liu, X., Gao, Q.: Image super-resolution using dense skip connections. In: Proceedings of IEEE International Conference on Computer Vision, pp. 4809–4817. IEEE, Venice (2017)
23. Du, L., Wang, Y., Song, G., Lu, Z., Wang, J.: Dynamic network embedding : an extended approach for skip-gram based network embedding. In: Proceedings of International Joint Conference on Artificial Intelligence, pp. 2086–2092. Morgan Kaufmann, Stockholm (2018)

Information Network Cascading and Network Re-construction with Bounded Rational User Behaviors

Guanxiang Yun[1]($\boxtimes$), Qipeng P. Zheng[1], Vladimir Boginski[1],
and Eduardo L. Pasiliao[2]

[1] University of Central Florida, Orlando, FL 32816, USA
ygx8822@gmail.com

[2] Air Force Research Laboratory, Eglin AFB, FL 32542, USA

Abstract. Social media platforms have become increasingly used for both socialization and information diffusion. For example, commercial users can improve their profits by expanding their social media connections to new users. In order to optimize an information provider's network connections, this paper establishes a mathematical model to simulate the behaviours of other users to build connections within the information provider's network. The behaviours include information reposting and following/unfollowing other users. We apply the linear threshold propagation model to determine the reposting actions. In addition, the following or unfollowing actions are modeled by the boundedly rational user equilibrium (BRUE). A three-level optimization model is proposed to maximize total number of connections, which is the goal of the top level. The second level is to simulate user behaviours under BRUE. The third or bottom level is to maximize the other users' utility used in the second level. This paper solves this problem by using exact algorithms for a small-scale synthetic network.

Keywords: Boundedly rational user equilibrium · Information network · Large neighborhood search · Linear threshold

1 Introduction

With the development of information technology, social media platforms play a vital role in most people's life. For some commercial users or non-profit organizations, their profits can increase by using the social media system [13,15] to extend their influence. This is especially for important commercial users that highly depend on social media platforms such as News Media, YouTube or We Media Organization. Many people are willing to expand their network connection in social media in order to expand their influences. The number of followers will dramatically influence their influence and thus, increase their profits.

This material is based on work supported by the AFRL Mathematical Modeling and Optimization Institute.

© Springer Nature Switzerland AG 2019
A. Tagarelli and H. Tong (Eds.): CSoNet 2019, LNCS 11917, pp. 351–362, 2019.
https://doi.org/10.1007/978-3-030-34980-6_37

The behaviour of a user connected to an information provider is primarily influenced by two aspects [24]: the content of information posted by the information provider [25], and the personality of the user who follows the information provider. Thus, to learn how an information provider's network can be expanded, both content and users must be studied. Follower growth will highly depend on what kind of information providers post. We define users that determine posting plans as information providers. In this paper, we optimize the information provider's information post plan in order to expand its network connections. We consider an information posting plan to mean the decisions made during a set of unit time period regarding what content to post. Because the criteria for what is considered an interesting (and therefore effective) post differs depending on the personality of a user, posting plans must also take user type into account.

One user can only influence another if the other user is able to view the information the original user posts. Thus, we must consider information cascading. The linear threshold model [1,2,5] and the independent cascading model [10] are two widely used models for information cascading. In this paper, the linear threshold propagation model is used representing information cascading. This model was first proposed by Granovetter [6] to describe people's behaviour. In this model, when the linear summation of the influence of one user's followees exceed the threshold of this user, then this user will become active. In our study, it means that when some user's followees re-post information and the linear summation of these followees' influence exceeds the threshold of this user, then this user will re-post that information.

After information cascades in the network, users then decide whether they wish to change their followers. Users determine their followees based on utility, they want to be in a network that provides them with their desired information. However, they also wish to avoid redundant information. We apply the concept bounded rationality user equilibrium (BRUE) as the decision principle of user's for actions of connectivity. In essence, it means that users seek a connection network that achieves the high utility without exceeding the maximum utility.

This idea of BRUE originally came from Simon's Theory [18] in 1957. In this paper, human behavior is restricted by bounded rationality. In 1972, Simon published another paper [19] which provides a fundamental illustration about the theory of bounded rationality. The theory states that human behavior is based on a behavior's ability to achieve a percentage of a human's optimal goals, rather than the optima, with given conditions and constraints. Simon continuously worked on bounded rationality [20,21] to expand the application of the theory.

The concept of bounded rationality can also be applied in many fields, such as energy [26], psychology [8], military [16], transportation [3,12,14], etc. [4,7,17]. However, to the best of our knowledge, it has rarely been applied on information network systems. We propose that user actions in information networks corresponds to BRUE, that is, users do not obligated to seek the highest information utility they can get, but simply greater than a certain percentage of the maximum. Any connection plan can be chosen if it fulfills this criteria.

Some researchers used a game theory model in social media network to determine a user's decisions [22,23]. However, we theorize that the BRUE model will more closely match reality than the game theory model. This is due to the fact that real users are not concerned with small changes in utility. Additionally, functions in network utility systems only have approximate values, thus, it is an inexact function. Based on reinforcement learning, users in the information network system will obey the BRUE principle. Finally, the BRUE model should be used over the game theory model since the topology of a network system changes before a user reaches a utility value equilibrium. Recent research suggests that a user's bounded rationality influences their network. Kasthurirathna and Piraveenan [9] developed a simulation for a number of strategic games. Then they regenerated the network so that the network, on average, converged towards a Nash equilibrium, despite the bounded rationality of nodes. The link between bounded rationality distributions and social structure is important for explaining social phenomena.

We generate a three-level mathematical optimization model. The first level optimizes the information posting plan of an information provider in order to maximize its connections. The second level optimizes the human behaviours of other users under BRUE. It has two formats, optimistic and pessimistic condition. In the optimistic condition, we maximize human behaviours for the connections of an information provider. In the pessimistic condition, we minimize these variables. The reason for two conditions is because, as discussed before, by introducing BRUE, users' behaviours will drop in an uncertainty set. We seek to determine how the best and the worst uncertainty will influence an information provider's network connections, which is why both conditions are necessary. The third level calculates the maximum information utility for one user, which needs to be used in second level for BRUE constraints.

We solve a small-scale synthetic network by exact algorithms. However, for large-scale networks, calculation time increases exponentially. We tackle this problem by using large neighbourhood search (LNS) algorithms. It is a heuristic algorithm [11] used to solve large-scale problems. It is an effective way to find a good solution quickly when the time to find a global optimal solution is unrealistically long. This method determines the general area of a local solution and then looks within this area to find a new solution. This new solution may actually be worse than the original, however, it can get rid of the local optimal and block other possible solutions, gradually leading to better solutions.

2   Mathemathical Model Formulation

We propose the following model of an information network system. Our objective is to maximize our information provider's connections by controlling its information posting plan. With different posting plans, the information cascading path will be different. Additionally, after information cascades, some users may connect to a new followee or disconnect from an exiting followee. Different information posting plans will lead to different numbers of followees. We utilize the linear threshold principle to determine users' information re-posting behavior, we apply the BRUE principle to users to simulate the network reconstruction after information cascading.

2.1   Linear Threshold Model for Information Cascading

We use the linear threshold propagation model to determine whether a user decides to re-post information after they receive it one or several times. When the summation of the influence of one user's followees who post the information exceed this user's threshold, it will re-post that information. The linear threshold constriant inside the CP_i model will be described later. Figure 1 gives one example of the information cascading process and the final connection network after the information cascades.

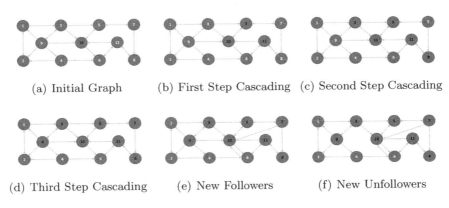

(a) Initial Graph   (b) First Step Cascading   (c) Second Step Cascading

(d) Third Step Cascading   (e) New Followers   (f) New Unfollowers

Fig. 1. Cascading for the information and the final connection of network

Figure 1(a) is the initial network. If node i has an arrow point to node j, it means node i follows node j. Some links between two users have two directions of arrows, this means that these two users follow each other. In this example, node 10, our information provider, is in black. Here, we only simulate for the cascading of one kind of information. Figure 1(b) is the first step cascading. By principle of the linear threshold, the influence of node 10 is greater than the threshold of node 5 and node 11. After node 10 posts information, node 5 and node 11 re-post it. We mark the re-post node in red. Figure 1(c) is the second step of cascading. We find that node 3 and node 8 also re-post this information. Even though node 3 already follow node 10 directly in the initial network, the single influence of node 10 does not beat the threshold of node 3. At that time, the influence of 10 to 3 is less than the threshold of node 3. However, after the first step, node 5 also re-posts this information and node 3 receives this information from both node 5 and node 10. Currently, the summation of the influence of node 5 and node 10 is over the threshold of node 3, so node 3 re-posts this information in the second step. Figure 1(d) is the third step of cascading. Node

9 and node 7 now repost the information for similar reasons of node 3. After Fig. 1(d), the information cascading will stop, because nodes 1, 2, 4, 6 will no longer re-post the information. Thus, the network becomes stable. Figure 1(e) adds two new followers to our target node 10 after the cascading based on our BRUE model. Figure 1(f) shows that node 9 un-follows node 10 based on the BRUE model. From the principle of linear threshold, if we know the post plan of the information provider, we can also know the information cascading route. Our next step is to optimize for the action of connection for other users in the system, which will follow the BRUE constraints.

2.2   BRUE Model

BRUE is the mathematical model's equilibrium constraints from the bounded rationality. We suppose that one user in the system has multiple choices, and for choice i it has utility $U(i)$. Without loss of generality, we can set choice i^* with the optimal utility value. Then, BRUE tells us that for any choice i has the following property that determines the possible choice for this user,

$$U(i) \geq \rho \cdot U(i^*). \tag{1}$$

where ρ is called the bounded rationality coefficient. We must have $\rho \leq 1$ because of the optimality of the choice i^*. From this constraint, we can know that by introducing BRUE to our math model, we will have an uncertainty feasible region for the users. And when $\rho = 1$, it is the perfect rationality user equilibrium (PRUE), and is the Nash equilibrium. This means the user accepts the plan's utility to be the maximum utility, and thus has no motivation to move to another plan. Game theory the Nash equilibrium is a special condition of BRUE when $\rho = 1$.

In this paper, after information cascades, users may change their connections. We assume a user's choice to connect or disconnect will obey BRUE constraints, which is closer to reality when compare to the Nash equilibrium.

Pessimistic Condition. The following model (CP_i) works for our information provider i to maximize the connections by determine its post plan. It is constructed under the pessimistic condition by introducing the BRUE constraints. In the pessimistic condition under BRUE constraints, the behaviour of the other users in the system acts in the worst case for our information provider. The other users' choice to connect or dis-connect will lead to the minimization of the information provider's connections. The first level finds the best choice for the information provider to maximize its connections in the worst case. The second level minimizes the connections based on the users decision variables. In this model, it also has third level which maximizes the information utility of each user in the system except the information provider. This information utility needs to be used in BRUE constraints. But this value also depends on the variables in the first level.

(CP_i) :

$$\max_{p_{il}} \min_{x_{ki}} BP(x_{ki}) = \sum_{k \in N, k \neq i} d_{ki} x_{ki} \tag{2a}$$

$$\text{s.t.} U_k = \sum_l U_{kl}, \qquad\qquad \forall k \in N, \tag{2b}$$

$$U_{kl} = F_{kl}(z_{kl}), \qquad\qquad \forall k \in N, \forall l \in L \tag{2c}$$

$$z_{kl} = \sum_{j \in N, j \neq k} x_{kj} \cdot p_{jl}, \qquad\qquad \forall k \in N, \forall l \in L \tag{2d}$$

$$p_{jl} = G(p_{il}), \qquad\qquad \forall j \in N, j \neq i, \forall l \in L \tag{2e}$$

$$x_{ki} \leq \sum_l \sum_{k' \in N, k' \neq i, k' \neq k} p_{k'l} * x_{k'k} + \hat{x}_{ki}, \quad \forall k \in N, k \neq i, \forall l \in L \tag{2f}$$

$$x_{ij} \in \{0,1\}, \qquad\qquad \forall i, j \in N, i \neq j \tag{2g}$$

$$U_k \geq U_k^* * \rho_k, \qquad\qquad \forall k \in N, k \neq i \tag{2h}$$

$$U_k^* = \max_{x'_{kj}} U_k', \qquad\qquad \forall k \in N, k \neq i \tag{2i}$$

$$\text{s.t. } (2b') - (2g') \tag{2j}$$

In model CP_i, the objective function is the total connection benefit the information provider i can get from the network.

The first level's decision variable p_{il} is a binary variable which indicates whether the information provider i will post information l to the system. This kind of variable can be controlled by the information provider.

In the second level, x_{ij} is a binary variable. When it is equal to 1, user i follows user j in the network. Otherwise, $x_{ij} = 0$. Constraint (2b) states that the total information utility received by user k equals the summation of the utility from all information in the system. We denote the function as $F_{kl}(\cdot)$. Where

$$F_{kl} = \begin{cases} v_{kl} - (z_{kl} - 1) * b_{kl}, & \forall z_{kl} \geq 1 \\ 0, & z_{kl} = 0 \end{cases}$$

the relation of the variable p_{jl} and variable p_{il} is restricted by the linear threshold principle, we denote their relation in function $G(\cdot)$. This function cannot be written out in formula. We thus show the mechanism to determine p_{jl} from p_{il} in the algorithm section. If we get the value of p_{il}, we can directly get the value of p_{jl} by the linear threshold principle.

Constraint (2d) gives that for user k, the frequency of information l is equal to the number of its followees who re-post information l. It will be a mixed linear constraint by given p_{il}.

Constraint (2f) shows that user k does not have the choice to follow the information provider i if it does not follow user i originally and no followee of user k re-posts any information generated by information provider i. $\hat{x}_{ki}$ is the original connection from user k to user i.

Constraint (2h) is the BRUE constraint. It states that user k can accept any follow-unfollow plan for which the information utility drops within the BRUE gaps. ρ_k is the BRUE coefficient for user k. Constraint (2i) is the third level problem. It calculates the maximum information utility that user k can get in the system. The constraints of the third level have the same formula as the constraint (2b)–(2g) in the second level. However, they do not share the same variable x_{jk} and U_k. We replace all of the relative variables x_{jk} in the second level with new variable x'_{jk} and U'_k in third level. This is the reason we write the constraints in third level as $(2b') - (2g')$.

3   Algorithm

We use the linear threshold principle to determine the information cascading process. When the summation of the influence of user $j's$ followees who post information l is greater than the threshold of user j for information l, user j will re-post information l.

In the model (CP_i), it is a three-level optimization problem, and in constraint (2d) it has the quadratic terms. But we can notice that, if we know the value of variables p_{il} in the first level. The problem will decompose to several one level mixed linear integer program (MILP) problem. We can imagine if we have the value of $\{p_{il}|\forall l \in L\}$, we can get all values of $\{p_{jl}|\forall j \in N, j \neq i, l \in L\}$. Then constraint (2d) becomes a linear constraint. And we can also calculate the value for the third level problem. It means we can get the value of $\{U^*(k)|\forall k \in N, k \neq i\}$. Then the total problem was decomposed to (n-1) one level MILP problem in the third level. And (1) MILP problem in the second level. Where n is the number of total users in the system include the information provider.

One possible method to solve this problem is to numerate all possible plans for the first level problem. But we can know that the number of different schedule to post information for user i is $2^{|L|}$, where $|L|$ is the number of information our information provider may post. When $|L|$ is increasing, the number of schedule will increasing exponentially. It is not a good method for the problem with large number of information to decide whether or not to post.

In a large-scale problem, we use the large neighbourhood search method for the first level. The detailed algorithm is shown in Algorithm 1 ALG-LNS. These two methods can be used for both pessimistic and optimistic conditions. We can not easily define the complexity by using large neighbourhood search method. Under worst case the complexity is still $O(2^{|L|})$. It means it stops after searching all possible options. However, it can get a valuable result after $O(|L|)$ calculations.

Algorithm 1. ALG − LNS

1: Set $k = 0$, $\{p_{il}^k = 0, |\forall l \in L\}.\{h[s] = 0| \forall s \in S\}$

2: Let $\{p_{il} = p_{il}^k | \forall l \in N\}$, calculate constraint (2i) in model (CP_i) to get $\{U^*(k)| \forall k \in N, k \neq i\}$, implement this value to BRUE constraint (2h) to get objective function value η^k. Set $h[p_{il}^k]=1$.

3: Set $m = 0$.

4: Let $\{p_{im}^{k,m} = 1 - p_{im}^k\}$, $\{p_{in}^{k,m} = p_{in}^k | \forall n \in L, n \neq m\}$. Let $\{p_{il} = p_{il}^{k,m} | \forall l \in N\}$.
Use it to calculate constraint (2i,), use the solution for BRUE constraint (2h) to get the objective function value $\eta^{k,m}$.

5: If m $< |L| - 1$. m=m+1, go to step 4. Otherwise, go to step 6.

6: $\eta^{k+1} = \{max_m \, \eta^{k,m} | s.t. \, h[p_{il}^{k,m}] = 0\}$, $m^* = \{argmax \, \eta^{k,m} | s.t. \, h[p_{il}^{k,m}] = 0\}$.
Let $\{p_{in}^{k+1} = p_{in}^{k,m^*} | \forall n \in N\}$

7: $n = \sum_{m \in N} h[p_{il}^{k,m}]$.

8: If $n < |L|$ and $k \leq K$ and $ct \leq TL$, k=k+1, go to step 2. Otherwise, stop.

4   Computational Results

4.1   Data Set

We use the synthetic network to calculate the model. We generate the network by different types of information, different numbers of users in the network, different link densities between users, and with or without budget as a constraint to evaluate the performance of the system. The following Table 1 gives the structure of the network. We in total have 3 different types of data structure to be calculated.

The coefficient b_{kl} is the coefficient for user k to get boring about information l. We generate it by using the random function in $[0, 2]$. The coefficient v_{kl} is the coefficient for user k to get how much value of the information l if just receive it for one time. We generate it randomly in $[0, 10]$. The coefficient d_{ki} is the importance of user k to user i. We generate it by using the random function in $[0, 100]$. Threshold value for one user to repost the information is generated in two categories. First category includes the user with high threshold. With probability of 40% in total users. We generate them randomly in $[2, HT]$. The second category includes the users with low threshold. We generate them randomly in $[2, LT]$. Where $HT = 10000 * N * D$ and $LT = N * D$. N is the number of users in the network. D is the density of arcs in the network. The influence between two users is generated randomly between $[1, HI]$, where $HI = N * D/2$. The edit cost for the information l is c_l. It is generated randomly between $[0,300]$. The total budget for the edit cost is 2000.

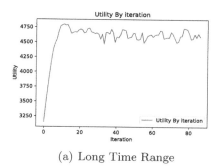
(a) Long Time Range

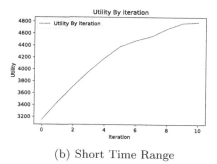
(b) Short Time Range

Fig. 2. Result of large neighbourhood search

Table 1. Data structure

Case	Node	Information	Density
1	20	5	0.3
2	100	20	0.1
3	1000	5	0.1

4.2 Results for Large Neighbourhood Search Method

We calculate the result by using the data set in case 2. Figure 2(a) is the result from data case 2. We solve it from the starting point '1', which means the information provider posts all information at the first iteration. We can see the optimal solution is obtained at iteration 10, and the optimal solution value is 4798.84. The time cost for the first solution is 1 h. Figure 2(b) shows the first 10 min of the calculation, which also obtains the optimal solution. After we enumerate all possible schedules, we also obtain the global optimal solution, 4798.84. However, the time cost is about 2 days, which is much longer than the time taken by using the large neighbour hood search method.

Influence of BRUE Coefficient ρ. Figure 3 shows the result of the influence of BRUE coefficient ρ in worst condition, and best condition with case 1 in Table 1. We can see that under the worst condition, when ρ is increasing, the total utility is also increasing. This is because by increasing ρ, the feasible region of the BRUE constraint is decreasing.

4.3 Comparison of BRUE and Game Theory

In this section, we calculate the post plan for our information provider if we use the game theory model to forecast the users' behaviour in the network under the worst conditions. Then we use this post schedule in our BRUE model, under different BRUE coefficients, it gets different maximum or minimum connection utilities for our information provider. We compare the relative difference to show

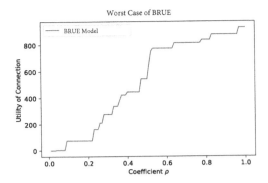

Fig. 3. Influence of BRUE coefficient ρ

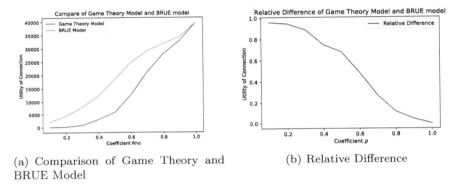

(a) Comparison of Game Theory and BRUE Model

(b) Relative Difference

Fig. 4. Comparison of BRUE and Game Theory Model 3

that the system is more efficient when using BRUE instead of the Game Theory Model under different BRUE coefficients.

Figure 4 is the comparison of the connection utility of BRUE and the Game Theory Model, with data set case 3 in Table 1 under different BRUE coefficients ρ. We can see that by using the post behaviour obtained from the Game Theory Model in BRUE, the total utility is less than or equal to the post behaviour directly obtained from the BRUE model. By decreasing ρ, the relative difference generally becomes larger.

5   Conclusion

Based on the BRUE model, we calculate the best posting plan for our information provider. By using the best plan, the user can expand its connections. In the BRUE model, the smaller BRUE coefficient ρ, the less connections our information provider has in pessimistic conditions. Thus, no matter what kind of information the information provider posts, it is more easy to lose such users in the network. So, the information provider should pay more attention to the users with high BRUE coefficient ρ. The BRUE model performs better than the Game Theory Model for maximizing the information provider's connections, especially when BRUE coefficient ρ is smaller. Even though the calculation method for Game Theory is relatively simple because there is no uncertain set, it is still useful to use BRUE model to simulate users' behaviour especially when more users in the system have smaller ρ.

We can conclude that the large neighbourhood search method is a useful algorithm for large-scale problem, as we can get the solution in a reasonable time. In addition, the local optimal from LNS is equal to the global optimal solution in our case study, but much lees time is spent in obtaining the optimal solution. Another advantage in our model by using LNS is seen when the variable of first level is fixed. The three-level optimization problem directly decomposed to several one level MILP problems. The starting point by using LNS can also influence the calculation to reach an acceptable local optimal solution. In general, when we have more people with a high boring coefficient, it is better to start from the plan that posts 0 information. But when we have more people with a low boring coefficient or negative coefficient, it is better to start from the posting plan that posts all information within the cost budget.

Acknowledgement. We would like to thank Luke Fuller for assistance with detailed proof reading and comments that greatly improved the manuscript.

References

1. Borodin, A., Filmus, Y., Oren, J.: Threshold models for competitive influence in social networks. In: Saberi, A. (ed.) WINE 2010. LNCS, vol. 6484, pp. 539–550. Springer, Heidelberg (2010). https://doi.org/10.1007/978-3-642-17572-5_48
2. Chen, W., Yuan, Y., Zhang, L.: Scalable influence maximization in social networks under the linear threshold model. In: 2010 IEEE International Conference on Data Mining, pp. 88–97. IEEE (2010)
3. Di, X., Liu, H.X., Pang, J.S., Ban, X.J.: Boundedly rational user equilibria (BRUE): mathematical formulation and solution sets. Transp. Res. Part B Methodol. **57**, 300–313 (2013)
4. Elsadany, A.: Competition analysis of a triopoly game with bounded rationality. Chaos, Solitons Fractals **45**(11), 1343–1348 (2012)
5. Goyal, A., Lu, W., Lakshmanan, L.V.: Simpath: an efficient algorithm for influence maximization under the linear threshold model. In: 2011 IEEE 11th International Conference on Data Mining (ICDM), pp. 211–220. IEEE (2011)
6. Granovetter, M.: Threshold models of collective behavior. Am. J. Sociol. **83**(6), 1420–1443 (1978)
7. Han, K., Szeto, W., Friesz, T.L.: Formulation, existence, and computation of boundedly rational dynamic user equilibrium with fixed or endogenous user tolerance. Transp. Res. Part B Methodol. **79**, 16–49 (2015)
8. Kahneman, D.: Maps of bounded rationality: psychology for behavioral economics. Am. Econ. Rev. **93**(5), 1449–1475 (2003)
9. Kasthurirathna, D., Piraveenan, M.: Emergence of scale-free characteristics in socio-ecological systems with bounded rationality. Sci. Rep. **5**, 10448 (2015)

10. Kempe, D., Kleinberg, J., Tardos, É.: Maximizing the spread of influence through a social network. In: Proceedings of the Ninth ACM SIGKDD International Conference on Knowledge Discovery and Data Mining, pp. 137–146. ACM (2003)

11. Laporte, G., Musmanno, R., Vocaturo, F.: An adaptive large neighbourhood search heuristic for the capacitated arc-routing problem with stochastic demands. Transp. Sci. **44**(1), 125–135 (2010)

12. Lou, Y., Yin, Y., Lawphongpanich, S.: Robust congestion pricing under boundedly rational user equilibrium. Transp. Res. Part B Methodol. **44**(1), 15–28 (2010)

13. Lovejoy, K., Saxton, G.D.: Information, community, and action: How nonprofit organizations use social media. J. Comput. Mediated Commun. **17**(3), 337–353 (2012)

14. Mahmassani, H.S., Chang, G.L.: On boundedly rational user equilibrium in transportation systems. Transp. Sci. **21**(2), 89–99 (1987)

15. Paniagua, J., Sapena, J.: Business performance and social media: Love or hate? Bus. Horiz. **57**(6), 719–728 (2014)

16. Roberts, K.H., Stout, S.K., Halpern, J.J.: Decision dynamics in two high reliability military organizations. Manage. Sci. **40**(5), 614–624 (1994)

17. Rötheli, T.F.: Boundedly rational banks contribution to the credit cycle. J. Soc. Econ. **41**(5), 730–737 (2012)

18. Simon, H.A.: Models of man; social and rational (1957)

19. Simon, H.A.: Theories of bounded rationality. Decis. Organ. **1**(1), 161–176 (1972)

20. Simon, H.A.: Bounded rationality and organizational learning. Organ. Sci. **2**(1), 125–134 (1991)

21. Simon, H.A.: Models of Bounded Rationality: Empirically Grounded Economic Reason, vol. 3. MIT Press, Cambridge (1982)

22. Singh, V.K., Jain, R., Kankanhalli, M.S.: Motivating contributors in social media networks. In: Proceedings of the First SIGMM Workshop on Social Media, pp. 11–18. ACM (2009)

23. Su, Z., Xu, Q., Fei, M., Dong, M.: Game theoretic resource allocation in media cloud with mobile social users. IEEE Trans. Multimedia **18**(8), 1650–1660 (2016)

24. Van Dijck, J.: The Culture of Connectivity: A Critical History of Social Media. Oxford University Press, Oxford (2013)

25. Van Dijck, J.: Facebook and the engineering of connectivity: a multi-layered approach to social media platforms. Convergence **19**(2), 141–155 (2013)

26. Wüstenhagen, R., Menichetti, E.: Strategic choices for renewable energy investment: conceptual framework and opportunities for further research. Energy Policy **40**, 1–10 (2012)

Gender Prediction Through Synthetic Resampling of User Profiles Using SeqGANs

Munira Syed, Jermaine Marshall, Aastha Nigam, and Nitesh V. Chawla[✉]

University of Notre Dame, Notre Dame, IN, USA
{msyed2,jmarsha5,anigam,nchawla}@nd.edu

Abstract. Generative Adversarial Networks (GANs) have enabled researchers to achieve groundbreaking results on generating synthetic images. While GANs have been heavily used for generating synthetic image data, there is limited work on using GANs for synthetically resampling the minority class, particularly for text data. In this paper, we utilize Sequential Generative Adversarial Networks (SeqGAN) for creating synthetic user profiles from text data. The text data consists of articles that the users have read that are representative of the minority class. Our goal is to improve the predictive power of supervised learning algorithms for the gender prediction problem, using articles consumed by the user from a large health-based website as our data source. Our study shows that by creating synthetic user profiles for the minority class with SeqGANs and passing in the resampled training data to an XGBoost classifier, we achieve a gain of 2% in AUROC, as well as a 3% gain in both F1-Score and AUPR for gender prediction when compared to SMOTE. This is promising for the use of GANs in the application of text resampling.

Keywords: Gender prediction · Resampling · Adversarial · Topic modeling

1 Introduction

Demographic prediction based on browsing behavior has applications in content recommendation, targeted advertising, and personalized news feeds among others. A few studies on the problem of gender prediction use content-based features (e.g. words, tagged categories, learned topics), and click-based features such as time and sequence of clicks [9,11]. Some studies characterize and predict users' demographic information based on various attributes of their browsing and search behavior [12,15]. For example, Hu et al. [9] utilized web page views and clicks to make predictions on the users' gender and age, Kabbur et al. [11] predicted gender using the content and structure of webpages, and Phuong et al. [18] reported that topic-based features worked better than time and sequential features for gender prediction. To make predictions about individual topic interests,

© Springer Nature Switzerland AG 2019
A. Tagarelli and H. Tong (Eds.): CSoNet 2019, LNCS 11917, pp. 363–370, 2019.
https://doi.org/10.1007/978-3-030-34980-6_38

Nigam et al. [16] observed and collected users' health-seeking behavior, i.e., user demographics, temporal features, and socio-economic community variables. Similarly, in our analysis, we use topic features derived from the text data of the articles read by users. By only using the content, there is a potential to generalize and create user profiles across website platforms and other domains. However, using bag-of-words representation leads to high dimensionality so instead, we use topic modeling to represent the user profiles as topic profiles. In our data set, there is a gender imbalance problem because women tend to search and read more health-based articles online than men. In addition, the preferences and health seeking behavior of females is very different from male users [16]. Furthermore, online article content is generated and expires quickly, so learning article-specific content does not generalize well. In our analysis, we use learned topics as features to mitigate this short-lived nature of articles, with the added benefit of topics being generalizable and transferable to other domains. By concatenating all of the articles a user reads, we can build a user profile. This representation of users would be beneficial because user interests do not change as quickly as the content they consume on a website. While most websites can have varying distributions of demographic representation, it is necessary to understand how content is consumed and interest varies based on the variety of demographic features [16]. Since we want to be able to identify the reading/consumption patterns of these under-represented users accurately, we use resampling techniques that can better represent the minority class. Imbalance can be tackled at the data level through various techniques such as oversampling (data augmentation), where we duplicate some of the minority samples, and undersampling, where we discard some of the majority samples. Undersampling techniques have the drawback of losing potentially valuable data whereas random oversampling may lead to a higher weight for the minority samples [8]. To mitigate the bias from duplicating the minority samples, Synthetic Minority Oversampling Technique (SMOTE) was introduced by Chawla et al. [5] for generating synthetic samples of the minority class. Other SMOTE variants have also been proposed since then [8].

Most of the previously mentioned popular resampling techniques exist for resampling real, continuous data. However, when this is applied to numerical representations of text data, it could lead to the generation of noisy samples. For example, in a bag-of-words representation of text where the text samples are represented by counts of words in the vocabulary, synthetic resampling methods could generate non-integral number of words. Thus, to avoid the percolation of noise from the numerical representation of text, we can resample the minority text data using synthetic text generation techniques. LSTMs and RNNs have been used for generating text in various applications such as generating lyrics [19] and fake reviews [2]. Adversarial methods such as SeqGANs are similar to these techniques in that they use RNNs in their generator for generating text data [21]. Generative adversarial networks have been successfully used for generating synthetic samples of the minority class to augment the training set [14]. Zhu et al. focused on solving a class imbalance problem with GANs in the domain of emotion classification using images with relative success [22]. In the text domain, Anand et al. [1] used text-GANs to generate synthetic URLs for phishing detection. While these techniques exist for synthetic text generation, their application for the task of resampling minority text data for classification, and specifically the use of GANs to do so, is under-explored. Existing resampling methods for text classification either rely on bag-of-words through term weighting [10] or generating synthetic text data using probabilistic topic models [6]. In fact, Sun et al. [20] systematically explored the effect of popular resampling strategies on tf-idf represented imbalanced text classification problems, and found that in most cases basic SVM performs better without resampling. Our goal therefore, is to explore the use of SeqGANs for generating text data for imbalanced binary classification. For this, we propose a pipeline that represents users with user profiles and topic modeling.

2   Dataset Description

The browsing data used in this paper was generated on a health-based website which collects users' demographic information from their subscribers and receives the browsing activity of these users. The data was collected from user clicks on articles from 2006 through 2015. Over this time frame, data from 263 topics related to health was collected [16]. The content of the URLs accessed by users was crawled from the website and processed by removing stop words. We experimented with a varying number of topics and decided to use 200 topics uniformly in all of our experiments. Since different age groups have varying topic interests [16] we split the dataset by age groups: 18–24 (32% of the data), 25–34 (33.3%), 35–44 (21.6%), 45–54 (14.4%), 55–64 (11.6%), and 65–80 (5.6%). For our experiments, we used the age group of 65–80 because they are at higher risk for health issues. This portion is small enough to avoid scalability issues with SeqGAN. There are 17,499 users in this age group with 13,021 females and 4,478 males (25.59% of users are male). We also discovered a long right tailed distribution with a steadily decreasing number of users as the number of article clicks per user increases.

3   Model

3.1   Steps I and II - User Representation

Users read various articles, which is the input to the model (click level representation, Fig. 1). At the user level, we create user profiles by concatenating all the articles read by the individual to generate a single text document correspond to each user.

3.2   Step III - User Representation Using Topics

We next represent a user in a structured format using topic modeling (topic profile at user level, Fig. 1). A topic model is trained on the corpus of the individual articles accessed by all of the users in the training and testing sets. While many topic modeling techniques such as SVD, LDA and their many variants exist, we use NMF because it is well-suited for the task of topic modeling and relies on

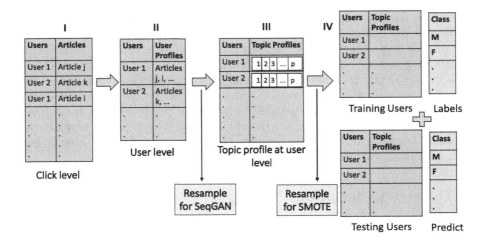

Fig. 1. Classification pipeline

matrix factorization. In our case, the vocabulary of the corpus is huge even after filtering stopwords. Thus, a bag-of-words representation would be infeasible for representing each user. The NMF topic model [17] is trained on all of the individual articles that appear in the corpus. The topic representation for each user is generated by transforming their profiles into the topic space.

Let the corpus D consist of articles $d_1, d_2, ..., d_m$. Each document d_j is represented by a vector of w words. Thus, the document matrix $\mathbf{D}$ has the dimensions $m \times w$. We generate an NMF topic model in the topic space of p dimensions by decomposing matrix $\mathbf{D}$ into factors $\mathbf{W}$ and $\mathbf{H}$. Thus, $\mathbf{D} = \mathbf{WH}$, where $\mathbf{W}$ has the dimensions $m \times p$ and $\mathbf{H}$ has the dimensions $p \times w$. Here $\mathbf{W}$ can be interpreted as representation of documents in the topic space and $\mathbf{H}$ is the representation of topics in the word space. NMF optimizes the objective function

$$\frac{1}{2} \|\mathbf{D} - \mathbf{WH}\|_F^2 = \sum_{i=1}^{n} \sum_{j=1}^{m} \left(D_{ij} - (WH)_{ij} \right)^2 \qquad (1)$$

where $\mathbf{D} = \mathbf{WH}$ and $\mathbf{W}$ and $\mathbf{H}$ are minimized alternately. A user U_i is a linear combination of all the documents in D. We represent the user by concatenating the articles read by the user. Thus, U_i is given by $\sum_{j=1}^{m} (c_j d_j)$ where c_j is the number of times user i read article d_j. The topic representation $\mathbf{W}'$ of a matrix of n users $\mathbf{U}$ (dimensions $n \times m$) consisting of $U_1, U_2, ..., U_n$, whether training or testing, would be given by $\mathbf{U} = \mathbf{W}'\mathbf{H}$, where $\mathbf{W}'$ is obtained by minimizing the same objective function in Eq. 1 while $\mathbf{H}$ is kept constant.

3.3   Step IV - Split into Training and Testing Sets

The topic representation of the s users in the training set W'_{train} is the input to train a classifier, and those of the $n - s$ users in the testing set given by W'_{test} are used to predict the gender of the users as the output.

3.4   Resampling

In the case of the minority class, we use two resampling approaches for improving the performance of the classifier (i.e. SMOTE-based and text-based).

The data can be resampled after Step III in which topic profiles of the users are generated. This is where we will apply SMOTE and its variants. However, the text-based resampling would occur after Step II by generating synthetic user profiles of the minority class from the text of real users of the minority class. The intuition is that by applying resampling at an earlier stage, we avoid biases introduced through the conversion of text to numerical representation. Resampling at this stage can be done by Random Oversampling of the minority texts (ROS), Random Undersampling of the majority texts (RUS), and SeqGAN to reduce the imbalance between the classes.

SeqGAN. We formulate the sequence generation problem for gender classification as shown below to produce a sequence of tokens $X_{1:T} = (x_1, x_2, ..., x_T)$, $x_T \in Y$ where Y is the vocabulary of the set of candidate tokens. We train a Discriminator model D in order to guide a Generator model G. The discriminator's goal is to predict how likely a sequence X_{1T} is to be from the real sequence information. G is then updated by a policy gradient from the expected reward received from D. The formulation for the policy gradient is shown in Eq. 2 below:

$$J(\Theta) = E[R_T|s_0] = \sum_{y_1 \in Y} G_\Theta(y_1|s_0) \times Q_{D_\Theta}^{G_\Theta}(s_0, y_1) \tag{2}$$

"where R_T is the reward for a complete sequence and $Q_{D_\Theta}^{G_\Theta}(s, a)$ is the expected cumulative reward starting from state s taking an action a following policy G_Θ" [21].

4   Experiments

We compare the resampling methods in our gender prediction task. Specifically, we report on two sets of experiments to compare the performance of SMOTE-based and SeqGAN text-based methods for resampling. We use 5-Fold cross-validation for evaluation with AUROC, AUPR, and F1-Score as the performance metrics. The 65–80 age group has an imbalance of approximately 25% male.

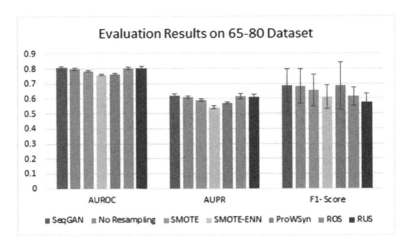

Fig. 2. Evaluation results of different resampling methods 65–80 dataset

4.1 Experiment 1: SMOTE-Based Resampling

We evaluate the capability of some SMOTE-based resampling techniques. SMOTE Edited Nearest Neighbor Rule (SMOTE-ENN) handles class imbalance by removing samples from both the majority and minority class [4]. SMOTE-Out considers the nearest majority and minority example to create synthetic data [13], and ProWSyn generates weights for the minority samples based on boundary distance [3]. We generated synthetic samples so as to balance the two classes.

4.2 Experiment 2: Text-Based Resampling

From each male user profile, we sampled 20 words with high TF-IDF values to represent the individual male user as input to the SeqGAN. Using SeqGAN, we generated 500 sequences of 20 words each which is the same sequence length used in [21]. Thus, we generated 500 synthetic male profiles for each fold of the 5-fold cross-validation. We used the implementation of SeqGAN with a CNN in the discriminator network and an LSTM in the generator network.[1]

We utilized XGBoost (with parameters set to a learning rate of 1, estimators of 9, a max depth of 5, subsample of 0.99, min-child-weight of 5, scale-pos-weight of 3, seed of 3, and gamma of 3) [7] after testing multiple configurations. We used XGBoost instead of a neural network such as DNN for this problem because XGBoost performed well and is a powerful ML algorithm also used in many papers and competitions. In the health domain, interpretability of models is vital to their practical usage and so we use XGBoost instead of neural networks which are not as easily interpreteble. Though there has been recent work

---

[1] https://github.com/bhushan23/Transformer-SeqGAN-PyTorch/blob/master/seq_gan/.

on explainable neural networks, that is beyond the scope of this paper. We compare SeqGAN against baselines with no resampling, resampling with SMOTE, SMOTE-Out, ProWSyn, and SMOTE-ENN as shown in Fig. 2. WE did not find significant differences when parameters were varied for the SMOTE-based baselines. In Fig. 2, we see that SeqGAN does not suffer from the sub-class problem and outperforms SMOTE and SMOTE-ENN in terms of AUROC, AUPR, and F1-Score. Text-based resampling methods of ROS and RUS perform very similarly to SeqGAN. XGBoost without resampling is second only to the text-based resampling methods. However, we expected this as XGBoost has a parameter known as 'scale-pos-weight' that varies the ratio of positive and negative examples. This allows the algorithm to better control for imbalance than many classic supervised learning algorithms.

5   Conclusion

We report on a new application for SeqGANs which synthetically resamples minority text data to improve imbalanced classification. The experimental results show that SeqGAN outperforms SMOTE-based resampling techniques when combined with the predictive power of XGBoost. In the future, we will explore other resampling techniques through the use of GANs, better text-summarization strategies to reduce the length of the input to SeqGAN, and more efficient methods of using higher sequence lengths with SeqGAN.

Acknowledgements. We thank Trenton Ford for helpful discussions. This work was supported in part by the National Science Foundation (NSF) Grant IIS-1447795.

References

1. Anand, A., Gorde, K., Moniz, J.R.A., Park, N., Chakraborty, T., Chu, B.T.: Phishing URL detection with oversampling based on text generative adversarial networks. In: 2018 IEEE International Conference on Big Data (Big Data), pp. 1168–1177. IEEE (2018)
2. Bartoli, A., De Lorenzo, A., Medvet, E., Tarlao, F.: Your paper has been accepted, rejected, or whatever: automatic generation of scientific paper reviews. In: Buccafurri, F., Holzinger, A., Kieseberg, P., Tjoa, A.M., Weippl, E. (eds.) CD-ARES 2016. LNCS, vol. 9817, pp. 19–28. Springer, Cham (2016). https://doi.org/10.1007/978-3-319-45507-5_2
3. Barua, S., Islam, M.M., Murase, K.: ProWSyn: proximity weighted synthetic oversampling technique for imbalanced data set learning. In: Pei, J., Tseng, V.S., Cao, L., Motoda, H., Xu, G. (eds.) PAKDD 2013. LNCS (LNAI), vol. 7819, pp. 317–328. Springer, Heidelberg (2013). https://doi.org/10.1007/978-3-642-37456-2_27
4. Batista, G.E.A.P.A., Prati, R.C., Monard, M.C.: A study of the behavior of several methods for balancing machine learning training data. SIGKDD Explor. **6**, 20–29 (2004)
5. Chawla, N.V., Bowyer, K.W., Hall, L.O., Kegelmeyer, W.P.: SMOTE: synthetic minority over-sampling technique. J. Artif. Intell. Res. **16**, 321–357 (2002)

6. Chen, E., Lin, Y., Xiong, H., Luo, Q., Ma, H.: Exploiting probabilistic topic models to improve text categorization under class imbalance. Inf. Process. Manage. **47**(2), 202–214 (2011)
7. Chen, T., Guestrin, C.: XGBoost: a scalable tree boosting system. In: KDD (2016)
8. Fernández, A.: SMOTE for learning from imbalanced data: progress and challenges, marking the 15-year anniversary. J. Artif. Intell. Res. **61**, 863–905 (2018)
9. Hu, J., Zeng, H.J., Li, H., Niu, C., Chen, Z.: Demographic prediction based on user's browsing behavior. In: WWW (2007)
10. Jindal, R., Malhotra, R., Jain, A.: Techniques for text classification: literature review and current trends. Webology **12**(2), 1–28 (2015)
11. Kabbur, S., Han, E.H., Karypis, G.: Content-based methods for predicting web-site demographic attributes. In: 2010 IEEE International Conference on Data Mining, pp. 863–868 (2010)
12. Kim, D.Y., Lehto, X.Y., Morrison, A.M.: Gender differences in online travel information search: implications for marketing communications on the internet. Tourism Manage. **28**(2), 423–433 (2007)
13. Koto, F.: SMOTE-Out, SMOTE-Cosine, and Selected-SMOTE: an ehancement strategy to handle imbalance in data level. In: 2014 International Conference on Advanced Computer Science and Information System, pp. 280–284 (2014)
14. Lee, S.K., Hong, S.J., Yang, S.I.: Oversampling for imbalanced data classification using adversarial network. In: 2018 International Conference on Information and Communication Technology Convergence (ICTC), pp. 1255–1257. IEEE (2018)
15. McMahan, C., Hovland, R., McMillan, S.: Online marketing communications: exploring online consumer behavior by examining gender differences and interactivity within internet advertising. J. Interact. Advertising **10**(1), 61–76 (2009)
16. Nigam, A., Johnson, R.A., Wang, D., Chawla, N.V.: Characterizing online health and wellness information consumption: a study. Inf. Fusion **46**, 33–43 (2019)
17. Pedregosa, F., et al.: Scikit-learn: machine learning in Python. J. Mach. Learn. Res. **12**, 2825–2830 (2011)
18. Phuong, T.M., et al.: Gender prediction using browsing history. In: Huynh, V., Denoeux, T., Tran, D., Le, A., Pham, S. (eds.) Knowledge and Systems Engineering, pp. 271–283. Springer, Cham (2014). https://doi.org/10.1007/978-3-319-02741-8_24
19. Potash, P., Romanov, A., Rumshisky, A.: Ghostwriter: using an LSTM for automatic rap lyric generation. In: Proceedings of the 2015 Conference on Empirical Methods in Natural Language Processing, pp. 1919–1924 (2015)
20. Sun, A., Lim, E.P., Liu, Y.: On strategies for imbalanced text classification using SVM: a comparative study. Decis. Support Syst. **48**(1), 191–201 (2009)
21. Yu, L., Zhang, W., Wang, J., Yu, Y.: SeqGAN: sequence generative adversarial nets with policy gradient. In: Thirty-First AAAI Conference on Artificial Intelligence (2017)
22. Zhu, X., Liu, Y., Qin, Z., Li, J.: Data Augmentation in Emotion Classification Using Generative Adversarial Networks. ArXiv abs/1711.00648 (2017)

Author Index

Printed in the United States
By Bookmasters